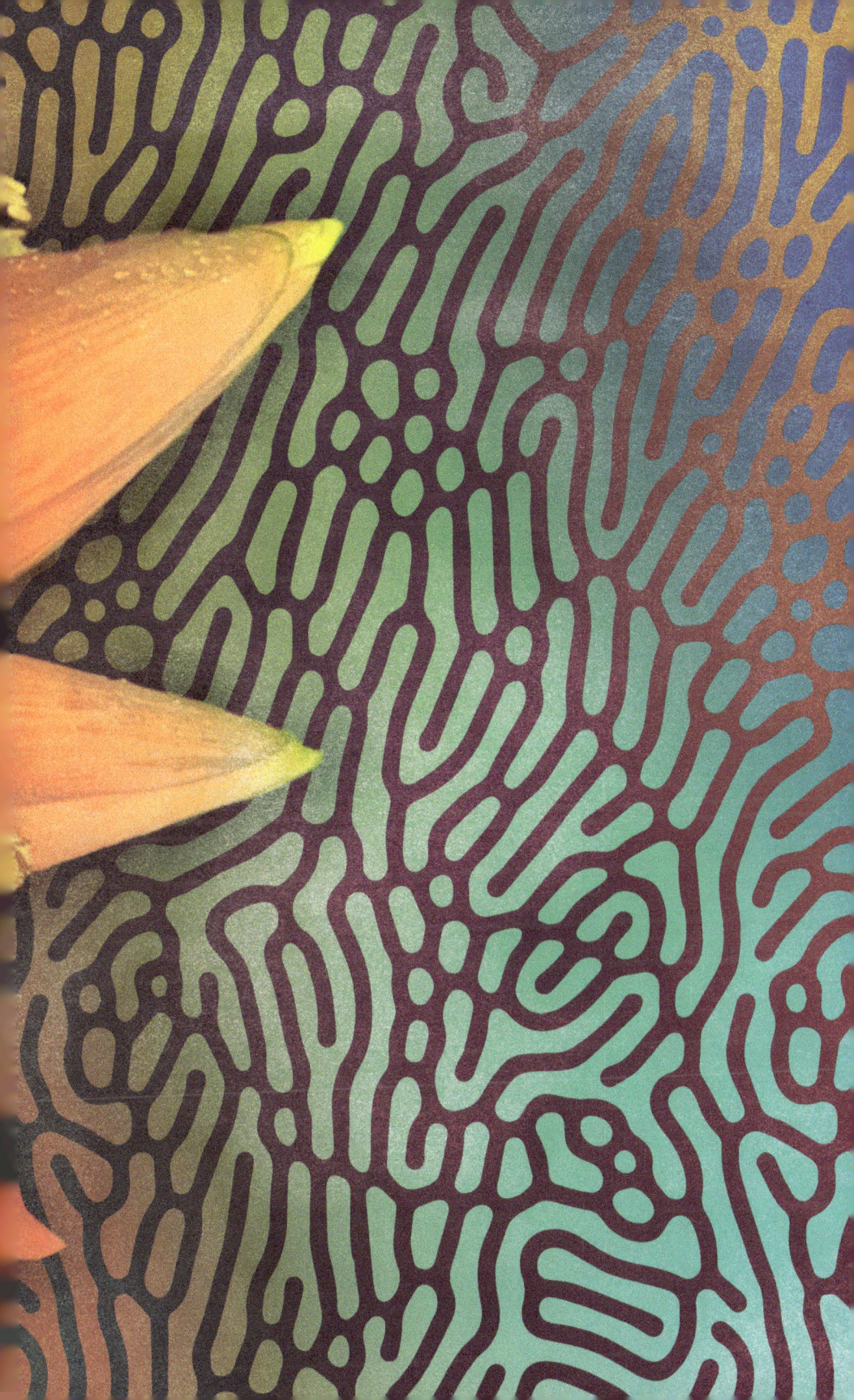

A Marianas Mosaic

Signs and Shifts in Contemporary Island Life

Edited by Ajani Burrell
with Kimberly Bunts-Anderson

Copyright © 2022 by University of Guam Press.
All rights reserved.

Copyright is meant to respect the research, hard work, imagination, and artistry that go into bringing a text to life. Please respect all copyright laws by not reproducing this resource in any manner without permission from the publisher except in brief quotations used for research, private studies, critical texts, or reviews.

Published by Proa Publications
An Imprint of University of Guam Press
Richard F. Taitano Micronesian Area Research Center (MARC)
303 University Drive, UOG Station
Mangilao, Guam 96923
(671) 735-2153/4

www.uogpress.com
ISBN-13: 978-1-935198-66-6
Library of Congress Control Number: 2022940607

This project was made possible with support from the Northern Marianas Humanities Council, a nonprofit, private corporation funded in part by the National Endowment for the Humanities.

Support was also provided through matching funds from the Northern Marianas College.

Orthography Note: *This publication includes work from authors throughout the Mariana Islands. Work contributed by authors from Guåhan adhere to the Guåhan CHamoru orthography, while authors from the Commonwealth of the Northern Mariana Islands (CNMI) adhere to the CNMI Chamorro and Refaluwasch orthographies. In some instances, authors have opted to use older or more unique spelling variations as a form of creative expression.*

Citation Style Note: *While this publication follows the American Psychological Association's (APA) 7th edition citation style, slight variations exist among the authors' work in mechanical details that include, but are not limited to, punctuation, capitalization, and verb tense usage.*

Editorial and Design Team

Ajani Burrell, Lead Collection Editor
Kimberly Bunts-Anderson, Ph.D., Collection Editor
Victoria-Lola Leon Guerrero, Managing Editor
Donald H. Rubinstein, Ph.D., Editor
Desiree Taimanglo Ventura, Editor
Verna Zafra-Kasala, Copy Editor
Joseph D. Franquez, Guåhan CHamoru Orthography Editor
Patrick Romolor, CNMI Refaluwasch Orthography Editor
Manuel Flores Borja, CNMI Chamorro Orthography Editor
Maria Cristobal Calori, Graphic Designer
Ralph Eurich Patacsil, Cover Artist

Table of Contents

1   Introduction
Ajani Burrell

Signs

15   CHamoru Leadership Lessons
Mary Therese Perez Hattori

25   Repping the Marianas: Cultural Pride and the Rise of Mariana Islands-Inspired Clothing Brands
Ajani Burrell

45   From Exotica to Erotica: Historical Fiction or Fictional History in Mariana Islands Novels, 2012-2017
Anne Perez Hattori

65   Mamåhlao: Negotiating Space for Indigenous Culturing
Royce Camacho

73   Fourth Day
Gerard van Gils

79   The Halo Halo ('Mix Mix') Generation
Tabitha Caser Espina

105   Poetry from a Son of the Marianas
Craig Santos Perez

123   Intersection of Identity in Three Generations of CHamoritas and Filipinas in Guam
Sharleen Santos-Bamba and Tabitha Caser Espina

137   Bridging Cultures
Mary Therese Perez Hattori

143   Discovering Saipan Community Art Values
Angelyn Labadan

159   The Thai Community in Saipan
Poonsri Algaier

167   Family Violence, Historical Trauma, and the CHamoru Manggåfa (the Family)
Lisa Linda S. Natividad

Shifts

195 Ti Siña Ma Funas Ham:
Shapes of CHamoru Erasure in Guam
Kenneth Gofigan Kuper

213 Language Change in Saipan: Attitudes and Visions
Dominique B. Hess

223 What Saved Me
Victoria-Lola M. Leon Guerrero

235 Contemporary Dynamics of Traditional Healing in Guam and the Commonwealth of the Northern Mariana Islands
Tricia Lizama

253 Fanachu Famalåo'an: Women are Emerging as Leaders in the Community-wide Resistance to Militarization in the Commonwealth of the Northern Mariana Islands
Sylvia C. Frain

277 May I Borrow Some Soy Sauce? The Changing Dynamics of Neighborly Interactions in Rota
Ajani Burrell

291 Militarism and Sovereignty in the Contemporary Northern Mariana Islands
Theresa "Isa" Arriola

317 The Evolution of Respeto (Respect) as Viewed through Three Generations of Refaluwasch (Carolinian) Families
Cinta Matagolai Kaipat

357 Misan Ánimasan Åsuli: field notes and conversations from the Talakhaya Watershed, Luta
Malcolm Johnson

375 Hågu, Guåhu, yan Hita (You, Me, and We): What Does it Mean to be Part of Guåhan's (Guam's) Multi-faceted Community?
Kelly G. Marsh-Taitano

399 Notes

409 Contributors

A Marianas Mosaic

Introduction

Ajani Burrell

A Marianas Mosaic: Signs and Shifts in Contemporary Island Life is the culmination of a project supported in great measure by a generous grant from the Northern Marianas Humanities Council, along with matching funds from the Northern Marianas College (NMC). The book is a collection of essays, articles, and narratives that explores some of the many topics relevant to contemporary life in the Marianas.

As we embarked on this project, we had two primary goals. One was to meaningfully contribute to the intellectual and cultural mosaic of the Marianas. The other was to do so in a comprehensive fashion. To accomplish the former, we reviewed the existing literature on the region to establish what gaps we might help to fill. While substantial literature on the Marianas exists, and seems to increase in volume every year, much of this literature does not utilize an academic or scholarly approach. Consequently, while this collection is not exclusively a scholarly endeavor, a significant number of the contributions are scholarly in form and approach. Moreover, existing literature that does examine aspects of contemporary life in the Marianas often suffers from a lack of accessibility, whether sequestered behind publisher paywalls or accessible only in physical archives. In compiling these works, we sought to make a broad collection of writings on the Marianas available—in one accessible place— to the people of the Marianas and beyond.

Any investigation of human life for a locale or set of peoples is invariably underpinned by an investigation of culture. Exploration of the existing literature on culture and related subjects in the Marianas was instructive in helping us ascertain what space this book might occupy. In addition to the usual internet databases, directories, indexes, and search engines, two valuable resources were the Pacific Collection and the Commonwealth of the Northern Mariana Islands (CNMI) Archives, both housed at the Northern Marianas College. These resources offered a wealth of local literature, much of which are primary sources or texts unavailable in digital format.

Also invaluable were the digital catalogs of the Micronesian Area Research Center (MARC), housed at the University of Guam (UOG), and the peer-reviewed journal *Pacific Asia Inquiry*, a UOG publication. The former provided information on or access to locally produced or locally relevant scholarship, such as unpublished theses, that were often difficult to find via other digital platforms. The latter helped us better appreciate the scope of Micronesia-specific cultural scholarship produced in the past decade. These resources, among others, confirmed to us that while there was considerable literature about the Marianas, and considerable academic scholarship on the region, there was not nearly enough scholarly literature examining local life and culture to reflect the diversity and vitality teeming in the islands today. Notable examples of existing scholarship include such works as *The New Shape of Old Island Cultures: A Half Century of Social Change in Micronesia* and *Making Sense of Micronesia: The Logic of Pacific Island Culture*, both by Francis X. Hezel (2001 & 2013); *Tiempon I Manmofo'na: Ancient Chamorro Culture and History of the Northern Mariana Islands* by Scott C. Russell (1998); *Cultures of Commemoration: The Politics of War, Memory and History in the Mariana Islands* by Keith L. Camacho (2011); and *Saipan: The Ethnology of a War-Devastated Island* by Alexander Spoehr (1954).

This selection of books, as well as many other similar titles, highlights two key gaps in the scholarly literature on life and culture in the Marianas. One shortcoming is that much of what literature does exist often subsumes the Marianas in the broader regional scope of Micronesia, and in some cases the wider Pacific (e.g., Liston et al. [2011]; *Pacific Island Heritage: Archeology, Identity & Community*; Farzana Gounder's [2015] *Narrative and Identity Construction in the Pacific Islands*; or Strathern et al.'s [2002] *Oceania: An Introduction to the Cultures and Identities of Pacific Islanders*). To be sure, a great many commonalities exists amongst the people of the various islands of Micronesia, and to a lesser extent the wider Pacific Islands or Oceania region, yet these commonalities are likely dwarfed by the unique dynamics at play in each of the constituent entities. For example, in a move that only took full effect in 1986, the CNMI freely entered into a political union with the United States as a commonwealth, a circumstance that distinguishes it from fellow territories and other nations in the Pacific (as well as US territories elsewhere). Guam, meanwhile, serves as the home for some of the largest US military installations in the Pacific, and allows non-indigenous ownership of land, both circumstances that distinguish it from many Oceanic nations. The dynamics in these examples have been at play for decades, yet continue to exert a profound impact on the people and life in the respective islands today.

Another issue highlighted in those texts is the historical focus of much of the scholarship produced about the region. Humans, according to current research, have inhabited the Marianas for over 3,500 years. The islands have also been impacted by Western colonialism for much of the past 400 years, and played a vital role in the Pacific theater of World War II. As a consequence, the region has been of great interest to historians and archeologists from around the world. And yet, even though the Marianas has now collectively spent several decades under the auspices of the United States, recent scholarship on the region continues to reflect an imbalance between the historical and the contemporary. As such, the bulk of the existing Marianas-related scholarship examines aspects of life that far predate the present.

Despite its relatively small land mass and population, the Mariana Islands can claim several compelling reasons (beyond their intriguing history) to document life today. As previously mentioned, the islands have a unique territorial relationship to the United States, a relationship all the more unique given the remote location of the archipelago. This remote location is also of particular strategic importance as the United States continues to engage the burgeoning regional power of China. Because of its current relationship with the United States, as well as the globalizing effects of such developments as the internet and cheap international travel, indigenous Marianas cultures—already themselves greatly altered by hundreds of years of colonialism—are undergoing significant and rapid shifts. Moreover, given the geopolitical dynamics of the past century in the region, the Marianas has one of the most ethnically and culturally diverse populaces on the planet, a feat all the more notable when considered in the context of the relatively small size of the islands and a total population of less than 250,000 people across the archipelago. For these and other reasons, we found it imperative to try to capture in some measure a scholarly picture of present-day dynamics in the region.

To be fair, the literature on the region goes far beyond the aforementioned texts, and far beyond scholarly or academic books in general. To a degree, the wider collection of literature on life in the Marianas also suffers similar issues of scope (frequently historical), but given the diversity it also provides more examples of contemporary dynamics in the region. As we developed this project, we relied on and were inspired by the work of such academics and writers as Laura Souder, Samuel F. McPhetres, Vicente M. Diaz, Robert A. Underwood, Don Farrell, David Atienza de Frutos, Michael L. Bevacqua, Mavis Warner Van Peenen, Bo Flood, and many others (some of whose work appears in this volume) to guide us. This body of literature is comprised of both scholarly and creative work, but together it helps to highlight another gap in the scholarly literature this volume aims to address: accessibility.

Over the lifespan of this project, we were pleased to see, year after year, ever more contemporary scholarship produced on aspects of life in the Marianas. Much of this scholarship was produced locally, or by sons and daughters of the Marianas who live, work, and study elsewhere in the world. A significant portion of this scholarship comes in the form of academic work done in pursuit of master's and doctoral degrees, in particular the theses that are a requirement for completion. These theses, while valuable contributions to the scholarship, often go unpublished. Sometimes copies will be procured by local institutions (such as the UOG's MARC or the CNMI Pacific Collection at NMC) or made available online, but apart from those avenues, accessing that literature is difficult, all the more so for non-researchers or non-academics.

Other limits on accessibility exist as well. Much of the scholarship on the region, even relatively recent scholarship, is unavailable in digital format. Often it can only be found in print versions, usually in the library collections of UOG or NMC. The same goes for much primary source material of a cultural nature. Typically, it has not been digitized, and frequently it is only accessible in person at one or two institutions in the region. Likewise, more recent scholarship that has been published digitally often can only be found behind paywalls. All of these circumstances confirm two prevailing issues regarding cultural scholarship on the region. First, the scholarship is often difficult to access for academics (and often next to impossible for non-academics), and second, and perhaps more importantly, the academic literature on the region, while expansive and burgeoning, is often disparate and diffuse in nature. It is these limitations, as well as the aforementioned gaps in the contemporary cultural scholarship on the region, that this book hopes to help redress.

To say that this book is merely a scholarly or academic one, however, would be inaccurate. While we place an emphasis on the academic and see one of the primary purposes of this endeavor to help fill certain gaps in the scholarship on the region, the text is rounded out with more creative works. These creative works include narratives and poetry, which further help to illuminate life in the Marianas today. The inclusion of these creative works is a means to help us accomplish the other principal objective of this text.

The other primary goal for this text was to provide a measure of comprehensiveness as it addressed the subject of life in the Marianas today. One aspect of this goal was to seek a broad scope of topics and issues within the relatively narrow geographic focus. Our hope was to reflect the diverse nature of life through the varied pieces in the book. Given life's complexities, this is necessarily an endless pursuit, but we sought to at least attempt it through an approach that advanced a panoramic perspective comprised of multiple, micro-focused investigations. Among the more than 20 contributions to this volume, none explore the same topic. Connections and thematic threads exist, but each piece explores in its own unique way a particular facet of life in the Marianas today. In this way we hoped to offer an expansive—if still incomplete—picture of life in the region.

Another aspect of the comprehensive approach is an effort to reflect and pay homage to the diversity and collective spirit of the region. Fundamentally, this meant ensuring that voices from the different populous islands of the chain be heard. Given the diversity present in the region, we also thought it imperative to gather voices of or from as many groups and communities as possible. Thus, the book contains works from academics, writers, educators, and other professionals. The contributors hail from communities and embody characteristics too disparate to enumerate here, though a notable feature is that women have authored a majority of the works included. As we mentioned earlier, in addition to diverse subject matter, each author approaches her topic in her own way and with her own voice. Some use a narrative style, others a scholarly one. Others still take a blended approach, or one that seems to use an observational or commentary style. And yet, despite differences in form and subject matter, each work enlightens us to life in the Marianas as it is today—a panorama via the micro-focused. In this way, this volume seeks to piece together disparate elements into a contemporary mosaic of the Marianas.

While diversity is a notable feature of the region, and consequently an intellectually honest examination of the region should acknowledge and document that characteristic, such an approach nevertheless has its perils. Though the region has been impacted—often brutally and adversely—by 400 years of colonialism, militarism, and other hegemonic attitudes and policies, it must be recognized that indigenous populations have persevered in the face of these conditions. Those populations persevere to this day. The chief peril, then, in taking an approach that highlights the diversity of the region, is to abet, as Kenneth Gofigan Kuper argues elsewhere in this volume, the marginalization of indigenous voices under the guise of multiculturalism. To allow this would be a mistake. To combat it, this book seeks a balance between indigenous and non-indigenous voices that befits the cultural landscape of the region.

In addition to the goal of contributing to the literature of and on the region, and doing so in a comprehensive way, we had one final guiding principle in the development of this book, one that pertained to the audience. Our hope as editors was that we might not simply create literature *about* the Marianas but also *for* the Marianas. In particular, we hoped that this book would be available to anyone who wished to read about life in the Marianas today. As such, care was taken to render the writing in an accessible fashion, so that this book—composed of diverse content written by diverse authors—could be read and appreciated by a diverse audience beyond the traditional scope of academe.

As we examined the contributions to be included in this volume, several themes emerged. Many of the pieces spoke to matters of place. Others dealt with matters of person. Others still explored politics. Some addressed a combination of topics. Beyond these themes of person, place, and politics, we found others to be more salient as a guide to arranging this text. The works in this book fall into two general thematic categories: those that document or otherwise examine what we'll call "signs" of life or cultural dynamics in the region, and those that identify or otherwise analyze the "shifts" underway in the region. The former category helps detail the social, political, and cultural world the people of the Marianas inhabit today. The latter seeks to clarify how we have arrived at this particular world with this particular set of dynamics, some of the effects of these dynamics and the longer-term historical factors, such as colonialism, that shaped them, and how that world continues to change. Indigenous and non-indigenous voices help to establish both the "signs" and "shifts" chronicled here. In some cases, particularly the pieces of a more narrative bent, the signs or shifts manifest on a more personal note. In others, the signs or shifts help us appreciate the dynamics taking place at a broader level.

We should say that the demarcation between "signs" and "shifts" is neither exact nor absolute. Each piece is complex, delving into context, circumstance, and causality. Invariably, each piece reveals elements of both sign and shift, given the intertwined nature of the two ideas. Yet most of the pieces seemed to fall to one side of the divide or the other. We hope this structure helps readers appreciate both the conditions and the consequences of life in the Marianas today.

Signs

In Chapter 1, Mary Therese Perez Hattori offers a framework for authentic and culturally sustaining leadership that could benefit both CHamoru heritage individuals and the American institutions in which they work. The framework harnesses CHamoru cultural precepts to facilitate authentic leadership in academic institutions while maintaining cultural heritage, and thereby proposing an alternative to Western models and ideals of leadership—models and ideals often at odds with CHamoru and other Indigenous cultures.

In the next chapter, Ajani Burrell chronicles the recent explosion of local clothing brands in the region, with a particular focus on the CNMI, and explores to what degree this explosion is a manifestation of cultural pride. He finds that the dynamics of the local clothing market are complex and suggests several contributing factors for the exceptional popularity of these types of brands.

Chapter 3, by Anne Perez Hattori, analyzes how recent novels set in the Marianas represent—and sometimes misrepresent—the people, habitat, and culture of the region. The essay also assesses the historical veracity of the novels, and posits that the histories represented in these novels are not always fair or ethical with respect to the culture they purport to depict.

Royce Camacho explores the notion of mamåhlao in CHamoru culture in Chapter 4. Drawing upon thinkers from Plato to Foucault, and punctuated by local anecdotes and illustrations, Camacho examines manifestations and implications of mamåhlao in the classroom and in the tourism-driven gift shop, among other settings.

In Chapter 5, Gerard van Gils recounts an anecdote from his first year teaching high school in Saipan, and uses that experience to explore some vital cultural and social issues that create challenges not just for the education system, but for most institutions in the region.

Tabitha Caser Espina examines identity formation for third-generation Filipinos in Guam in Chapter 6. She takes a multidisciplinary approach that employs autoethnography and the analysis of poems written by two Guamanian poets. Espina utilizes the popular Filipino dessert halo-halo as a metaphor to underpin her assessment that this generation of Filipino immigrants in Guam undergoes a significant degree of "mixing" as they negotiate their identity formation.

In a series of poems that comprise Chapter 7, Craig Santos Perez explores themes of Chamorro culture, food, politics, migration, family, ecology, and history.

In Chapter 8, Sharleen Santos-Bamba and Tabitha Espina investigate how Chamorrita and Filipina women use literacy in different ways as they develop their identities. The research takes an intergenerational and intercultural approach to better understand how each of these populations forms its identity and relationships to one another.

Chapter 9, by Mary Therese Perez Hattori, discusses how the author has come to thrive as a CHamoru transplant in Hawaiʻi. In relating her journey, she uses her experiences, scholarly and cultural work, and research to provide strategies for CHamoru transplants to stay connected to their culture and maintain their cultural identity.

In Chapter 10, Angelyn Labadan explores the reasons behind the notable lack of arts resources and programming in the CNMI, as well as public perspectives on the value of art in the community.

Chapter 11, by Poonsri Algaier, paints a picture of contemporary life for the Thais who remain in Saipan from the large influx of immigrants during the boom years of the garment industry.

In Chapter 12, Lisa Linda S. Natividad examines family violence in the Marianas and offers a framework that includes historical trauma and traditional CHamoru concepts of the family system to better understand the deeper dimensions of this issue. She also discusses some of the implications for social service practitioners, with the goal of developing more effective and culturally appropriate intervention practices.

Shifts

In Chapter 13, Kenneth Gofigan Kuper provides a segue from Signs to Shifts through an exploration of multiculturalism in present-day Guåhan. Kuper posits that multiculturalism is just the latest manifestation of settler colonialism designed to deprive Indigenous CHamorus of agency and independence in their homeland. As part of his analysis, Kuper chronicles key aspects of the colonial history of Guåhan and examines the role of a pivotal court case in reinforcing the more negative impacts of multiculturalism on the island.

In the next chapter, Dominique B. Hess examines ongoing language change in the largest and most populous island of the Commonwealth of the Northern Mariana Islands, in particular the influence of the English language on the local community and languages. Her research highlights the tensions that underpin the shifting language landscape in Saipan, and notes the emergence of a distinct, local variety of English that reflects these tensions.

Chapter 15, by Victoria-Lola M. Leon Guerrero, recounts the heart-rending story of trying to process the loss of her first child shortly after his birth. In reckoning with her grief, she experiences a spiritual transformation born out of a conflict between her Indigenous culture and her Catholic upbringing.

Tricia Lizama explores the current state of traditional healing in the Marianas in Chapter 16. Based on hundreds of hours of interviews with more than 40 traditional healers in the region, this essay contours the worldview of the Mariana Islands healer. Lizama also chronicles developments in 21st century traditional healing, and in so doing, provides a glimpse of what the future of this millennia-old practice may hold.

In Chapter 17, Sylvia C. Frain examines the way in which CHamoru and Refaluwasch women are spearheading the resistance to militarization in the Marianas region. The article presents three distinct examples of these efforts and highlights critical factors that that help foster and propagate the resistance.

Chapter 18, by Ajani Burrell, examines a particular and perplexing change in neighborly dynamics in Rota. Interviews with Rota residents, along with historical and demographic information, help to inform a narrative that explores the phenomenon of Rota residents becoming increasingly unlikely to ask small favors of their neighbors. The essay also discusses some possible causes of this change, as perceived by residents themselves.

Theresa "Isa" Arriola argues in Chapter 19 that the people of the CNMI should reconsider how they conceptualize sovereignty. At the heart of this reconsideration is the role and interpretation of the CNMI Covenant. She advances the idea that conceptions of sovereignty in the CNMI should be rooted in Indigenous epistemologies rather than Western ones, which could result in a more fluid and effective sovereignty for the people, one that resists future militarization and opens the door to a more expansive interpretation of the CNMI's political status.

In the next chapter, Cinta Matagolai Kaipat investigates notions of respeto (respect) in Refaluwasch (Carolinian) culture and how it has changed over the past three generations. As a bedrock of Refaluwasch culture, respeto influences or impacts many other aspects of the culture, several of which are discussed here in this wide-ranging examination. Kaipat asserts that the erosion of respeto over the past three generations has been swift and precipitous, with dire consequences for the culture —both present and future—should the decline not be remedied.

Chapter 21, by Malcolm Johnson, highlights the changes affecting the Talakhaya watershed in Rota. He reports on several aspects of his time in Rota while working as a National Coral Reef Management Fellow, including the shifting human relationships to the watershed, local perspectives on the watershed and programs to help sustain it, and the challenges—human and environmental—facing this vital feature of Rota's ecology.

To conclude, Kelly G. Marsh-Taitano, in Chapter 22, explores the dynamics that have produced the multiethnic and multicultural island that is Guåhan today. As part of this exploration, Marsh highlights recent demographic shifts, as well as some of the impacts these shifts are having on life and people in Guåhan.

Signs

CHamoru Leadership Lessons

Mary Therese Perez Hattori

CHamoru Leadership Lessons
Born and raised on Guam, I am one of nine children of Fermina Leon Guerrero Perez and Paul Mitsuo Hattori. I moved to O'ahu after I graduated from high school in 1983 to further my education at the University of Hawai'i at Mānoa (UHM). I completed a baccalaureate degree in Secondary Social Studies with a concentration in Pacific Islands History, a Professional Diploma in Secondary Social Studies, a master's degree in Educational Technology, and a Doctor of Education degree in Professional Educational Practice.

While in college, I took several jobs at UHM, progressing from positions as a student employee during my undergraduate studies, to professional positions as a computer specialist, academic advisor, lecturer, and professor in the fields of computer science, information technology, educational technology, and teacher education. For over 10 years, I was Technology Director at Kapi'olani Community College, the largest community college in the University of Hawai'i system, and currently I serve as Interim Director of the Pacific Islands Development Program.

Crosscurrents of Culture

Early in my career, I struggled with being a teacher and leader, trapped in the crosscurrents of two cultures—CHamoru and American. My teacher training and leadership development programs promoted American principles and practices that often ran counter to my Native cultural ideals. Individualism, ambition, competition, and rapid decision-making were valued over communal identity, collaboration, and deliberate, tradition-honoring decision-making. An individual's accumulation of material wealth and increased social status were key factors in academic and career planning; colleges even supply students and parents with charts showing the highest paying college majors and lifetime salary-earning potential based on college degrees. Students are encouraged to select majors as soon as possible, while exploring a variety of disciplines is strongly discouraged with institutional policies such as the practice of placing students on academic warning if they do not declare an academic major by the time they are sophomores. Education is not viewed as a developmental process that may take time, but a means to rapid degree completion and lucrative employment.

In the initial phase of my career, I engaged in teaching educators a curriculum based on American principles, all the while ignoring ways that a program of study may contradict my own Indigenous ways, beliefs, and standards. I also participated in several leadership development programs that were grounded in ideals and customs of US society. These programs promoted a variety of Western leadership models such as Breakthrough Leadership, Sustainable Leadership, and Adaptive Leadership, and provided examples from American institutions such as the military, for-profit corporations, and politics. There was no acknowledgement of culture, which is a critical aspect of leadership, as noted by Chamorro-Premuzic and Sanger (2016),

> Although the core ingredients of leadership are universal (good judgment, integrity, and people skills), the full recipe for successful leadership requires culture-specific condiments. The main reason for this is that cultures differ in their implicit theories of leadership, the lay beliefs about the qualities that individuals need to display to be considered leaders.

For a time, I was caught in opposing cultural crosscurrents and believed that as a CHamoru living in the United States, survival and success would depend on the ability to set aside my own culture and live up to expectations of the dominant American society. Faculty in institutions of higher education in the state of Hawai'i are largely judged by individual effort; tenure and promotion in many fields requires publication of articles or books authored as an individual, not as a co-author. There are no mechanisms to support team-teaching by hiring more than one faculty member to teach a course. Documents submitted for contract renewal, tenure, and promotion must be written in a self-centered and I-focused style that highlights one's individual accomplishments. People like me who come from societies that value humility and a communal identity are advised to use "I" and "me" rather than "us" and "we," and are instructed to remove all self-effacing and modest language from our documents because those may be viewed negatively by peer and administrative reviewers. In one promotion application, I ignored this advice and crafted statements that reflected my unit's collective identity, including the statement, "Many of my professional accomplishments are the result of helping others make connections to the information, resources, decision-makers, and skills they need to realize their objectives and contribute to the achievement of organizational goals." This approach was not well-received, and one reviewer complained that he could not distinguish my identity and my achievements from the identity and achievements of the department I led. In my view as a leader of one of the largest units on the campus, the development of a communal identity was a positive achievement, and as a good leader my professional successes were possible because of the group's efforts and support. I was directed to provide a supplemental statement reframing my leadership philosophy and accomplishments from an individual perspective. This was a wholly inauthentic document but a requirement to move my promotion application forward, so I complied with this request. This is but one example of cultural expectations of the dominant society being imposed on my professional life and producing a living contradiction in which my values were denied in my workplace (McNiff, 2013, p. 35). These conflicts motivated me to find ways to validate and legitimate my CHamoru culture in leadership. To be authentic and to honor my heritage, I used Western models such as Robert Greenleaf's Servant Leadership and Authentic Leadership as conceptual bridges, stepping-stones to understanding that allowed my American colleagues and superiors to see and understand the value of a culture-based leadership praxis. With these Western-based constructs of Servant Leadership and

Authentic Leadership, I was able to navigate antagonistic crosscurrents and articulate those CHamoru approaches which make me a better leader. These approaches can be helpful models for others; our Native ways and wisdom can also be used to mitigate problems of American culture and colonization.

Riding the Currents: Culturally Sustaining Leadership

The work of educator Django Paris provides another way for me to advocate for cultural authenticity in American schools and workplaces. Paris (2012) asserts that our schools can "support young people in sustaining the cultural and linguistic competence of their communities while simultaneously offering access to dominant cultural competence" (p. 95). In other words, culturally sustaining education enables students to retain and sustain their cultures while learning the skills needed to succeed in the dominant culture. Paris and Alim (2014) state, "equity and access can best be achieved by centering pedagogies on the heritage and contemporary practices of students and communities of color" (p. 87).

Culturally sustaining leadership means leveraging the best parts of my CHamoru identity and culture in enacting an effective leadership practice and permitting those I lead to honor their heritages while succeeding in their respective jobs. Even in the midst of foreign institutions we can use aspects of our culture to be effective leaders wherever we are, at home or away.

Authentically CHamoru Leadership

As stated earlier, literature on the topic of authenticity in leadership was an important conceptual bridge allowing for CHamoru ways to be integrated into my professional practice. Avolio and Gardner (2005) suggest that authentic leadership is a foundational or root construct which "forms the basis for what then constitutes other forms of positive leadership" (p. 328). Authenticity is required of leaders; in fact, "Leadership calls us to be authentic: to be true to ourselves and be true to the world" (Terry, 1993, p. 189). CHamoru culture thus forms the foundation of my leadership philosophy and guides my decisions and conduct. Terry (1993) writes, "Authenticity informs and directs action; action grounds authenticity in life. ... Without authenticity, action drifts. Without action, authenticity remains idle conjecture and wishful thinking" (p. 138). In this essay I highlight two cultural elements that I have integrated into my leadership praxis. This act of articulation is also an act of authentic leadership; leaders must identify and share their values with their followers (Aponte-Moreno, 2014).

Belonging

As CHamorus, we practice and prioritize belonging; it is a notable aspect of our culture that can have a transformational impact on organizational culture. Like many people of the Pacific, CHamorus are oriented toward a communal identity which gives everyone a sense of recognition and belonging. Belonging, as described by Spiller and Wolfgramm (2015) "embraces spiritual ideals of interconnectedness and relationality" (p. 305). A primary lesson I learned throughout my childhood was that everyone is a valued member of the family and the greater society simply by virtue of being born and that nothing I did or did not do could eradicate my status as a CHamoru. A strong sense of security comes from being born into a state of belonging and it is "a defining source of happiness and is central to well-being, meaning, and purpose" (Spiller & Wolfgramm, 2015, p. 303). We do have high standards and aspirations for our children and ourselves, but achievements such as material wealth or social status are not measures of worth and acceptance.

Members of cultures that are individualistic rather than communal often struggle for recognition and belonging. It is a source of great concern noted by Swiss philosopher de Botton (2005), who says "it is an almost universal anxiety: an anxiety about what others think of us; about whether we're judged a success or a failure, a winner or a loser" (p. vii).

The famous medical doctor Oliver Sacks was impressed by this ethos of belonging after having visited Guam while investigating the disease Lytico-Bodig. In an interview with TV Ontario's Allan Gregg (2010), Dr. Sacks spoke of an "immensely different and moving sense of belonging" and contrasted CHamoru and American responses to disease:

> One of the horrors of disease in American communities, especially with those who have severe degenerative diseases, is that one gets isolated, abandoned, stigmatized, marginalized and falls out of the world. On Guam, I never saw that. People would remain completely part of the family and community, a full person right to the last. If they had to go to the hospital, the whole family would go with

them. The hospital was like a village. Everyone is integrated all the while, even before Lytico-Bodig. In this way, they are much more civilized than we are.

These social problems mentioned by de Botton and Sacks are caused by a lack of and struggle for recognition and belonging and are uncommon in our islands, which have a strong spirit of belonging. Perhaps this CHamoru tradition is an antidote for these social woes (Hattori, 2016).

Educational researchers note a connection between academic success and a sense of belonging in school. They note, "Feeling part of a school or classroom community has significant psychological benefits for students and makes them more likely to engage in productive academic behaviors" (Farrington et al., 2012, p. 28). An example of putting belonging into practice is to infuse program orientation with the CHamoru ethos of belonging. I tell students in orientation programs that by virtue of admission, they belong. In a highly selective educational leadership doctoral program at UH, I remind new students, many in positions of leadership and all over-achievers, that they need not worry about proving themselves; instead, they should focus their efforts on improving themselves. Former students have remarked that these assurances of belonging were among the most affirming moments in their orientation and for some, gave them a new sense of freedom they do not necessarily have in their professional lives. As an educator, I felt responsible for creating a sense of belonging in the classroom and relational accountability to my students. This requires establishing a relationship with the students to the greatest extent possible given limited class time and office hours. I fostered belonging through team-building, collaborative learning pedagogies, and engendering in students a sense of responsibility for the learning of others. This awareness of doing good for the benefit of others or the benefit of the whole is typical of CHamoru culture where older siblings nurture younger siblings, where youth are taught to be mindful of the needs of elders.

These benefits of a culture of belonging apply to the workplace as well as schools; employee engagement has been linked to a sense of belonging. This can be achieved by a leadership that affirms each employee's suitability for the unit, prioritizing a communal identity, and engendering collaboration rather than competition. In the workplace, I fostered a communal identity at several levels by organizing employees into functional teams, creating project teams that include people from across different functional teams, and by ensuring regular team and departmental meetings.

The meetings had several purposes for each functional team: to inform others of their work, to recognize and acknowledge achievements of individuals and teams, and to maintain awareness of departmental and organizational goals. Employees develop professional identities as members of a functional team and as members of the department as a whole. The word "we" was used more often than "I" or "me," and as the unit head, I always reported the department's achievements as collective accomplishments. These team and department meetings were a commitment to fostering relationships among professionals who might not work directly with each other on a regular basis, and generated a sense of collective identity and accountability. As the head of the unit, I was not only accountable to the institution, but was also able to use the collective identity to impart a relational accountability to my employees. As an educator and leader, I have seen the ideal of belonging transform and empower students and employees.

Cultural Metaphors

Like many Indigenous people, CHamorus communicate using analogy and metaphor, which are powerful tools for educators and leaders. Philosopher Ortega y Gasset (2019) says, "The metaphor is probably the most fertile power possessed by man" (p. 33). We gain and transmit knowledge through analogy and metaphor. On metaphors as a leadership tool, Terry (1993) writes, they "open paths for understanding human discourse" (p. 68). Metaphors "open windows onto reality" (p. 160). Our culture is replete with powerful metaphors that illuminate CHamoru ways of being; here I share two that can be applied to leadership—latte and wayfinding.

The latte—stone house-posts used in ancient CHamoru society—is an important cultural icon and can be a metaphor for strength, support, foundations, and the strength borne of unification. The latte is created through the combination of haligi house-post and tåsa capstone; latte standing in groups can form strong structural foundations. Leaders use this iconic image to inspire unity, connection, and relational accountability. I have employed this metaphor in several instances, sometimes sharing the chant, "Ini Na Latte" by Leonard Iriarte as a call for unity. I have shared it in speeches to Pacific Islanders in Hawai'i and on the mainland in programs such as the National Pacific American Leadership Institute (NAPALI), a leadership development program hosted annually in Hawai'i for emerging Indigenous leaders, and the City College of San Francisco's Talanoa program, which hosts public events bringing those of Pacific Islander heritage in San Francisco together for periodic talks by noted Pacific Islanders. Another commonly used metaphorical device comes from the revival of the traditional canoe sailing, which inspires the use of navigation as a metaphor. We often talk about navigating successfully in school, in college, in the workplace, and life. Goals and vision can be communicated as important destinations. Leaders, mentors, parents, and friends can be described as celestial bodies that provide guidance, or as winds, tides, and currents helping others reach their destinations.

Communicating organizational goals through metaphor is an effective leadership skill. Terry (1993) notes a connection between leadership, metaphors, and authenticity:
> Leadership calls us to be authentic: to be true to ourselves and be true to the world. In order to be true to ourselves, we must look at any misalignment that exists between our professed metaphor and the behavior that is entailed by that metaphor. (p. 189)

Closing Reflection

An authentic professional life, grounded in culturally sustaining practices such as belonging and the use of metaphor, and other cultural elements not addressed here such as chenchule', respect for manåmko', and temporal intelligence, has made me a more successful leader and educator (Hattori, 2016). Beyond my own professional growth, sharing and modeling culturally sustaining leadership in professional development workshops enable me to contribute to change in the people and institutions I serve. There is recognition of the worth of our Indigenous knowledge applied to organizational culture. The Native cultures of the Mariana Islands are rich in positive customs and values that can benefit others and make this world a better place. Let's identify, articulate, and practice the best elements of our culture and share them, enriching ourselves and everyone else in the process.

Culturally sustaining leadership brings to mind an account of the Greek myth of Narcissus in a novel by Coelho (1993). In the legend, the young man is so enraptured by his reflection in a lake that he cannot look away, falls into the water, and drowns.

When Narcissus died, the goddesses of the forest appeared and found that the lake, which had been fresh water, was transformed into a lake of salty tears. "Why do you weep?" the goddesses asked. "I weep for Narcissus," the lake replied. "Ah, it is no surprise that you weep for Narcissus," they said, "for though we always pursued him in the forest, you alone could contemplate his beauty close at hand." "But ... was Narcissus beautiful?" the lake asked. "Who better than you to know that?" the goddesses said in wonder. "After all, it was by your banks that he knelt each day to contemplate himself!" The lake was silent for some time. Finally, it said, "I weep for Narcissus, but I never noticed that Narcissus was beautiful. I weep because, each time he knelt beside my banks, I could see, in the depths of his eyes, my own beauty reflected" (p. ix).

Culturally sustaining leadership provides ways leaders can give their followers this kind of experience—so that in our workplaces, our activities, and in our personal encounters, they see reflections of their own beauty.

References

Aponte-Moreno, M. (2014). Embodying authentic leadership: An actor's perspective. In K.G. Schuyler, J.E. Baugher, K. Jironet, & L. Lid-Falkman (Eds.), *Leading with spirit, presence, and authenticity* (pp. 197–212). Jossey-Bass.

Avolio, B. J., & Gardner, W. L. (2005). Authentic leadership development: Getting to the root of positive forms of leadership. *The Leadership Quarterly, 16*, 315–338.

Chamorro-Premuzic, T. & Sanger, M. (2016, May 6). What leadership looks like in different cultures. *Harvard Business Review.* https://hbr.org/2016/05/what-leadership-looks-like-in-different-cultures

Coelho, P. (1993). *The alchemist.* Harper Collins.

de Botton, A. (2005). *Status anxiety.* Vintage.

Farrington, C. A., Roderick, M., Allensworth, E., Nagaoka, J., Keyes, T. S., Johnson, D. W., & Beechum, N. O. (2012). *Teaching adolescents to become learners; The role of noncognitive factors in shaping school performance: A critical literature review.* University of Chicago Consortium on Chicago School Research.

Gregg, A. (Host) (2010). Dr. Oliver Sacks – Island of the colorblind [Audio podcast episode]. In *Allan Gregg in conversation.* TV Ontario. https://player.fm/series/allan-gregg-in-conversation-audio/dr-oliver-sacks-island-of-the-colorblind-full

Hattori, M. T. P. (2016). Culturally sustaining leadership: A Pacific Islander's perspective. *Education Sciences, 6*(4), 1–10.

McNiff, J. (2013). *Action research: Principles and practice* (3rd ed.). Routledge.

Ortega y Gasset, J. (2019). *The dehumanization of art and other essays on art, culture, and literature.* Princeton University Press.

Paris, D. (2012). Culturally sustaining pedagogy: A needed change in stance, terminology, and practice. *Educational Researcher, 41*(3), 93–97.

Paris, D., & Alim, H. S. (2014). What are we seeking to sustain through culturally sustaining pedagogy? A loving critique forward. *Harvard Educational Review, 84*(1), 85–100.

Spiller, C. & Wolfgramm, R. (2015). *Indigenous spiritualties at work: Transforming the spirit of enterprise.* Information Age Publishing, Inc.

Terry, R. W. (1993). *Authentic leadership: Courage in action.* Jossey-Bass.

Repping the Marianas: Cultural Pride and the Rise of Mariana Islands-Inspired Clothing Brands

Ajani Burrell

In 2017, the Commonwealth of the Northern Mariana Islands, or CNMI, had an estimated 52,000 inhabitants (Central Intelligence Agency, 2018). The CNMI is an archipelago of fourteen islands stretching across hundreds of miles in the northwest Pacific Ocean, but the population largely resides on three islands: Saipan, Tinian, and Rota. These three islands are marked by diverse geography that includes elevated limestone plateaus, valleys, cliffs, rocky and sandy beaches of various sizes, and large swaths of thick jungle, but cover in total just 116 square miles. This total land area is about one-fifth the size of Oʻahu, and about one-tenth the size of Rhode Island, the smallest of the United States, while the CNMI's population is just one-twentieth that of Rhode Island.

Though the area and population density are relatively small, the CNMI holds an abundance of beautiful beaches and natural scenery. Over half a million tourists flock annually to the islands (Marianas Visitors Authority, 2018), which are home to a variety of cultures and communities, including at least eight different Pacific Island groups and people from more than half a dozen Asian countries (US Census Bureau, 2011). The CNMI also has something else in abundance: local clothing brands. In 2018, the people of the CNMI could choose from more than 20 local clothing brands, an astounding number for a population of only 52,000 people. Even more astounding is that of these twenty-plus brands, no fewer than 13 of them are located in or were founded in the CNMI.

To put this situation into context, imagine the town of La Crosse, WI (estimated 2017 population: 51,834) or Palm Desert, CA (52, 932), or Valdosta, GA (56,085) (US Census Bureau, 2017). Imagine if thirteen different companies were producing and selling distinct La Crosse-related clothing and accessories in La Crosse (or Palm Desert or Valdosta). Try to imagine visiting a place where half the population is wearing an article of clothing that depicts or represents some aspect of the local culture. How many people on a given day in La Crosse, WI, are wearing clothing that represents La Crosse or its culture? Even iconic and populous cities such as New York or Los Angeles do not see such rates. The only location that seems even remotely analogous would be a college campus, where a significant portion of the student body on any given day is wearing clothing associated with the institution. Such is the pervasive nature of the local clothing brand movement in the Marianas.

What are local clothing brands? For the purposes of this chapter, local clothing brands (LCBs) are those that produce and sell clothing and accessories that relate directly to the Marianas region, which includes both the CNMI and Guam, a neighboring US territory to the south. These LCBs are designed by people who live in or come from the Marianas region. More importantly, the designs for these brands represent some aspect of life or culture in the region, and are all marketed to people who live in the region or come from the region.

While a plethora of LCBs exists today, only two or three such brands existed as recently as 2005, barely 15 years ago. Then a veritable explosion of LCBs occurred around 2015, when entrepreneurs launched or rebooted some of the largest CNMI-based brands still in existence today. For Marianas residents then, the growth was obvious. It seemed—and still seems—that at least half the population at any given moment is wearing a product from one of these brands. Why have these brands—and their popularity—proliferated so quickly? And what can this growth tell us about the people and the culture of the Mariana Islands today?

Clothing, Culture, Values, and Identity

Clothing, in particular dress and fashion, is a public display of culture, values, and identity. In recent decades, scholars from a multitude of academic disciplines—including philosophy, economics, geography, cultural studies, and sociology, among others—have contributed to the interdisciplinary study of fashion (Aspers & Godart, 2013, p. 175). Crane and Bovone (2006) posited that fashion can serve as an example of the connection between symbolic values and material culture, and that "material goods express values; consumption of these goods is a means for the consumer to communicate messages about the values she holds" (p. 320). The study of clothing as a value-laden material good has a long history, dating back to the 1930s, according to Hsu and Burns (2012), who built on the work of Allport, Vernon, and Linday (1951, 1960). Hsu and Burns—following earlier writers Blackwell, Miniard, and Engel (2001), Hofestede (1994), and Lapitsky (1961), among others—put this value formation in a cultural context, asserting that values, including cultural values, "are learned and can shape our consumer behavior, which includes clothing selection" (pp. 1585–1587). Since culture shapes clothing choices and clothing choices can thereby reflect values, an examination of the clothing or fashion choices of a culture can potentially reveal some of the values at work in a culture.

Similarly, clothing as a means to understand and examine identity (both personal and cultural) has been well documented. Giddens (1991) asserted that "dress is vastly more than simply a means of bodily protection: it is, manifestly, a means of symbolic display, a way of giving external form to narratives of self-identity" (p. 62). Crane and Bovone (2006), following earlier work by Giddens (1991), Goffman (1961), Bovone (2003), and others, have argued that the wide variety of fashion choice in today's society imparts a sense of agency to the individual, and can be viewed as the individual making a choice for a particular, meaningful self-identification (p. 323). Crane (2000) posited that "clothing choices provide an excellent field for studying how people interpret a specific form of culture for their own purposes" (p. 1). Other scholars have also examined the connection between identity and personal values (Hitlin & Piliavin, 2004, p. 382).

History of Marianas Dress

As with many other aspects of life in the Marianas, clothing and dress can be viewed within the historical dynamics of three major eras: pre-European contact, colonial occupation, and the post-colonial period. Reports from the first European contact, Magellan's 1521 visit, and from the ensuing decades indicate that the Indigenous Chamorros were scantily clothed. Flores (2010) stated that men generally went without clothing, while "most observers noted women wearing at minimum a leaf (*tifi'*) attached to a cord around their waists, or a piece of paper-thin bark (*gunut*), which covered their private parts" (p. 508). Flores also cited reports describing regular use of natural accessories from both land and sea as adornment, body modification, or indication of social status.

Indigenous dress began to shift radically in the late 17th century when Spain established colonial occupation, and religious missionaries came to the islands. In and around Hagåtña, the present capital of Guam and former headquarters for the Spanish colonial administration, the Indigenous Chamorros—including men, women, and children—adopted Spanish clothing, although outside of the capital, "where contact with religious authority was limited, indigenous attire was still worn" (Flores, 2010, p. 508). Although the influence of the Spanish Empire weakened over the 18th and 19th centuries, a Spanish style of dress persisted in the form of the mestisa, which generally consisted of woven fabric pants and shirts for men and a kamisola and skirt for women (Flores, 2010, p. 509). George Fritz (2001) reported similar attire for Chamorros in the Northern Mariana Islands under the German administration in the early 20th century. Men's work attire consisted of "short pants (*katsunes*) reaching to the knee and a short shirt (*chinia*) worn over the pants," while women wore a "skirt (*lupes*) ... a short blouse (*chinina*) and a kerchief (*paniou-ulo*)" (p. 35). However, the Refaluwasch (Carolinians who had settled in Saipan in the early 1800s) resisted the adoption of Spanish-style clothing well into the 20th century. Refaluwasch men wore "a piece of cotton cloth tied between their legs" and women wore a similar cloth, only wider and wrapped around their hips (Craddock, 1982). Outside influences, including from the Japanese, who administered the Northern Mariana Islands between WWI and WWII, would continue to affect dress styles through the 20th century, though Flores (2010) noted that the style throughout the archipelago remained largely "consistent despite political changes between the Northern Mariana Islands and Guam" (p. 510).

Americanization during the post-WWII period marked another shift in dress styles, with American styles predominating. More recently, dress styles in the Mariana Islands have been impacted by the globalization of the clothing and textile industry, with a wide variety of brands available for purchase. In the late 20th century, a "renaissance of Chamorro language and culture began" that, in part, resulted in an "interest in redefining Chamorro identity via the use of 'heritage' items" (Flores, 2010, p. 510). This fusion of American influence and renewed interest in Chamorro identity provides the historical context for an examination of the eventual rise of local clothing brands, the focus of this research.

Local Clothing Brands and Cultural Pride in the Marianas
To explore the scope and background of local clothing brands of the Marianas, I interviewed brand principals and conducted a survey of the Northern Marianas College community. I also analyzed the symbols, taglines, mottos, and motifs of the brands to better understand brand goals, as well as the specific cultural signifiers they employ or embody.

Repping the Marianas
Until the turn of the 21st century, people in the Marianas were largely limited to clothing designed and produced outside the region. The lifestyle of the islands drew people to surfing brands such as Quicksilver and Hollister, as well as global companies such as Nike. Sporadically, local entrepreneurs would produce a limited run of t-shirts. Often these shirts would be emblazoned with images of Chamorro warriors or sayings. By most accounts, the local clothing brand movement has its origins at the beginning of the 21st century, with the founding of Fotten Gäga' in the CNMI and Fökai Industries in Guam. According to their respective Facebook pages, Fotten Gäga' was founded in 2001, while Fökai Industries opened its first store in 2003. Both brands are still in operation today and retain their early popularity. Around 2005, the first big wave of local clothing brands began, and over the next few years more brands were launched, including Rocksteady (Magas/Mas Magas, 670, Deepside, Stressfree), Chokechain, Atdit, Poksu, Marianas Built, and Salbahe'. A second wave of brands launched around 2015, including Trendsetters, Legends, Roil Soil, and, perhaps the most popular CNMI brand today, Tribe Marianas.

Since 2005 or so, more than two dozen local clothing brands have launched in the Marianas, with many setting up shop in the CNMI. One goal shared among nearly all these brands is a desire to positively represent the people, culture, and region to the world. A common theme in interviews with owners and designers of some of the best-known local brands was their concern over the general lack of knowledge about the Marianas and her people in the wider world, particularly the mainland United States. Often, Islanders find that when they visit the United States, few people have heard of the Marianas or know much about a region that comprises two US territories and boasts some of the highest rates in the country of enlistment in the US armed forces (Hicks, 2014; Weare & Cruz, 2017). Misperceptions are common, and people from the mainland may wonder whether people in the Mariana Islands wear grass skirts, or whether they have McDonald's and the Internet. Consequently, according to Tribe Marianas co-founder Rob Travilla (personal communication, May 8, 2017), "one of the major—if not first—missions of Tribe Marianas, is to spread the Marianas worldwide, so hopefully one day we no longer need to introduce ourselves." Many brands express a similar sentiment in their online descriptions. Fökai, one of the largest brands in the Marianas, describes itself as "an imminent venture to present the native people of the Mariana Islands to the world as an intelligent, persevering, and respectful and respectable community" (Fokai Industries, n.d.a), while the Rocksteady shop was founded "in an attempt to promote and represent the culture, people and life of the Marianas" (irocksteady, n.d.a). Eric Palacios (personal communication, December 4, 2017), creator of the Atdit and Trendsetters brands, agrees, and believes that the "common goal" for all of the brands in the Mariana Islands is to represent the islands.

Symbols, Taglines, and Motifs

Brands achieve the goal of representing the people and culture of the Marianas in distinct ways, but they all share a concerted effort to infuse aspects of the local culture into each brand. For most, this starts with the company or brand name. Some have chosen to incorporate explicit references to the region, such as Tribe Marianas, 670 (the telephone area code for the CNMI), MarianasBuilt, Chamorrita Swimwear (Chamorrita refers to young Chamorro women; it is also the name of an ancient song style in the Marianas), Hafaloha ("Hafa" is the first word of the Chamorro greeting "Hafa Adai"), and Hafa Brand. Others chose a specific word or phrase from Chamorro (Table 1).

Table 1

English Translations of Chamorro Brand Names

Brand	Translation	Additional Meanings
Magas	"Chief" or "Boss"	
Fotten Gäga'	"Strong and powerful beast"	"Party animal"
Poksu	"Accurate" or "Precise"	"Sharpshooter in any skill requiring the ability to secure good aim and a clean grip" (slang)
Fökai	"Go for it" (contemporary)	"Distribution," "Persevere"
Atdit	"Too much"	

Note. Translations for Magas and Fotten Gäga' gathered from Trademark Details, by Justia, n.d. (https://trademarks.justia.com/772/10/magas-stressfree-c-n-m-i-77210306.html). Translations for Poksu from *Home* [Facebook Page], by 82 Threads Co., n.d (https://www.facebook.com/82threads/about?lst=716466056%3A100002572383344%3A1528687248&section=bio). Translations for Fökai from What is the meaning of of fokai? Part 2, by Camacho, 2012 (http://crankeffect.com/1220/what-is-the-meaning-of-fokai-part-2/). Translations for Atdit from Eric Palacios (personal communication, December 4, 2017).

This dedication to representing the Marianas people and culture is also evident in brand taglines and logos, as well as the symbols and images that appear in the designs. The tagline for Tribe Marianas, for example, is "Divided By Tide x United By Pride," a reference to the demography and geography of the region, the fact that a significant portion of the Indigenous people from Guam and the CNMI now reside in the US mainland, and the shared cultural pride of people from the Marianas. Other taglines from Tribe Marianas include "Common Tradition, Common Culture, Commonwealth," in reference to the Commonwealth of the Northern Mariana Islands, and "XV Deep," referring to the 15 islands of the Marianas chain and their proximity to the Marianas Trench, the deepest place on earth. Other brands echo this cultural sentiment. Roil Soil's motto is "Rep Your Soil," which, according to lead designer Peter Aldan (personal communication, January 25, 2018), means to "represent your homeland and culture, to have pride" in the Marianas as a place of origin. A motto for Crowns Guam reads, "Our Waters Run Deep. Our Roots Run Deeper."

While taglines and mottos often express geographical or cultural pride elements, the logos of the companies usually depict cultural heritage artifacts. Perhaps the most common symbol is the latte stone (Figure 1), which figures prominently in the history and culture of the islands. It appears at the center of the official CNMI seal (Figure 2) and in the logos of brands including Legends (Figure 3), Atdit, and Magas. The Tribe Marianas logo includes two crossed adzes, a carving tool of the ancient Chamorros (Figure 4). Some logos, such as those of Roil Soil and Fotten Gäga', feature native plants, while others include iconic symbols of the culture, such as spears.

Figure 1
Chamorro Latte Stones

Figure 2
CNMI Official Seal Featuring Latte Stone at Center

Figure 3
Brand Logo for Legends Clothing Brand Featuring Latte Stone at Center

Figure 4
Tribe Marianas Logo with Adzes

Fig.1 Note. Latte Stones in Latte Stone Park, Hagåtña, Guam. Photograph by H. Nakano, 2006, Wikipedia (https://en.wikipedia.org/wiki/Latte_stone#/media/File:Latte1.jpg). CC BY 2.0

Fig.2 Note. From Seal of the Northern Mariana Islands [Image], Connormah, 2011, Wikimedia (https://commons.wikimedia.org/wiki/File:Seal_of_the_Northern_Mariana_Islands.svg). In the public domain.

Fig.3 Note. From E. Palacios, personal communication, August 22, 2018.

Fig.4 Note. From R. Travilla, personal communication, September 8, 2018.

The products displayed on the websites of the various brands illustrate many of the popular aspects of Marianas culture and history, from marine activities like surfing, outrigger paddling, and spearfishing, to local flora and fauna. Cultural expressions (Table 2) include traditional Chamorro sayings and phrases, as well as references to both contemporary and historical characteristics of the islands.

Table 2

Cultural Expressions Used on Products by Local Clothing Brands

Brand	Sample Expressions (excluding logos)
Atdit / Legends / Trendsetters	"Hafa Adai," "Marianas"
Crowns Guam	"Chief," "Islander," "Guahan"
Roil Soil	"Hafa Adai"
The Undeniable	"The CMMNWLTH," "Islas de los Ladrones,"[a] "Thieves," "Islander," "Hafa Adai"
Tribe Marianas	"Familia," "Hafa Adai"

Note. Expressions are taken verbatim and presented in quotation marks. Expressions for Atdit / Legends / Trendsetters from Photos [Facebook page], by Atdit x Trendsetters CNMI, n.d. (https://www.facebook.com/atditbrand/photos/?ref=page_internal). Expressions for Crowns Guam from Photos [Facebook page], by Crowns Guam, n.d.b (https://www.facebook.com/CrownsGuam/photos/?ref=page_internal). Expressions for Roil Soil from Photos [Facebook page], by Roil Soil Clothing, n.d. (https://www.facebook.com/roilsoil/photos/?ref=page_internal). Expressions for The Undeniable from Photos [Facebook page], by The Undeniable, n.d.b (https://www.facebook.com/UndeniableCNMI/photos/?ref=page_internal). Expressions for Tribe Marianas from Photos [Facebook page], by Tribe Marianas, n.d. (https://www.facebook.com/tribemarianas/photos/?ref=page_internal).
[a]The name Islas de las Ladrones [Island of Thieves] was given to the Mariana Islands by Ferdinand Magellan in the 16th century, and according to Russell (2002), "appeared on many maritime maps until well into the 20th century" (p. 24).

Cultural symbols (Table 3), as with brand logos, often depict heritage items or those durable artifacts that have remained a part of the contemporary fabric of life in the Marianas.

Table 3
Cultural Symbols Used on Products by Local Clothing Brands

Brand	Sample Symbols (excluding logos)
Atdit / Legends / Trendsetters	Machetes, Floral pattern[a], Ancient Chamorro chief, CNMI Seal
Crowns Guam	Palm trees, Proa[b], Flame Tree flowers, Spear, Hibiscus flowers, Plumeria flowers
Fökai	Slingstones, Floral pattern, Latte Stone
Magas / Mas Magas	Sirena[c], Guma[d], Floral pattern, CNMI Seal, Spearfisher, Sea turtle
Roil Soil	Pineapple, Spearfisher, Sirena
The Undeniable	Palm trees, Palm fronds
Tribe Marianas	Floral pattern, CNMI Seal, Coconut, Kamyo

Note. Sample cultural symbols for Atdit / Legends / Trendsetters from Photos [Facebook page], by Atdit x Trendsetters CNMI, n.d. (https://www.facebook.com/atditbrand/photos/?ref=page_internal). Sample cultural symbols for Crowns Guam from Photos [Facebook page], by Crowns Guam, n.d.b (https://www.facebook.com/CrownsGuam/photos/?ref=page_internal). Sample cultural symbols for Fökai from Fokaistuff.com, by Fokai Industries, n.d.b (https://www.fokaistuff.com/). Copyright 2018 by Fokai Online Store. Sample cultural symbols for Magas / Mas Magas from Photos [Facebook page], by 670 Rocksteady Shop, n.d. (https://www.facebook.com/670rocksteady/photos/?ref=page_internal), and from irocksteady.com, by iRocksteady.com, n.d.b, (https://irocksteady.com/products). Copyright 2018 by irocksteady. Sample cultural symbols for Roil Soil from Photos [Facebook page], by Roil Soil Clothing, n.d. (https://www.facebook.com/roilsoil/photos/?ref=page_internal). Sample cultural symbols for The Undeniable from Photos [Facebook page], by The Undeniable, n.d.b (https://www.facebook.com/UndeniableCNMI/photos/?ref=page_internal). Sample cultural symbols for Tribe Marianas from Photos [Facebook page], by Tribe Marianas, n.d. (https://www.facebook.com/tribemarianas/photos/?ref=page_internal).
[a]Floral pattern typically includes some combination of flora prevalent in the Mariana Islands, such as hibiscus, plumeria, flame tree, orchid, and bird of paradise, among others.
[b]Traditional outrigger sailboat prevalent among Pacific Island cultures.
[c]Mythical mermaid creature.
[d]Traditional Chamorro dwelling.

Influences: Producers and Consumers

While examination of the brands and their products reveals an abundant use of cultural, geographic, and geopolitical features of the region, interviews with the brand principals reveal that such thematic foci are conscious choices tailored to a local population. As Pete Aldan (personal communication, January 25, 2018) said about the design influences for Roil Soil, we try to incorporate the mindset of the islander, one who practices patience and enjoys the simpler things in life. There is definitely a connection between us and our natural environment. The Chamorros and Carolinians can be defined by the islands—interconnected, small, yet diverse and beautiful.

This sentiment applies not only to Indigenous descendants, but to just about anyone who calls the Marianas home. When asked who the customers of Tribe Marianas are, co-founder Rob Travilla (personal communication, May 8, 2017) said,

When you define the word *tribe* it's basically a group of people with common interests or common tradition or common culture ... and I feel like even if you've only lived on Saipan for a week but if you say, "man I love the beaches, I love the culture, I love the food," it automatically connects you to Saipan, and wearing a Tribe Marianas shirt makes you feel like you will always be a part of the tribe.

In my interviews with brand principals, they affirmed their strong bond with their home in the Mariana Islands, and their conviction that their customer base shares that affinity. That local loyalty seems in part to be driving the popularity of the brands.

Whatever the reason for their popularity, the broad appeal of the local brands is apparent. In addition to the anecdotal evidence gathered from interviews with owners and designers of the brands—mostly boutique brands with intimate customer relationships—I conducted a survey in December 2017 of consumers of LCBs in the Marianas. Among the 154 respondents from the Northern Marianas College community, nearly 4 out of 5 (78.3%) indicated that they purchased or wore products from one or more LCBs. Of those respondents, 76% indicated that they purchased or wore products from at least two LCBs, which equates to 60% of all respondents. All these figures help to confirm the popularity of LCBs in the Marianas.

While the respondents were predominantly aged 18-24 (63.4%), and therefore not representative of the general population, affirmative response rates were relatively consistent across the three largest age groups represented in the survey (18-24, 25-34, and 35-44-year-olds). The survey data, coupled with anecdotal and observational evidence from brand creators, reinforces the conclusion that these brands have achieved notable penetration and popularity.

Witnessing this explosion of locally branded and inspired clothing, as well as the pervasive use of culturally significant symbols and language by the brands themselves, one might deduce that the popularity of the brands is an expression of cultural pride, analogous to the cultural resurgence of local arts described by Flores (2010) and other regional scholars. After centuries of colonial control by Spain, Japan, Germany, and the United States, and decades under a formal territorial relationship with the United States, the rise of LCBs in the Marianas signals a move to reclaim and reassert cultural heritage. Pete Aldan (personal communication, January 25, 2018), speaking on the influences of the Roil Soil brand, expressed precisely this sentiment:

> Our history of being colonized and not being given the chance to exist as our own, our own identity and voice. Roil means to "stir up," and we like to think that we are stirring up our people and our culture to do more, wake up and live. Of course, it's a play on words, roil meaning what it is as well as "royal," giving immense value to our soil, our land.

As Flores (2010) has noted, the cultural resurgence in the Marianas began in the 1970s and has continued since then, invigorating various aspects of the culture, from language and traditional practices such as maritime navigation and healing, to environmentalism and political self-determination. The rise of LCBs, from the late 1990s to the present day, has similarly manifested this cultural resurgence. Several respondents in the survey indicated that cultural pride was a motivating factor in their choice of personal favorite brands or their pick of the most popular brand. Sixteen percent of all respondents to the question "Why is this your favorite brand?" gave an answer that expressed cultural pride. Likewise, respondents to the question "Why do you think that X brand is so popular?" gave answers such as, "It represents the whole Chamorro community," "Local pride," "The designs … represent the CNMI," "Each design has an aspect of the CNMI," and "Because they express pride and culture." Furthermore, 85% of all respondents agreed or strongly agreed with the statements that "Local clothing/lifestyle brands are more popular today than ever before" and "When people wear local clothing/lifestyle brands they show their pride in the CNMI." Almost 75% of respondents agreed or strongly agreed with the statement that "Today, people from the CNMI have pride in being from the CNMI." All of these results underscore the strong connection between these brands and cultural pride in the region.

Beyond Local Culture

The consumer surveys, and the statements by brand principals, also reveal that other key factors besides cultural pride are likely at play. While both brand principals and consumers recognized the role of cultural pride in the recent rise of LCBs, they also pointed out that cultural pride is not a recent phenomenon of the Marianas. Eric Palacios (personal communication, December 4, 2017) shared his belief that the "sense of [cultural] pride" was always there in the people of the Marianas, whether living in the islands or in the mainland. Shayne Villanueva (personal communication, March 5, 2018) concurred, stating that "Chamorro people are the proudest," and part of the success of Roil Soil and other brands is attributable to people always wanting to share that pride. The great majority of survey respondents expressed a similar viewpoint, that people of the Marianas are proud of their home and culture, and they display that pride when wearing local brands. However, only 59% of respondents agreed or strongly agreed with the statement that "The people of the CNMI have more pride in being from the CNMI than at any other time I can remember," while 75% of respondents agreed or strongly agreed with the statement that "Today, the people of the CNMI have pride in being from the CNMI." These findings suggest that while cultural pride may be a key factor in the rise of LCBs, the feeling of cultural pride is not a sentiment specific to this particular time, but was also prevalent in other recent historical periods. Other factors than cultural pride are likely fueling the growth in popularity of LCBs.

Interviews with some of the key principals behind the brands revealed several other possible drivers of their popularity. One is the influence of urban American culture. Eric Palacios (personal communication, December 4, 2018), creator of the brands Atdit and Trendsetters, reflected on the origins of the LCB movement in the Marianas:
> We wanted to rep where we were from, because in Hawai'i they were repping where they were from. When they go—when Hawai'i people go to the mainland or wherever they really wear it loud and proud, Hawai'i with their flag in the back. So we wanted to do the same.

While Palacios sees the cultural pride movement in Hawai'i as a likely impetus for Pacific Islanders in the Marianas, more germane here is his use of the words *rep* and *repping*—as in "repping the homeland" or "repping the Marianas"—which come from the word *represent*. This word and its meaning are associated with the urban experience in the mainland United States and signal the quintessential urban artistic expression: hip-hop. The idea of "repping" is pervasive in urban and hip-hop culture. One reps their "hood," their "set," their "crew," their "block," their "people."

This reference to repping, and the clear association to urban and hip-hop culture, was present in many of the interviews with brand principals.

TJ Manglona (personal communication, September 28, 2017), co-founder of Tribe Marianas, recalled,
> When I was in like the fourth grade, my dad had a collection of CDs, Tupac, Dr. Dre—'The Chronic', Too $hort, and I'd take that box of CDs and listen to it when they [my parents] weren't home. For me, it was a connection to California, to the West Coast. I felt like it made sense for me too. That whole culture has always been an influence for me.

TJ's sentiment was echoed by almost all of the other brand principals interviewed. Most grew up listening to hip-hop and as fans of hip-hop and urban culture. Several lived in urban areas such as Oakland or San Diego, and considered hip-hop and urban culture as strong influences on their designs.

This influence is apparent when we examine the actual brands and products. Many of the brands reproduce "streetwear," the fashion embodiment of urban culture. Crowns Guam's (n.d.a) website states that they "look to represent the island and our culture, within the fashion and streetwear realm as the 'Underground King.'" The Undeniable (n.d.a), a recent brand that is already attracting a sizeable fan base, presents its products on its Facebook page as "Superior Island Streetwear." TJ Manglona (personal communication, September 28, 2017), speaking about the genesis of the Tribe Marianas style, said,
> We didn't necessarily want to impose so much of the hip-hop/urban culture, but we wanted to make it so that, if we take our stuff, it's influenced by the islands, by the beauty of our culture, but we also want to present it in a way that makes sense in that world [urban], because that's the world we look up to, that's the world that inspires us, inspired what we love—the music that we love, the fashion that we love—we wanted to make it make sense in that world too.

As Marianas LCB designers have taken inspiration from American urban hip-hop culture, unsurprisingly their most popular items are snapback and fitted baseball caps and basketball-style jerseys, all of which are trendy with hip-hop artists and the wider urban community. Among Marianas consumers, it is also no surprise that the brands' urban-inspired streetwear sells well. Hip-hop and rap are mainstream, as a glance at the Billboard Top 100 Artists confirms: for the week of June 16th, 2018, for example, three of the top ten artists were from the world of hip-hop, including the number one artist for the week, Kanye West (one of the most popular music artists of the last two decades). The popularity of urban music and culture extends to the Marianas, and where it has likely been the most popular musical import from the United States during the 21st century.

While the local brands' popularity rests on their fusion of urban style and island culture, another major driver of their success is marketing, chiefly in the form of social media. Both the brand principals I interviewed and the consumers I surveyed cited marketing as a key factor. Eric Palacios (personal communication, December 4, 2017) surmised that "marketing is what really made the big explosion" for local clothing brands. TJ Manglona (personal communication, September 28, 2017) agreed, indicating that "the boom in social media … got everyone's eyes open." Manglona and Travilla's Tribe Marianas exemplifies the power of marketing and social media: their skillful focus on marketing and social media led them, within only 18 months, to become the most followed company in the CNMI, with more than 10,000 followers across their various social media platforms and over 30,000 views on their YouTube channel (R. Travilla, personal communication, May 8, 2017). Their social media followership is paralleled by brand loyalty: according to the survey I conducted, Tribe Marianas was the most popular LCB in the CNMI, after just over a year of full-time operations.

Survey respondents also recognized the singular role of marketing and social media in the popularity of the brands. While some respondents indicated that cultural pride or "repping" the islands was a main factor for choosing their personal favorite or the brand they thought most popular, many more respondents thought that some aspect of marketing played a primary role. Twenty-four percent of respondents to the question "Why do you think that X brand is so popular?" named some aspect of marketing (e.g., "marketing," "ads," "advertising," "social media") as the cause of the popularity. This type of response was by far the most common. Variations on other types of answers—such as the design of the gear or longevity of the brand—were less common, and many answers were unique enough not to fit neatly into a category (e.g., "a day won't go by without noticing one near by"). More than likely, some other responses, such as "trendy" or "see them everywhere," also relate to marketing without explicitly stating it, thereby increasing the likelihood of marketing as a primary driver of popularity.

Another factor driving the demand for LCBs—cited by brand principals and confirmed by consumers—is the quality of the products. TJ Manglona (personal communication, September 28, 2017) from Tribe Marianas explained that the CNMI only recently had anyone "really producing quality goods that could stand up to anything in the States". Eric Palacios (personal communication, December 4, 2017) of Atdit and Legends noted that producers in the CNMI have found a way to "produce everything legit," from the tags to the stitching to the packaging. As recently as a decade ago, the majority of local garments were produced by silkscreening designs onto blank or generic items, predominantly t-shirts and hats. Today, LCBs are capable of customization and quality production. Shayne Villanueva (personal communication, March 5, 2018), for example, said that Roil Soil does not mass market their products. Rather, the brand customizes designs and produces small batches with an attention to quality, which also serves a marketing purpose found elsewhere in fashion, including the sneakerhead market. Other brands run their operations similarly. Rob Travilla (personal communication, September 8, 2018) from Tribe Marianas stressed that the company's ethos is quality over quantity. Tribe, like other brands, has turned to sublimation printing and cut-and-sewn garments. Tribe even embroiders their garment tags and utilizes custom tapering and inlays, quality improvements that far exceed the basic silkscreened products of a decade earlier.

The public has responded to the emphasis on quality. According to the survey of the NMC community, 9% of respondents cited the quality of a brand as the primary reason that brand was their favorite. Interestingly, half a dozen different brands were represented in this group, an indication of the quality of many of the goods being produced by Marianas LCBs.

Conclusions

Local Mariana Islands clothing brands have grown increasingly popular in recent years. Much of this popularity stems from the brands' attention to representing aspects of the culture—both traditional and contemporary—and consumers' feelings of cultural pride. Yet, those aspects of cultural expression and pride might not be the most influential drivers of the popularity of these brands, which have also benefited from the globalization of urban and streetwear styles that influence many of the brand design choices. A desire from the public for high quality, locally produced garments, and a parallel commitment by brands to produce quality garments, also contributed to the popularity of the brands. However, the greatest driver of the local clothing brands' popularity is likely the marketing enabled by the contemporary global phenomenon of social media, rather than specific style or quality, or the immense cultural pride present in the region.

This research project also leaves some questions unanswered. Foremost, what is the import of these findings? What does it mean that the popularity of these brands might be driven more by social media marketing than by cultural pride? How durable is a style that relies heavily on cultural expression and signification? Other questions also arise, particularly about the nature of the cultural pride on display in the brands and the public that consumes their products. Is that cultural pride authentic, or mainly a construct of our digital, social media age, the byproduct more of savvy marketing than cultural pride? Is cultural pride necessary to the popularity of the brands, sufficient, or both?

This research has affirmed the strong sense of cultural pride within the Marianas, and that wearing products from local clothing brands is an expression of that pride. Future research might explore the source of this pride. Where does it come from? Why is it so strong? Or such research might ask how we can better understand the complex relationship between local clothing brands and cultural pride in the Mariana Islands. Exploring some of these questions would deepen our understanding of how the people of the Marianas view themselves and their contemporary culture in this particular domain.

References

670 Rocksteady Shop. (n.d.). *Photos* [Facebook page]. Facebook. Retrieved July 2, 2018, from https://www.facebook.com/670rocksteady/photos/?ref=page_internal

82 Threads Co. (n.d.). *Home* [Facebook page]. Retrieved April 10, 2017, from https://www.facebook.com/82threads/about?lst=716466056%3A100002572383344%3A1528687248&section=bio

Aguon. J. (n.d.). Niyok: Coconut. In *Guampedia*. https://www.guampedia.com/niyok/

Aspers, P., & Godart, F. (2013). Sociology of fashion: Order and change. *Annual Review of Sociology, 39*, 171–192. https://doi.org/10.1146/annurev-soc-071811-145524

Atdit x Trendsetters CNMI. (n.d.). *Photos* [Facebook page]. Facebook. Retrieved February 11, 2018, from https://www.facebook.com/atditbrand/photos/?ref=page_internal

Camacho, F. (2012, May 24). What is the meaning of fokai? Part 2. http://crankeffect.com/1220/what-is-the-meaning-of-fokai-part-2/

Central Intelligence Agency. (2018). Northern Mariana Islands. In *The world factbook*. https://www.cia.gov/library/publications/the-world-factbook/geos/print_cq.html

Connormah. (2011, December 10). *Seal of the Northern Mariana Islands* [Image]. Wikimedia. Retrieved October 14, 2017, from https://commons.wikimedia.org/wiki/File:Seal_of_the_Northern_Mariana_Islands.svg

Craddock, E. W. (1982). *Life in the Northern Mariana Islands during the German administration (1899–1914)* [Exhibition Catalogue]. Commonwealth Council for Arts and Culture.

Crane, D. (2000). *Fashion and its social agendas: Class, gender, and identity in clothing*. https://books.google.com/books?id=vphcHONAXmwC&printsec=frontcover&source=gbs_ge_summary_r&cad=0#v=onepage&q&f=false

Crane, D., & Bovone, L. (2006). Approaches to material culture: The sociology of fashion and clothing. *Poetics, 34*(6), 319–333. https://www.sciencedirect.com/science/article/pii/S0304422X06000428

Crowns Guam. (n.d.a). *About*. http://crownsguam.com/about/

Crowns Guam. (n.d.b). *Photos* [Facebook page]. Facebook. Retrieved July 26, 2018, from https://www.facebook.com/CrownsGuam/photos/?ref=page_internal

Flores, J. (2010). Dress of the Chamorro. In M. Maynard, & J. Eicher (Eds.), *Berg encyclopedia of world dress and fashion* (Vol. 7, pp. 508–511). Bloomsbury Academic.

Fokai Industries. (n.d.a). *About us*. Retrieved December 17, 2017, from https://www.fokaistuff.com/pages/about-us

Fokai Industries. (n.d.b). *Home*. Retrieved January 16, 2018, from https://www.fokaistuff.com

Fritz, G. (2001). *The Chamorro: A history and ethnography of the Mariana Islands* (3rd ed.) (S. Russell, Ed.) (E. Craddock, Trans.). CNMI Division of Historic Preservation.

Giddens, A. (1991). *Modernity and self-identity: Self and society in the late modern age*. https://books.google.com/books?id=Jujn_YrD6DsC&printsec=frontcover&source=gbs_ge_summary_rcad=0#v=onepage&q&f=false

Hicks, J. (2014, October 29). Guam: A high concentration of veterans, but rock-bottom VA funding. *The Washington Post*. https://www.washingtonpost.com/news/federal-eye/wp/2014/10/29/guam-a-high-concentration-of-veterans-with-little-va-funding/?utm_term=.6ef1000c911e

Hitlin, S., & Piliavin, J. A. (2004). Values: Reviving a dormant concept. *Annual Review of Sociology, 30*, 359–393. https://doi.org/10.1146/annurev.soc.30.012703.110640

Hsu, H., & Burns, L.D. (2012). The effects of culture, long-term orientation, and gender on consumers' perceptions of clothing values. *Social Behavior and Personality, 40*(10), 1585–1596. https://doi.org/10.2224/sbp.2012.40.10.1585

irocksteady. (n.d.a). *Our story*. Retrieved June 8, 2018, from https://irocksteady.com/about

irocksteady. (n.d.b). *Products*. Retrieved July 2, 2018, from https://irocksteady.com/products

Justia. (n.d.) Trademark details. https://trademarks.justia.com/772/10/magas-stressfree-c-n-m-i-77210306.html

Marianas Visitors Authority. (2018). *Marianas visitors authority 2017 annual report*. https://drive.google.com/file/d/1jnLDxAguqXQNg2Q55Cvx0x92VWpPZWiG/view

Nakano, H. (2006, June 7). *Latte Stone in Latte Stone Park, Hagatna, Guam* [Photograph]. Wikipedia. https://en.wikipedia.org/wiki/Latte_stone#/media/File:Latte1.jpg

Roil Soil Clothing. (n.d.). *Photos* [Facebook page]. Facebook. Retrieved April 14, 2018, from https://www.facebook.com/roilsoil/photos/?ref=page_internal

Russell, S. (2002). *The island of Rota: An archaeological and historical overview*. CNMI Division of Historic Preservation.

Tribe Marianas. (n.d). *Photos* [Facebook page]. Facebook. Retrieved January 11, 2018, from https://www.facebook.com/tribemarianas/photos/?ref=page_internal

The Undeniable. (n.d.a). *Home*. [Facebook page]. Retrieved January 23, 2018, from https://www.facebook.com/pg/UndeniableCNMI/about/?ref=page_internal

The Undeniable. (n.d.b). *Photos* [Facebook page]. Facebook. Retrieved January 29, 2018, from https://www.facebook.com/UndeniableCNMI/photos/?ref=page_internal

US Census Bureau. (2011). *Northern Mariana Islands: 2010 census summary report*. http://i2io42u7ucg3bwn5b3lofquc.wpengine.netdna-cdn.com/wp-content/uploads/2012/12/2010-Census-Demographics-Profile-Summary-by-District.pdf

US Census Bureau. (2017). *Annual estimates of the resident population for incorporated places of 50,000 or more, ranked by July 1, 2017 population: April 1, 2010 to July 1, 2017 – United States*. https://factfinder.census.gov/faces/tableservices/jsf/pages/productview.xhtml?src=bkmk

Weare, N., & Cruz, R. (2017, August 14). Guam, America's forgotten front line. *The New York Times*. https://www.nytimes.com/2017/08/14/opinion/guam-north-korea-american-ally-.html

From Exotica to Erotica: Historical Fiction or Fictional History in Mariana Islands Novels, 2012-2017

Anne Perez Hattori

Author Note: In March 2017, I received an email inquiry from Professor Carolina Rodriguez of the University of Oviedo in Spain, faculty of American literatures and cultures. As part of a research group studying literature written by American authors about "exotic" places, she encountered Guam through her discovery of the novel, Conquered: A WWII Erotic Historical Romance Set in Guam, *written by CHamoru writer Paula Lujan Quinene. Prof. Rodriguez took an interest in Guam's past and present and emailed to ask me to recommend readings in order to learn more about us and our history. Her curiosity about Guam and novels about the island spurred me to read* Conquered, *and from there, other recent novels. It struck me that as a University of Guam professor who teaches classes in Guam History and CHamoru Studies, I ought to be familiar with these publications. So, for that bit of motivation and inspiration, I offer my thanks: Si Yu'os Ma'åse, Prof. Rodriguez.*

For much of the 19th and early 20th centuries, the "Pacific novel" referred to works by Herman Melville, Robert Louis Stevenson, James Michener, and other Western writers. More recent decades have seen the emergence of Indigenous novelists, led by writers such as the late Epeli Hau'ofa of Tonga, Albert Wendt (Samoa), Sia Figiel (Samoa), and Patricia Grace (Aotearoa New Zealand Māori). Indeed, fictional works about islands in the South Pacific—that is, Oceanic islands below the equator—have proliferated over the past 40 years.[1] The same, however, could not be said of our region, as is attested by the near absence of Micronesian novels in Pacific Literature classes across the region.[2] Since 2012, however, more than 10 novels have been published that feature the Mariana Islands, the CHamoru people, and our Indigenous culture, including four written by Natives and five others by authors who at one time resided here. These novels make heavy use of island landscapes, CHamoru legends, and Marianas history, sometimes as mere backdrops for their storylines but other times as key ingredients in their plots' unfolding. This chapter, firstly, summarizes some of these novels in the hopes that local readers might be inspired to seek them out and read what others are writing about our islands and culture. Secondly, this work analyzes some of the ways in which these novels represent CHamoru culture and history—at times exotically and erotically. Thirdly, this project evaluates the historical accuracy of the novels, assessing the degree to which the stories fairly and ethically represent the actual historical events that inform their plots.

The Exotic Environment
The Greeks defined *exotikos* as "foreign," this notion extending into modern times to include characteristics or qualities "from another country" and thereby deemed to be "mysteriously different or unusual" (Oxford, n.d.b). The central idea behind the exotic emphasizes the non-Native and strange origins of a person, place, or thing in order to foreground its difference or "otherness." Descriptions of Pacific Islands as exotic locales have become commonplace in literature, art, film, and other forms of popular culture, so much so that we ourselves exploit this discourse in multiple ways, most notably to bill our islands as alluring and attractive places for prospective tourists.

Rather than as ordinary spaces for the unfolding of extraordinary historical events, the Mariana Islands are often described in touristic, otherworldly ways, as places foreign, different, and marvelous—indeed, as exotic. In each of the novels, written by both CHamoru and non-Native authors, the otherness of both the CHamoru people and culture, as well as the island landscape, is central to the story. On perhaps the most basic level, exoticism is expressed in terms of the tropical environment, ranging from its oppressive heat to its gentle breezes, from its sandy beaches to its dense jungles. The novel *Spirits of the Island*, for example, demonstrates this practice, describing Guam as a tropical island with "warm sun and endless beaches" (Latham, 2014, Chapter 1, para. 1), a "gentle breeze" (Chapter 1, para. 82; Chapter 1, para. 89; Chapter 10, para. 13), "magnificent" views (Chapter 5, para. 123), "wonderful beauty" (Chapter 1, para. 5), and pinkish-orange sunsets that make "photo[s] look surreal" (Chapter 1, para. 5).[3] Not only the sunsets, however, evoke surrealism in this novel written by East Texas author K. Latham (2014) and dedicated to Daniel Aflleje for "the many wonderful memories of Guam" (Dedication). The plot revolves around a small group of teenaged CHamoru said to have been appointed by the taotaomo'na (spirits of the ancestors) to be "Guardians," individuals with the ability to shapeshift into the forms of a dog, a puma, a reef shark, a large bird, and a snake in order to "protect the people from the jungle, and the jungle from the people. ... like a go between for the living and the dead" (Chapter 15, para. 5). Perhaps attempting to capitalize on the success of the popular *Twilight* book and film series that also feature shapeshifting teens, in Latham's *Spirits of the Island* the jungle becomes a vibrant, living, and ominous space in which the ultimate exoticisms play out.

The island landscape similarly becomes an exotic backdrop in *Conquered: A World War II Erotic Historical Romance*, written by CHamoru author Paula Lujan Quinene (2016). This novel opens with the invitation to enter "the exotic world of the Pacific, complete with coconut trees, banana doughnuts, dolphins swimming in the ocean, and moonlight on Pago Bay" (p. 12). Quinene tells the love story of Mangilao teenager Jesi (Jessica) Taimanglo and American GI Johan Landers, a member of the USMC invasion force. The plot begins with Jesi hiding in a Pago Bay cave in the hours before Guam's "liberation" from wartime occupation. She then is discovered by Japanese soldiers and on the verge of being raped when rescued by Johan, who kills her attackers in the process. The remainder of the novel recounts her undying love and lust for Johan, manifested initially by copious servings of delectable CHamoru dishes (some recipes of which are included at the back of the book), interspersed with equally large doses of explicit sexual activity. Detailed and repeated descriptions of the coconut husking, splitting, and grating process, as well as mouth-watering descriptions of specific food items such as breadfruit, coconut crab, and kelaguen, effectively serve to paint an image of Guam as a place that would be unfamiliar, indeed exotic, to its presumably non-Native readers.

Foods-as-exotic receive similar treatment in Joan Awa's 2017 *Shadows in the Water*, a novel set in Guam during the whaling era of the 1800s. Authored ostensibly as an homage to CHamoru culture with considerable parts of the novel written in the native language, Awa (2017) writes of "exotic dishes the ship's crewmen have eaten—an array of sea turtles, an endless supply of coconut, and a variety of savory fish that only swim in the ocean of the Pacific" (Chapter 3, para. 8.). As in *Conquered*, everyday CHamoru foods become exoticized as marvelous wonders. But tropical food-as-exotic turns fictitious in some of the novels, particularly when describing animals that are not found in the island jungles. In *Some Boy*, for example, author Susie Sample (2014) erroneously states that the CHamorus survived World War II by eating most of the monkeys on the island (Chapter 2, para. 8). In another novel, *The Ghost of Guam*, Japanese straggler Shoichi Yokoi survives his 28 years in the jungles near Talofofo by trapping wild squirrels, chipmunks, and rabbits (Flannery, 2016, p. 107). Despite the factual errors in these two novels, the images of people in "Survivor: Guam" mode play into notions of the island environment as exotic.

Native fauna as exotic recur in the novels more than simply as food sources, with predictable references to hilitai (iguana) roaming the land, fanihi (fruit bat) on the dinner tables, wild boars on the attack, and snakes slithering through the jungles. Going even further, one novel resorts to creating a fictional beast. In Kent Johnson Olsen's (2014) *Chamorro*, a community of CHamorus living in an underground "cavern city" find themselves at the mercy of vicious "guegpo" birds—flesh-eating specimens with 18' long bodies, 30' wing spans, and jaws longer than an alligator's body (Chapter 6, para. 68). Killing them and then finding a way back to the "sun world" forms the primary storyline of this self-labeled historical fiction.

In novels such as *Spirits of the Island, Shadows in the Water, Some Boy, Ghost of Guam*, and *Chamorro*, whether in realistic or imaginary form, the Mariana Islands' tropical environment, foods, and animals are depicted in different ways as exotic—remarkable, different, and unusual. The particular convergence of heat, humidity, wildlife, spirit-filled jungles, sunsets, and sunrises that occurs in the Marianas animates the action within each novel. Consequently, as a result of being exoticized rather than treated simply as the geographical backdrop for the various plotlines, the Mariana Islands' tropical environment becomes a principal actor in these stories—indeed, a determiner of history. Amidst the storied struggles with giant birds (*Chamorro*), shapeshifting creatures (*Spirits of the Island*), and jungles filled with a wide variety of both natural and supernatural threats (*Some Boy, Ghost of Guam, Shadows, Spirits*), readers get the sense that the described events could not happen in just any other place.

Such exploitation of this notion of the exotic problematically positions our foods, fauna, flora, and weather as central features in determining our uniqueness, rather than crediting CHamorus throughout past centuries for making intelligent and thoughtful decisions concerning their families, villages, and islands. The result is an environmental determinism in which the Mariana Islands' tropical landscape becomes a principal actor, thereby reducing the active agency of the CHamoru people. The islanders become mere pawns of nature, rather than the agents or makers of their history and culture. Yet history demonstrates that the CHamorus are a people who have successfully negotiated the changing demands of four colonial eras over the course of more than three centuries, as well as navigated complex histories of births and deaths, marriages and fiestas, typhoons and earthquakes, and more. It is thus belittling to suggest that anything other than human ingenuity and perseverance, familial dedication and sacrifice, and personal decision-making deserves credit for explaining the course of our cultural development. We are who we are today because of specific people's actions and inactions in the face of whatever challenges were present at specific moments in time, not because of our region's heat, sunsets, animals, and plants.

From Exotica to Erotica

Dictionaries define the erotic as that which arouses sexual desire or sexual excitement (Oxford, n.d.a), and indeed, among the novels under consideration in this essay are two works categorized within the genre of erotica—*Conquered* and *Tropical Medicine*. *Tropical Medicine*'s plot tracks a high-powered New York art designer's business trip to Saipan and the sexual liaisons that await her in the surrounds of the Hyatt Hotel. This work does not merely contain tidbits of sexually explicit material; its purpose is to deliver erotic content, and the weak plot is simply the delivery vehicle. It does, however, contain descriptions of modern Saipan and some of its tourist attractions, lust-worthy men being among them. The second erotic fiction, *Conquered*, declares itself with its subtitle, *A World War II Erotic Historical Romance*. Unlike *Tropical Medicine*, however, Guam's history is an important part of the storyline. Indeed, the Pacific War provides the ideal historical context to support the plot of a heroic American soldier who rescues a CHamoru damsel in distress from the violent clutches of evil Japanese brutes.

Quinene's *Conquered* fuses the exotic with the erotic in numerous ways. Despite its wartime context, this novel is ultimately a love story set in a romantic environment, every breeze a sensual treat, every sunset more glorious than the one before, and every CHamoru dish a stimulating explosion of scent and taste. In an interesting twist on the definition of exotic as foreign, different, or unusual, *Conquered* exoticizes its leading female, Jesi Taimanglo, in terms of traits that would seem not unique but instead familiar to its readership, presumably comprised mainly of non-CHamorus who would be unfamiliar with the local foods described in detail throughout the book. Specifically setting Jesi apart from other local women are her oft-mentioned green eyes (Quinene, 2016, Chapter 2, para. 51; Chapter 3, para. 7; Chapter 14, para. 25; Chapter 37, para. 17) and light-colored skin (Chapter 3, para. 109; Chapter 3, para. 113; Chapter 37, para. 17). These physical characteristics, attributed by Jesi to a "light-skinned" ancestor from a "long, long time ago" (Chapter 3, para. 113), distinguishes her from other CHamorus described only as "pretty dark" (Chapter 3, para. 109). Jesi's green eyes, plus recurring descriptions of sexual arousal triggered by the scent of her coconut-oiled skin (Chapter 5, para. 4; Chapter 9, section 3, para. 42), become the primary aspects of her exotic and erotic appeal to Johan. Thus, part of *Conquered*'s exoticism entails a hybridity of traits both foreign and familiar; that is, rather than treating CHamoru women in general as exotic because of their physical and cultural "otherness," *Conquered* distinguishes Jesi as unique because of her combined Native and non-Native characteristics. In *Conquered*, the exotic CHamoru woman is not some dark, sensuous Islander cliché, but instead a coconut-scented woman who might pass for white. Jesi's hybrid characterization suggests a blended CHamoru-Spanish lineage, whether consensual or, possibly non-consensual, described as "rape-colored skin" by Black poet Caroline Randall Williams (2020). In either case, Jesi's light skin color can be read as heightened accessibility to Johan.

Erotica is not limited to those works classified within the named genre. Even in some of the non-erotic historical fictions, only a thin line separates the exotic from the erotic as gentle breezes, spectacular sunsets, and warm waters are often accompanied by sensuous and sexualized bodies. *Shadows in the Water* perpetuates the stereotypical "hula dancer" sexualization of Pacific Island women with Awa (2017) describing a group of female dancers in terms of the "swaying of hips, the clanging of shells and the dark hair flowing with the wind" (Chapter 4, para. 1). Another novel, however, seemingly subverts this exotic-as-erotic motif. In *A Mansion on the Moon*, author Cathy Sablan Gault (2015) repeatedly refers to her protagonist Vivian as "exotic," yet conspicuously avoids equating that with eroticism or sexuality. Instead, Vivian's exoticism is defined in terms of curiosity (Chapter 18, para. 46); resilience, strength, and physical fitness (Chapter 21, para. 17); confidence (Chapter 25, para. 25); and rarity (Chapter 45, para. 28). Despite the author's frank exoticism of this character, she does not treat Vivian as a sexualized object of physical desire. In this way, Gault redefines the terms of the island exotic, emphasizing outstanding character traits rather than physical difference.

Interestingly, the novels under review here eroticize the male body more so than the female one. The second work of erotic fiction, *Tropical Medicine* by Lynda Ambrose, describes little of the female lead character, instead focusing on the three men with whom the lead character has sexual encounters. Ambrose (2013) exploits the "sex on the beach" fantasy with the main character who, while on a business trip to Saipan, imagines herself on a hidden beach, "lying under a hanging cliff, with waves breaking and salt air, watching the sunset" while engaging in sexual activity (Chapter 4, para. 37). She describes her main interest, Gregorio, as "a shaggy-haired, barely-clothed, chocolate-skinned fisherman ... [who] smelled like salt, sweat, and Budweiser" (Chapter 5, para. 12). Describing his skin as "the color of the gooey syrup at the bottom of a Starbucks mocha" (Chapter 9, para. 1), Gregorio is her "tropical medicine, a close and special friend who gave [her] something amazing" (Chapter 14, para. 6).

Similarly eroticizing its male characters, Latham's (2014) paranormal shape-shifting fiction, *Spirits of the Island*, describes its leading male, Michael or Miguet, as having a "chiseled chest and sexy six-pack abs" (Chapter 2, para. 57) and his circle of male friends as "all varying degrees of hotness" (Chapter 9, para. 176). After meeting the cohort of teenaged males, Tori, the lead female character, asks, "*Do all island guys look buff and sexy?*" (Chapter 6, para. 103, emphasis in original). Latham extends the sexualization of CHamoru men even to their speech, with Tori commenting, "the light accent in his [Miguet's] voice was enough to send a rush of heat to my cheeks" (Chapter 1, para. 92).

In these works, the authors commingle the exotic island landscape with the erotic sexuality of their CHamoru characters, males even more so than females. This motif of linking the exotic and erotic should come as no surprise, however, since the global tourism industry's portrayal of the Pacific as a place for weddings, honeymoons, and escapist romance is well-entrenched, particularly in Polynesia and Micronesia. Pacific Islands, depicted in terms of their hot climate, scantily clad Natives, warm waters, and beautiful landscapes, become ideal places in the world's imagination for the fusion of the exotic and the erotic.

Historical Fiction or Fictional History?
All of the novels under review could be classified as works of historical fiction, a genre that has become increasingly popular. Historian Jerome de Groot noted in his 2010 *The Historical Novel* that "the last few decades have seen an explosion in the sales and popularity of novels set in the past" (p. 152). Yet what qualifies as historical fiction is not a simple matter. To address this issue, Eastern Illinois University Professor Sarah Johnson (n.d.), writing on behalf of the *Historical Novel Society*, offered a working definition of the historical novel as "a novel which is set fifty or more years in the past, and one in which the author is writing from research rather than personal experience" (para. 7). Other scholars define the genre more inclusively, focusing on the subject matter, rather than a historical timeline. For example, Daniel McGarry and Harriman White, authors of the *World Historical Fiction Guide*, defined historical fiction more broadly as works that include "reference to customs, conditions, identifiable persons, or events in the past" (De Groot, 2010, p. 986).

By McGarry and White's definition, each of the 11 novels under review qualify as historical fiction, dealing with the Mariana Islands and its people and culture at some point in the past. Four of the novels, however, situate their stories in the present—the erotic novel *Tropical Medicine*, set amidst Saipan hotels, duty-free shops, and Japanese tourists; the shapeshifting *Spirits of the Land*, with references to cell phones, tablets, and BFFs; *Mariana Sky* by Steven Aflleje LeFever, situated during Guam's hosting of FestPac in 2016; and P.F. Kluge's *Master Blaster*, set in Saipan in the mid-2000s, a time marked by the closure of garment factories, the Jack Abramoff scandal, and the launch of the now-defunct website, Saipansucks.com. In these contemporary-era novels, the historical content and context is assumed, rather than explained and developed. Hence, despite their references to aspects of

Marianas history and culture, their categorization as historical fiction would appear to be generally unwarranted.

Self-categorized as historical fiction, LeFever's (2016) *Mariana Sky* tells the fantastical story of an English-speaking Marianas Fruit Dove named Tsewi that travels to each of the Mariana Islands in search of philosophical growth and spiritual enlightenment. Each chapter is dedicated to one of the islands as the bird flies from the northernmost Farallon de Pajaros to southernmost Guam and conveys its impressions of the landscapes and personalities encountered in the voyage. Along the way, the bird comes into contact with CHamorus struggling to maintain their connections to the land and ocean, as well as their cultural and linguistic traditions. The American military appears as the chief threat to the islands, ocean, and CHamoru lifestyle. *Mariana Sky* is part travelogue, part armchair philosophy, and part historical and cultural critique, representing the Marianas as places of immense physical and cultural beauty that are continually threatened by arrogant and condescending imperialists. The author intends his story to be both a personal statement of cultural pride and a broad cry for Pacific Islander unity. But historical reality it is not.

The last of the contemporary novels, *Master Blaster*, by renowned author P. F. Kluge (2012), tells a sordid tale of corruption and exploitation in Saipan. The title refers to an anonymous website author, "the Master Blaster," who takes it upon himself to expose acts of malfeasance occurring on the island. His litany of offenses lists "Slavery, human trafficking, prostitution, gambling from cockfights to poker to casinos, drugs from pot to ice to crack, corruption, nepotism, swindling, crimes against tourists, sanctuary for Japanese and Chinese gangsters, disbarred lawyers, tax evaders and trust fund fiddlers" (p. 185), and his website "blasts" CHamorus, both individually and collectively, for their assumed characteristics of laziness, greed, and foolishness. As the main character (and heroic figure), who arrived in Saipan as a Peace Corps volunteer in the 1960s and never left, the Master Blaster bemoans the loss of the island's simpler times, before the Commonwealth Covenant.

In the novel, various Americans come and go, all attempting to fill some emptiness in their lives and wishfully thinking that Saipan might do the trick. In the meantime, CHamorus lurk in the shadows as devious characters waiting for their golden opportunity to swindle this latest batch of fresh white meat on the island. In *Master*

Blaster's version of history, the Northern Marianas received the so-called gifts of America on a silver platter, and, having done absolutely nothing to deserve this largesse, proceeded to squander the bounty, quickly and corruptly. In the process, the CHamorus have willfully destroyed their island and culture. Although praised by the *New York Times* as "stingingly funny" (Maslin, 2012), this book serves as a rich illustration of Māori author Patricia Grace's admonition that "books are dangerous" when they perpetuate negative and insensitive images of Indigenous, colonized people (Smith, 2012). CHamorus are portrayed as uniformly unethical and unprincipled, as well as lacking any semblance of self or cultural pride, with the author, moreover, cynically implying that there is no turning back. This bleak perspective is voiced by one of Kluge's (2012) key CHamoru characters, "Big Ben" Romero of the Saipan Governor's Office, who states, "We didn't control the past. We don't control the present. Or the future" (p. 299).

In addition to these four contemporary novels, two works, *Chamorro* and *Shadows in the Water*, are set in the 1800s, and five are situated around or shortly after the Second World War—*Conquered, The Ghost of Guam, Some Boy, A Mansion on the Moon,* and *Natural Destiny*. These all make considerable use of historical events and contexts, yet for the most part would more appropriately be labeled as fictional history rather than historical fiction. In several, their free invention of historical events and wild versions of CHamoru culture fall so far outside the bounds of reality that I would be reluctant to grant them historical credibility. The issue of historical accuracy has been hotly debated by those who seek to delineate and evaluate the field of historical fiction. Some argue that these novels are, after all, works of fiction and do not represent themselves as histories, even if they categorize themselves as historical fiction.

But leading scholars of the historical fiction genre disagree. The Historical Novel Society (n.d.), for example, asks, "How much distortion of history will we allow before a book becomes more fantasy than historical?" (Para. 1). Similarly, scholars such as Jerome de Groot (2010) of the University of Manchester urge novelists to embrace a "duty" to history (p. 288) and to historical accuracy, as well as to avoid misrepresenting the past or committing anachronisms. This is particularly significant in light of a trend that has been developing since the beginning of the 20th century to use historical novels "as something educational … and as a form which in some ways was in dialogue with history rather than with the aesthetic strategies of fiction" (de Groot, 2010, p. 947).

While *Mariana Sky*, *Tropical Medicine*, and *Spirits of the Land* steer fairly clear of much historical commentary, both of the novels set in the 19th century, *Chamorro* and *Shadows in the Water*, immerse themselves in it. Yet their storylines commit numerous errors of fact, in addition to considerable faults of anachronism, attributing to the 1800s aspects of CHamoru lifestyle from either pre-colonial or contemporary times. *Chamorro* obviously intends to be a fantasy rather than a history, as evident in its author's creation of a species of gigantic birds, the "guegpo," that threaten CHamoru lives. The novel opens with the suggestion of cultural and historical authenticity by citing an "old Chamorro legend," but it then delivers an invented tale. Rather than the traditional CHamoru creation story of Puntan and Fu'una, the author imaginatively writes, "The Ladrone Island was created when the Sun God placed three stone pillars in the ocean and covered them with dirt and trees and plants and animals" (Olsen, 2014, Chapter 1, para. 1). Later portions of the novel describe 19th century CHamorus maintaining their "ancient religion" by continuing to keep the skulls of their leaders in order to worship them as aniti (Chapter 5, para. 4), a practice which ended in the 1600s. It also invents the cultural attire of CHamoru chiefs, itself a position nonexistent by the 1800s, as comprised of a necklace made with a "guegpo" bird talon (Chapter 29, para. 59) as well as "a tall headdress filled with guegpo feathers" (Chapter 21, para. 72-73). The blurring of fact and fiction that permeates this novel can be difficult for unfamiliar readers to discern, and indeed, two reviewers on Amazon.com praise the author for sharing stories of their home island, for loading the book with educational facts, and for sacrificing so that future generations of CHamorus can learn their stories.

Shadows on the Water similarly misrepresents CHamoru culture in its exoticized description of cultural rites and ceremonial wear, as well as in its numerous anachronisms. Awa (2017) describes performance of CHamoru cultural dances and chants by young, nubile islanders in the late 1800s, similar to the contemporary Taotao Tåno or I Fanlalai'an troupes, while also fictionally depicting the chiefly ceremonial dress to include "an overlay resembling a poncho made of dried coconut leaves and a tie in the center. ... [while] dried nut shells dangle from a rope bound to their calves" (Chapter 4, para. 4). Moreover, the clans and warriors of Guam are shown to unify in order to wage war against visiting whalers, while the Spanish priest is called upon by the CHamorus as a respected ally to lend the services of his government's military in support of the warriors. The characters have names like Torahi, Pulan, Fu'una, Isa, Inina, and Apu, again more reminiscent of 20th and 21st century naming practices, while the central figures live in latte stone houses, almost 200 years after their actual disuse. In much of the novel, events in history from the 1600s, 1800s, and 1900s become (con)fused within the fictionalized plot line. Despite its admirable intent to tell a story of the beauty and strength of the CHamoru people and culture, its misrepresentation of history undermines its credibility.

CHamoru supernatural beliefs are misrepresented in several of the novels, particularly whenever the specter of the taotaomo'na, or spirits of our ancestors, emerges. In *Spirits of the Island*, for example, the shapeshifting characters in the novel exist entirely for the purpose of protecting ordinary CHamorus from the dangers lurking within Guam's jungles and waters. Similarly, *Shadows in the Water* represents the taotaomo'na as primarily malevolent and the jungle as an ominous space. For instance, when one of the female characters, Apu, goes missing from the village for a secret rendezvous with some American whalers, her family and friends express their concern for her disappearance in terms of a taotaomo'na occurrence (Awa, 2017, Chapter 6, para. 1). Similarly, the duendes are understood as malicious and dangerous beings that reside in threatening jungle spaces. The mythological creatures, named from the Spanish word *duende*, meaning fairy, are typically described by CHamorus as dwarflike beings who lure young children away, sometimes for extended periods of time, and return them physically unharmed but often in a mute state.[4] In *Spirits of the Island*, author K. Latham takes fictional liberty by defining duendes as CHamoru children who had been slaughtered by the Spanish during their conquest of the Marianas in the 1600s. Latham (2014) writes that the existing duendes "trick living children to follow them into the jungle, then shrink them down and keep them there. Eventually these children become more Duendes" Chapter 18, para. 13).

Perhaps the most egregious historical inaccuracies can be read in *The Ghost of Guam*, a fictional story based on the historical experiences of Shoichi Yokoi, the famous Japanese straggler who survived for 28 years in the jungles of Talofofo. The novel flips between World War II and modern Guam, spanning Yokoi's wartime experiences to his eventual discovery and return to Japan. Right from the start, the novel errs with the Japanese invading Guam a year too soon, in December 1940. It also creates a handy disclaimer by naming the main character Satoshi Yoko, rather than Shoichi Yokoi. True-to-life descriptions of CHamoru suffering and malnutrition, American valor, and Japanese brutality infuse the story, but are marred by flagrantly false information. For example, author Flannery (2016) writes that when the Japanese caught CHamorus hiding food, they would "cut off the victims' heads and put them up for display for months" (p. 37). He also erroneously claims that "It was nothing special to see the soldiers cut open one of the CHamoru, while still alive tear out his heart and intestines to the screams of the person" (p. 54) and, yet again, speaking through Yoko, says, "I saw once how babies were tossed around on bayonets among a group of laughing soldiers, and another time thrown against a rock, and yet another time dumped into boiling water" (p. 57). The author also combines the wartime suicides of Japanese civilian and military personnel on Saipan's Suicide Cliff and Bansai Cliff and situates them instead at Guam's Two Lovers Point (pp. 86, 96). Flannery's exaggeration of wartime violence ultimately undermines the truth of the CHamoru people's suffering.

Three other World War II novels fare better in terms of representing the day-to-day challenges and fears faced by CHamorus who lived through the experience, although serious questions of historical accuracy nonetheless arise. The novel *Natural Destiny* tells Guam's wartime history from the perspective of Sumay child, Bernidita or Bernie, only 8 years old at the war's onset. Novelist Sherry Dixon forewords her novel with a powerful story about her mother, an elderly CHamoru woman who more than 50 years after the war suddenly and shockingly opened up one day about her wartime experiences. According to the author, over the course of several months, her mother, the novel's Bernidita, shared her traumatic memories. Dixon (2012) describes, "I wrote notes in a journal so I would not forget. After I had filled a couple of journals, she said, 'Sherry, this needs to be a book'" (p. 4). Thus was *Natural Destiny* initiated, Dixon dedicating the book "to my mother and the thousands of other Guamanians who struggled under the Japanese occupation during World War II" (Dedication, p. 1). Despite the noble intentions, however, a number of glaring factual errors detract from the book's historical value.

Natural Destiny tells the perspective of Bernie, who lost both of her parents by the time she was only 4 years old, then moved from Hagåtña to live in Sumay with her bachelorette godmother (Nina) and her godmother's mother "Nanan Beha [sic]." On December 8, 1941, while the island celebrated the Feast of the Immaculate Conception, Japan's bombings of Guam began. From this point on, the events, dates, and places become badly jumbled. According to Dizon's story, most of Sumay's residents, including her Nina and "Nanan Beha [sic]," were attending the fiesta mass in the Sumay church when the building was bombed, killing a large part of the village's population and leaving Bernie essentially orphaned. The Japanese proceed to invade two days later, forcibly marching Bernie and the other Sumay survivors to a concentration camp in Manenggon where they remained for the war's entire duration of two and a half years (in actuality, it was 11 days). The story erroneously claims that all the infants and toddlers, as well as the elders and those with any physical disability, were ushered out of the camp and killed (pp. 66-69). All the unmarried females, ages seven and up, were taken to serve as comfort women to the Japanese (p. 72), a horror that Bernie escaped because her short buzz-cut hair enabled her to be mistaken for a boy. Although, in actuality, some CHamoru women were forced into sexual submission, it has never been reported on the scale described in *Natural Destiny*.

Indeed, historical memory can be slippery in the best of circumstances, even immediately after an event has occurred, and what a child remembers and comprehends of an event is also questionable. Nonetheless, while *Natural Destiny* may contain understandable errors of memory and judgement coming 50 years after the event from someone who was a child at the time, the novel's compounding of errors discourages me from recommending it to anyone not already knowledgeable of Guam's wartime experience. Although the novel admirably captures the emotional strength, determination and cohesion of the CHamoru wartime community, its glaring factual errors undermine its utility as a representation of Guam's wartime history.

Another of the war novels, *Conquered*, similarly captures the history of CHamoru suffering, fear, and sacrifice, although it does not offer much historical detail. Despite being set during the war and classifying itself as historical fiction, *Conquered* is ultimately a love story that uses the historical event primarily as a stage for the meeting of its two main characters, an American Navy officer and a young CHamoru woman. The author is more instructive in addressing CHamoru cultural attitudes towards Americans and the military, and she makes it clear from the start where her loyalties lie. Quinene (2016) begins her book with a dedication not only "To the survivors of WWII on Guam," but also "To the military families who lost loved ones fighting for Guam during WWII; To the veterans and their families who have served Guam and the United States of America; To the men, women, and their families who still serve, protecting and defending Guam and the United States of America" (Dedication). To them, Quinene states, "I thank you. We thank you." In *Conquered*'s story of the 1944 biracial courtship between Jesi Taimanglo and Johan Landers, the author highlights notions of CHamoru gratitude to the US for its defeat of occupying Japanese forces, but not in the usual terms of CHamoru men enlisting in the service as a form of cultural reciprocity. Instead, the Islanders' gratitude plays out as CHamorus' eagerness for their daughters to marry white men. Although some of the American characters in the novel express surprise at the interracial wedding, Johan explains that "The locals were so grateful they didn't have any reservations" (Chapter 16, para. 10). This story of American valor and heroism, accompanied by CHamoru gratitude, is a common narrative in most of Guam's history books and other publications concerning World War II. The accuracy of this perspective, however, is problematic and has been questioned in recent years[5], although it does undoubtedly represent views held by some portion of the population.

The most ambitious of the novels, *A Mansion on the Moon* by Cathy Sablan Gault (2015), is a saga across three generations of CHamoru women in the de Leon family, beginning in 1899 with Amanda encountering the first Americans to colonize the island. The family saga continues with Amanda's daughter, Sylvia, who marries Tino Flores Camacho and gradually acculturates during the early American colonial era. The saga concludes with Amanda's granddaughter, Vivian, whose romance with a US Navy officer survives the hardships of World War II. Unlike *Conquered*'s romanticized treatment of the American military presence in Guam, *Mansion* offers a more even-handed approach, portraying American racist and condescending attitudes towards CHamorus as well as the benevolence and goodwill of some of the men stationed on the island. Gault's storylines depict CHamoru characters as resilient, facing major earthquakes and typhoons without fanfare or drama. After one typhoon, for instance, one of the Navy men reflects that "the strong Chamorro instinct for survival had developed not only out of their will to live, but also on their recognition of nature's foibles, their stoic acceptance of the consequences, and on their dependence on one another" (Chapter 26, para. 10). The CHamoru response to the war would align with this cultural pattern, the novel concluding, "Nothing in

Guam or for any of its people was ever going to be the same again. Yet the people of Guam would triumph over it all, as they always had" (Chapter 46, para. 28). In *Mansion on the Moon*, CHamorus emerge as the true heroes of the war, raising critical questions about the American military's postwar land-grabbing in Guam.

Exotica to Erotica: Historical Fiction or Fictional History
Although this chapter examines only a few historical novels, it highlights the need for local readers to engage critically in the discussion and analysis of works written about us. With the proliferation of on-demand presses and online vendors, publishing novels has seemingly never been easier. Moreover, while locating these historical novels, I also came across other literary publications worthy of attention, including collections of poetry and short stories, as well as personal memoirs and general travelogues.[6] An explosion of children's books has also hit the market in recent years, some retelling cultural legends and folklore, others creating fictional stories, and yet others sharing personal experiences. One, for example, *The Boy Who Dreamed to Be with His Parents on Saipan*, a children's book by Riza Oledan-Ramos (2012), tells the story of a young Filipino boy whose parents left him with relatives in Manila as an infant while they pursued job opportunities, until the family reunited in Saipan a few years later. Although the book focuses on the emotional needs of children caught up in migrant labor hardships, it also exoticizes Saipan as a stereotypical paradise, replete with "white, sandy beaches" (Chapter 7, para. 7), delicious fruits, and pleasant weather. The genre of children's literature, with books written both in CHamoru and English, offers much opportunity for further analysis.

Works of historical fiction, whether accurate or inaccurate, are easily accessible as both paperbacks and e-books to audiences around the world through global vendors such as Amazon and Apple's iBook store. Written by CHamorus and non-CHamorus alike, these books contain elements of tropical exoticisms that portray the Mariana Islands as otherworldly paradises that look, taste, and smell unlike anything found in the Western world. Although seeming to compliment the Marianas, these descriptions border on an environmental determinism that privileges nature as the agent of history, rather than focusing on the achievements of the CHamoru people who negotiated whatever came their way, shaping history through their decisions and actions. This exoticist environmental determinism positions CHamorus as passive subjects rather than active agents of their own history. Thus, one fundamental flaw with overly exoticized emplotment is that it strips islander agency from CHamorus, a tactic that denies us the ability to shape our own history.

Some of the exotic otherness within the novels panders to the erotic desires of their primarily white, single, heterosexual characters—and is, in fact, based on misinformation. Errors also confound the exoticized novels, and perhaps this could be remedied through a more determined effort on the part of locals to hold authors accountable for their representations of CHamoru culture and history. The targeted audience appears to be primarily non-Natives, and perhaps secondarily the thousands of off-island CHamorus in the US mainland, readers with scant direct knowledge of the islands and who therefore require detailed descriptions of weather, landscapes, and everyday cultural practices. The romantic image of Mariana Islanders existing in some otherworldly paradise, free from the problems of modern civilization, might be enticing to such readers. But presenting inaccurate information that fails to reflect the complex challenges that CHamorus have faced over time performs a disservice to the CHamoru people, regardless of how seemingly positive the overall portrayal.

Most of the novels under review here exhibit a pervasive and grievous inattention to historical accuracy, and some grave cultural misrepresentation. These inaccuracies range from careless depictions of monkeys, giant birds, and chipmunks in the islands' jungles to flagrant falsehoods about the experiences of violence during the Second World War. Breaches of creative license occur in the recitation and explanation of CHamoru legends and cultural beliefs (especially concerning supernatural phenomena such as taotaomo'na and duendes), and offensive descriptions of CHamoru character and morality further impair some of the novels. Despite their ostensibly entertaining genre as novels, these fictional works nonetheless become damaging sources of misinformation about the Mariana Islands, as well as unwitting tools that undermine the vitality and vibrancy of the CHamoru characters.

Although novelists may rely on the convenient disclaimer that their work is fictional, thereby somehow excusing them from being accountable for factual errors, critics and readers alike should insist that authors exercise integrity towards the people and events of the past. Novels that fictionalize our history and culture constitute a form of cultural exploitation by demeaning our past and our present for the writer's personal gains of authorship and the revenue it might generate. Such works dishonor the richness and complexity of the CHamoru experience and would better be labeled "fictional history" rather than historical fiction. Surely our 4,000-year-old culture and history deserve better.

References

Ambrose, L. (2013). *Tropical medicine*. Amazon Digital Services.
Awa, J. (2017). *Shadows in the water*. Joan Awa.
de Groot, J. (2010). *The historical novel*. Routledge.
Dixon, S. (2012). *Natural destiny*. CreateSpace Independent Publishing Platform.
Flannery, R. (2016). *The ghost of Guam*. WestBow Press.
Forbes, P. E. (2011, October 30). I duendes. *Paleric*. https://paleric.blogspot.com/2011/10/i-duendes.html.
Gault, C. S. (2015). *A mansion on the moon: A Guam love story*. Xlibris US.
Historical Novel Society. (n.d.). *Defining the genre*. https://historicalnovelsociety.org/guides/defining-the-genre/
Johnson, S. (n.d.). *Defining the genre: What are the rules for historical fiction?* Historical Novel Society. https://historicalnovelsociety.org/guides/defining-the-genre/defining-the-genre-what-are-the-rules-for-historical-fiction/
Kluge, P.F. (2012). *Master blaster: A novel*. The Overlook Press.
Latham, K. (2014). *Spirits of the island*. Eirelander Publishing.
LeFever, S. (2016). *Mariana sky*. Lesteze.com.
Maslin, J. (2012, March 25). A far-off island: Where the American dream curdles. *The New York Times*. https://www.nytimes.com/2012/03/26/books/the-master-blaster-by-p-f-kluge.html
Oledan-Ramos, R. (2012). *The boy who dreamed to be with his parents on Saipan*. Riza Ramos Books.
Olsen, K. J. (2014). *Chamorro*. Outskirts Press, Inc.
Oxford. (n.d.a). Erotic. In *OxfordDictionaries.com*. Retrieved March 19, 2019, from https://en.oxforddictionaries.com/definition/erotic
Oxford. (n.d.b) Exotic. In *OxfordDictionaries.com*. Retrieved March 19, 2019, from https://en.oxforddictionaries.com/definition/exotic
Quinene, P. A. L. (2016). *Conquered: A WWII erotic historical romance set in Guam*. Infinity Publishing.
Sample, S. (2014). *Some boy*. Susan Sample Hughes.
Smith, L. T. (1999). *Decolonizing methodologies: Research and indigenous peoples* (2nd ed.). Zed Books.
Williams, C. R. (2020, June 26). You want a confederate monument? My body is a confederate monument. *The New York Times*. https://www.nytimes.com/2020/06/26/opinion/confederate-monuments-racism.html

Mamåhlao: Negotiating Space for Indigenous Culture

Royce Camacho

Successful composition is often measured by the writer's ability to present a unique contribution to scholarship. In Foucault's (1984) description of authorship, "The coming into being of the notion of 'author' constitutes the privileged moment of individualization in the history of ideas, knowledge, literature, philosophy, and the sciences" (p. 101). To fulfill this expectation, many beginning composition students in Guam, who may have lived their entire lives prioritizing interdependence, must step outside of their cultural framework and instead see themselves as *individuals* to complete their assignments. This is especially true for CHamorus, the Indigenous people of Guam and the Marianas. CHamoru students entering the institution are welcomed by first-year composition course textbooks that present claims such as, "The positions of authority that academics are expected to hold and the kind of value that academics place on conveying knowledge result in language and essay structures that may be, to the outsider, mysterious or imposing" (Fontaine & Smith, 2008, p. 3). Consequently, the students believe that the dissonance they experience is just a natural part of negotiating their assimilation into scholarship. However, there may be more at work in Guam and the surrounding island communities; many voices that could bring Indigenous insight into academic spaces are practicing a silence, one culturally reinforced by the CHamoru value known as "mamåhlao."

Mamåhlao has been described as "shame or embarrassment" and is seen as important because it "represents all the Chamorro ideas of what is proper and civilized behavior" (Kasperbauer, 1996, p. 29). At least one common scenario exists in which adherence to mamåhlao can be observed and better understood, but there are many. It occurs at social gatherings when food or refreshments are offered to guests, and according to principle, the intended recipients should refuse the first and even second offering because accepting offers brazenly is viewed as "selfish, crude and disrespectful," and is a mark of "having no shame." I have come to understand that many cultures have adopted a similar perspective on accepting food. The value can also be observed in collaborative settings like the classroom, when participants are careful not to dominate the discourse or be perceived to "know-it-all" (have no shame) because these are marked characteristics of a taimamåhlao (not mamåhlao) attitude. A student may have to be called on a few times before offering an opinion. In other words, the student "who 'has shame' (mamåhlao) is always humble and respectful [whether inside or outside the classroom]; he or she is honorable and generous and caring of others" and will often put the group experience before any urge to express their thoughts (p. 29). For those observing the tenets of mamåhlao, it is more important to be seen as humble than to get "ahead," even at the cost of going without food so that others can get their fill, or conceding in an argument even if the other party is incorrect.

If this is the case—that the expectations of adhering to mamåhlao somehow represses the fire of the Indigenous perspective, the CHamoru perspective—what is the effect of encouraging students in the Marianas to draw on their experiences and insights to contribute something valuable to Western academic discourse? As a teacher in the Pacific, I often wonder what I am really asking of my students.

In Plato's (2001) *Phaedrus*, Socrates relates the story of Theuth, the Egyptian god and inventor of letters, who is challenged by King Thalus after boasting of writing's unparalleled utility. To Theuth's claim, King Thalus responds:

Most ingenious Theuth, one man has the ability to beget arts, but the ability to judge of their usefulness or harmfulness to their users belongs to another; and now you, who are the father of letter, have been led by your affection to ascribe to them a power the opposite of that which they really possess. For this invention will produce forgetfulness in the minds of those who learn to use it, because they will not practice their memory. Their trust in writing, produced by external characters which are no part of themselves, will discourage the use of their own memory within them. You have invented an elixir not of memory, but of reminding. (p. 165)

There is a prevailing belief in many institutions that standard English and effective composition are one and the same. And this makes many weary of articulating knowledge that is held as intimate when the primary measure of student ability and intelligence is an adherence to proper grammar, organization, tense consistency, and other academic conventions. Like Theuth, there are proponents of writing who will encourage the student to mine Indigenous knowledge in order confirm or challenge some aspect of Western academic discourse. Many soon realize that, although scholarship is valuable in academia, writing about the precepts of mamåhlao does not refine mamåhlao culturing or prioritize Indigenous thought in the classroom. In other words, it is difficult to serve the institution *and* your people. A worry is that as CHamorus begin to see themselves as part of the academic tradition instead of outside of it, they will refer to the literature (or the internet) to guide their behavior before searching the contents of their soul, before seeking the wisdom of their elders, before realizing that government policy and federal legislation (written word) continue to twist their people into colonial submission.

An uncle of mine passed recently, and 9 days of rosary followed before the funeral. The rosaries took place outside the residence under five-or-six large canopies. One canopy was designated just for tables of food. To a visitor, it may have looked more like a celebration than a site of grieving. The rosary ended and the techa, my great-aunt, asked everyone to stand and bless the table(s). From the living room, where the immediate family was gathered, her voice carried outside through a small PA system. A line formed after a couple minutes, with the kids first and the most senior in the family close behind. The hosting family may pick at the finger food or have a cup of soup, but they are mainly responsible for restocking the table or making room for another pot or plate of something that has just arrived. Someone has a little notebook in hand to quietly record the names of the families that contribute a dish. That way, when those families host a rosary or wedding, my family can return the favor.

An elder will say, "We have to go because so-and-so came to your cousin's birthday and brought two trays of buchi buchi." The written reminders in the little notebooks help to keep this system of reciprocity intact today, but who can recall how long this exchange has been in practice, or remember all the families that have taken part? That record does not live in memory. However, when it was time for my Nåna, who has been gone for 20 years now, to bring a pot of something to her mother-in-law's uncle's cousin's rosary many years ago, she did not have to keep a notebook of reminders; the details inhabited her soul, as if mamåhlao was a featured software in the Indigenous programming of CHamoru people. It determines how CHamorus should allocate their attention, to whom or what they owe a reciprocal responsibility, and it ensures interdependence. Mamåhlao is also understood as the soul of CHamoru culturing, and described as an "attitude of deference for others" (Cunningham, 1992, p. 92) or a "kind of intuitive measure which tells you when your behavior is proper and decent" (Underwood, 1978, p. 17). Those that have no sense of mamåhlao are said to have no shame (taimamåhlao) (Topping et al., 1975, p. 132).

Presenting this kind of intimate cultural knowledge here and now, in this very text you are reading, could be considered taimamåhlao, and students in Guam confront this risk because they are expected to situate themselves in the academic tradition (and concomitantly appreciate the privilege of individualization). In the process they will be required to acknowledge the ongoing academic conversation, which includes a colonial history that has declared Indigenous futility and promulgated the identity of the demeaning place-name "Ladrones." These early narratives, fueled by Western European rhetoric, have asserted notions like, "there are no pure CHamorus," that the "CHamoru language is dying," that the cultural practices of today are somehow "less authentic than pre-contact traditions," and that CHamorus needed and continue to depend on an external (colonial) force to propel them into modernity. Because the literature they confront contradicts their lived experience, students often opt not to touch cultural issues in their composition and defer to others, as if there are "experts" ready to write a revisionist CHamoru history, and as if they are not *themselves* practitioners of the culturing taking place in their community.

These colonial narratives continue to color the perception of CHamoru culturing, allowing these notions to be reiterated in the classroom, as if race and ethnicity are a measure of what is pure and authentic—and not constructs of our imagination. Indigenous students could feel disadvantaged from the onset because it is difficult to reconcile their framework of interdependence alongside expectations to be independent scholars. Not only are they expected to distinguish themselves from others, but they must also engage with literature that defines the CHamoru experience as lesser. When asking students in Guam to synthesize cultural insights and present these findings in a classroom, they are skeptical and even distrusting because they know that Indigenous thought is often seen as a response to and result of Western European discourse, instead of a parallel philosophy of equal value. Teachers have a responsibility to equip students with the appropriate regional literature to contextualize this historical perspective. Students who are not equipped may find it easier to practice a conscious disassociation from academia altogether and pursue other avenues of achievement.

With social media and the internet facilitating a culture of accessibility, there are endless paths to explore being CHamoru. In what has been called a cultural resurgence, there is a palpable desire to brand the next trend, lifestyle, or accouterment, and Indigenous undertones often get wrapped up in this commercialization. For example, sinahi, which are crescent-shaped symbols of seasonal renewal, are sported like fashion jewelry that can be made and worn by anyone without coveting the lunar motifs that provide their cultural significance. Using the symbol to communicate Indigenous knowledge about timing has remained in tandem with the reification of a culturing that suggests "we could all be chiefs now." Another example is the contemporary depiction of latte, which are large stone house posts, traditionally. These artifacts have been redesigned, resized, reinvented, and included as images on websites or in DVDs shown to the Chinese, Russian, Japanese, Korean, and American (military) markets. These visitors, expecting to meet latte-makers, can instead stop at the Galleria or visit Chamorro Village, where they can also buy sinahi and spondylus next to I ♥ Guam shirts.

Those that dwell on the misappropriation of these symbols are often seen as old-fashioned or "gate-keepers," dwelling on issues that ultimately do not matter, and may be labeled "taimamåhlao" for their unabashed expression of distaste. Meanwhile hotel chains and real-estate agencies, restaurants and the fitness industry, tour agencies and all manner of businesses use Indigenous artifacts to advertise their services without a responsibility to serve and enrich Guam's Indigenous population, to which these entities owe their marketability, at least in part. Maybe special consideration should be extended to those whose life-long goal is to represent CHamoru-ness judiciously so that the symbols that communicate Indigenous knowledge are not reduced to commercial products used to sell visitors a more exotic experience. While some maintain that participants in our local community should value mamåhlao attitudes, others see the distribution of cultural merchandise as a natural way of negotiating space for CHamoru-ness in the modern era.

Epitomizing Freud's narcissism of small differences, business entrepreneurs who redesign cultural products for commercial distribution will be criticized for exploiting Indigenous culture and other professionals condemned for putting on their island-print shirts and "selling out." Many toil away, endlessly debating the most appropriate way to represent CHamoru-ness, while pressing issues like decolonizing consciousness and self-determination are passed over—a result of Guam being inculcated by a history designed to haunt CHamorus into social disorder. Whether in the academic tradition or on the open market, Indigenous participation is often perceived to require a departure from Indigeneity—that CHamoru-ness must be presented in a certain way to be marketable today. More haunting than a colonial history is the reality that many CHamorus are not applying themselves because of a sensed systemic disassociation between their language and cultural community on one hand, and academia and capitalism on the other. An average of one self-inflicted death per week occurs in Guam (Cruz, 2017), with systemic disassociation likely a contributing factor. Teachers and educators, business entrepreneurs, politicians, entertainers, and others all have a responsibility to guard the mental health of Guam's people by creating space for Indigenous success.

Just before the funeral service for my uncle at the Immaculate Heart of Mary Catholic Church in Toto, a site of worship and grieving for generations of my family, my great-aunt led the rosary. During one of the Lord's Prayers, she struggled to get the words out. One of her nieces (my aunt) knelt by her side, just in range of the microphone. They shared rosary beads, and with cues from my great-aunt, the prayer picked up where it left off, but this time, in English. While the shift was by no means subtle, after 10 minutes a distinct cadence and style became apparent, resembling the melodic mantra that has guided generations of CHamoru grieving. Just like that, the voice of a new techa was recognized, validated not by an adherence to an authentic language or a pure bloodline, but by an intuitive conviction to serve interdependence. Mamåhlao culturing prioritizes interdependence. And to the Indigenous writer, mamåhlao often means speaking through the writing and ideas of others and only conveying a unique contribution in the absence of a more authoritative voice. In other words, "Since decisions [are] never individual decisions, it [is] not proper to express personal opinion directly. To do so [slows] down the process of reaching an interdependent group consensus" (Cunningham, 1992, p. 92). Indigenous writing will benefit from an audience that is willing to read between the lines and discern the argument being made with the same attention to the text that we afford the greats.

The notion of "individualization in the history of ideas" is a great opportunity afforded to the modern writer, but the modern writer is also plagued by too much information, and there is enough arguing in the comment sections across the internet to go around. I have begun coaching my students to select the writers they agree with or the material they find worth consuming, and have that be a feature in their writing, instead of instructing them to set themselves apart from an already established perspective. Point out a scholar or business owner or politician in Guam that has it all wrong, and be prepared to explain yourself to family members of yours and theirs alike at the next rosary. Even if you make a solid point, you may still be viewed as taimamåhlao for causing a stir in the first place.

References

Cruz, M. (2017, August 6). Suicide rates increasing: Adult males most at risk. *The Guam Daily Post*. https://www.postguam.com/.

Cunningham, L. J. (1992). *Ancient Chamorro society*. The Bess Press.

Fontaine, S. I., & Smith, C. (2008). *Writing your way through college: A student's guide*. Heinemann.

Foucault, M. (1984). What is an author? (J. Harari, Trans.). In P. Rabinow (Ed.), *The Foucault reader* (pp. 101–120). Pantheon Books.

Kasperbauer, C. A. (1996). The Chamorro culture. In Political Status Education Coordinating Commission (Ed.), *Kinalamten pulitikåt: Siñenten i Chamorro (Issues in Guam's political development: The Chamorro perspective)* (p. 29). Political Status Education Coordinating Commission.

Plato. (2001). Phaedrus. In P. Bizzell, & B. Herzberg (Eds.), *The rhetorical tradition: Readings from classical times to the present*. Bedford and St. Martin's.

Topping, D. M., Ogo, P. M., & Dungca, B. C. (1975). *Chamorro-English dictionary*. University of Hawaii.

Underwood, R. A. (1978). *Hispanicization as a socio-historical process on Guam*. University of Guam.

Fourth Day

Gerard van Gils

And on the third day of school, two boys rose from their desks, wildly punching each other in the face.

I had divided my students into groups of four. They were working on their projects in "American History" (scarcely mentioned, as my students do not often see American history as their history). As I rounded the room, failing to keep everyone on task, I apparently paired two boys into the same group without knowing anything of their extensive history. So, one boy tried to cheat an answer from another, some comment was sent back, threats were made, memories resurrected of prior offenses given and received. And so it was that on my third day as a teacher at Kagman High School, I calmly tried to break up a fight in my classroom. It was perhaps the most frightened I had ever been. I almost ran out of the room to go find a *real* teacher.

At the time I entered my Saipan classroom, I had a certification that said I was a "Highly Qualified" public educator. I had never stepped into a classroom or observed a full day in school—but I was "highly qualified" because I took a test called the Praxis and passed. My college degree is in Political Science, but I had spent my career as a banker in Utah. When I began my career in education in the Northern Mariana Islands, I was a stay-at-home dad and was, quite frankly, looking for a place to fit in. I volunteered to coach a high school soccer team and enjoyed the young people I coached. So, I started applying for open positions, of which there were plenty, and was hired at Kagman High School. I was not likely to last. I had no cultural understanding of my students, no professional practice or education, and I was not well paid, working full time for less than $30,000.

What I did not realize during those first days on the job is that public education in this country has serious illnesses, and I was merely a symptom: it is difficult to find quality teachers and to keep them. It is even harder to hire and retain quality teachers in remote and rural areas.

Around the country, school districts create pathways for college-educated people, like me, to become teachers either right out of college or coming from other careers. New teachers are essentially learning alongside their students, while often acting as if they have all the answers. It had been 13 years since I graduated from high school, and now, returning as the teacher, nothing had really changed: I was still looking for answers in the back of the book.

I had crashed from teacher idealism to harsh reality in just 3 days. On my first day, I was sure that I was answering the call to be a "hero teacher." I had somehow convinced myself that I was going to be exactly what these kids were waiting for. I remember telling one girl, Talianna, that I was "the best shot she had!" I still do not know what the hell I meant. In short, I was arrogant and had a savior complex. I was sure that these kids needed me. I did not realize it was the other way around.

Then the third day came, forcibly reversing my worldview. My young students' black eyes were swelling up like water balloons on a slow fill. I dragged the boys to the office and as we walked, I asked them, "Why were you fighting? How could you disrespect my classroom?" They both tried to explain with phrases like, "He atan båba'd me!" and "Pår, I never disrepeck notheen!" I could not understand anything they said, and I told them so. Exasperated, I pleaded with them, saying, "Just help me understand!"

"Sir, no disrespect. You can't get it because you don't know me."

Today, as a teacher at the same school for more than 6 years, I remember this as one of my earliest and most powerful lessons. "You can't teach me, because you don't know me." A powerfully accurate criticism, delivered sharply to his teacher, by a 9th grade boy who had just been punched in the face. And so keenly disarmed, I surrendered the point. "I think you're right. I hope you'll give me the chance to get to know you." The last bit was all the difference.

The remoteness and size of the islands mean that classrooms are often filled with local kids but led by fresh and hopeful teachers who are new to the islands. Some of these teachers are rigid, expecting island students to conform to their expectations without investing the effort to understand the context from which their students come. This was exactly my mistake.

At the beginning, I saw myself as the "Shining White Knight" kind of teacher, sent to save the villagers. I have seen similar teachers arrive every August, many of whom are like me and without previous teaching experience. While I still feel the tendencies, I recognize that the desire to save the world is terribly arrogant. Even the desire to "save one kid" is rooted in a narcissism of which I have been guilty. If you go into the classroom with a cape on, trying to be a superhero, you will wear yourself out and fail. Teachers must enter the classroom with an appreciation of the unknown and learn as much as they teach. To know the young people of the islands is to love them, and they love their teachers back. And they learn from teachers they love.

This phenomenon is acute in education, whether it's a suburban teacher entering an inner-city classroom or a continental teacher entering an island one. On the islands, the cultural divide occurs outside education as well since many professionals are educated elsewhere and visiting the islands on a two-year contract. A sizable portion of the island's doctors, lawyers, engineers, and other professionals are from elsewhere. They all, to some degree, suffer this disconnect. But if an engineer does not connect with his peers on a level of cultural understanding, the generators can still get fixed. A surgeon can take out an appendix on an Indigenous person as easily as on an immigrant. But in education, the entire outcome seems to hinge on a teacher's ability to relate to the student. That ability to relate is required. We educators learn and adapt to the ways of these islands. The Public School System requires teachers to take continuing education credits in CNMI history, but I think the real burden should be on the teachers. We educators need to learn the lay of the land, make some local friends, and internalize Indigenous culture. Acclimate to the tropics in ways beyond the climate. Life is a lot more comfortable when we settle in with the people and learn more than we teach.

I am terribly afraid to fail, and sometimes that fear paralyzes me. I think to myself, "I'd rather not try at it—I'll probably suck." My fear of failure is something I work on, and luckily teaching has provided me ample practice. Being a teacher is a terribly difficult job, and I think those who are brave enough to try it deserve honor and respect from their communities. Teaching is a career of daily failure. It is a job where most days, you fail to reach at least some of the kids placed before you. Even more difficult, the students who are most in need often do not have the vocabulary and emotional understanding to ask for help. So, on any good day, a wonderful teacher will miss opportunities to love and teach. That burden weighs on educators. Despite all the good they do, teachers stay up late at night worrying about the students they cannot reach.

The emotional struggle of teaching is compounded for off-island educators who struggle in a new climate, culture, and job. High school teachers everywhere are managing upwards of 120–150 kids a day, of various abilities, attention spans, and smells. Some kids smell so bad that your eyes water, but teachers love those smelly kids anyways. Everything is hard for teachers. They are broke and mosquito-bitten. They need friends and support or we'll lose them at the conclusion of their two-year contracts. The Northern Mariana Islands have lost too many wonderful and worn-out teachers.

My help came from new friends. I became friends with a younger guy, a high school dropout as it turns out. My attempts to help him "improve" his life were unwelcome, and so I was not sure what I was supposed to do "for" him. DJ told me we could just "chill," and so we did. Soon afterwards I visited his farm, attended a baby shower, and witnessed my first cockfight—all on the same first visit. I saw a pregnant mother open *Goodnight Moon*, and then I saw one rooster murder another rooster. I lost $20 betting on the red.

Another friend, Peter, invited me to a poker game at his house. Peter is the art teacher at Kagman High School, and he is a master educator. I said to Peter, "I'm nervous to go to your poker game where I'm the only non-local. I'm not sure how to behave, got any advice?" He was a good friend and cultural guide. His advice for making local friends at the poker table was simple: "lose." And I did, and I kept going back, and I kept losing money and making friends. Humbling to say, it turns out I was never losing on purpose. I'm terrible at poker, but I have a lot of friends who will welcome me to their tables.

Auntie Josie, a matronly Carolinian, took me in like a nephew and told me I was family. She wove birds out of coconut leaves for my daughters and taught me to make a mwáár. Her boys tried to teach me to mass. She told me about Pågan, where she was born, and how she hopes to go back and teach there some day. Teachers like her build communities, whole islands even.

My early semesters teaching were busy and filled with learning. I grew into this place. I released some of my closely held surety and asked more questions. I listened, and I learned. I relaxed and had fun, too. Soon, my students were laughing with me. Disciplinary issues were gone. A class spontaneously applauded me when one naughty boy showed attitude, and I snapped back, " ... wettz?" which is a Northside Saipan slang word roughly expressing disbelief and shock.

There were still days, like the third day, when I came home feeling like I had just carefully managed a brush fire. But there were more good days to add balance. There was progress in my students, and we were all happier. Students were hanging out in my room even when I wanted them to leave. I would see them around town, and they would come to hug me in the stores. The community had always wanted to welcome me, but I needed to get to know them first. I had to do my part.

In education, the good days get you through the difficult days. Sometimes, the good days and the difficult days are one and the same. Once, when I was feeling really low and was noticeably alone in a large crowd, a woman grabbed my hand and said, "Mr. G? I am Victor's mom." She hugged me, and we were both instantly crying, while everyone around us found a reason to look away. Victor is a brilliant young man with special needs. Victor treated his teachers to a steady flow of mathematical brilliance that was fractured by social difficulty. He would often storm out of class, fists clenched, and usually it was for something I had done. I had triggered him and Boom! —we were on a screaming outburst. Over Christmas break, we worked on a scholarship application for about three weeks straight. Victor wrote a beautiful essay about how he did not want to be a leader, and about how his puzzled brain made him see the world differently and how that made his education a worthy investment. Victor won a Gates Millennium Scholarship. When I met his mother for the first time, she knew what Victor had put me through, and I knew some of what she had endured raising him. We were both filled with overwhelming gratitude for the struggles and the successes. Victor is amazing and kind, and I got to be his teacher. It was one example of many explaining why teaching is the best job in the world, and why teachers should stick with it. I scarcely remember the hard days with Victor. I remember Victor, with his backpack stuffed, walking up the ramp at the airport, flying to Eastern Oregon University on a full ride.

For 500 years, these islands have had a stream of people come ashore with plans for what they would make of the people and the place; I brought plans with me when I came as well. What I fortunately learned is to reverse the order. I invited these people and this place to change me, make something of me, and I learned to teach.

I recently spoke, again, with my student, Talianna. She had witnessed my early days teaching, when I acted as the noble "first-day teacher-hero." Talianna was now one of my Million Dollar Scholars, Kagman High School students who were preparing as cohorts to attend college. I asked Talianna if she remembered my first day. She did not let me even finish the question, "Yes! Oh my God, Mr. G, you were the weirdest! You came in talking like you were going to rescue us from all the terrible things or something. You sounded ... like ... a crazy person." She was right, but it still hurt to remember. Then she continued, "But you weren't weird for too long. You got better, I think, as you got to know us."

I dedicate these words, from my heart, to the noble educators of these islands who come back on the fourth day and every day.

The Halo Halo ("Mix Mix") Generation

Tabitha Caser Espina

I am called "Balikbayan" because the girl in me is a country of rope hammocks and waling-waling orchids—a land with irresistible gravity because, in it, I forget the world's magnificent indifference. In this country, my grandmother's birthland, even the dead are never cold and I become a child at ease with trawling through rooms in the dark.
-*"Corolla" by Eileen Tabios (2000),*
Babaylan: An Anthology of Filipina and Filipina American Writers, xxi.[7]

Translated literally, halo halo means "mix mix" in the Filipino language. In preparing the halo halo dessert, an assortment of native ingredients, such as jackfruit (langka), saba bananas, sweet potatoes (kamote), red mung beans, young coconut (buko), flavored gelatin, and the quintessential purple yam (halayang ube) are mixed together, typically in a clear glass. These ingredients are added and apportioned according to taste. Shaved ice is piled on top before evaporated milk is poured over all the ingredients. As all the ingredients are mixed, they are subsumed and sublated into the dominant, white milk mixture. In halo halo, although each item maintains its distinctive flavor, the overall taste experience is the result of the blending of flavors.

As in the Filipino halo halo dessert, there is both a distinctiveness and a mixing that occur in the identity negotiations of immigrant third-generation Filipinos. Third-generation youth in America find themselves situated, as sociologist Peggy Levitt (2009) argues, between a variety of different and often competing generational, ideological, and moral reference points, including those of their parents, their grandparents, and their own real and imagined perspectives about their multiple identities and their homelands. Filipinos comprise a significant part of the population worldwide, within the United States, the Mariana Islands, and Guam. An estimated 2.2 million Overseas Filipino Workers (OFWs) were employed overseas in 2016 (Philippine Statistics Authority, 2017). Filipinos now comprise the second-largest immigrant group and second-largest Asian American group in the United States, according to Yen Le Espiritu's (2003) chronicle of Filipino lives across cultures, communities, and countries. Filipinos comprised the single largest ethnic group employed in the Commonwealth of the Northern Mariana Islands (CNMI) in 2005 (CNMI Department of Commerce/Central Statistics Division, 2008). In Guam, Filipinos are the second-largest ethnic group, comprising approximately 26.3% of the island's population (Central Intelligence Agency, 2017). The Filipino population in Guam has grown steadily from post-World War II to today, from approximately 7,258 in 1950 to approximately 42,057 in 2012 (US Census Bureau, 2017; Central Intelligence Agency, 2017). As Filipino immigrants have made their homes all over the world, their descendants continue to reconcile conceptions of home and belonging.

This chapter explores the enunciations of identity of third-generation Filipinos in Guam, whom I term the Halo Halo generation, through my own narratives of autoethnography and through poems by two prolific local slam poets: Verna Zafra, whose work interrogates Western conceptions of feminism and laments the loss of her culture; and John "Metaforce" Sarmiento, whose work uses Filipino characters to capture the attitudes of the young, contemporary generation. Halo halo, "mix mix," then, is an apt metaphor for the "mixing" that occurs in the identity enunciations of third-generation Filipinos in Guam.

Inspired by Filipina poet Eileen Tabios (2000) in her poem "Corolla," I will be "collaging" the works of my peers to contextualize and frame my own narratives. This collage strategy references not only the identities of contemporaries but also the experiences of previous generations to ground elusive identities. Young Filipinos can rewrite the words of their parents and grandparents to create a collage of collective experience that may help them better understand their position as members of the Filipino community in Guam.

By using the literary expressions of young Filipinos, I emphasize the significance of our personal experiences in exploring the attitudes and ideas of this large population in Guam. Narrative, according to narrative theorist David Herman (2009), is "a basic human strategy for coming to terms with time, process, and change," and interpreting such expressions from where they emerge is essential to understanding the thoughts, ideas, and attitudes of this contemporary generation (Introduction, para. 2). I incorporate these theories into the halo halo theoretical metaphor I have devised, as Wai-Chee Dimock (1991) suggests in her study of feminist new historicism, to describe the complexities of life as a coherent system to be organized and interpreted into some semblance of clarity and order. Using the halo halo dessert as a scholarly term, as opposed to standard Western terminology, signifies progression and hybridity, according to feminist cultural theorist Gloria Anzaldúa (2001), and enables Filipino Americans to provide name and shape to this concept as our own.

In the Halo Halo generation, a variety of Filipino and Guamanian cultural elements is chosen from and added together according to "taste." While I recognize that the term "Guamanian" is fraught with identity politics and has been criticized for contributing to the erasure of Guam's Indigenous people, I use this term primarily for consistency and familiarity, referring to Filipinos' colonial settler position on Guam. I want to portray how these distinct cultural experiences are then mixed with, subsumed, and sublimated into the dominant American culture through complex processes that include acculturation and assimilation. This "mixing" is attributed to a multitude of processes, which often diminish cultural distinctions by varied degrees. I argue that the Halo Halo generation acts within the spectrum of acculturation and assimilation, often altering the Filipino values of parents and grandparents and privileging American values over both Filipino and Guamanian cultures. This combination occurs against a backdrop of Westernization, one legacy of which is the colonial mentality that either values or devalues, favors or rejects various characteristics. Just as the local ingredients are often mashed into and inundated in milk to become an opaque, milky mixture, American values and cultural norms flood Filipino values and cultural norms, coloring and flavoring them. Under the influence of the "white milk" of Westernization, the identity of the third-generation Filipinos becomes more homogenized as compared to previous generations, assimilating Filipino, as well as Guamanian, cultural distinctions into a pervasive American culture. I am optimistic, however, that the halo halo dessert's inclusion of the halayang ube ingredient symbolizes the "roots" of Filipino culture as an essential ingredient of Halo Halo identity.[8] At the same time, the Guamanian identity, symbolized by the presence of the buko, or young coconut, in the halo halo dessert, adds a dimension of complexity to the Halo Halo identity. Though still existent, the "root" element of the ube and the "seed" element of the buko become dissolved into the mixture, imperceptible but nonetheless present to create a distinct flavor. Just as halo halo is no simple shaved ice, the Halo Halo generation is more than the sum of its cultural ingredients and experiences.

Am I Not an Island Girl?
While I, like many of my Filipino peers, grew up in Guam, my attempts to understand the different cultures that comprise my identity have often left me unsatisfied and unsettled. Like the mixture of ingredients in halo halo preparation, I am provided with a mix of cultures and contexts, from which I choose to suit my changing tastes. Interestingly, however, the result has been the sharp, sometimes bitter taste of disillusionment and ambivalence, instead of a mixing of "flavors" that might produce a unique and enjoyable blend.[9]

I am a third-generation Filipina. At the age of four, I became Guam's youngest recording artist, singing with my mother, Alpha Espina (1994), on her Christmas album, *Back to You*. At seven-years-old, I then released a solo album (Figure 1), *Tabitha Espina: Island Girl* (1997), in which the title track contained words in CHamoru, Guam's native language.[10] Throughout my childhood, I regularly performed as "The Island Girl" at malls, local fiestas, charity fundraisers, and community and government-sponsored events, even being sponsored by Fox Network in Saipan to perform in my own concert. Although I enjoyed performing, throughout primary school, I was constantly teased, "You're not an island girl! You're Filipina!"

Figure 1
Tabitha Espina: Island Girl Album Cover

Until then, I had not realized that I was not an "authentic island girl." I was born and raised in Guam and had only thought of the Philippines as a place where my family vacationed. Though I had claimed Guam as my home, claiming to be one of its "island girls" was crossing a line—an invisible border that delineated where I did not and could not belong. By internalizing this putative border, I had allowed it to cause me to doubt my own definition. I felt like Hélène Cixous's (1993) uncertain border crosser, "who trembles while crossing a border [and thus] casts doubt on [her] own definition … What 'nature' [am I]? What 'species' [am I]?" (p. 131). Once conscious of these borders, I could not navigate between cultures as seamlessly as I had once done. From then on, I had to question what I was allowed to say or do because I am Filipina.

This research admittedly began as an exploration of my own identity. I employ the use of personal experience in my autoethnographic study of identity as a method to demonstrate some aspects of third-generation Filipina identity that have only begun to be theorized. An autoethnographic approach, like that used by Peruvemba S. Jaya (2011), can act as a catalyst for reflection on issues surrounding diaspora and the meanings of identity within the context of globalization. The inclusion of my personal experience in this research is therefore part of a reflexive process, wherein I influence and am influenced by my findings.[11]

Espiritu (2003), in her chronicle of Filipino American lives across cultures, communities, and countries, describes how political and cultural mechanisms designed to restrict membership are created everywhere within a nation, setting clear but imaginary boundaries between who is "inside" and who is "outside." The third generation, then, lives in a mixed, "halo halo" world, and it is the divisions of this world that engenders their Halo Halo identity. Espiritu (2003) finds, however, that although Filipinos are discursively produced as foreign and are pressured to carry figurative borders around with them, their self-made multiple subject positions and transnational connections repeatedly push against these borders, as I found myself doing. Because of these persistent borders and the push against them, Filipinos of the Halo Halo generation lead a double or multiple existence—they have integrated into Guam society as generational colonial settlers, but the original sense of foreignness experienced by their immigrant ancestors continues to pervade their experience. They feel that Guam is their home but may not feel fully at home. They recognize that they are ethnically Filipino but sometimes feel shame in their heritage, are reluctant to claim certain aspects of Filipino culture, and may also feel out of place in the Filipino community.

These feelings of being unfamiliar and ill-equipped are captured in Verna Zafra's (2015) poem, "Tools," published in *As Us: A Space for the Women of the World*. Zafra is a young Filipina poet raised in Guam who uses written and slam poetry to explore themes of negotiation and empowerment. The emphasis of her engagement in poetry is service, as she served as a mentor and the Program Director of Sinangån-ta Youth Movement, Guam's official youth slam and spoken word organization until 2015. With an ear towards the youth, Zafra (2015) describes her experience of visiting relatives in the Philippines:

We crossed into mountain-backed fields
It was my first time;
Theirs, they had lost count.
Like hardened soldiers,
They trudged the paths
Of sword grass,
Retracing the steps of their mothers
And brothers and fathers –

The vague ghosts of my bloodline.
And with graceful dexterity,
They put their tools to use.
Tools that tilled and weeded,
Tended and sowed,
Indifferent to the black mud,
Even to their own calloused abuse.

Zafra's poem shows her passage through rugged terrain, which is new for her but part of the everyday lives of her relatives. The beginning of her poem contrasts their lifestyles, with her relatives marked by generations of "hardened" trudging. Zafra admires their commitment to the traditions of their ancestors, while plaintively describing her ghostly tenuousness. Using the metaphor of "tools," she compares their skill, ease, and capability, with her inability and reluctance. Zafra's observation is, overall, marked by shame in her different lifestyle, lack of skills, and fragile connection to her cultural heritage.

Like Zafra, the slam poetry of John Norman "Metaforce" Sarmiento confronts the issue of belonging among youth. Sarmiento has been widely affiliated with the Halo Halo generation. In 2015, he represented Guam in Paris, France, as he was chosen by the Global Call for Climate Action group to perform his poetry at the United Nations Framework Convention on Climate Change. Sarmiento's dynamic poetry articulates his fascination with his Filipino-American-Guamanian culture but also his tensions with it.

Sarmiento's unpublished poem, "Blind Tongue," voices the Halo Halo generation's battle with boundaries set up by definitions of the authentic and inauthentic. Because young Filipinos are classified by the first and second generations of immigrants as neither "this" nor "that" after all of the "mixing" of being caught between cultures, there is a sense of being caught between identities:

You were born in a white room
beneath white lights
wrapped in a white blanket,
but raised in the grey area

of being from here
but not really from here.

. . . .

'cause your eyes
don't speak enough Tagalog.
Your tongue is blind
to what it can't understand.
Taste test your Filipino culture on China.
Refuse it 'cause the flavor isn't English enough.

. . . .

You're not Filipino
or CHamoru enough
to be from anywhere.
This is not your island.
It belongs to the activists.
They just let you live here.
You have no right to contribute to the island's destiny.
You are one in a thousand products of immigration
stuck in this CHamoru class.
You are Filipino-American.

Sarmiento describes his birth as shrouded in a sterile, ominous whiteness that houses him, enlightens him, and encases him. He recognizes that he is born into a position surrounded by the "whiteness" of American Western culture, which is common for Filipino Americans born in the United States and oriented towards American norms and values. For Sarmiento, the "grey area of being from here but not really from here" is a combination of white and dark, as he is born into the "white" of the United States in Guam but is still affected by the "dark" unknown of his Filipino ancestry. It is because of this "grey area" that Sarmiento feels his tongue is "blind"—both his language and tastes are not Filipino and he blindly rejects what is not "English enough." Restricted by feelings of insufficiency, he grieves not being enough of a Filipino or CHamoru (i.e., one of Guam's Indigenous people), making him unable to fully inhabit or contribute to Guam's community, or any community. He expresses feelings of not belonging, having no claim to the island as his home, and having no rights. He condemns himself for being just another product of immigration, lacking originality and significance, and being "stuck" in a culture that is not his own. These distressing emotions encapsulate the position of Sarmiento and others of the Halo Halo generation. Caught in the act of trying to cross a guarded border, they are left stranded with feelings of insufficiency, inauthenticity, estrangement, and inadequacy.

Borders create anxiety. In *The Filipino Americans (The New Americans)*, Barbara M. Posadas (1999) remarks that cohesion and fragmentation simultaneously characterize young Filipino Americans. Considering their transnational struggles, Diane L. Wolf (2002) finds that the distress of Filipino youth, particularly females, is greater than that experienced by other groups and must be further explored through individual circumstances and contextualized within historical, political, and racialized relations. Nadal (2011) describes Filipino youth's struggles as "acculturative stress," due to the conflicting processes of negotiating between the boundaries of acculturation and assimilation (p.53). Sarmiento's metaphoric "blind tongue" is representative of the second stage of Nadal's (2004) Pilipino Identity Development Model, "Assimilation to Dominant Culture," in which Filipino Americans realize they are different from dominant cultural norms and may attempt to assimilate into the dominant culture and reject being Filipino. While the majority of young Filipino Americans may appear apathetic and uninterested in understanding their complex identities, beginning to acknowledge and interrogate this apathy signifies the beginnings of a shift in ideology. While apathy is revealed in my narrative through my self-defeating creation of restrictive borders, in Zafra's disillusioned conclusion, as well as in Sarmiento's conceding that the island can never be his home because of his felt inadequacies, the mere speaking out and pronouncement of these feelings is the opposite of apathy and disinterest. While they speak of a sentiment that suggests passivity, these narratives simultaneously and proactively contemplate these emotions, instead displaying agency and assertion.

"Aiy, No Me?": Resisting Anomie

Confronted with feelings of alienation and inauthenticity within their American and Guamanian contexts, the Halo Halo generation may attempt to break down barriers or boundaries to help ground their sense of identity. Linda A. Revilla (1997) argues in "Filipino American Identity: Transcending the Crisis," that part of the "identity crisis" of youth in the Filipino American community is reconciling issues of self-love and self-respect as Filipinos. In "On Both Sides of The Hyphen: Exploring the Filipino-American Identity," Ma. Teresa G. Tuason et al. (2007) write that it is not that US-born Filipino Americans devalue Filipino customs and traditions, but rather they grew up mostly deprived of and unfamiliar with their Filipino heritage. However, while the work of Tuason et al. considers only Filipinos born in the US mainland, an unfamiliarity with Filipino customs can be found in the narratives of the Halo Halo generation who grew up and came into adulthood in Guam. Wolf (2002) describes young Filipino Americans' ethnic affiliation as a "largely symbolic sense of ethnicity," in which Filipino language, culture, and traditions are derived from experiences that are intermittent, brief, and disconnected from the rest of their lives (p. 263). The narratives of the Halo Halo generation reflect what Wolf (2002) describes as an "allegiance to an imagined past" (p. 263). While the Halo Halo generation identifies as Filipino, they also must contemplate what it means to be a Filipino in Guam.

In my own personal attempt to actively seek out my Filipino heritage, I entered a Filipino pageant sponsored by a local United Filipino Students Association. While other contestants answered the questions in "Taglish" (code-switching between Tagalog and English), I was ashamed that I could only respond in English and even sheepishly appealed to the host for a translation whenever he spoke in Tagalog. As other contestants incorporated Filipino dances and songs into their performances, I sang and danced to a song in English and spoke only the one Tagalog phrase of "Hindi kita malilimutan"—ironically translated, "I will never forget you." I was, much to my surprise, given the title crown of Miss Teen Philippines-Guam 2006 and then as title-holder, I participated in various Filipino cultural events and spoke on Filipino television and talk shows. Each experience made me uncomfortably aware that I was pretending to celebrate a Filipino culture and history that remained largely unknown to me. I felt unfit to represent Guam's Filipino community, to which I had never truly felt I belonged. I wondered, "Does being Filipina make me any less connected to Guam? Does being from Guam make me any less of a Filipina? Does being an American enrich or hinder my understanding of my Filipino culture, as it is expressed in Guam?" Once again, I felt inauthentic and questioned the symbolism of the hyphen in my Miss Teen Philippines-Guam title: the hyphen between "Philippines" and "Guam" was the border I inhabited. Like the hyphen, I felt nested—constricted even—between the two communities, two cultures. Like Espiritu's (2003) invisible borders, that hyphen attempted to define who I was and who I was not, to what extent I was from the Philippines and to what extent from Guam. This hyphenated identity meant, to me, that I was neither fully one nor the other.

My experience in the pageant was somewhat detached, as I was able to appreciate the culture and participate in the festivities only to a certain extent because they were not a regular part of my daily life. Although I prefaced my performance proclaiming, "I will never forget you," truthfully, I could not forget a Filipino culture that I never actually knew or remembered in the first place. This avowal instead attested to a longing and a desire to remember what had yet to be known.

It also attested to a more subtle crisis—the tension between love and respect of the self and shame and rejection, as Revilla (1997) argues in "Filipino American Identity: Transcending the Crisis." This complex crisis results not from a devaluing of whatever is Filipino but from a deprivation that then imagines Filipino as alien, as something outside of the self (Revilla, 1997). There is thus a divide in identity, as pride in one's culture is intermingled with shame in not knowing it enough.

In her unpublished poem, "Moving Mountains," Zafra also examines her tension between self-respect and shame. She begins by challenging the impositions of society that attempt to dictate her behavior:

Growing up,
I was told that the only way
To survive in this world
As a woman
Is not to show weakness:
I was told to always keep my head high,
My voice loud,
And my skin tough,
Because anything that looked less than strength
Instantly made me a liability,
A burden to myself

But I have walked through 23 years
With my head bowed,
Not because I am ashamed,
But because I have learned
That I cannot show respect
By having my chin up in the air,
But lowered in a sign of regard
For others and their struggles
That I'll never know about

Zafra begins by criticizing what she has been told. She interrogates these gender roles imposed by Western culture, and she explains in the rest of her poem that these expectations are incongruous with her own expressions of womanhood. She feels the need to justify her behavior, claiming that her seeming timidity is not for lack of strength, but because of it. Her perceived timidity is instead a regard for what she claims she will "never know about."

Sarmiento's unpublished poem "Jewelry" is more indignant in describing the dilemma of the Halo Halo generation, as well as their lack of knowledge of their Filipino culture:

[B]ut they don't see the dilemma that they've put me in.
I'm in a push and a pull between my cultural identity.
My mom always said that I was born and raised on Guam,
but I'm really from the Philippines.
I guess that means I'm supposed to be
part FOB
and part almost-chaud.
. . .
I was born full Filipino,
but now I'm half American Colonized.
I can't be proud of my heritage!
I know virtually nothing about the first half of it!
and the second half?!

I know so much about that sometimes I'm ashamed of it.
I know exactly what it means to be American Colonized.

Sarmiento accuses colonialism of building the borders that divide him into many parts. While he is expected to be a "FOB," a "Fresh Off the Boat," newly immigrated Filipino, he feels he is not. Instead, he identifies as "part almost-chaud," aligning himself more with CHamoru culture but acknowledging that he is only "part," not fully, and "almost," but not yet. Sarmiento's nuanced use of the word "chaud" aligns with Robert Underwood's (2017) description in "Underwood: At the Edge of Chamoru and English," referencing CHamoru people suffering from language loss and who are of a particular generation and social class. The term is often stigmatized and used disparagingly in Guam and the CNMI. Similarly, Sarmiento blames his dilemma of cultural identity on the previous generation, but acknowledges that they were unaware of the circumstances they put him in.[12]

A prominent divisive factor in Sarmiento's poem, as well as in my narrative, is the inability to speak the Tagalog language. Within the Filipino community of Guam, there is a broad, rigorously guarded border between those who speak Tagalog and those who do not. This is possibly intensified by the CHamoru language revitalization efforts, such as CHamoru language instruction in the Guam Department of Education curriculum, which emphasize the importance of language for the perpetuation of culture. Many young Filipino Americans regret that they were not taught to speak or understand any Philippine language and surmise that they may have been able to better identify with their Filipino culture and community if they had been taught their Philippine language, according to Jennifer G. Osalbo (2011) in her research on Filipino American identity development and its relation to heritage language loss. Especially with regards to teaching the Philippine language, previous generations were often reluctant to pass on Filipino culture and values to children and grandchildren, often citing busy work schedules, fear of discrimination, and hopes of upward social mobility through greater English proficiency. The result is a new generation of Filipino Americans who are disconnected from their language, creating the largest divide between themselves and Filipino culture.[13] The American colonialism that negatively impacted the previous generations unfortunately continues to affect the successful adaptation and development of Filipinos in Guam into the succeeding generations. The Halo Halo generation depends on the previous generations to orient them towards Filipino cultural values and to help them establish a place for themselves within the Filipino community. There is a discernible sense of searching for that which remains unknown to the Halo Halo generation. Though all but invisible in the mix of bright colors in halo halo, it is still there—the roots of halayang ube—giving the halo halo the distinctive flavor of earth, of grounding.

"White" Milk and Young "Coconut"

In *Legacies: The Story of the Immigrant Second Generation*, Portes and Rumbaut (2001) find that by the third generation, ethnic ties and identities have weakened to the point of nonexistence as immigrant groups become fully integrated into the American mainstream. By the time the grandchildren of Filipino immigrants come of age, their severance from the homeland is complete. They have the highest composite assimilation index ranking on a 100-point scale among immigrant groups in the United States: 100 in economic assimilation, 72 in cultural assimilation, and 65 in civic assimilation, according to a comprehensive report by Jacob L. Vigdor (2008) of the Manhattan Institute. Nevertheless, despite the whole-hearted embrace of assimilation, a longing for what was never known remains.

In "Alone," a song I composed[14] in 2011 for "The Navigator," a musical digital storybook for use in a multicultural classroom, I express feelings of alienation and drifting away from origins:

How did I get here?
It's still a ways to go.
The distance is even harder
When you're out on your own.
The stars remain silent
And as they shine down on me,
I can't even tell if I'm where
I'm supposed to be.
So I cry out to the sky
And ask it, "Why?"
How much more have I to go
As I drift further

Far from home?
I am sick and tired
Of being tossed and blown!
But most of all,
I can't take
Feeling so alone.

Pondering where I am, how I got there, and how much further I have to go produces the feelings of loss and disillusionment experienced by the Halo Halo generation subsumed in American culture. Moreover, as the descendants of immigrants to Guam, the Halo Halo generation can also feel alienated by their ancestry from some other place than the island they call home. Separated from Filipino culture and nested within another colonized culture, the "distance" of growing up and developing a sense of self is even more difficult in isolation and without a point of reference. Displaced, ironically despite having a physical home, and disempowered, despite standing in their new communities, the Halo Halo generation may feel "tossed and blown," unable to fully ground their identities or find complete belonging in Filipino, Guamanian, or American culture.

Metaphor continues to be helpful in understanding the complexities of the Halo Halo generation identity. In her interviews with Filipino American youth, Osalbo (2011) finds that a common symbol for the "Americanized" Filipino is a coconut—brown on the outside, white on the inside. This symbol is particularly applicable to the Guam context, as it is a local fruit that is also a common ingredient in the halo halo dessert. Filipinos on Guam are "coconuts" in a different sense. Just as the coconut is also a seed, the Halo Halo generation has been planted and grown on Guam. Like mature coconuts, members of the Halo Halo generation come to maturation in Guam as "brown" locals, but their insides are white—inevitably marked by the legacies of American colonialism.

In his integral text on contemporary colonial mentality, *Brown Skin, White Minds: Filipino -/ American Postcolonial Psychology*, E. J. R. David (2013) vividly recounts the moment in his adolescence that provoked questions about his ethnic and cultural identity: finding "SELL-OUT! COCONUT! YOU'RE FILIPINO, ACT LIKE IT!" written on his school locker (p. xvii).[15] Such a lack of congruence between one's internal and external ethnic belonging could result in psychological tension over one's sense of self, as suggested by Lisa Kiang and David Takeuchi (2009) in their study of Filipino Americans. Through their narratives, the Halo Halo generation attempts to find words for this incongruence.

In "Tools," Zafra's (2015) recognition of her white, smooth tools in contrast to the worn, stained tools of her relatives attests to the internalizing of her "whitewashed" designation:

I looked on in awe
Before looking down
At my own tools:
Smooth, white,
And in that moment,
I realized,
Dumb.
They were hands that did not know.

She is in awe of the tools of her relatives that have been burnished by trials and experience. She finds her tools inadequate, as they are uninitiated, under-utilized, and essentially "dumb." Her hands are rendered useless, unaccustomed to the work before her.

While Zafra genuinely describes her difference from her ancestors, Sarmiento (2012) explicitly condemns the inauthentic way many young Filipino Americans attempt to portray themselves in his poem, "Just a Rant":

Brown boys got pale hoes
white washed
like French toast
with milk mixed by Foremost.
. . . .
A bunch of island kids
pretendin' that they ghetto

talkin' like they gangbangers
cause they can't talk Filipino.

Sarmiento (2012) sarcastically describes the "brown boys" preferring "white washed," "pale hoes," symbolizing Filipino youth being seduced by the allure of White American society. The "milk mixed by Foremost" is Sarmiento's (2012) contextualizing of this claim, as Foremost Foods Guam Inc. produces and distributes commercial fruit and dairy products to the island. The milk being "mixed" signifies that it is processed and inorganic, suggesting that the promises and allure of White society are similarly artificial and empty. Sarmiento later derides the tendency of Filipino youth to pretend to be who they are not, in an attempt to compensate for not knowing or not wanting to admit to who they are. Sarmiento confronts the superficial desire of the Halo Halo generation to hide and denigrate their Filipino culture and regard the norms and culture of White America as superior. Sarmiento's poem scrutinizes colonial mentality at work in his friends and peers in the Halo Halo generation.

The previous narratives display the various forms of colonial mentality (CM). David (2013) conceptualizes CM as being "characterized by a perception of ethnic or cultural inferiority that is ... a specific consequence of centuries of colonization under Spain and the US" and "involves an automatic and uncritical preference for anything American" (p. 241).[16] CM entails associating superiority, pleasantness, or desirability with the physical characteristics (i.e. whiteness) and cultural characteristics considered American or Western (David, 2013). Based on a large national sample of Filipino Americans, David (2012) finds that one out of three Filipino Americans has some form of CM, resulting in lower personal self-esteem and higher depression levels. The Halo Halo generation's negative experiences in their ethnic identity formation can thus be greatly attributed to the prevalence of CM.[17]

A colonial mentality prevails among the Halo Halo generation, despite living in a society as culturally diverse as Guam. This attests to the lasting effects of Western colonialism in the lives of Filipinos, CHamorus, and the other ethnic groups in Guam. American and Western cultural norms continue to pervade the lives of the Halo Halo generation and affect their emotional, social, and psychological development. Nevertheless, with the changing socio-political landscape, Filipino Americans of the later generations are adapting to an increasingly diverse society. The Halo Halo generation engages in active adoptions, adaptations, and contestations of the different cultures they encounter and, as a result, dynamic identity enunciation and expression take place. While being "coconuts" appears to be a general trend in the narratives of the Halo Halo generation, young Filipinos in Guam are recognizing their CM, are actively resisting it, and are forming coalitions with others affected by American colonialism.

A recent example of the Halo Halo generation fighting against CM for themselves and others is through the Filipino Revolutionary History Teach-In that took place on July 20, 2017 at the University of Guam. The "teach-in" was one of the monthly sessions conducted by Independent Guåhan, a taskforce that provides education on CHamoru self-determination and advocates for Guam's political independence. Kristin Oberiano (2017), whose grandfather came to Guam through Camp Roxas, explained to The *Guam Daily Post* that

> As Filipinos living on Guam, we need to acknowledge that the fight for CHamoru self-determination is a fight for the ideals of self-governance, sovereignty and freedom – the same principles that led to the establishment of the Philippines, the USA, and other independent countries around the world.

Oberiano and co-presenters Josephine Ong, Jamela Santos, and Ruzelle Almonds are all Filipinas who consider Guam home and hope to begin dialogue with fellow Filipinos in Guam to stand in solidarity with the CHamoru people by supporting the CHamoru self-determination movement (Oberiano, 2017). By presenting information on Philippine revolutionary history, Philippine migration history, and CHamoru self-determination movements, Oberiano, Ong, Santos, and Almonds hope that for Filipinos in Guam, understanding their own history of independence will increase the Filipino community's support for the CHamoru self-determination movement and will encourage other communities of non-CHamorus to do the same. In this way, the Halo Halo generation develops ethnic and cultural identities that transcend negative self-representations.

In Guam, the members of the Halo Halo generation are developing their identities alongside the identity politics and cultural revitalization efforts of the local CHamoru people. While the erosion of ethnic identity usually takes place in the course of three generations, the assimilability of the third generation must be considered within a more complex, post-civil rights context characterized by an increasingly non-European composition, identity politics, and ethnic revivals (Rumbaut & Portes, 2001). By coming together to understand how their identities are affected by American colonialism in Guam and the Philippines, the Halo Halo generation can counteract feelings of unbelonging and disconnectedness. Kiang and Takeuchi (2009) emphasize the importance of revisioning the Filipino American self in order to moderate the negative effects of perceived discrimination by contributing to a sense of group belonging, social support, and connectedness. A strong ethnic identity enables the Halo Halo generation to participate more fully in the community. The Halo Halo generation can be equipped to redefine themselves ethnically and culturally to enhance their confidence and gain self-worth. This can be done by creating spaces of agency—past, present, and in-between.

The Fluidity of Halo Halo

Diasporic spaces are places, as sociologist Peggy Levitt (2009) asserts, where norms are constantly renegotiated across borders and the lines between home and host cultures and between the generations become blurred, making them one interconnected social experience. These diasporic spaces, as Espiritu (2003) argues, are the "space between," a transnational space that productively articulates the tensions, irresolutions, and contradictions that underscore the multiplicity of Filipino lives and work against definitions that would fix them in one identity or place (p. 10). Living between old and new, between homes, between cultures, and between languages, the Halo Halo generation does not merely insert or incorporate themselves into existing spaces; they instead transform these spaces with memories and histories to create new ones—a "space between" (Espiritu, 2003, p. 10). When describing my own identity, I claim to have internalized Guam's political status as an "unincorporated territory," finding myself in the conflicts and contradictions that this ambiguous status provokes, but also emboldened to push against its limitations.

Accessing the collective memory of the community, according to Leny M. Strobel's (1997) study of the narratives of post-1965 Filipino Americans, brings the Halo Halo generation full circle in the process of decolonization to recover what had once been unknown to them:

> To reclaim memory at the personal level is to engage in the process of creating a collective memory of a people's history. From their memory banks, the participants were able to connect their personal struggles to the struggles of the Filipino

people in the Philippines, the United States, and all parts of the world ... As reconstructed memories, these were imbued with new meanings for the present. (p. 73) The Halo Halo generation can compensate for a lack of cultural and historical knowledge by integrating the experiences of other Filipinos into their personal memories and experiences. These additional experiences become extensions of understanding and allow the Halo Halo generation to formulate a productive identity that is able to transform and adapt to increasingly globalized contexts.

Other young Filipinos of the Halo Halo generation are similarly re-membering, collaging, and referencing the cultural knowledge of those in the two previous generations to foreground their identity enunciations and expressions. Writing and research has helped my peers and me come to terms with and give shape to our experiences as descendants of our grandparents' immigration. By gaining access to the experiences of Filipinos in Guam throughout the generations, the Halo Halo generation feels richer and more encompassing.

Personal memory must, however, be fortified by historical memory. Increased awareness of Filipino culture and history enhances the identity of the Halo Halo generation. The current state of the diasporic Filipino is a consequence of historical facts of racism and oppression (Strobel, 1996). By reflecting on the larger political and historical context of Filipino immigration and how it relates to the political and historical context of Guam, the Halo Halo generation can begin the often painful and emotional journey of rediscovering and reconstructing their ethnic and cultural identity (Strobel, 1996), which will in turn yield acts of reclamation and activism.

In addition to this autoethnographic research, one of the ways that I have attempted to explore ethnic identity in the diverse context of Guam and consider the voice of other Filipinos is through writing fiction. In "Departures," my short story included in the *Local Voices* anthology for the 2016 Festival of the Pacific, I created the character Lily, who goes by "Lila," a half-Filipino, half-CHamoru island girl. Her mixed identity intrigues her unnamed love interest who describes her as "worldly—or other-worldly," (p. 108) with a "passion that never stayed too latent beneath her solemnity" (p. 110). Lila's character, however, is not simply defined by the paradoxes of her identity. She navigates these seamlessly and displays tremendous agency, eventually choosing to abandon her departing love interest and stay at home, with her family. She has a commitment to the island she calls home, but remains perceptive of the difficulties of living there:

> "It's a microcosm of the feeling of living on Guam ... I think it brings people together when they know what they'll be missing," she continued, "Families on Guam are together all the time. And sometimes we take that togetherness for granted. But when someone leaves, you're forced to remember all that you loved. It just really hurts being the one here all the time." (Espina Velasco, 2016a, p.110)

Lila is emblematic of the fluidity of the Halo Halo identity, as she makes conscious choices that display her devotion to her home and yet challenges cultural expectations. She is intrigued by her White military love interest and relishes the opportunity to leave home for college, but she remains tied to her family and chooses not to pursue a relationship that would take her away from home. She admits that she is broken, but still necessary to the ecology of "[her] ocean" (Espina Velasco, 2016a).

However, balancing between the needs of the self and the expectations of the community is delicate. While integrating and considering the words of others, Zafra cautions that there is the need to preserve the self. In "Moving Mountains," Zafra reconciles her sense of self amidst cultural expectations by claiming power in her perceived weaknesses:

I have walked through 23 years
With the same blanket of skin
Wrapped around my body
It is not tough,
But it is mine.
It knows
That I want nothing more
Than to walk into rooms unnoticed
To sit in far corners
Where I can make my quiet observations
Not because I am afraid,
But because I have been raised to believe
That strength does not always come wrapped
In perfect packaging,

But in tiny frameworks of dark blemishes
And sneaky birthmarks.

While numerous voices have informed the development of her womanhood, Zafra recognizes the most important voice is her own, as she makes her own identity. This overtly displays the value of Western individualism. However, she also recognizes the significance of the way she has been raised to overcome obstacles, alluding to the influence of her family. This displays the collectivism of the island culture. Her ability to claim who she is despite "blemishes" and imperfections is an empowering act of negotiation and resolve, based on her upbringing.

Re-Mixing: Conclusion
Spaces invite fluidity. Like the smooth, fluid halo halo dessert, the Halo Halo generation has a fluid positioning, which, in the words of cultural theorist Stuart Hall (1989), is not a fixed, "once-and-for-all," but a point of identification or suture made within the discourses of history and culture. Within these spaces, the social identities of Filipino, Guamanian, and American collide, and the Halo Halo generation can understand how these cultures comprise their sense of self and how their identities and Guam's context mutually influence each other. This is a space of possibilities, re-mixing conceptions of identity for their own particular purposes and contexts.

It is what historian Howard Zinn (1984) describes as a postmodern space of identity that is both multidimensional and unified, both emotional and cognitive, and both individual and social, so that being oneself as a Filipino, Guamanian, and American is no longer a question of authenticity, but rather being true to self in context and in relationship to these different senses of self. The Halo Halo generation can experience belonging and self-realization by understanding who they are as third-generation Filipinos in Guam. Zinn (1984) observes that the result of re-mixing selves is an identity that is different from its competing parts. The Halo Halo identity is a constant process of revising who one is in relation to other Filipinos in Guam, including those within and outside their own families; in relation to changing circumstances, such as Guam's changing socio-political landscape; and in relation to different cultures, such as that of CHamorus and other communities who call Guam home. Just as the different ingredients undergo changes when mixed together in the halo halo dessert (e.g. mashing, breaking apart, dissolving), the Halo Halo generation is simultaneously embedded in more than one context where fluid social spaces are constantly reworked and re-mixed.

In *Authentic Though Not Exotic: Essays on Filipino Identity*, Fernando N. Zialcita (2005) aptly articulates the foundation of this postmodern space: "Often people think in terms of 'Either ... or,' ... [but] I believe it is really a case of 'Yes ... but ... ' Yes, to certain features of Westernization; no to others and at the same time going beyond them to work out a better order" (p. 26). It is this selectivity that epitomizes the Halo Halo generation's perspective. Their future depends on flexibility and shifting to divergent thinking, which, according to cultural and feminist theorist Gloria Anzaldúa (2001), is moving away from analytical, singular Western thinking and instead towards a holistic perspective that breaks down paradigms and straddles cultures. This self rejects Western polarization, is collective and encompassing, stands in solidarity with others, and is uniquely and distinctly its own. It offers an invitation: "Kumain na tayo! Let's eat!"

References

Anzaldúa, G. (2001). La conciencia de la mestiza: Towards a new consciousness. In K. Bhavnani (Ed.), *Feminism and 'race'* (pp. 93–107). Oxford University Press.

Central Intelligence Agency. (2017, July 18). Guam. In *The world factbook*. https://www.cia.gov/library/publications/the-world-factbook/geos/gq.html

Cixous, H. (1993). *Three steps on the ladder of writing*. (S. Cornell, & S. Sellers, Trans.). Columbia University Press.

CNMI Department of Commerce/Central Statistics Division. (2008, April 1). *Report on the 2005 CNMI household, income, and expenditures survey (HIES)*. http://sdd.spc.int/en/resources/document-library?view=preview&format=raw&fileId=302

Constantino, R. (1970). The mis-education of the Filipino. (B. M. Drona, Trans). *Journal of Contemporary Asia, 1*(1), 1–16. https://doi.org/10.1080/00472337085390031

Côté, J. E., & Levine, C. G. (2002). *Identity formation, agency, and culture: A social psychological synthesis*. Erlbaum.

David, E. J. R. (2012, November 14). *The colonial mentality project: The psychological study of colonial mentality or internalized oppression among Filipino Americans and other marginalized groups*. The Colonial Mentality Project. http://colonialmentality.netfirms.com/CM.html

David, E. J. R. (2013). *Brown skin, white minds: Filipino-/American postcolonial psychology*. Information Age Publishing.

Dimock, W. (1991). Feminism, new historicism, and the reader. *American Literature, 63*(4), 601–622. https://doi.org/10.2307/2926870

Espina, A. (1994). *Back to You* [Album]. Masterpeace Studios.

Espina, T. (1997) *Tabitha Espina: Island girl* [Album]. Trax Studios.

Espina, T. (2011, May 21). *Alone*. The Navigator Digital Storybook. http://thenavigator.weebly.com.

Espina Velasco, T. (2016a). Departures. In the Literary Arts Committee (Publications) for FESTPAC 2016 (Ed.), *Local voices: An anthology*. (pp. 107-112). 12th Festival of Pacific Arts.

Espina Velasco, T. (2016b). The ube ("roots") generation. *Humanities Diliman, 13*(2), 75-101.

Espiritu, Y. L. (2003). *Home bound: Filipino American lives across cultures, communities, and countries*. University of California Press.

Hall, S. (1989). Cultural identity and diaspora. *Framework, 36*, 222–237.

Herman, D. (2009). *Basic elements of narrative*. Wiley-Blackwell.

Jaya, P. S. (2011). Themes of identity: An auto-ethnographical exploration. *The Qualitative Report, 16*(3), 745–763.

Kiang, L., & Takeuchi, D. T., (2009). Phenotypic bias and ethnic identity in Filipino Americans. *Social Science Quarterly, 90*(1), 428–445. https://doi.org/10.1111/j.1540-6237.2009.00625.x

Levitt, P. (2009). Roots and routes: Understanding lives of the second generation transnationally. *Journal of Ethnic and Migration Studies, 35*(7), 1225–1242. https://doi.org/10.1080/13691830903006309

Nadal, K. L. (2004). Pilipino American identity development model. *Journal of Multicultural Counseling & Development, 32*(1), 45–62. https://doi.org/10.1002/j.2161-1912.2004.tb00360.x

Nadal, K. L. (2010). *Filipino American psychology: A collection of personal narratives*. AuthorHouse.

Nadal, K. L. (2011). *Filipino American psychology: A handbook of theory, research, and clinical practice*. Wiley.

Oberiano, K. (2017). What it means to identify as a settler. *The Guam Daily Post*. https://www.postguam.com/forum/letter_to_the_editor/what-it-means-to-identify-as-a-settler/article_0bc225e6-a998-11e7-aacf-e7bc0e57e7cc.html

Osalbo, J. G. (2011). *Filipino American identity development and its relation to heritage language loss* [Master's thesis, California State University, Sacramento].

Philippine Statistics Authority. (2017, May 24). *2016 survey on overseas Filipinos*. https://psa.gov.ph/content/2016-survey-overseas-filipinos

Portes, A., & Rumbaut, R. G. (2001). *Legacies: The story of the immigrant second generation*. University of California Press.

Posadas, B. M. (1999). *The Filipino Americans (the new Americans)*. Greenwood.

Rath, S. P. (2000). Home(s) abroad: Diasporic identities in third spaces. *Jouvert, 4*(3).

Revilla, L. A. (1997). Filipino American identity: Transcending the crisis. In M. P. P. Root (Ed.), *Filipino Americans: Transformation and identity* (pp. 95–111). Sage.

Rumbaut, R. G., & Portes, A. (2001). *Ethnicities: Children of immigrants in America*. University of California Press.

Sarmiento, John Norman [Meta Sarmiento]. (2012, May 10). *Just a rant* [Video]. YouTube. http://www.youtube.com/watch?v=_9NpLbRT-bM

Skinner, M. C. (2009). *In the company of strangers*. Bamboo Ridge Press.

Strobel, L. M. (1996). 'Born-again Filipino': Filipino American identity and Asian panethnicity. *Amerasia Journal*, 22(2), 31–53. https://doi.org/10.17953/amer.22.2.v7841w4h7881hk04

Strobel, L. M. (1997). Coming full circle: Narratives of decolonization among post-1965 Filipino Americans. In M. P. P. Root (Ed.), *Filipino Americans: Transformation and identity* (pp. 62–79). Sage.

Tabios, E. (2000) Rupturing language for the rapture of beauty. In N. Carbo, & E. Tabios (Eds.), *Babaylan: An anthology of Filipina and Filipina American writers* (pp. xiii-xxii). Aunt Lute.

Tuason, M. T. G., Taylor, A. R., Rollings, L., Harris, T., & Martin, C. (2007). On both sides of the hyphen: Exploring the Filipino-American identity. *Journal of Counseling Psychology, 54*(4), 362–372. https://doi.org/10.1037/0022-0167.54.4.362

Underwood, R. (2017). Underwood: At the edge of Chamoru and English. *Pacific Daily News*. https://www.guampdn.com/opinion/underwood-at-the-edge-of-chamoru-and-english/article_e84619ba-63f7-5306-be27-b0a438ce49e0.html

US Census Bureau. (2017). *1950 census of population: Volume 2. Characteristics of the population*. https://www2.census.gov/library/publications/decennial/1950/population-volume-2/41601749

Vigdor, J. L. (2008). Measuring immigrant assimilation in the United States. *Civic Report, 53*, 1–46.

Wolf, D. L. (2002). There's no place like "home": Emotional transnationalism and the struggles of second-generation Filipinos. In P. Levitt, & M. C. Waters (Eds.), *The changing face of home: The transnational lives of the second generation* (pp. 255-294). Russell Sage Foundation.

Zafra, V. (2015). Tools. *As us: A space for women of the world*. http://asusjournal.org/2015/12/06/verna-zafra-poetry/

Zialcita, F. N. (2005). *Authentic though not exotic: Essays on Filipino identity*. Ateneo de Manila University Press.

Zinn, H. (1984). *The twentieth century: A people's history*. Harper Colophon.

Poetry from a Son of the Marianas

Craig Santos Perez

During Your Lifetime, 2016
for Guam's "Greatest Generation," which refers to the generation of native CHamorus who died and survived the massacre of World War II in Guam, including my grandma, who passed away in 2018, at the age of 95

~

You survived violent Japanese military
occupation and the bloody march
to Manenggon. You endured American

bombing, and felt the wounds of our island
stitched by barbed wire fences. You said
goodbye to the sons and daughters of Guam

as they donned uniforms and deployed

overseas. You hugged all your children
as they migrated, one by one, off-island.

You witnessed invasive beetles devour
half our coconut trees. You prayed
as diabetes and cancer diseased half

our relatives. You listened as English
endangered our language and snakes
silenced our birds. Dear grandparents,

I doubt if we'll ever receive reparations,
or sovereignty over our own nation. I
can't count how many more body

bags will arrive with tough boxes and
folded flags. I'm not sure if our language
and birds will sing wild once again

beneath healthy coconut trees. And I
don't know if all your children,
grandchildren, and great-grandchildren,

will return home, together, during
your lifetime, to show the abundance
that you will be survived by.

Ode and Elegy to Drinking a Can of Coconut Water with My Dad in California

Once, I bought a can of coconut water for my dad
because he felt homesick for the island of our birth.

After the first taste, he can't stop talking story
about the tropical past. He claims, as a barefoot

child, he climbed tall coconut trees that touched
the Western Pacific sky. And he swears his grandpa

removed the husk with his teeth and cracked the shell
with his knuckles. And he swears his grandma grated

the meat with her fingernails, and squeezed it into milk
and oil. These products are trendy and expensive now,

I tell him, imported from plantations in Sri Lanka,
the Philippines, and Thailand. He laughs and says

his great-aunties sat in a circle weaving coconut leaves,
and if you pressed your ear to their woven mats,

you could still hear their gossip and singing, even after
they died. And because circles make memory seem less broken,

he recalls his great-uncles, too, sat in a circle braiding
dried coconut fibers into rope, used to lash canoes

and thatched houses, just as our veins bind our genealogies
to endure the lashing of waves and conquest. I read aloud

the nutrition facts label: 45 calories, 30mg sodium,
470mg potassium, and 11g sugar. Fat and cholesterol free.

He responds with this origin tale: once, a young girl,
beloved by our entire island, dies during a time

of drought. The family buries her and weeps upon
the grave, from which an unfamiliar tree sprouts.

They watch it grow and bloom until its hard, strange
fruit falls and opens on impact. The girl's mother braves

the first sip, then smiles for the first time in years,
as if her body, after having been completely emptied,

is finally replenished. From that harvest, we planted
a sapling whenever a child was born. As generations

passed, the trees became kin, teaching us how to bend
without breaking, how to create without wasting,

and how to take without depleting. My dad tells me,
during his last visit home, that invasive beetles

are devouring our coconut trees. We discard the aluminum
cans in the recycling bin and swallow the bitter aftertaste.

Family Trees
written for the 2016 Guam Educators Symposium on Soil and Water Conservation

1

Before we enter the jungle, my dad
asks permission of the spirits who dwell
within. He walks slowly, with care,
to teach me, like his father taught him,
how to show respect. Then he stops
and closes his eyes to teach me
how to *listen. Ekungok*, as the winds
exhale and billow the canopy, tremble
the understory, and conduct the wild
orchestra of all breathing things.

2

"Niyok, Lemmai, Ifit, Yoga', Nunu," he chants
in a tone of reverence, calling forth the names
of each tree, each elder, who has provided us
with food and medicine, clothes and tools,
canoes and shelter. Like us, they grew in dark
wombs, sprouted from seeds, were nourished
by the light. Like us, they survived the storms
of conquest. Like us, roots anchor them to this
island, giving breath, giving strength to reach
towards the Pacific sky and blossom.

3

"When you take," my dad says, "Take with
gratitude, and never more than what you need."
He teaches me the phrase, "eminent domain,"
which means "theft," means "to turn a place

of abundance into a base of destruction."
The military uprooted trees with bulldozers,
paved the fertile earth with concrete, and planted
toxic chemicals and ordnances in the ground.
Barbed wire fences spread like invasive vines,
whose only fruit are the cancerous tumors
that bloom on every branch of our family tree.

4

Today, the military invites us to collect
plants and trees within areas of the jungle
slated to be cleared for impending
construction. Fill out the appropriate forms
and wait 14 business days for a background
and security check. If we receive their
permission, they'll escort us to the site
so we can mark and claim what we want
delivered to us after removal. They say
this is a benevolent gesture, but why
does it feel like a cruel reaping?

5

Listen, an ancient wind rouses the jungle.
Ekungok, i trongkon Yoga' calls us to stand tall!
Listen, i trongkon Lemmai calls us to spread our arms wide!
Ekungok, i trongkon Nunu calls to link our hands!
Listen, i trongkon Ifit calls us to be firm!
Ekungok, i trongkon Niyok calls us to never break!
Listen, i halom tano' yan i taotaomona call us
to rise, to surround our family of trees and chant,
Åhe'! No! We do not give you permission!

Off-Island CHamorus

My family migrated to California when I was 15 years old. During the first day at my new high school, the homeroom teacher asked me where I was from. "The Mariana Islands," I answered. He replied: "I've never heard of that place. Prove it exists." When I stepped in front of the world map on the wall, it transformed into a mirror: the Pacific Ocean, like my body, was split in two and flayed to the margins. I found Australia, then the Philippines, then Japan. I pointed to an empty space between them and said: "I'm from this invisible archipelago." Everyone laughed. And even though I descend from oceanic navigators, I felt so lost, shipwrecked

on the coast of a strange continent. "Are you a citizen?" he probed. "Yes. My island, Guam, is a US territory." We attend American schools, eat American food, listen to American music, watch American movies and television, play American sports, learn American history, and dream American dreams. "You speak English well," he proclaimed, "with almost no accent." And isn't that what it means to be a diasporic CHamoru: to feel *foreign in a domestic sense.*

Over the last 50 years, CHamorus have migrated to escape the violent memories of war; to seek jobs, schools, hospitals, adventure, and love; but most of all, we've migrated for military service, deployed and stationed to bases around the world. According to the 2010 census, 44,000 CHamorus live in California, 15,000 in Washington, 10,000 in Texas, 7,000 in Hawai'i, and 70,000 more in every other state and even Puerto Rico. We are the most "geographically dispersed" Pacific Islander population within the United States, and off-island CHamorus now outnumber our on-island kin, with generations having been born away from our ancestral homelands, including my daughter.

Some of us will be able to return home for holidays, weddings, and funerals; others won't be able to afford the expensive plane ticket to the Western Pacific. Years and even decades might pass between trips, and each visit will feel too short. We'll lose contact with family and friends, and the island will continue to change until it becomes unfamiliar to us. And isn't that, too, what it means to be a diasporic CHamoru: to feel foreign in your own homeland.

And there'll be times when we'll feel adrift, without itinerary or destination. We'll wonder: What if we stayed? What if we return? When the undertow of these questions begins pulling you out to sea, remember: migration flows through our blood like the aerial roots of i trongkon nunu. Remember: our ancestors taught us how to carry our culture in the canoes of our bodies. Remember: our people, scattered like stars, form new constellations when we gather. Remember: home is not simply a house, village, or island; home is an archipelago of belonging.

Ode to Fina'denne' & Kikkoman Soy Sauce

1

A wood carving of the last supper
hangs on the wall above our dining table
in Mongmong, Guam, circa 1980s.
Where's the fina'denne'? I wonder.

2

Fina'denne' *(pronounced fin-ah-den-ee)*
is the most important condiment, sauce,
and/or marinade in CHamoru cuisine:

1 part soy sauce
1 part lemon/lime juice or white/coconut vinegar
chopped onions (white and/or green)
chopped donne' (red chili peppers)
chopped tomatoes and/or garlic (optional)

Mix in a bowl, chill, serve.

3

Fina'denne' is holy water
at every special CHamoru event.
Spooned over rice, grilled meat and fish,
cooked vegetables, and even green salad.
On Guam, fina'denne' is served
at McDonald's and KFC.
It was recently featured in *Saveur Magazine*,
and now has its own Wikipedia page!

4

On ordinary days, my dad
simply places the soy sauce
bottle in the middle of the table.

"Who's Kikkoman?" I once asked him.
In his myth-making voice, he bellows:
"Kikko is an ancient CHamoru chief
who once caught 10,000 green sea turtles
and stored their tears in bottles."

"And soy," he says. "Soy is a magic bean
that grows in the Far East. The turtles eat them
before swimming to Guam. It means, long life."

5

I stare at the Kikkoman bottle and imagine
the Nakajima Ki-84 Hayate fighter jets
that bombed our island on December 8, 1941.
I stare at the red cap and imagine
the imperial rising sun of the Japanese flag,
how my grandparents were forced to bow
during those violent years of occupation,
how the blood of 1,000 CHamorus
marinated the land. Yet

where the Greater East Asia
Co-Prosperity Sphere failed,
the Greater Asian Amino Acids
Concentration Sphere conquered:
our stomachs continue to bow
to the fifth taste of "umami"
(pronounced oo-ma-mee),

and the sixth taste of empire.

6

Now, listen to the legend of Kenji Ekuan:
as a child, he watched his mother pour soy sauce
from a half-gallon bottle into a tabletop dispenser.
He witnessed the atomic bombing of Hiroshima.
His younger sister died in the explosion.
His father, a Buddhist monk, died from cancer.
Kenji traced his father's shadow and became a monk
at a temple in the ruined, irradiated city.

Having faced nothingness, Kenji decided to make
human things. He studied art, started a design company,
and after three years and 100 prototypes,
created the transparent Kikkoman bottle in 1961.

"The shape is gentle," he once said. "During the war,
we were forced into acting differently. But for 1,000 years,
the history of the Japanese people was very gentle."

Kenji also became famous for designing
motorbikes and bullet trains.

7

More than 300 million Kikkoman soy sauce dispensers
have been sold in more than 70 countries since then.
They infiltrate every CHamoru kitchen and table.
Soy sauce gently bullets through our intestines.

"Is it healthy for me to consume soy sauce every day?"
"Is Kikkoman soy sauce made from genetically-modified soybeans?"
"Are companies like Kikkoman testing on animals"

"Does sodium increase blood pressure and heart disease?"

8

I watch my dad chop the ingredients
and place them in an empty bowl.
"Pass me the *ketchåp*," he says.

In CHamoru, the word for soy sauce is *ketchåp*,
which is also our word for American tomato ketchup.
"Same difference," he says.

I ask him: "If soy sauce is Japanese,
what makes *fina'denne'* CHamoru?"

"It's CHamoru," he smiles, "because
we made it better, we spiced it up."

He raises and tilts the teardrop
shaped bottle until it bows to us.

Guam, Where America's Voting Rights End

1

My 7th grade social studies teacher made us,
the children of Guam, memorize the names of
all 41 American presidents, whose portraits stared
down at us in the furthest American territory
from the White House. As I recited their names
at home, my parents watched Bill Clinton play
saxophone on television. "Are you voting for him?"
I asked. My dad, wearing his Army t-shirt, said:
"Didn't your teacher tell you that our votes don't
count. It doesn't matter that we're citizens or veterans."

2

A few years later, my family migrated to California,
where I became a resident, graduated high school,
and registered to vote. But after Al Gore lost,
I learned that living in the States doesn't guarantee
your ballot will actually count. I learned how easy
it is to memorize the name of a president who wages
two wars and sharpens your island into a weapon.
And isn't that what an American president is: a name
to which our lands and bodies are ultimately sacrificed.

3

When Barack Obama campaigned in 2007, his name
gave me hope because it descended from slavery,
from the civil rights movement, from a mixed raced family,
from the Pacific. Yet Obama only visited Guam once.
In 2011, his plane landed at night on the air force base,
refueled, then departed. That's when I learned the arc

of history doesn't bend justice towards Guam. I learned
no matter what the president's name is, he remains our
commander, and our island remains a forgotten name.

4

For thirty years, a straw poll in Guam has accurately
predicted the result of US presidential elections. In 2016,
Hillary Clinton won the poll, yet still lost to Donald Trump,
thus breaking our historic (and ironic) streak. I voted for
neither candidate, which felt like a betrayal to my kin
back home, who don't have a voice in the election.
Some activists now petition to extend voting rights
to the territories; instead, I want our decolonial
voices to be counted, I want Guam's liberation
from American presidents to be inaugurated.

SPAM's Carbon Footprint

Guam is considered the SPAM® capital of the world. On average, each CHamoru consumes 16 tins of SPAM each year, which is more per capita than any country in the world. Headline: Guam Struggles to Find Its Roots From Beneath Growing Piles of SPAM. Guam, Hawaii, and Saipan have the only McDonald's restaurants that feature SPAM on the menu. I went to the "World's Largest K-Mart" in Guam and I was amazed at the SPAM display ... it was like a whole "Wall of SPAM." SPAM has a place not only in the stomachs of Guam's people, but in our hearts as well. Here SPAM is considered a gourmet luxury and is often presented as a gift at birthdays, weddings, and funerals. Hormel even made a Hot and Spicy SPAM especially formulated for Guam with Tabasco already added to it! A culinary legacy of American troops stationed in the Pacific during World War Two, the GIs noticed how much the people of Guam loved SPAM, so they started to jokingly call it "CHamoru Steak." Not coincidentally, SPAM is also popular in Hawai'i, the Philippines, Okinawa, and Saipan, all places with a history of a US military presence. In fact, SPAM may have been responsible for Hitler's defeat. The Allies would not have won WWII without SPAM. Plus, it's processed so I guess we can keep it forever right? Wow, I haven't seen this much SPAM since I lived on Guam and the car dealership there started offering 50-lb bags of rice and cases of SPAM with every purchase. The end result can be found in the newspaper's obituary pages. In 2004, Public Health reported that heart disease was the leading cause of death in Guam, representing 33.7% of deaths. You can rub the entire block of SPAM, along with the accompanying delicious gelatinous goo, onto wood furniture. The oils from the SPAM moisturize the wood and give the furniture a nice luster. Plus, you'll have enough left over to polish some of your neighbors' furniture. You'll be like Santa Claus meets Mr. Clean. How did I miss hearing about the "In Honor of Guam's Liberation" SPAM! I thought I had collected them all! But as I got older and tried to be "healthier" (whatever that means, haha), SPAM faded from my consciousness. Then I met my future wife, who is Hawaiian, and SPAM became part of my life again. Maybe the economic downturn will help people truly appreciate SPAM instead of loathing it. SPAM doesn't have to be unhealthy. I eat SPAM on a regular basis and I'm not dead yet. Just switch to SPAM Lite. In the devastating wake of Typhoon Omar, SPAM arrived. Hormel Foods donated 40,000 cases of the belly-filling foodstuff to the Salvation Army's disaster relief effort. That's about six million SPAMburgers! Despite rumors, SPAM is NOT made of such odds and ends as hooves, ears, brains, native people, or whole baby pigs. SPAM is for realz made of pork shoulder, ham, salt, water, sugar, and sodium nitrate, if you can belief it. The name itself stands for Specially Processed Army Meat, Salted Pork And More, Super Pink Artificial Meat, Squirrel Possum And Mouse, or Some People Are Missing. My uncle is the reigning Guam SPAM king. He won the last SPAM cook-off with his Spicy SPAM meatballs. I will never forget the two-pound SPAM bust of George Washington he made for Liberation Day, toasted crispy on the outside with raw egg yolk in the hollow center. The kids loved it! Only a fool would start a company in Guam that provides SPAM protection. We don't want to be protected from SPAM bots. For Xmas, I bought a SPAM snow-globe featuring a can of SPAM sitting on an island; turn it over and a typhoon swirls madly, unable to unseat SPAM from its place of honor. I have a souvenir can I bought after seeing Monty Python's SPAMALOT on Broadway. It cost me $10 and is the most expensive SPAM I've ever bought. I will never eat it.

SPAM's Carbon Footprint II

SPAM® was born on July 5, 1937, in Austin, Minnesota—the home of Hormel headquarters and the SPAM museum #cubistartyoucaneat. Eight pounds of SPAM die in every CHamoru stomach each year, which is more per capita than any other ethno-intestinal tract in the world. Motto: "Guam is Where the Impure Pork Products of America Begin!" Our guttural love of SPAM was born in 1944, when cases of the shiny cans were berthed from aircraft carriers. That fateful day when my grandparents first tasted SPAM is commemorated as the Feast Day of the Immaculate Consumption. St. Hormel, pray for [us]. The rest of the story is gestational genealogy, a delicious cycle. Sadly, military recruiters are now worried that young CHamorus have become too unhealthy and obese to enlist in the armed forces. My food philosophy is simple: I eat therefore I SPAM. How can I prove that I'm an authentic Indigenous person and not a SPAM script? At this year's Hormel SPAM Cook-Off in Guam, the Polish inspired "Pika Pieirogi" ousted the "Crispy Wanton Spam Ravioli" for first place. I've eaten turkey SPAM, smoke-flavored SPAM, hot and spicy SPAM, garlic SPAM, SPAM lite, Portuguese Sausage flavored SPAM, and more! When did our lives become so complicated and post-modern? WSFWJE? What SPAM Flavor Would Jesus Eat? Come closer, closer, and I will whisper to you, in my sexy voice, "google the SPAM factory's dirty little secret." Oooohhh baby, here I am, come rub up on my belly like SPAM jelly—Oooo baby here I am, come rub up on my belly like SPAM jelly, Spam-Spam-Jelly, Spam-Spam Jelly! #mandatorymarley. In the morning, we can bring our SPAM labels to the Sorensen Media Group Offices in Hågatña, and redeem 12 labels for a SPAM shirt and 9 for a SPAM hat. Guam is an acronym for "Give Us American Meat." My favorite scene in John Steinbeck's *The Grapes of Wrath* (b. 1939) is when the tractor driver takes a lunch break near a tenant house and eats his sandwich of white bread, pickle, cheese, and SPAM. The curious, starving children surround the driver, watching his hands carry the SPAM to his mouth. Once upon spiral time, a CHamoru brother and sister refused to eat SPAM, so their Authentic CHamoru Grandmother banished them into the diaspora and cursed them to a life without meat. The vegetarian siblings migrated to Minnesota, where they opened the world's first vegan butcher shop and sold meatless meats at farmers markets and pop-up events. They dedicated their lives to creating the perfect vegan SPAM. They tried vital wheat gluten. They tried garbanzo tapioca flour. They tried peanut butter. "The flavor's good but the texture's off," they say in unison. "SPAM is just a difficult whale to catch." If they succeed, I will never eat it.

Intersection of Identity in Three Generations of CHamoritas and Filipinas in Guam

Sharleen Santos-Bamba
Tabitha Caser Espina

Gracing Alupang Beach is a statue that epitomizes the women of Guam and their rootedness in culture and home. "The Women of the Island—Three Generations" statue (Figure 1) was based on a design by local CHamoru artist, Ron Castro. Castro's mother, daughter, and niece posed for artwork meant to show the women of Guam waiting at the shore for the men to return from fishing (R. Castro, personal communication, March 2017). Later, Alupang Beach Towers commissioned Italian sculptor, Roberta Giovanni, to take Castro's art and create a bronze statue to be placed along the beach shore. Three generations of women, together, waiting, listening, anticipating the return of their men from sea.

In the same way, this chapter acts as a return. The women of the following narratives are together, waiting and listening not for men, but for their own voices to come ashore in solidarity. CHamorus and Filipinos are historically the two largest populations in Guam, at 37.3% and 26.3%, respectively (Central Intelligence Agency,

2017). CHamorus and Filipinos have a long, complex, and interwoven history of immigration, competition, and intermingling. While most research describes this interaction broadly, we turn to the voices of these women to relate the dynamics and motivations of these two populations through the literate and spiritual lives of CHamoru and Filipina women themselves.

Figure 1

"The Women of the Island — Three Generations" Statue Along Alupang Beach

Note. Photograph courtesy of Lakeisha Tenorio Espina, 2021.

As a way to unpack the complex identities of CHamoru women in Guam, Dr. Sharleen Santos-Bamba (2010) makes use of a trove of interviews and historical records to trace the literacy trajectories of three generations of CHamoru women in modern Guam. Tabitha Espina Velasco (2013) uses autoethnography to explore the identity formation of three generations of Filipinas in Guam. As members of both these populations, we decided that an intergenerational and intercultural examination of our work would be productive in exploring the plurality, complexity, and interrelatedness of these female identities in Guam and how they are affected by the intersections of gender, race, and culture. In this chapter we examine the ways these women perceive quality of life, spirituality, and cultural perpetuation in Guam.

Our approach manifests CHamoru feminist scholar Laura Souder's claim in the conclusion of her seminal text, *Daughters of the Island: Contemporary Chamorro Women Organizers on Guam*. Although Souder (1987) does not explicitly address CHamoru and Filipina relations, she does recognize the value of comparing CHamoru women with other groups in Guam (p. 237). Our partnership through our work acknowledges a relationship between CHamoru and Filipina women in Guam that has largely gone unexamined. The current era of contact between Filipinos and CHamorus has deep historical roots in the advent of Western colonization. From 1521 to 1898, Spain colonized Guam and the Philippines, and Guam fell under Spanish colonial domination for more than two centuries, resulting in intermarriages between CHamoru women and immigrant Filipino laborers, according to local Filipina scholar Clarisa Quan (n.d.).

Filipino immigrants were brought to Guam en masse after World War II as laborers (Quan, n.d.). Men from Iloilo and the Visayas were recruited by construction companies to assist in the rebuilding of Guam's infrastructure. They worked hard and performed well to avoid being returned to the Philippines. The money they earned as laborers was far more than what they would have earned at home. The disparity in wages today is comparable to 60 years ago. In 2010, the average household income in Guam was $49,263 (Guam Chamber of Commerce, n.d.), while in the Philippines the average household income in 2012 was ₱235,000 PHP, approximately $4,643 USD (Philippine Statistics Authority, 2013). For 75 years, Filipino immigrants have sought greater financial opportunities in Guam.

Campbell (1987) notes that Filipinos have left a major imprint on Guam's history, and Quan (n.d.) affirms that some of the richness of Guam's history owes to Filipinos' contributions. Filipinos have helped to build Guam's infrastructure, establish local businesses, participate in local politics, and contribute to the culture of the community through humanitarian and service efforts, such as various chapters of the Lion's Club, the Filipino Community of Guam, and the Bayanihan issues within the *Pacific Daily News*.

Despite their shared history, forged through the oppressions of colonialism, animosity between Filipinos and CHamorus began with what James Perez Viernes (2015) documents as "The Filipino Question" (p. 218). In 1926, Philippine Congress Representative Edward Marcaido petitioned for Guam to be annexed to the Philippines because of the "overlapping histories and racial similarities between the CHamoru and Filipinos" (Viernes, 2015, p. 218). This provoked vehement responses from CHamorus. The following are quotes from various CHamoru congressmen:

> "It is a well known [sic] fact that, while the people of Guam and the Filipinos belong to the brown race, they do not have the same peculiarities, interests, and habits ... [These differences are a] very clear reason why the Filipinos and Chamorros will never be friends ... The Chamorro has at heart that he is a better man than the Filipino." (Viernes, 2015, pp. 220-223)

Overall, congressmen asserted racial difference, and CHamoru racial superiority, citing presumptions that CHamorus were more highly evolved when it came to emotional character, spiritual faith, and philosophies of respect and good governance. These perceived differences, in turn, continued to perpetuate divisiveness and competition between CHamorus and Filipinos. Today, such divisiveness persists. So long as there are ethnic, national, or religious variations in a community, there are bound to be differences in ideology, epistemology, and perceptions of quality of life.

In addition to this history, our own lived experiences have shown us that CHamorus and Filipinos have not always gotten along. As recently as the 1960s through the 1980s in Guam, CHamoru-Filipino battles and street fights broke out daily—battles over territory and gang fights, often drawn between ethnic lines, the immigrant versus the Indigenous. These differences, fortunately, have defused in recent generations. Much of the antagonism that had lasted almost two decades can possibly be attributed to the legacy of colonialism that both groups have had to endure.

Increasing recognition of the ramifications of colonialism has resulted in increased collaboration and cooperation.

What changed this relationship in later years, however, was intermarriage. CHamoru men married Filipinas, and Filipino men married CHamoritas. They had children, and their bi-cultural children grew up alongside CHamoru and Filipino children. Today, most CHamoru families claim Filipino family members, and most Filipino families claim CHamoru family members. Campbell (1987) refers to this relationship as "cultural consanguinity," historically and biologically intertwined (pp. 3-7). The historiographies of the CHamorus and Filipinos in Guam, however, have largely been documented as parallel. There is much less literature devoted to the interconnectedness or historical relationships between CHamorus and Filipinos, and there are no studies that focus specifically on the female perceptions, complexities, similarities, and nuances between the generations of CHamoritas and the generations of Filipinas who call Guam home. To address this void, we engage together and begin to share space.

Generations

Santos-Bamba (2010, 2013) delineates three generations of CHamoritas in relation to World War II. The first generation of CHamoritas, G1, were born before WWII and experienced the hardships of war. CHamoritas of the second generation, G2, were born during the postwar reconstruction period. This was a time in Guam when Americanization through education and the media led to banning the use of the CHamoru language and marginalizing Native culture and traditions, as a way to compel CHamoru acculturation. The third generation CHamoritas, G3, were born in the 1970s and 1980s and are descendants of G2 and grand-descendants of G1. They attended school in Guam when English and CHamoru were both recognized as official languages of Guam, hence they were not subjected to the English-only policies of the early postwar period. English, more than likely, was their first language in the home. While a fourth generation was not included in Santos-Bamba's study, she notes anecdotally that children of G3 have expressed the significance of the CHamoru language and culture in their lives, similar to their mothers' experiences. This fourth generation makes use of CHamoru in personal and spiritual domains through prayer and song. During an informal conversation with Santos-Bamba, an 8-year-old said, "My grandma and mom speak to each other in Chamorro sometimes. They do that when they don't want us to understand. [Laughing] But we understand what they are saying!"

In her chapter, "The Halo Halo Generation: Identity Formation in the Narratives of Third Generation Filipinos on Guam," Espina Velasco (2013) describes three generations of Filipina women, using metaphors from Filipino desserts. Espina Velasco uses the Tagalog term ube (purple yam) to characterize the generation of Filipinas who were the initial generation in their families to emigrate to Guam from the Philippines. Espina Velasco uses the term sapin sapin, literally "layers," to characterize the second generation of Filipinas in Guam. This generation is characterized by a "layering" and hybridity within their syncretic identity. Espina Velasco terms the third generation of Filipinas the Halo Halo generation, after the Filipino halo halo dessert, as various ingredients significant in Filipino culture are subsumed and are literally "mix mixed" in a white milk concoction to become indistinguishable. In the same way, this generation's Filipino cultural identity is dispersed among other elements.

Quality of Life

CHamoru women generally are expected to hold the family together, nurture faith, and protect the home. The ways they do this involve language. For G1, literacy was sought for education and professional work and was not necessary for home life. While English was the vehicle for academic and professional endeavors, for G1 the CHamoru language was the language of the home.

Having observed life within the military from their vantage "outside the fence," and seen stateside lifestyle via the media, G2 yearned for a quality of life that mirrored their American counterparts. Guam swiftly moved from subsistence to a cash-based economy following WWII (Santos-Bamba, 2010). G2 then entered the workforce and contributed to their household finances. Some had college degrees, but most did not. Because of dual household incomes, they made enough money to travel, build modern homes, buy new cars, and eventually send their children to college. Education and being literate in English were priorities instilled in their children because it was American education and the English language that afforded opportunities for an elevated quality of life. In interviews, the women of G2 expressed their sense that entering the workforce and contributing to their household incomes provided an improved quality of life that included the comforts of modernity, travel, and material goods.

Born in the 1970s and 1980s, G3 was greatly influenced by their grandmothers, the first generation, because their G2 mothers had entered the workforce. Most third generation CHamoritas spent a significant amount of time with their grandmothers, which in turn led them to embrace the traditional coupled with the modern. Some examples of this include the preparation of traditional foods like kadun mannok, faith-based practices like rosaries and novenas, and domestic duties like caring for a home and family. Another prime example is the practice of showing respect when greeting an elder, fanngigne'. Fannginge' is the act of sniffing an elder's right hand to inhale or receive their wisdom, strength, and courage (ånimu).

The three generations of Filipinas in Guam, like their CHamoru counterparts, also deployed language to improve their quality of life. The writings by and interview with Espina Velasco's grandmother, Ruthie Alvarez Caser, describe her feelings of alienation and disillusionment upon her initial arrival in Guam: "I cried! I was trapped ... I was really crying for a few days, in spite of me with my husband. Yeah. I was so sad ... " (as cited in Espina Velasco, 2016, p. 87). Like the CHamoritas in G1, Caser and others in the Ube generation attempt what Espina Velasco terms "(ho) me-making," the simultaneous making of both home and self, in Caser's case while being a homemaker in the family. Like the CHamoritas in G1, the diary entries and letters Caser wrote to Espina Velasco's great-grandmother depicted her identity formation, but through the difficulties of immigration. Caser, like the CHamoritas in G1, describes choosing family over education. Narratives from Bruce Campbell's 1987 survey of Filipino immigrants in Guam and from Bernadette Provido, an original Camp Roxas immigrant, also portray the Ube generation's migrant identity as constituted through a range of intersecting, competing forces and processes reconciled through agency. Education, family, the impacts of World War II, and motherhood were also topics that recurred. Like the CHamoritas, Filipina women have the responsibility of maintaining and upholding the family. Many Filipinas began to work outside of the home to contribute to the livelihood of their families, and they use their language to effect change outside the home, in the community.

Like G2 of CHamoritas, the Sapin Sapin generation has a quality of life greatly influenced by the postwar Americanization of Guam. They use their literacy and familiarity with American culture to navigate among competing identities. Songs and books written by Espina Velasco's mother, Alpha Caser Espina, a teacher and recording artist, and other supplementary narratives by Vivian Dames, a Filipina scholar-activist, and by Bernadette Schumann, producer of the film *Under the American Sun*, display a paradox of assimilation, wherein assimilability is valued, yet ethnic differentiation is also embraced (Espina Velasco, 2014). Their language displays the intersectionality of multiple, layered identities that simultaneously register oppression and privilege. While these women work outside of the home, their labors are concerned with what is deeply felt inside home—trying to reconcile multiple roles and expectations.

No other generation is more influenced by the Americanization of Guam than the third generation. The narratives of the Halo Halo generation show a fluid positioning, situated between a variety of different and often competing generational, ideological, and moral reference points, including those of parents, grandparents, and their own real and imagined perspectives about multiple homelands. Because of the ambiguity of what constitutes home for this generation, language is more concerned with reclamation for personal identity, rather than the maintenance of a household. Like the CHamoritas of G3, the upward social mobility enabled by previous generations of Filipinas in Guam have granted the Halo Halo generation the privilege of considering identity apart from livelihood. Their connection with Filipino culture is further removed, as Filipino customs and traditions are often combined with aspects of their American culture. However, like G3 CHamoritas, many young Filipinas are taught Filipino cultural values through cooking traditional dishes like adobo and pancit, fulfilling domestic duties while going to work or school, and maintaining spiritual practices, mostly through the Catholic Church. Just as the younger generations of CHamoritas are taught the honorific practice of fannginge', young Filipinas are taught to beso beso, or kiss the cheeks of friends and family, and are taught to amen, showing respect by placing the hand of an elder on her forehead. Kevin Nadal (2011) finds in his handbook *Filipino American Psychology* that many young Filipino Americans in the US mainland have a culture that is "a hybrid of indigenous and colonial values, beliefs, customs, and traditions" (p. 36), and the same could be said of the young Filipino Americans in Guam. The Halo Halo generation is unencumbered by the immigrant mentality of previous generations and instead is diasporic in ideology and practice. For the third generations of both CHamoritas and Filipinas, American media, in particular, perpetuates the process of Americanization, as young people are increasingly exposed to contemporary fashion trends and slang, world travel, and opportunities beyond Guam's shores. While Americanization has embedded itself in island culture through media and education, both Filipino and CHamoru youth maintain their cultural values, as seen in their collectivist cultures. While they may behave more independently than previous generations, their independence fuels their commitment to their families and communities. For example, many young adults are employed and live at home. Not only do they support themselves, but they also contribute to their family's well-being. An added layer to this commitment is the choice that hundreds of college students make to attend a higher education institution in Guam; remaining on island makes obtaining a degree, contributing to household income, and fulfilling familial responsibilities possible and economical—enabling young CHamoritas and Filipinas to continue to aim for an increased quality of life.

Spirituality

Family and faith, for most CHamoru women, are the foundations for a secure quality of life. Consequently, a shared element among all three generations of CHamoritas is that CHamoru language remains significant in the private and religious domains via song and prayer. In interviews with G1 CHamoritas, they remarked that the CHamoru language was used for spiritual and religious activities and that CHamoru was the language of the home. Literacy in the Native language manifested in the form of religious materials like rosary and novena prayers and songs. Among G2 CHamoritas as well, the utility of the CHamoru language relates directly to religious activities and familial relationships. As mothers, they exposed their children to and encouraged religious devotion through family prayer, songs, and worship. Family togetherness and interconnectedness were nurtured and transmitted through the generations and they attributed much of this family strength to their faith. In G3, the CHamoritas lament the erosion of their CHamoru language, which in turn affects their faith. Certain practices and traditions are expressed in CHamoru or bilingually as a way to preserve the language. However, while their understanding of CHamoru may be satisfactory—having been exposed to the CHamoru language by their parents, grandparents, and extended family—they are not confident in their ability to converse in the language, and they sense some loss and longing for the language of their people. They also realize that CHamoru language and literacy is personal and important for maintaining CHamoru culture and identity, especially through faith and practice in the Catholic Church in Guam. This realization and spiritual practices and beliefs are also present in the lives of the children of G3. These children—alongside their parents, grandparents, and often great-grandparents—engage in activities that perpetuate their cultural and religious beliefs.

Similar patterns of spirituality appear among the generations of Filipinas in Guam. The Ube generation used both English and Tagalog in letters and diaries to express faith. For example, Caser's letters begin with exhortations to God for the family's good health and happiness and often end with "God bless you!" and written prayers. In the Sapin Sapin generation, faith is what motivates Espina to continue her work in both music and teaching. In her scholarly work on abortion and the Catholic Church, Dames (2003) contemplates the faith of Guam's people and how it plays a role in access to health services. Like the CHamoritas of G3, the Halo Halo generation also laments an erosion of language; many can only express themselves in English. Their narratives do not directly address their faith and spirituality. Their disillusionment and ambivalence owe in part to being limited in the ways to connect with the faith of their family and culture through Native language.

Cultural Perpetuation

One distinct difference between CHamoru and Filipino women with regard to identity is their sense of place. Specifically, CHamoru women are of the land, but Filipino women and their descendants have a motherland other than Guam. It is the difference between those who imposed and those who were imposed upon. This distinction, however, is not meant to negate a relationship, but rather to help make sense of the bifurcated, complex relationship between CHamoru and Filipino women in Guam. The positionalities of these populations with regard to home come to bear on the perpetuation of their individual cultures.

For the generations of CHamoritas, identity, culture, language, and literacy in Guam have been displaced by the politicization of language. The three generations of CHamoru women in Santos-Bamba's study are the bearers of culture and language in their respective families. They acknowledge that colonization, Americanization, and modernization have influenced life and CHamoru culture in Guam, and although their lives today may be quite different from their ancient CHamoru ancestors, the stories of these generations of women coupled with what is documented in Guam history, show that these CHamoru women embody the same values of their ancestors: inafa'maolek, interdependence and helping one another, and mamåhlao, humility.

For the generations of Filipinas, cultural perpetuation remains complex, subject to the multiple homelands and reference points of immigration. Assimilative processes and the exigencies of moving to Guam prevented many in the Ube generation from perpetuating their language and culture within the home. Many feel that orienting their children and grandchildren toward a more American lifestyle would guarantee greater social mobility. For the Sapin Sapin generation, acculturative processes and being able to navigate several subject positions simultaneously enable them to transmit their culture through their narratives both inside and outside the home. While they see Filipino culture as important, for the immigrants and their offspring, movement and migration force them to consider what is necessary to bring and to pass along.

Particularly for the third generation of both groups, cultural perpetuation is increasingly constrained. The third generation of CHamoritas believe that Americanization and modernization have forced the culture to evolve in positive ways, but have also pushed many traditional beliefs and practices to the periphery, so much that people have forgotten the meanings behind them. A prime example of forgotten meanings is the CHamoru Catholic practice of rosaries for the dead. The 9 days of public rosary and another 9 days of family rosaries—18 rosaries in total—is a way to show respect to the deceased relative over an extended period of time. There are many CHamorus who practice the 18 days of rosaries because "that's just how it has always been" without questioning the meaning behind the practice. Like the CHamoritas in the third generation, many in the Halo Halo generation tend not to speak any Filipino language and tend to be averse to Filipino customs. This is characteristic of the self-denigrating Filipino colonial mentality, described by Filipino scholars E. J. R. David (2013) and Renato Constantino (1966). Espina Velasco finds that, as a Filipina, claiming an island girl identity in Guam is both problematic and contentious, as she encounters questions of authenticity and belonging as both Filipina and Guamanian—identities that are seen as mutually exclusive. Along with the slam poetry of Verna Zafra, their narratives articulate the feelings of loss and disillusionment experienced by the Halo Halo generation, subsumed in American culture and unable to fully claim an "island" or even "authentic" Filipino identity.

Conclusion

Overall, this juxtaposition of CHamorita and Filipina lives is informative because both are postcolonial subjects who have experienced oppression in similar and dissimilar ways, particularly in relation to language. By presenting Guam subjects as similar, yet distinct, we hope to increase solidarity and furthermore, to claim that the only way to counteract the effects of colonialism is through unity. This is admittedly a beginning work but one that we hope will begin the sharing of space between CHamoritas and Filipinas.

Our shared motivations in our individual research projects were the starting point for our collaboration. We both desire for our communities to share their identities on their own terms—with their own authority—in their own languages, as we explore how CHamorita and Filipina grandmothers, mothers, and daughters all share a sense of connectedness and express "women's ways of knowing" (Santos-Bamba, 2010, p. 58). For both CHamoritas and Filipinas, faith is significant in the maintenance of language, culture, and community, and each of our studies emphasizes the significance of intergenerational transmission of culture and language. CHamoritas and Filipinas lament the loss of language through generations, even though they recognize their own responsibility for the loss. The similarities between these populations in Guam are too significant to ignore.

In launching this research, we hope to increase understanding of the ways language, literacy, and identity in Guam have been and continue to be politicized as a result of Guam's colonial history and its ambiguous political relationship with the United States. Guam's language and culture have been directly influenced by colonialism, Westernization, modernization, migration and integration of peoples, and the globalization of English, and these influences can be seen in the ways that these women use language for empowerment, faith, and family.

We hope that another implication will be increased collaboration between these communities in Guam, which Teresia Teaiwa (1994) refers to as "s/pacific n/oceans

[that] honor the specificities of Islander experience, recognize the generic effects of (neo)colonialism on all Islanders, and are committed to political and cultural cooperation at the regional level" (p. 102). Ultimately, the act of combining and analyzing these two scholarly works together speaks to the need for increased collaboration between CHamoritas and Filipinas in contemporary generations. Furthermore, it confronts and counteracts historical perceptions of competition and animosity and works within the complex relationship of cultural consanguinity.

As a CHamorita scholar and a Filipina scholar, we stand alongside the women of these generations, resting upon their shoulders, like the female figures in "The Women of the Island—Three Generations" statue. We add our voices to theirs. Additionally, as a CHamorita scholar and a Filipina scholar, we stand alongside one another, attesting to the community of Guam that is formed by these two populations. Like the statue, we stand firm on the foundations of the women who came before us. At the same time, generations together, cultures together, we remain forged, resolute, and immovable. We look on, toward the ocean, toward new horizons.

References

Campbell, B. L. (1987). *The Filipino community of Guam (1945–1975)* [Master's thesis, University of Hawaiʻi, Mānoa].

Central Intelligence Agency (2017). Australia-Oceania: Guam. In *The world factbook.* https://www.cia.gov/library/publications/the-world-factbook/geos/gq.html

Constantino, R. (1966). The miseducation of the Filipino. (B. M. Drona, Trans.). In *The Filipinos in the Philippines and other essays* (pp. 1–16). Weekly Graphic.

Dames, V. L. (2003). Chamorro women, self-determination, and the politics of abortion in Guam. In S. Hune, & G. M. Nomura (Eds.), *Asian/Pacific Islander American women: A historical anthology* (pp. 365–382). New York University Press.

David, E. J. R. (2013). *Brown skin, white minds: Filipino-/American postcolonial psychology.* Information Age Publishing.

Espina, L. T. E. (2021). *Three generations statue.* [Photograph].

Espina Velasco, T. (2013). *Palatable experiences: Identity formation in the narratives of three generations of Filipinas on Guam* [Master's thesis, University of Guam].

Espina Velasco, T. (2014). The Sapin Sapin generation. *Pacific Asia Inquiry,* 5(1), 80–96.

Espina Velasco, T. (2016). The Ube ('roots') generation. *Humanities Diliman,* 58(4), 75–101.

Guam Chamber of Commerce. (n.d.). *Guam at a glance.* https://www.guamchamber.com.gu/guam/at-a-glance.

Nadal, K. L. (2011). *Filipino American psychology: A handbook of theory, research, and clinical practice.* Wiley.

Philippine Statistics Authority. (2013, March 27). *2010 annual survey of Philippine business and industry-economy-wide for all establishments: Final results.* http://psa.gov.ph/content/2010-annual-survey-philippine-business-and-industry-economy-wide-all-establishments-final.

Quan, C. G. (n.d.). Filipinos on Guam. In *Guampedia.* Retrieved July 15, 2021, from http://guampedia.com/filipinos-on-guam/

Santos-Bamba, S. J. Q. (2010). *The literate lives of Chamorro women in modern Guam* [Doctoral dissertation, Indiana University of Pennsylvania].

Santos-Bamba, S. J. Q. (2013). The languages of three generations of Chamorro women. *Pacific Asia Inquiry,* 4(1), 84–93.

Souder, L. (1987). *Daughters of the island: Contemporary Chamorro women organizers of Guam.* University of Guam Micronesian Area Research Center.

Teaiwa, T. K. (1994). bikinis and other s/pacific n/oceans. *The Contemporary Pacific,* 6(1), 87–109. http://www.jstor.org/stable/23701591

Viernes, J. P. (2015). *Negotiating manhood: Chamorro masculinities and US military colonialism in Guam, 1898–1941* [Doctoral dissertation, University of Hawaiʻi, Mānoa].

Bridging Cultures

Mary Therese Perez Hattori

The word *home* immediately evokes thoughts of Guam though I have lived away from home for over three decades. In this article, I will share some challenges that we who move away from home face, and some strategies for surmounting those challenges without relinquishing cultural identity and values.

One of the biggest challenges faced when first living away is homesickness, indicated by the frequent use of the word *mahålang* (yearn, desire, lonely) and its variants by CHamorus who live away from home. The world of social media is replete with instances or variants of the word as a theme, hashtag, keyword, and comment posted by CHamorus who live away from the islands. One's well-being is negatively impacted by the separation from one's homeland. Expressions of mahålang are often posted in response to photos, stories, news, events, and even recipes about our home islands in social spaces such as Pinterest, Tumblr, Facebook, YouTube, and blogs. For those who no longer live in the islands, these images evoke feelings of yearning, expressed in the comment, "Mahålang yu'." Those from other Micronesian islands have similar expressions—pwos (Chuukese/Carolinian), ngachalong (Ulithian), ōn (Marshallese). I have not observed such a strong and consistent response by American social media consumers who have moved away from their home states.

Even though we move away from the Marianas and call our new spaces "home," for many of us, there will always be a deeply felt yearning for our ancestral lands. The deep sense of i minahalang can be softened by sustaining my CHamoru customs and values, and connecting to others. The pain of longing for home is eased by belonging to various groups; one can mitigate those intense feelings of longing that impede wholeness and affect well-being by finding spaces of belonging. I have sought affiliation with communities that embody what Kawagley and Barnhardt (n.d.) describe as groups that "have a remarkable capacity to open themselves up and draw people into their lives." I've made connections to Native scholars from other Pacific islands, to advocacy groups who serve Micronesians in Hawai'i, and to Indigenous-serving educational institutions that seek new perspectives as they expand and improve services for students from Micronesia.

I am aware that in many interactions with others, I may be one of the few CHamorus the other people might meet. Due to the human tendency to generalize, the other person may assume that anything I say or do, any impressions or emotions I might evoke, may then be generalized to all CHamoru people. To help people understand that I am a member of, but not a paragon of an entire people and culture, I often begin my talks with a statement like, "I can only speak from my own personal perspective at this time and cannot speak for all CHamoru people, all Pacific Islanders, or all Indigenous people."

This cognizance of generalization carries a sense of responsibility for being an exemplary representative of our people, a responsibility that sometimes seems a burden. It is a factor that influences my public behavior and anything I produce. CHamoru society is communal in nature, in contrast to the individualistic society of the United States. This contrast is highlighted by the way personal introductions are made in social and professional encounters and by the communal designations used to refer to individuals. CHamorus introduce themselves by clan, village, and family names before using personal names. Throughout my childhood, I was often referred to by my surname and since I am a twin, was often simply called "dinga"

(CHamoru for "twin, double, fork of a road or tree branch"). Personal introductions in social settings rarely involved the use of my first name. Another designation is hagan Guåhan, daughter of Guam (literally "blood of Guam"); this encourages a sense of being a representative of the island and her people.

When I conduct research, write a paper, or deliver a speech, there is an accountability to others, a sense that I am crafting this work not only for myself, but for my family and people. Professional endeavors are not undertaken for my own benefit, but for the good of our community. In contrast, peers from the United States have the freedom to perform these same acts as individuals, with no care or expectation of representing their home states, other American people, or American culture in general.

Despite any feeling of burden, there are empowering possibilities in being a representative of our culture. For the last 4 years, I have served alongside other Micronesians as cultural consultants guiding the Honolulu Museum of Art's planning of an annual Celebrate Micronesia Festival. Informed by members of the region, the festival is an authentic representation of contemporary culture from the perspective of Native peoples of the region. Another strategy for sustaining my CHamoru identity while living away has been a process of reflection, articulation, and application. Living in a foreign place forces me to reflect on my own identity. Academic studies have given me the ability to articulate CHamoru ways of being, ways of knowing, and values. I engage in what Dr. Michael Perez (2016) calls "academic sovereignty," wherein I employ and appropriate the language and tools of academia to assert my CHamoru identity and shine a positive light on our culture. I have used Western principles such as Authentic Leadership, Temporal Intelligence, and Culturally Sustaining Education to construct conceptual bridges, pathways to understanding so that sophisticated CHamoru ideas are accessible to people from mainstream America. I apply CHamoru ways to my professional practices of teaching, research, and leadership. Applying the ethos of inafa'maolek in my leadership practice, I prioritize relationships and communal identity by employing community-building activities, establishing teams, and mentoring relationships to foster collaboration rather than competition and cultivate feelings of belonging. My leadership philosophy reflects a posture of stewardship, "the attitude that I am a custodian of the university's resources, be they material, financial, or human. I strive for equitable distribution of assets and sustainability of efforts, mindful that present-day decisions and actions will impact future generations" (Hattori, 2016a, p. 5).

Creative endeavors such as poetry and photography allow me to communicate the esoteric, spiritual aspects of our culture in ways that resonate with other people, thus building bridges between our cultures. As an example, I share a poem which illustrates a CHamoru sensibility regarding spiritual connections to our elders:

i piluña (the feather)

From a still and empty sky
a lone feather emerges
the down of a bird
descends gradually
gently
slowly

it floats
down
down
down

alighting onto my outstretched palm

a soft sweet kiss
from the aniti
a powerful portent
a message

maolek......good
todu maolek.....all is well

Perhaps my tåta, now a taotaomo'na
always a pikaru
plucked it from a passing bird

and sent it as a gift
a feather drifting on the susurration of saina
the whispers of wise elders. (Hattori, 2016b, p. 53)

Creative expression has been an important aspect of the lives of other CHamoru academics and artists who have lived for a time away from the Marianas. The poetry written during this phase in their lives acts as bridges, connecting them to homeland, to the Indigenous people of their temporary homes, and to subsequent generations of CHamoru who have spent part of their lives away from home. Examples are the poetry of my contemporaries Cecelia Lee Perez and Anne Perez Hattori, the work of younger poets such as Kisha Borja-Quichocho, Anghet Hoppe-Cruz, Craig Santos Perez, and emerging Matao/Ilokano artist Dåkot-ta Alcantara-Camacho (2017), who includes a reference to "i piluña" in his song, Fangguålo', excerpted here:

if we don't do the work to clear up all the hurt
we just pass it on to our children who really don't deserve
more excuses for the nooses we tie around our selves
the truth is we can do this our ancestors here to help
i can hear them crying out people tell me they have seen
spirits in the form of feathers and grandma's chanting in dreams
i know this is their message asking us to just believe
but I am not a priest and definitely not here to preach
just trying to craft a medicine to set our people free

It seems that many of us who live away from our home islands engage in this process of reflection, articulation, and application of CHamoru ways, finding our own paths to authentic lives that honor our heritage. By identifying and sharing the best aspects of our culture, we can be agents of positive change in this world, wherever we are, simply by being who we are.

References

Alcantara-Camacho, D. (2017). Fangguålo' [Song]. On *Na'lå'la'*. Track and Release Records. https://infinitedakota.bandcamp.com/track/fanggu-lo.

Hattori, M. T. P. (2016a). Culturally sustaining leadership: A Pacific Islander's perspective. *Education Sciences*, 6(4), 1–10.

Hattori, M. T. P. (2016b). i piluña. In the Literary Arts Committee (Publications) for FESTPAC 2016 (Ed.), *Local voices: An anthology*. (p. 53). 12th Festival of Pacific Arts.

Kawagley, A. O., & Barnhardt, R. (n.d.). *Education indigenous to place: Western science meets native reality*. Alaskan Native Knowledge Network. http://www.ankn.uaf.edu/Curriculum/Articles/BarnhardtKawagley/EIP.html.

Perez, M. (2016, October 28). *Diasporic educational trajectories and Chamoru articulations in historical context* [Conference presentation]. The Chamorro Studies Speaker Series, University of Hawai'i at Mānoa, Honolulu, HI, United States.

Discovering Saipan Community Art Values

Angelyn Labadan

Having been interested in art from a young age, I often found myself taking art classes and getting involved in as many art activities as I could. From elementary to high school, and to the present day, I crave to satisfy my creative passions through making crafts at home, creating works in the studio, participating in various art contests, visiting exhibitions and galleries, and much more. However, during high school and my early university years, I soon realized that the number of art activities, promotions, and funding for such in the CNMI was limited or unavailable due to federal funding blocks. This realization sparked an interest to uncover the reason for this issue and to identify the benefits that art could provide for the CNMI community (if and when the blocks are lifted).

There are often many questions asked about art. Is there a right or wrong in art? Is there a real value to art? However, perhaps the most apt question for the CNMI is, "Where is the art?" Are the arts in the CNMI fading due to lack of support and value? These questions form the basis for the primary inquiry of this chapter: "What is the value of art in the Saipan community?" The arts have played a major part in our history, such as documenting events before the written word, and are proven to have positive intrinsic and instrumental cognitive benefits. Despite this, there is a noticeable lack of artistic outlets and production in the Saipan art community. Thus, the study reported here is a prompt for future research to further increase art engagement, art promotion, and creative projects such as public murals, art galleries, or art institutions within the Northern Marianas community.

Art has value beyond merely aesthetic creation. Much literature has served to establish "benefits of the arts" that range from educational benefits like enhanced creativity, critical thinking, and problem-solving skills, to socio-emotional benefits such as positive impacts on one's social skills, and growth in areas of independence and cognition. Exemplars of such literature include the book *Arts with the Brain in Mind* by Eric Jensen (2001) and the *Cultural Trends* journal article entitled "Measuring the Intrinsic Benefits of Art Attendance" by Jennifer Radbourne, Hilary Glow, and Katya Johanson (2010). In *Arts with the Brain in Mind*, Jensen (2001) states, "the visual arts are an important part of brain-based education. They can enhance cognition, emotional expression, perception, cultural awareness, and aesthetics; they can play a significant role in the learning process" (p. 49). Likewise, numerous secondary sources, ranging from newspaper articles, magazines, journals, and blogs from artists all over the world and in Saipan, highlight the benefits of the arts. Although there is much literature and research advocating the arts, there are indications in Saipan that the value of art is not as well accepted as elsewhere. In many cases the arts are viewed as optional or unnecessary. This perceived low value has resulted in budget cuts in both school art programs and community art programs. Budget cuts are mainly evident in public schools—which emphasize core subjects like math, reading, and writing—and in communities where social issues like governmental assistance are of higher priority. In light of these circumstances, this research explores the importance and value of the arts in the Saipan community.

The Psychological and Educational Value of the Arts

Blum's 2011 study of the psychological birth of art states, "Prehistoric cave art was created many thousands of years before the Egyptian pyramids and Stonehenge. Later, written language appeared, long after spoken language and derived from pictorial script such as, hieroglyphics" (p. 197). This means that art was present before humans developed into the "dominant" species but served as a useful tool for evolving humans. Evidence also shows the use of art at burial sites of ancestors and as an expression of emotion and display of culture. Art still serves these purposes, but has become even more vital as studies show how art can enhance brain functions as well.

The value of arts in education has been an ongoing debate in recent years and still sparks arguments today. Despite many scientific studies advocating the implementation of arts in education, there are many other critical issues to consider, such as funding and assessment. In *Arts with the Brain in Mind*, Jensen (2001) states that "the visual arts are an important brain-based education ... and can enhance cognition, emotional expression, perception, cultural awareness ... [The visual arts] play a significant role in the learning process" (p. 49). An article entitled "Does Arts Education Develop School Readiness" (Nevanen et al., 2014), reports on a study conducted in Finland that measured the implementation of art programs in day care centers and schools. The results showed "that the program motivated children and aroused their interest in thinking, problem-solving, practicing, and learning" (p.71). Similarly, other studies also advocate for greater inclusion of arts in the educational curriculum or further endorse art programs for increased intrinsic and instrumental benefits. Eisner (2008), in his commentary "What Education Can Learn from the Arts," states, "The recognition of the demands and the contributions that the arts make is of fundamental importance in justifying the place of the arts in our schools, that is, as being central, rather than educational accomplishments" (p. 23). Jensen's (2001) research on the arts in education reveals positive test score correlations and asserts that "the College Board says that the arts are vital ... and knows the value of the arts" (p. 60).

Despite strong support for increased art inclusion in education, other research and observation show a fair number of schools cutting art programs due to lack of funding, lack of understanding, and confusion in relation to the value of art. An article from the National Federation of State High Schools (2013) states, "When cutting programs, superintendents strive to cut those that have the least impact to learning and that create the least amount of controversy. Wrongly, superintendents often recommend cutting some of the fine arts programs" (para. 2). There are also questions that continue to baffle some educators in regard to how the arts should be assessed. If art is subjective and there is no right or wrong, then how will it be assessed? And, if art does have intrinsic and instrumental benefits, how can these benefits be measured in the classroom? In his book, Jensen (2001) asserts that art can be assessed with three concepts: knowledge/content of art, responses to art, and performance-related questions. Although the concepts of art assessment are still being explored, studies of art and its effects not only on education but on the brain can be said to be proliferating.

With regard to the current standing of the arts, arts partnerships, and funding in the CNMI, the most relevant information can be found in the local newspapers, in particular the *Marianas Variety*. While the newspaper has recorded the blocks on funding from 2005-2018, one of its articles entitled "NEA Reinstates Arts Council's Eligibility to Apply for Federal Grants," indicates that the council is once again able to apply for funding and is determined to properly manage funds if they are granted (Lirio, 2018). As of October 2021, Arts Council Executive Director Parker Y. Yobei (personal communication, September 29, 2021) stated via email that

> The annual partnership [grant] with NEA was reinstated back in 2018. [However] During the peak of the COVID-19 pandemic, we administered the grant from NEA towards recovery from Typhoon Mangkhut and Super Typhoon Yutu, in which community [art] projects like murals on gyms and power poles took place.

Surveying the Community

Two distinct surveys were developed, piloted, and distributed—one for the general public (see Appendix A) and one for professional artists (see Appendix B)—to help analyze the state of the arts in the Saipan community. Additionally, short interviews were conducted with children regarding their perceptions of the arts. The interview questions (see Appendix C) were based on the questions from the general survey, but appropriately revised for the children's ease of comprehension. Interviews were conducted with 10 children. The surveys were distributed both electronically and manually. The general survey garnered 29 respondents while the artist survey garnered 11 respondents, many of whom were manually acquired at a local artists' market. All surveys were open for about a month. The surveys and interviews garnered responses from varying age groups (Figure 1). Responses were unique and provided useful expressions of the Saipan community's views on the value of art.

Figure 1

Responses Divided by Age Group

Age Group	Responses
10-11	10 (20%)
14-19	18 (36%)
20-29	7 (14%)
30-39	7 (14%)
40-49	3 (6%)
50-59	3 (6%)
60+	2 (4%)
Total	50

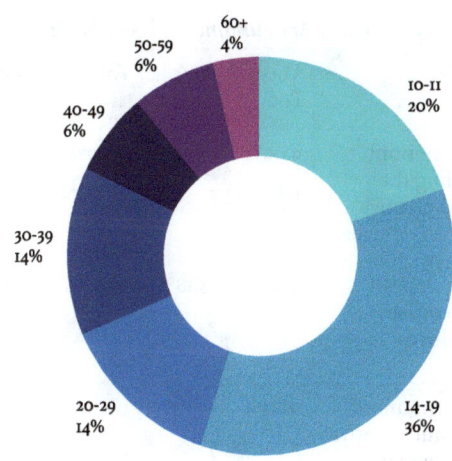

All professional artists held a similar view on the value of art, despite the varying years and experiences in their professional careers. As a general consensus, artists reported that the arts hold major importance in generating creativity and expressing oneself, as well as art being a key instrument in what makes people human. Participant #1 highlighted the importance of art in education:

> While some are quick to dismiss the importance of art in school curriculum, art is just as important as any of the core subjects because art, any form of art, promotes freedom of expression, creativity, ingenuity, and critical thinking—all of which are vital in the pursuit of innovation and human development.

Participant #2 encouraged both the community and artists to play an active role in the social art network: "A place where artists can perform together and have some great time. [I'm] Dreaming [of] a place in the vicinity of a busy place like in Garapan area, so that other artists would be interested to show up their artwork." Overall, the artists expressed interest in all areas of visual arts and ranked drawing and painting as the two top areas. When answering the survey question about Saipan's strongest and weakest aspects of visual arts, the consensus for strongest aspects of the art community were community support for artists and youth involvement in art events (see Appendix D). The consensus for the weakest aspects were lack of funding for the arts, lack of support for artists, and lack of markets for artists. When posed with the question about the quality of funding the arts received in Saipan, a majority of artists rated the quality "very poor" or "poor" (Figure 2).

Figure 2

Artists' Perceptions of Art Funding and Availability in Saipan

	Very Poor	Poor	Fair	Good	Excellent	Total	Weighted Average
… The amount of funding the arts and creative programs receives	9.09% 1	63.64% 7	27.27% 3	0.00% 0	0.00% 0	11	2.18
… The amount of arts courses available in schools.	9.09% 1	18.18% 2	63.64% 7	9.09% 1	0.00% 0	11	2.73
… the amount of artistic and creative aspects in your neighborhood	18.18% 2	63.64% 7	00.00% 0	0.00% 0	18.18% 2	11	2.36
… the quality and frequency of the arts and creative events	9.09% 1	27.27% 3	45.45% 5	18.18% 2	0.00% 0	11	2.18

The last questions of the survey asked if the artists would be willing to go to a hypothetical art gallery or public arts in Saipan and asked for suggestions of what they would like to see in the art community. All the artist surveys reported that they would go to a hypothetical art space. The following graph (Figure 3) displays the top three kinds of art spaces they would like to see: (1) public art space, (2) mural space, and (3) sculpture space. Meanwhile, the suggestions of other arts projects in the community were as follows: a gallery, museum, cultural center, murals, and public art activities for youth, more arts in education, and sculptures.

Figure 3
Type of Desired Art Places for Saipan (Artists)

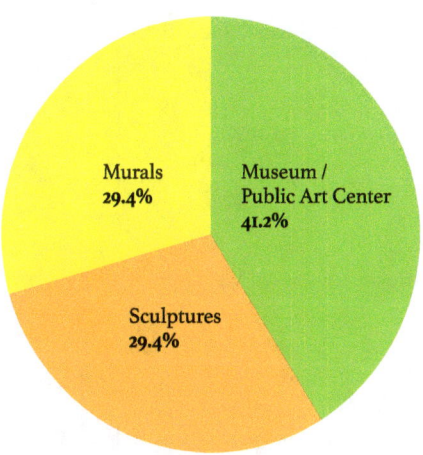

While the general public held varying views about funding, art interests, and the quality of the arts in the community (See Appendix E), the general consensus among those surveyed reflected the same perspective as the artists, "that the arts hold a major importance in generating creativity and expressing oneself, as well as art being a key instrument in what makes people human." The general public expressed interest in all areas of visual arts, although different age groups favored different art interests. The 14-to-19-year age group preferred photography, film, painting, and drawing (See Appendix F). The 20-to-29-year age group preferred drawing and design (See Appendix G). The 30-to-39-year age group preferred photography and film (See Appendix H). The 40-to-49-year age group preferred ceramics and design (See Appendix I). In regard to art experiences, the younger age group displayed more participation in art classes and events in comparison to the older age group. Despite this contrast, respondents of all ages rated the quality of funding for the arts as relatively "poor" or "fair" (Figure 4).

Figure 4

General Public's Perceptions of Art Funding and Availability in Saipan

	Very Poor	Poor	Fair	Good	Excellent	Total	Weighted Average
… The amount of funding the arts and creative programs receives	2 (6.90%)	21 (72.41%)	6 (20.69%)	0 (0.00%)	0 (0.00%)	29	2.14
… The amount of arts courses available in schools.	5 (17.24%)	15 (51.72%)	7 (24.14%)	2 (6.90%)	0 (0.00%)	29	2.21
… the amount of artistic and creative aspects in your neighborhood	9 (31.03%)	9 (31.03%)	9 (31.03%)	2 (6.90%)	0 (0.00%)	29	2.36
… the quality and frequency of the arts and creative events	2 (6.90%)	13 (44.83%)	10 (34.48%)	4 (13.79%)	0 (0.00%)	29	2.55

Since there were more participants for the general public survey than the artist survey, there were more suggestions about what types of projects would be a pleasant addition to Saipan's art community. These suggestions included permanent art galleries, museums, monthly art events, rehabilitation of abandoned buildings, roadside artwork, more business opportunities for local artists, free outdoor canvases, and art parks.

Among the children (ages 10–11) surveyed, most reported that they take part in drawing. The children also stated that they do not see much art in the Saipan community other than during events like the Flame Tree Arts Festival. All the children indicated that they would like to see more permanent art in Saipan, and that they would be interested in going to a place where they learn more about art and could experience creating art.

The general survey for the public garnered 29 responses and provided a useful view of the Saipan community's views on art. During data collection, other key topics of concern arose such as the reasons for the lack of adequate funding for the arts in the CNMI and Saipan. In one survey response, a professional artist stated that the prolonged lack of funding in the arts community is due to a ban placed on the CNMI by the National Endowment for the Arts (NEA) from 2005 and was in place for 7 years total. Presently, the ban placed by the NEA has been lifted and the recent efforts by the Northern Marianas Humanities Council aim to cultivate and support the arts. These efforts are currently being covered by the *Marianas Variety*.

Conclusions

The results of this research and survey suggest that the general consensus among both the public and professional artists is that art is important and essential to all human beings for creativity and expression. The survey group expressed positive and high values for art despite the previous lack of funds and resources to establish foundational creative communities and projects from 2005–2018. Survey participants also suggested a variety of ideas for possible future art projects. The prevalent suggestions were galleries, murals, and sculptures. Due to this perceived value of the arts, an artistically enthusiastic community, and newly reinstated funds, it can be said that the possibility of strengthening Saipan's creative community is stronger today than in the past 10 years. Furthermore, the results from this paper could be used by community leaders and members of the arts council as an aid when forming plans for future events and grants.

References

Blum, H. P. (2011). The psychological birth of art: A psychoanalytic approach to prehistoric cave art. *International Forum of Psychoanalysis, 20*(4), 196–204. https://doi.org/10.1080/0803706X.2011.597429

Eisner, E. (2008). *What education can learn from the arts.* http://www.learninglandscapes.ca/images/documents/ll-no3/eeisner.pdf

Jensen, E. (2001). *Arts with the brain in mind.* Association for Supervision and Curriculum Development.

Lirio, L. (2018, June 16). NEA reinstates Art Council's eligibility to apply for federal grants. *Marianas Variety.*

National Federation of State High School Associations. (2013). *Fine arts should be spared from school districts' budget cuts.* https://www.nfhs.org/articles/fine-arts-should-be-spared-from-school-districts-budget-cuts/

Nevanen, S., Juvonen, A., & Ruismäki, H. (2014). Does arts education develop school readiness? Teachers' and artists' points of view on an art education project. *Arts Education Policy Review, 115*(3), 72–81. https://doi.org/10.1080/10632913.2014.913970

Radbourne, J., Glow, H., & Johanson, K. (2010). Measuring the intrinsic benefits of arts attendance. *Cultural Trends, 19*(4), 307–324. https://doi.org/10.1080/09548963.2010.515005

Appendices

Appendix A
General Public Survey

1. What is your age?
   ▫ 14 – 19   ▫ 20 – 29   ▫ 30 – 39   ▫ 40 – 49   ▫ 50 – 59   ▫ 60+

2. When you think of visual arts, what comes to mind? Do you think the visual arts are important? Why or why not?

3. Which of the following have you participated in? 1 (lowest) to 5 (highest), please rate how often you participated.

	1	2	3	4	5	N/A
Art experience: creating/making art, crafting, etc.						
Art experience: creating/making art, crafting, etc.						
Art History (knowledge on historical artists, art history)						

If you have participated in other arts activities, please list them below. (e.g. arts as a hobby, arts and crafts with children, degree in arts, etc.)

4. What types of visual arts are you interested in (if any)? You may select more than one.
   ▫ Ceramics
   ▫ Drawing
   ▫ Sculpture
   ▫ Painting
   ▫ Crafts
   ▫ Printmaking
   ▫ Filmmaking
   ▫ Design
   ▫ Photography
   ▫ Video

- Architecture
- N/A

5. How much would you agree/disagree with the following regarding [visual] arts in Saipan?

	Strongly Disagree	Disagree	Neither	Agree	Strongly Agree
The arts promoting history and culture					
The arts bringing communities together					
The arts providing learning opportunities					
The arts attracting tourism					
The arts improving education					

6. Please rate the following aspects of the [visual] arts in relation to funding and availability on Saipan.

	Very Poor	Poor	Fair	Good	Excellent
The amount of funding the arts and creative programs receive					
The amount of arts courses available in schools					
The amount of artistic and creative aspects in your neighborhood					
The quality and frequency of the arts and creative events					

7. If there were to be more art spaces in Saipan, would you go? (E.g. art gallery, art museum, art center, etc.)

- Yes   - No   - Maybe

8. By the year 2025, what are 3 things you would like to see in Saipan's art community? (E.g. A public art gallery, more murals, outdoor sculptures, etc.)

9. Are there any other comments you would like to make?

Appendix B
Artists Survey

1. What is your age?
- 14 – 19   - 20 – 29   - 30 – 39   - 40 – 49   - 50 – 59   - 60+

2. When you think of visual arts, what comes to mind? Do you think the visual arts are important? Why or why not?

3. Which of the following have you participated in? 1 (lowest) to 5 (highest), please rate how often you participated.

	1	2	3	4	5	N/A
Art classes (drawing, painting, sculpting)						
Art experience: creating/making art, crafting, etc.						
Art History (knowledge on historical artists, art history)						

If you have participated in other arts activities, please list them below. (e.g. arts as a hobby, arts and crafts with children, degree in arts, etc.)

4. What types of visual arts are you interested in (if any)? You may select more than one.
- Ceramics
- Drawing
- Sculpture
- Painting
- Crafts
- Printmaking
- Filmmaking
- Design
- Photography
- Video
- Architecture
- N/A

5. What do you think are the 3 strongest and weakest aspects of the visual arts in Saipan? Please check the strongest aspects and list the weakest aspects in the according box.
- Funding
- Accessibility
- Programs/Events
- Community Support/Engagement
- Community Projects
- Youth Involvement
- Public Art
- Support for Individual Artists
- Market for Artists
- Media Coverage
- Collaborations with Businesses and/or charitable organization
- N/A

Weakest Aspects (please specify): _____

6. How much would you agree/disagree with the following regarding [visual] arts in Saipan?

	Strongly Disagree	Disagree	Neither	Agree	Strongly Agree
The arts promoting history and culture					
The arts bringing communities together					
The arts providing learning opportunities					

	Very Poor	Poor	Fair	Good	Excellent
The arts attracting tourism					
The arts improving education					

7. Please rate the following aspects of the [visual] arts in relation to funding and availability on Saipan.

	Very Poor	Poor	Fair	Good	Excellent
The amount of funding the arts and creative programs receive					
The amount of arts courses available in schools					
The amount of artistic and creative aspects in your neighborhood					
The quality and frequency of the arts and creative events					

8. If there were to be more art spaces in Saipan, would you go? (E.g. art gallery, art museum, art center, etc.)

▫ Yes   ▫ No   ▫ Maybe

9. By the year 2025, what are 3 things you would like to see in Saipan's art community? (E.g. A public art gallery, more murals, outdoor sculptures, etc.)

10. Are there any other comments you would like to make?

Appendix C
Children's Interview Questions

1. What is your age?
2. When you think of art, what do you think of?
3. What kind of art do you do? (drawing, painting, coloring, crafts, others)
4. Do you see a lot of art on Saipan? (Yes/No? Where?)
5. Do you want to see more art on Saipan? (Yes/No? What kind?)
6. If there was a place for you to make art or see art, would you go? (Yes/No? Why?)

Appendix D
Artists' View on Strongest Aspects of Visual Arts

What do you think are the 3 strongest and weakest aspects of the visual arts in Saipan? Please check the strongest aspects and list the weakest aspects in the according box.

Answer Choices	Responses
Funding	16.17% (2)
Accessibility	16.17% (2)
Programs/Events	25.00% (3)
Community Support/Engagement	33.33 (4)
Community Projects	25.00% (3)

Youth Involvement	33.33 (4)
Public Art	41.67% (5)
Support for Individual Artists	16.17% (2)
Market for Artists	8.33% (1)
Media Coverage	8.33% (1)
Collaboration with Business and/or Charitable Organization	16.67% (2)
N/A	8.33% (1)
Weakest Aspects	100.00% (11)

Weakest Aspects
Lack of funding
Lack of NEA Funding
Lack of support/Weak market for artists

Appendix E
General Public's View on Funding of Art

Please rate the following aspects of the [visual] arts in relation to funding and availability on Saipan.

	Very Poor	Poor	Fair	Good	Excellent	Total	Weighted Average
The amount of funding the arts and creative programs receive	6.90% (2)	72.41% (21)	20.69% (6)	0.00% (0)	0.00% (0)	29	2.14
The amount of arts courses available in schools	17.24% (5)	51.72% (15)	24.14% (7)	6.90% (2)	0.00% (0)	29	2.21
The amount of artistic and creative aspects in your neighborhood	31.03% (9)	31.03% (9)	31.03% (9)	6.90% (2)	0.00% (0)	29	2.14
The quality and frequency of the arts and creative events	6.90% (2)	44.83% (13)	34.48% (10)	13.97% (4)	0.00% (0)	29	2.55

Appendix F
Art Interests Ages 14 - 19

What types of visual arts are you interested in (if any)? You may select more than one.

N = 16

Type of Visual Arts	Response
Ceramics	38%
Drawing	75%
Painting	62%

Type of Visual Arts	Response
Sculpture	31%
Printmaking	25%
Design	62%
Crafts	48%
Photography	81%
Video	75%
Filmmaking	61%
Architecture	31%
N/A	0%

Appendix G
Art Interests Ages 20 – 29

What types of visual arts are you interested in (if any)? You may select more than one.

$N = 6$

Type of Visual Arts	Response
Ceramics	33%
Drawing	82%
Painting	33%
Sculpture	33%
Printmaking	27%
Design	68%
Crafts	33%
Photography	50%
Video	18%
Filmmaking	18%
Architecture	18%
N/A	0%

Appendix H
Art Interests Ages 30 – 39

What types of visual arts are you interested in (if any)? You may select more than one.

$N = 4$

Type of Visual Arts	Response
Ceramics	25%
Drawing	0%
Painting	25%
Sculpture	0%
Printmaking	0%
Design	0%
Crafts	50%
Photography	100%
Video	0%
Filmmaking	50%
Architecture	0%
N/A	0%

Appendix I
Art Interests Ages 40 - 49

What types of visual arts are you interested in (if any)? You may select more than one.

N = 2

Type of Visual Arts	Response
Ceramics	50%
Drawing	0%
Painting	0%
Sculpture	0%
Printmaking	50%
Design	50%
Crafts	0%
Photography	50%
Video	50%
Filmmaking	50%
Architecture	0%
N/A	0%

The Thai Community in Saipan

Poonsri Algaier

In the 1980s and 1990s, Saipan's labor force opened internationally, with immigration under local control by the Commonwealth government. Then, when the international garment industry decided to turn the Commonwealth of the Northern Mariana Islands (CNMI) into one of its main hubs for production and shipment to the USA, the local economy boomed. That boom attracted a pool of non-immigrant workers from across Asia, and over time included among them thousands of people from Thailand. The Thais who came to Saipan were very concerned about working fast enough to be given the lucrative overtime work that was often available for the most efficient workers in the factories. The vast majority of those who came are now gone, returned to the houses they built on US wages, but some remain. The Thai community continues to be represented among construction workers, massage specialists, restaurant workers, and others.

Most Thai people came to Saipan to work in garment factories. During the heyday of the multiple factories, with UIC as the largest employer, over 2,000 Thai workers called Saipan home throughout the 1990s and early 2000s. Thais were also working in construction, hotel businesses, and auto shops. There were up to four Thai grocery stores, two in San Antonio and two in Chalan Kanoa. One of these original grocery stores morphed over time into a restaurant—the Spicy Thai Noodle Place—that still operates in Garapan as of 2018. Other Thai restaurants from the time, many of which have since closed, include—The I-Thai, a Thai-Italian adventure; the Nid Noi Café; Supanahong, Mai-Tai, and a number of unlicensed "casual" outdoor places for Thai and connected non-Thais only. Some restaurants remained after Typhoon Soudelor hit in August 2015, including two in Garapan, the Thai House (since closed) and Wild Bill's.

As Thais love Thailand, a clamor for representation prompted organization; thus, in 1999, a Thai Association was formed. Dues-paying members supported annual Loy Kratong and Songkran festivals events in the Fall and Spring which brought together crowds of revelers from every part of island society and allowed the Thai community to showcase their rich and deep culture. On the full moon night of the twelfth lunar month, usually in November, a Loy Kratong festival was held. Events would include Miss Nopamas beauty contests (Nopamas is a mythical character said to have been the consort of King Ramkamhaeng of the ancient capital Sukothai; she is supposed to have started the first Loy Kratong festival), junior Miss Nopamas contests, banana float contests, traditional dance—*ramwong*—contests, food, songs, dances, and lavish cultural displays. The first official festival began in 1999 after personal gatherings, parties that grew from year to year, were held on beaches in San Antonio, and Thai Association venues, which lasted until 2006, included Susupe Park and the Pacific Islands Club. Similarly, the Songkran Water Festival, known simply as Songkran, would every year spark joyous celebration among Thais who use the festival as a break from the dogdays of the hot season. In Thailand, Songkran is a nation-wide water fight. In Saipan, it was celebrated as a day-long water ball, barbecue, home-cooked feast, and dance party. Celebrations went on in Thai barracks across the island; crowds at parties in the two Thai barracks in San Antonio, separated by 100 meters, would grow so large one could stand in the middle of the crowd and be in both parties at once. It was a joyous time.

The Thai Association also acted as a center to collect donations among community members in time of need. Deaths on island, deaths in families back home,

home-destroying fires, or disasters either in Saipan or in the Kingdom were always met with generous responses from community members. Thai Association members performed community services such as clean-ups on beaches, in villages, and along the roads. Thai dancers also performed at Flame Tree Festivals, Hot Chili Pepper Festivals in Tinian, and village Saint Days. They trained children to dance and provided traditional Thai costumes for school children on International Days and Cultural Days at various schools in Saipan. Unfortunately, by 2006, due to the rapid departure of many former garment workers following the closure of that industry, the Thai Association was effectively disbanded. Individuals still celebrate the Loy Kratong and Songkran Festival with their friends and families, but no organizational structures exist to make the holiday island-wide celebrations. The barracks that used to house hundreds of Thai workers have largely disappeared, though some Thais continue to stay in their former housing units as caretakers for the now-closed factories.

After the closing of the garment factories, many Thai workers had to leave. According to a Thai labor survey completed in the first quarter of 2017, there were 143 Thai citizens in Saipan (R. Charoenkhai, personal communication, November 7, 2018).[18] Those who remain in the CNMI are those who married into the local community or who got jobs after the garment industry disappeared. Some work as masseuses, taxi drivers, farmers, or with restaurants, hotels, or other companies. Some have private businesses, and some are homemakers. The movement of workers from Thailand to Saipan largely ended with the closure of the garment factories. While a few Thai workers continue to find their way to Saipan, these workers are usually arriving through personal contacts with other Thais who are currently living here.

The following anecdotes are from a few Thais who still live in Saipan. Their names are pseudonyms.

Som was a schoolteacher in Thailand, who, because of his eloquent speaking skills, was assigned to be a Community Scouts leader. Community Scouts was a Thai government program to gather ordinary Thai people to fight against the communist insurgency in Thailand. After working as a teacher, he tried his luck with construction in the Middle East. He arrived in Saipan in 1991. He first worked for NTC (now IT&E), then with Tano Group, a construction company. After that he worked as a reverse osmosis operator for a golf course and as a security guard for Pacific

Amusement before he joined G4S Secure Solutions (CNMI) Inc. in 2014, where he remains. While working here he was able to send his two children to school in Thailand. His daughter has earned a master's degree in early childhood education; his son has a master's degree in petrochemical engineering. Som assists the Thai people here when they need to renew their passports, obtain Thai birth certificates for their children, or deal with other documents. He is instrumental in arranging for Thai consular officers to visit the island, as they did in February 2017, to provide support for Thai citizens. He also assists the Thai Labor Department in Hong Kong in collecting biodata from the Thai people here. The Labor Department in Hong Kong has jurisdiction over Hong Kong, Guam, Saipan, Rota, Tinian, and Palau. Som likes working and living here in Saipan. His only concern with island life is the way US Citizenship and Immigration Services (USCIS) handles CW-1 visa[19] renewals. He says USCIS may send the worker's acceptance letter either to his home country or to Saipan. If the letter is sent to the home country, the worker will have to go back home, apply for a visa, and wait and wait and wait. It could be weeks or months before he can come back. During this indeterminate waiting period, financial problems become burdensome as workers must meet fixed-cost family obligations while their income has stopped.

Orn is a female who came to work for UIC garment factory over 20 years ago. Through hard work and smart financial management, at a time when the minimum wage in Saipan was barely over $3 per hour, Orn was able to buy a house in Thailand. Still in Saipan, she is now happily married and helps her husband with his business. She and her husband built a house here too, and they have no plans to relocate anywhere else for the foreseeable future. Orn loves to work in her garden. She enjoys hosting parties on various Thai holidays at her house. For Loy Kratong Festival, she prepares food and makes floats from banana trunks, banana leaves, and fresh flowers. Her guests would enjoy the food and later that night go to the beach to float the kratongs under the moonlight. Though their numbers are smaller, Thai people in Saipan still follow their Thai traditions. On some occasions, Orn will still gather with others at the shrine of Brahmin, to whom some Thai pray for help, at the old Onwel factory ground. Comfortable with syncretic religious practices, Orn will also join others, though she is not Christian, at the Santa Lourdes Shrine to entreat Santa Lourdes for divine intervention. After petitioners get what they ask for, they would offer different kinds of gifts, flowers, food, or dance to the sacred entity. Unlike Som, Orn does not have to worry about a visa. She has a green card through her husband.

Prakai arrived in Saipan in 1994. She paid a recruiter 50,000 baht (about $2,000 USD at the time) for bringing her here to work for the Sako garment company. She paid him in two payments. There were basically three ways to come to work in Saipan at that time. The first way was through the Thai Labor Department. The second way was through a sponsor who could be a private person or a business owner. And the third way was through a recruiter. After Sako, she got a job in a poker room and worked there for a few years. For self-improvement, she took ESL classes offered by the Adult Basic Education Program at Northern Marianas College. The course was offered on Sundays to accommodate guest workers, and each student paid $40 for the 3-hour-per-week, 10-week course; hundreds enrolled in the courses, helping both to better themselves and to strengthen their connections to the community.

Prakai is now 52 years old and works as a waitress in a restaurant. When asked if she wanted to go back to Thailand, she said, "yes, eventually, but not now." Her age and her educational background are big obstacles. She thinks that at 52 it would be hard for her to get a job in Thailand. She would also not make as much money as she can in Saipan. The minimum wage in Thailand varies from province to province, with the highest in Bangkok at 310 Thai baht, about $9 USD, per day in 2017. Prakai notes that her future seems bright. If she is careful, she can cover her rent and electricity for about $250 per month in Saipan. She is saving up for her retirement in Thailand. With more than 20 years of work in Saipan, she will also receive her US Social Security benefits when she reaches the eligible age. She has also inherited a house in Thailand from her parents. Her only concern now is about getting her CW-1 visa renewal. Sometimes even when the employers file the renewal documents in a timely manner, there are still glitches that cause the non-renewal of the CW-1 visa for their employees. Some Thai people who have US-born children are able to get Employment Authorization Documents (EAD) to work here, but Prakai is not one of them. Thus, the suspense and tension she feels while waiting for the renewal of her CW-1 visa continues.

Prapa came to Saipan as an office worker for a garment factory. She has a vocational degree from Thailand. She picked up both English and Chinese from hearing those two languages in the factory, and she became fluent in both. She is now working as a manager for a local company. Like many Thai men and women in Saipan, Prapa enjoys playing soccer. She currently plays in a competitive women's league on a team that is predominantly Thai. She also stays fit by working out in a fitness center. Married now, with two children, she is also a proud naturalized American citizen.

Over the past three-plus decades, the existing world trade regulations permitted a booming economy in Saipan that was fueled by garment factories. Times changed, however, and those factories went away. But Som, Orn, Prakai, and Prapa remained. They arrived of their own free will. They created lives: they provided for others, saved for retirement, raised families, bought land and built houses in their home provinces, and came to love their homes in both their lands. The Thais in Saipan came as fully engaged and cognizant economic actors finding their own roles as stars in their own lives. Though fewer in number, they nevertheless persist, and continue to contribute to the Thai community and the wider Saipan community today.

Reference

United States Department of Labor. (n.d.). *CW-1*. Retrieved December 14, 2021, from https://www.dol.gov/agencies/eta/foreign-labor/programs/cw-1

Family Violence, Historical Trauma, and the CHamoru Manggåfa (the Family)

Lisa Linda S. Natividad

I manggåfa (the family system) has consistently been the anchoring point of life for CHamorus since time immemorial. CHamorus are the Indigenous peoples of the Mariana Islands of Micronesia, who settled the islands nearly 4,000 years ago. Cunningham (1992) describes the significant role that families played in society: "Ancient Chamorros tried to meet all their obligations and always remain loyal to their family" (p. 94). Despite this longstanding tradition, family violence is a phenomenon that impacts CHamoru families today at alarming rates throughout the Mariana Islands. According to the Guam Family Violence Act of 1998, it is defined as follows:

> the occurrence of one (1) or more of the following acts by a family or household member, but does not include acts of self-defense or defense of others:
>
> (1) Attempting to cause or causing bodily injury to another family or household member;
>
> (2) Placing another family or household member in reasonable fear of imminent bodily injury; or

(3) Knowingly or intentionally, against the will of another, impeding the normal breathing or circulation of the blood of a family or household member by applying pressure to the throat or neck or by blocking the nose or mouth of a family or household member. (p. 3)

This chapter explores the intersectionality of family violence and the CHamoru manggåfa (family system) by examining intimate partner abuse, child abuse, and elder abuse. I review available family violence data in Guåhan and the Commonwealth of the Northern Mariana Islands (CNMI). To understand the plight of CHamorus today within the context of colonization and oppression, I introduce the theoretical framework of historical trauma. I also examine traditional CHamoru concepts of gender, the marital relationship, parenting practices, and the role of the elderly within the family. Lastly, I discuss implications for practitioners in the field of social services working with CHamoru families.

Family Violence Across the Marianas Archipelago

People across the Marianas Archipelago have a long and well-documented history of suffering under colonialism. Family violence is a social issue that affects many Indigenous peoples with a history of colonization and CHamorus are no exception. While the Guåhan statute provides the framework for defining family violence, in this chapter, I specifically explore abuse within the family system to include intimate partner violence, child abuse and neglect, and elder abuse. Each of these categories can be more precisely identified by the specific type of abuse to include physical, sexual, financial, emotional/psychological/verbal abuse, and neglect. To further contextualize these statistics, I note that in the 2010 US Census, CHamorus comprised 23.9% of the total population in the CNMI and 37.3% in Guåhan (CNMI Department of Commerce/Central Statistics Division, n.d.; US Census Bureau, 2014). The minoritization of the Indigenous population in the Mariana Islands is an indicator of a colonial history that has disadvantaged the CHamoru family system by setting the conditions for culture loss.

Data on family violence cases in the Marianas is uneven at best. In light of the underreporting of cases, coupled with the limited capacity for the integration of reported data, it is difficult to obtain a comprehensive look at this social issue. The Guam Police Department's Domestic Assault Response Team (2016-2018) intimate partner violence statistics indicate the total number of cases in recent years as follows: 1,442 (2016), 1,383 (2017), and 1,356 (2018). These numbers reflect cases in four categories: kidnapping, intimidation, simple assault, and aggravated assault. The Guam Statistical Yearbook 2017 reported family violence offenders by race and indicated that Pacific Islanders (including people from the Federated States of Micronesia) comprised between 81.3% to 85.5% of perpetrators for the years 2014 to 2017 (Guam Office of the Governor Bureau of Statistics and Plans, 2018, p. 250). In 2019, The Guam STOP Violence Against Women Primary Victim Data Collection reported that CHamorus comprised a total of 32% of victims of violence. Similarly, CHamorus comprised 30% of offenders. The reported gender of offenders was male in 79% of cases and female in 21% of cases.

In looking more specifically at child abuse and neglect (CAN) cases in Guahån, Table 1 shows the number of referrals received by Child Protective Services (CPS) from 2012 to 2017 as reported in the Guam Statistical Yearbook 2017 (Guam Office of the Governor Bureau of Statistics and Plans, 2018). Those figures indicate a gradual decrease in the number of cases. Table 2 breaks down the total referrals by maltreatment type that include physical, sexual, and emotional abuse, as well as physical neglect. There are also other forms of neglect not indicated in the table, including medical, educational, and emotional neglect, abandonment, lack of adult supervision, and deprivation of necessities. Table 3 reveals that the most reported co-occurring risk factor at the time of CPS referral was drug use by caretakers. This confirms the confounding relationship between violence and drug and alcohol abuse.

Table 1
Child Protective Services Referrals from 2012–2017

Year	Number of Referrals Received
2012	3,064
2013	2,747
2014	2,321
2015	2,185
2016	2,147
2017	2,205
Total	14,669

Note. From *Guam Statistical Yearbook*, 2017, by Guam Office of the Governor Bureau of Statistics and Plans, 2018, http://bsp.guam.gov/wp-bsp-content/uploads/2019/01/2017-GU-STAT-YRBK_Final.pdf

Table 2

Child Protective Services (CPS) Referrals by Maltreatment Type from 2013–2017

Maltreatment Type	2017	2016	2015	2014	2013
Physical Abuse	609	608	658	711	797
Sexual Abuse	371	303	370	302	423
Emotional Abuse	372	491	505	519	580
Neglect-Physical	1,048	1,052	649	222	260
Total	2,400	2,454	2,182	1,754	2,060

Note. From *Guam Statistical Yearbook*, 2017, by Guam Office of the Governor Bureau of Statistics and Plans, 2018, http://bsp.guam.gov/wp-bsp-content/uploads/2019/01/2017-GU-STAT-YRBK_Final.pdf

Table 3

Child Protective Services (CPS) Select Risk Factors from 2013–2017

Risk Factors	2017	2016	2015	2014	2013
Referrals involving alcohol abuse	45	71	54	107	124
Referrals involving children at-risk due to drug use by caretakers	211	229	169	172	294
Total	256	300	223	279	418

Note. From *Guam Statistical Yearbook*, 2017, by Guam Office of the Governor Bureau of Statistics and Plans, 2018, http://bsp.guam.gov/wp-bsp-content/uploads/2019/01/2017-GU-STAT-YRBK_Final.pdf

In examining the cases of reported elder abuse in Guahån, the Bureau of Adult Protective Services reported the number of referrals and indicated that CHamorus demonstrated the highest percentage of referrals ranging from 67–69% between the years 2016–2018 (Table 4). This percentage reveals the overrepresentation of CHamoru cases in relation to their percentage (37.3%) of the island's total population. In addition, the types of reported maltreatment are ranked, with the highest number of referrals for financial/property abuse, followed by neglect, and then emotional/psychological maltreatment. These data clearly show that family violence spans the life cycle, encompassing both child and elder abuse.

Table 4

Guam Bureau of Adult Protective Services (BAPS) Statistics from 2016–2018

Year	Number of Referrals Received	Percentage by Ethnicity	Type of Maltreatment Ranked
2016	205	CHamoru - 67% Filipino - 16% White - 6%	Neglect Financial/property Emotional/psychological
2017	259	CHamoru - 67% Filipino - 15% White - 8%	Financial/property Emotional/psychological Neglect
2018	240	CHamoru - 69% Filipino - 13% White - 10%	Financial/property Neglect Emotional/psychological

Note. From *Statistics from 2016–2018* [Unpublished raw data], by Guam Bureau of Adult Protective Services, 2016–2018.

In the Commonwealth of the Northern Mariana Islands (CNMI), family violence is also a social issue impacting the community. According to Maurin (2019), "the Office of the Attorney General prosecuted 73 cases of domestic violence. This was on top of the 239 calls received by the Department of Public Safety regarding domestic abuse." While this social issue was traditionally hidden, denied, or excused in the past, recent community educational efforts have helped to reframe the issue as one of power, control, and violence (Lirio, 2018). According to the CNMI Office of the Attorney General (2018), for the years 2015 to 2018, the lowest number of family violence cases occurred in 2017 (48 cases) and the highest number in 2016 (77 cases).

Official statistics report 200 cases of child abuse and neglect in the CNMI in 2018 (Table 5) including a total of 337 allegations that included physical abuse, sexual abuse, emotional abuse, negligence, and other factors (Table 6). The distribution of cases was primarily in Saipan (185 cases), followed by Tinian (10 cases), and Rota (five cases).

Table 5

Child Abuse and Neglect Referrals in the CNMI by Island in FY 2018

Island	Number of Referrals
Saipan	185
Tinian	10
Rota	5
Total	200

Note. Adapted from "DYS: 200 reports of child abuse in NMI in FY 2018," by E. Encinares, 2019 (https://www.saipantribune.com/index.php/dys-200-reports-of-child-abuse-in-nmi-in-fy-2018/).

Table 6

Child Abuse and Neglect Allegations by Type of Abuse in the CNMI in FY 2018

Type of Abuse	Number of Referrals
Physical abuse	49
Sexual abuse	45
Emotional abuse	118
Negligence cases	59
Other (suicide, teen pregnancy, domestic violence, drug use, and minor sex trafficking)	66
Total	337

Note. Adapted from "DYS: 200 reports of child abuse in NMI in FY 2018," by E. Encinares, 2019 (https://www.saipantribune.com/index.php/dys-200-reports-of-child-abuse-in-nmi-in-fy-2018/).

As in Guåhan, abuse of the elderly also occurs in the CNMI. According to Walter Manglona from the Office on Aging, the most common type of elder abuse in the Commonwealth is fraud, which he indicated includes financial exploitation and scams (Robago, 2018). Further, he gave examples such as the misuse of an elderly person's personal checks, credit cards, or other accounts, as well as stealing cash, income checks, household goods, forging signatures, and identity theft. Manglona clarified that elder abuse also includes physical, sexual, emotional, and psychological or non-verbal abuse and neglect.

The literature on violence within CHamoru families is sparse. Twaddle, Roberto, and Quintanilla (2003) conducted a study examining CHamoru perspectives on mental health issues and their context within Indigenous and Western cultural ideas. The following is an excerpt from a participant discussing intimate partner violence:

> I think there is a lot of spouse abuse in my community and I think a lot of that stems from changes in the ancient Chamorro culture. Women used to be in control; they were the ones everyone respected. Somewhere along the line things changed and now it's the man who acts as the master of the house ... If they feel they're not in control in the house, they react by thinking, "If I smack you a little harder, maybe you will notice that I am in control" [Female, 38 years, Maite]. (pp. 40-41)

This participant's sentiment was a reiteration of one offered by Rapadas (1997) when describing perpetrators of family violence on Guåhan. Rapadas is a behavioral health provider who facilitated group therapy for male perpetrators of family violence through the Superior Court of Guam. He discussed the regional shift from traditional societies that were matrilineal to the current patriarchal culture influenced by colonial powers, wherein men have risen to positions of power in society and the family structure. Rapadas noted that this shift in values and worldview may have led to a decline in the self-esteem and prominence of women and their positioning within i manggåfa. Indications are that this rise of patriarchy and decline of matriarchy provides a fertile ground for family violence to occur. He offered as evidence for this phenomenon the consistent increase in the number of cases of family violence in Guåhan.

Family violence has often been viewed as a poor coping mechanism of Indigenous peoples living in the highly Westernized context of a colonized society (Cheers et al., 2006). Colonization usually brings with it a shift in values and worldview, high levels of stress from the need to acculturate and adapt to the new world order, and feelings of inadequacy. Cheers et al. (2006) remind us that complicit with colonization are experiences of oppression, dispossession, disempowerment, dislocation, and poverty. Hence, CHamorus' manifestation of family violence is consistent with other Indigenous communities as they deal with the stressors of life in an environment that disempowers the very essence of their identity in a colonial context. These contemporary experiences are rooted in the erasure of traditional systems that define Indigenous peoples, as well as the invalidation of their very existence in modern society.

Historical Trauma, Family Violence, and Indigenous Peoples

The intersectionality of Indigenous peoples, family violence, and historical trauma is a consistent theme in the relevant literature. Historical trauma is defined "as a cumulative emotional and psychological wounding across generations, including the lifespan, which emanates from massive group trauma" (Braveheart et al., 2011, p. 282). The concept of historical trauma has been used to describe the American Indian experience of post-traumatic stress disorder (PTSD) and communal trauma as a result of genocide, colonization, assimilation, and social exclusion.

Fast and Collin-Vezina (2010) conducted a meta-analysis of the literature examining historical trauma and Indigenous peoples. They shared findings from Evans-Campbell, who highlighted the inadequacy of a PTSD diagnosis because the diagnosis does not capture the trauma experienced across generations. Evans-Campbell established three criteria for historical trauma: 1) it was experienced by many people; 2) high levels of stress were generated: and 3) outsiders perpetrated the events with destructive intent. She further posited that historical trauma impacts the individual, the family, and the larger community: individuals experience depression, anxiety, or grief; families struggle with effective communication and parenting issues; and the larger community exhibits a breakdown of traditional values and practices, internalized racism, and high rates of social problems.

Gurm (2020) describes how Indigenous peoples continue to experience the effects of trauma for generations, particularly as manifested in violence against women and girls. Specifically examining Indigenous women in Canada, Gurm (2020) reports that Indigenous women were twice as likely to experience intimate partner violence as compared to non-Indigenous women. Indigenous peoples in Canada's colonial history repeatedly experienced the removal of children from their homes and their placement in residential schools. Indigenous peoples were grossly over-represented in incarceration rates, comprising 27% of incarcerations in both 2017 and 2018 but only 3% of the population. Of those incarcerated, 50% reported experiences of family violence as children. Equally shocking is the number of murdered and missing Indigenous women and girls in Canada, who are 12 times more likely to be killed or go missing as compared to other ethnic groups (Gurm, 2020).

Gurm (2020) reports that Indigenous peoples globally suffer a comparable outcome with high rates of family violence, as evidenced in the Aboriginal peoples of Australia and the Māori of Aotearoa (New Zealand). Efforts to eradicate traditional practices, coupled with inequality, racism, and the lack of cultural safety within systems, are traumatic experiences that contribute to family violence. Further, Vickers and Moyer (2020) draw the connection between historical and ongoing colonialism and the loss of identity and support, fragmentation of the family system, loneliness, and psychological distress in Indigenous populations.

Unfortunately, CHamorus have suffered a similar fate as indicated in the aforementioned statistics. The intersectionality of ongoing colonialism, war and related invasions, the high risk for poverty, and structural racism helps to contextualize the high rates of family violence for CHamorus in the Marianas. Their experience of historical trauma is related to land dispossession, language loss, the demonization of traditional spirituality, identity and role confusion, experiences of World War II atrocities, and historical and ongoing colonialism. Pier (1998) investigated the intergenerational transmission of historic community trauma affecting CHamorus and indicates that such experiences pose mental health concerns. In an unsettling parallel, Braveheart et al. (2011) report that the prevalence of serious psychiatric disorders among American Indians and Alaska Natives living on reservations is rooted in the experience of collective, communal, and generational trauma that manifests today as racism, oppression, and discrimination. Having a mental health diagnosis is a confounding variable for family violence, and such dynamics are prevalent in Indigenous populations in the Marianas, as they are for Indigenous populations around the world.

Traditional CHamoru Concepts of the Family (I Manggåfa)
While CHamorus continue to endure colonization today, many traditional values remain intact, including the value of i manggåfa (the family system). In present times, i manggåfa continues to play a critical role in the lives of CHamorus and remains the foundation of society. Consequently, traditional concepts of i manggåfa provide a framework for understanding contemporary familial dynamics, particularly those of family violence. The CHamoru creation account describes how humanity was born out of Fouha Rock in Humåtak (Umatac), as fashioned by the primordial brother and sister, Pontan and Fo'na. The cross-sibling relationship in the account

speaks to CHamorus' value of familial relationships and the brother-sister pair as the "basic building block" of matrilineal societies found throughout Micronesia (Marshall, 1981). According to Underwood (1992),

> The family, in its various manifestations throughout Micronesia is the unit that traditionally has kept the society intact, responsive, and responsible in the face of change. Micronesians, by an overwhelming majority, see families as the basic building blocks of society; moreover, they tend to see each other not as individuals with particular professions or personalities, but as people from certain families. This family orientation is healthy and necessary for their continued survival as Micronesians, for it is in the family context that most serious discussions occur and most decisions are made. (p. 169)

With the extensive history of colonization of the Mariana Islands by the Spanish for over two centuries, the common reference for "family" used in the CHamoru language is the adopted Spanish word, *familia*. As the global community has slowly shifted to embrace indigeneity, CHamorus have further embarked upon the processes of political and personal decolonization. As part of the latter, there has been great emphasis on reclaiming more authentic, Indigenous, and decolonized concepts of culture and language, including the use of archaic terms in the CHamoru language, also referred to as Fino' Håya, "one of an estimated 1,200 languages in the Austronesian language family that originated out of Taiwan more than 5,000 years ago" (Lynch, 1998). Fino' Håya uses Indigenous and pre-colonial words that were not introduced by the island's colonizers—more specifically, the Spanish, Germans, Japanese, or Americans. Hence, in exploring CHamoru concepts of manggåfa, it is critical to examine the Fino' Håya references to family.

Early accounts of CHamorus and the role of the family have been documented by a number of foreign observers, including Fray Juan Pobre de Zamora and Louis Claude de Freycinet. Fray Juan Pobre de Zamora was a priest who lived in the Marianas for about 7 months in 1602. Louis Claude de Freycinet was a French navigator who visited the Mariana Islands as part of a Pacific expedition in the early 1800s. Each of these men wrote extensive accounts of their observations of the CHamoru culture and other aspects of living in the Marianas. Similarly, Russell (1998) describes ancient CHamoru culture as reported by early foreign accounts of the Marianas.

Freycinet (2003) revealed a number of word references to the concept of family for CHamorus. He noted that CHamorus referred to family as *manggåfa* and one's blood relatives as *atchafgnang*, who were obliged to carry out familial duties. In addition, he defined *atchagma* as those who were related by friendship and who were assigned specific duties. He also described *atugtcha-guma* as those who had family relations through a specific connection or obligation, as in the case of someone who saved the life of one's child. The atugcha-guma was typically given a *guneha famaguan* (guinahan famagu'on) or turtle shell necklace pendant with drilled holes in it to represent each of one's children. This custom is consistent with CHamoru reciprocity practices and is an effort to make empas, or even, for the debt of saving the child's life. Freycinet also described children who were pinigsai (pineksai)—adopted into the family and regarded as biological children entrusted to the care and protection of the women. He also reported that relationships were closest with the mother's side of the family system and that women's requests were obliged over those of men.

Gender Roles and Marriage

Consistent with CHamorus' matrilineal, matriarchal, and matricentric organization of society, women were noted as having a prominent role in the clan—particularly evident in the maga'håga or female chief. The role of the maga'håga complemented the role of the maga'låhi or male chief and together they managed affairs as the highest-ranking male and female in the clan. Women were traditionally responsible for managing the affairs of the house, raising the children, fishing inside of the reef, food preparation, weaving, and making pottery. Men, on the other hand, were the navigators, fishermen outside of the reef, and tool makers. Nonetheless, there existed a complementary relationship between them. According to Mendiola (2019), "Chamorros were able to find a societal equilibrium as both men and women—the eldest brother and sister—were co-equal guardians and administrators of clans and their resources" (para. 3). The status of men and women in CHamoru society was historically one of complementarity, giving respect and responsibilities to each in different spheres of communal life. Hence, men and women functioned on equal planes, rather than one holding a position of power over the other. Rather, both assumed complementary roles in society and were equally respected and revered for their contributions. This egalitarian relationship is nicely articulated in the creation account with brother-sister gods Pontan and Fo'na.

Freycinet (2003) described the role of CHamoru women as having "the direction of public affairs ... in their hands. At home, they were absolute mistresses and had the command of everything; nothing was done without first obtaining their opinion or consent" (p. 183). Russell (1998) added that

> It is clear from these accounts that while the men may have been the warriors and navigators, the women were the heads of household and were quick to assert their prerogatives. For instance, the husband did not dare give an order contrary to [his wife's] wishes, nor punish the children, for she [would] turn upon him and beat him. (p. 150)

These two accounts highlight CHamoru women's significant role in the household and in affairs concerning the children. One reason given for the prominent role of women is their sacred ability to carry and bear children.

Women clearly assumed the role of household heads, inclusive of decision-making and parenting. Souder (as cited in Russell, 1998) underscores these functions, and references the active role of women in matters of familial inheritance:

> Females—particularly elder women in the clan, who were married and mothers—were powerful in all spheres of ... society. Through [the] matrilineal kinship system, women exercised control over family life, property, and inheritance. They assumed a central role and possessed strong bargaining powers in their marriage ... Their esteemed status was also reflected in rituals, legends, and ceremonial events. (p. 150)

Although women were highly respected and regarded for their ability to bear children and for their role as traditional owners of clan land, men were not subordinate or secondary to them. Describing the honoring accorded to fathers, Freycinet (2003) observed that when a child of status was born, rice was thrown at the feet of the father as a sign of respect. Children's names were also based on the skills of their fathers, as in the case of Nineti (ingenious) and Tai-agnao (intrepid). These examples highlight the complementarity of the relationship between men and women, as well as the respect given to fathers of the clan.

The importance of manggåfa is reiterated when examining traditional CHamoru practices relative to marriage. Freycinet (2003) specifically addressed the sanctity of the union of marriage and described the consequences of marital infidelity:

An adulterous woman, who had been repudiated by her husband and sent back to her mother's house after judgment, was stripped of her possessions at the same time ... But he was perfectly free to avenge himself upon the seducer for the insult received, even to the point of killing him. (p. 183)

Likewise, when women were upset with their spouses, they were able to respond, as Freycinet (2003) observed:

All the women kept it, a spear in their hand and their husband's hat on their head. In that marital guise, they then advance as a unit on the house of the guilty man. First, they lay waste his crops and tear up his cereals, trampling them down, then they strip his fruit trees of their fruit and create an appalling mess. Finally, they descend upon the dwelling itself, and if the wretched husband has not taken precaution of betaking himself elsewhere and finding cover, they attack him too, and chase him right out. (p. 183)

Each of these accounts by Freycinet indicate responses that, in extreme cases, led to physical violence: in the former, towards the third-party male having an affair with one's wife, and in the latter, towards one's husband. Fray Juan Pobre de Zamora reported similar reactions to infidelity:

when a man and a woman marry and live together in a house, although they have been married twenty or thirty years, if the husband is unfaithful to his wife, or takes a mistress, and if it should anger his wife, she will leave the house, taking the children and all the household furniture and effects, and will go to the house of her parents or of other relatives, where she will remain. During all this time, the children will not acknowledge their father, even though he may pass very close to them. Before the wife will return to the husband, his relatives will have to go to great lengths to do so. If the wife is unfaithful to the husband, her relatives do not have to go to such lengths because it is easier to obtain the husband's pardon since this sin is considered less serious for the women than for the men. (Driver, 1989, p. 21)

Clearly, the marital relationship entailed a relationship between a man and a woman, but also a relationship between two clans and the conjugation of their resources.

In a matrilineal society, land is transmitted along the maternal line, giving women great power in society. Consistent with practices throughout the Pacific, land ownership represented wealth for CHamoru women. This dynamic, coupled with the ability to bear children, gave CHamoru women prominence and special standing in society. Perhaps this explains the privilege afforded women that is referenced in these historical accounts.

In contemporary times, however, the introduction of patriarchal values through the Catholic Church and Westernization has begun a shift from an egalitarian system to one with the male as the head of household, principal decision maker, and holder of the resources. Land, for example, is more likely today to be passed on to sons so that they may be able to take care of their families, a practice that was introduced during the Spanish colonial period. The introduction of patriarchy has placed a strain on CHamoru families, as males assert a non-traditional role at the helm of families and attempt to disempower women and reduce their status in the family. This dynamic has proven problematic and is a key factor leading to role confusion, thereby increasing the potential for intimate partner violence.

Parenting and the Role of Children
Children hold a position of great importance within the CHamoru manggåfa. Consistent with agrarian societies, CHamoru families were traditionally large. Similar to other Micronesian societies, children were viewed as resources and wealth. While both parents bore the responsibilities of parenting the children, children were clearly viewed as belonging to the mother and her clan.

Juan Pobre described the very beautiful role prescribed to children and the great love that accompanied parenting as follows:
> While they are very young, they make their sons and daughters work and teach them to perform their tasks. Consequently, the very young know how to perform their tasks like their parents because they have been taught with great love. So great is their love for their children that it would take a long time to describe it and to sing it praises. They never spank them, and they even scold them with loving words. When a child is offended and angered by what is said to him, he will move a short distance away from his parents and turn his back to them, not wanting to face them. They will then toss sand or pebbles on the ground behind him and after he has cried for a little while, one of his parents will go to him and, with very tender words, will take him in his arms or raise him to his shoulders and carry him back to where the others are gathered. Then they will always give him some of their best food and speaking to them as if he were an adult, tell him

how he should behave, admonishing him to be good. With such great love, these barbarians raise their children, that they, in turn, grow up to be obedient and expert in their occupations and skills. (Driver, 1989, p.17)

This historical account of CHamoru childrearing practices describes a very loving approach that can serve as a source of empowerment for parents today as they learn to improve their parenting skills.

Parents were tasked with socializing their same-gendered children into their respective gender roles. Fathers were noted to be central figures in the lives of their sons. Juan Pobre observed:

At the age of four or five, they teach their sons to go out to sea in little boats that they build for them, and which have their own outriggers that are identical to those on their fathers' larger boats. By the age of fourteen, they have come so skilled at using them, that the sons know as much as their fathers; by the time they are sixteen or eighteen, the sons put out to sea to fish alone, as I have seen them do. Alone in his funei, he sets the sails, bails the boat, and fishes with a hook and net; if it capsizes, he rights it, so great is their strength. (Driver, 1989, p. 15)

This account demonstrates the active role that fathers played in socializing their sons in their culturally prescribed gender roles. Similarly, mothers too were responsible for teaching their daughters how to carry out their duties in the service of the clan.

The propensity for child abuse and neglect in contemporary society seems inconsistent with Juan Pobre's accounts of how lovingly CHamorus treated their children. This raises the question of what accounts for the incidence of child abuse in contemporary times. Colonialism in the past and present has placed pressure on CHamorus to adapt to the new world order of westernization. Parents experience high levels of stress as a result of being ill-prepared for the demands of life. Confounding factors such as substance use disorders, land dispossession, poverty, limited educational attainment, and youthful parenting present additional challenges and increase the propensity for the abuse of CHamoru children today.

I Manåmko' (Elderly)/Mañaina (Parents/Parental Figures)

The elderly, or manåmko', have historically been, and continue to be valued and key members in i manggåfa for CHamorus. Contemporary CHamorus also refer to the elderly as mañaina or parents/parental figures. Mañaina are revered for their wisdom and knowledge as teachers and decision makers of the clan.

Mañaina are the cultural knowledge bearers for traditions, family history, the CHamoru language, genealogy, and inafa'maolek (collective peace). Their permission is sought when a young couple intends to marry. The immense respect afforded mañaina is encapsulated in the custom of mannginge' or the practice of sniffing the hand of elders so as in to inhale their spirit and wisdom. In return, the practitioner receives a blessing from the parental figure.

Historical accounts on the role of mañaina are far and few, but Marsh (2018) states,
> One of the first things written about CHamoru society was that manåmko (elders) were highly respected and held a lot of power. An early Spanish visitor to Guam, Fray Antonio de los Angeles, in 1596 said the elders gave orders and everyone obeyed them—completely. It was family elders who ruled their clans and thus ancient CHamoru society. (para. 2)

This prominent role of elders continues today with the eldest members of the clan receiving special privileges and care. Typically, elderly parents are cared for by the eldest daughter in the clan from the home. While Guahån has a senior care home, the CNMI does not. For most CHamoru families, the inability to care for elders in the home until their death is internalized as a failure on their part.

The cultural practice of caring for elders until their death is inconsistent with the high rates of elder abuse by CHamorus in the Marianas. It is noteworthy to mention that the most frequently reported form of elder abuse in Guahån is financial/property and in the CNMI is fraud (financial exploitation and scams).

In attempting to understand this phenomenon, the interconnectedness between the cultural practice of caring for the elderly in the home until death and the limited coping and resources in the home should be considered and contextualized through the lens of colonization. Traditional CHamoru practices treated the individual as a small part of the larger collective society. Hence, value was placed on the needs of the collective before the individual. When this worldview is applied to contemporary practices, the use of the elderly's financial resources and assets can be seen as a contribution to meeting the needs of the collective household. This sharing of resources becomes necessary in the context of colonization wherein the family system experiences extreme stress and is unable to meet the demands of daily living. While through a Western lens these acts are deemed illegal and in violation of the elder's rights, a traditional cultural perspective could view it as an extension of the care that the elders have consistently contributed to the family system in the past.

Implications for Social Service Practitioners
Indigenous peoples' experiences of historical trauma warrant the integration of culture-based interventions to facilitate healing from family violence (Braveheart et al., 2011; Fast & Collin-Vezina, 2010; Gurm, 2020; Klingspohn, 2018; Pihama et al., 2019; Vickers & Moyer, 2020). Given the dismal reality of family violence experiences for many CHamoru families, it is strategic for social service providers to integrate traditional conceptualizations of i manggåfa into their provision of services in an effort to provide services that are culturally competent and reflective of cultural safety.

According to the National Association of Social Workers (2015) Standards and Indicators for Cultural Competence in Social Work Practice, "Cultural competence requires self-awareness, cultural humility, and the commitment to understanding and embracing culture as central to effective practice" (p. 6). Self-awareness requires self-reflection and taking personal inventory of one's beliefs, prejudices, and biases that exist against persons from diverse backgrounds. Becoming aware of these beliefs is necessary to be able to sensitize themselves when working with CHamoru families. Further, seeking a deeper understanding of CHamoru values, beliefs, cultural practices, and history will allow one to develop a more deeply rooted understanding of behaviors. This deeper understanding will allow the practitioner to exercise empathy and avoid negative judgement.

Cultural humility is another consistently recommended approach for working with Indigenous peoples. Cultural humility positions the practitioner as an observer and learner to ensure alignment with the client's traditional beliefs, values, and worldview. This practice places the client at the center and as the expert of his or her life. Cultural humility acknowledges that the practitioner is merely a resource for change to the client system, presenting clients with options, information, and skills that complement their own and make cultural sense. Cultural humility also makes certain that the options presented to clients flow logically and are rooted in traditional knowledge, attitudes, and beliefs.

Coupled with cultural competency and cultural humility, cultural safety is defined as "an environment that is spiritually, socially, emotionally and physically safe for people; where cultural identity is recognized and valued through shared respect, meaning, knowledge and the experience of learning together" (Klingspohn, 2018, p. 3). Social service delivery systems should prioritize creating an environment of cultural safety to rebuild trust and confidence in the system. This effort to validate the lived experiences of clients and to meet them in the context of their cultural selves becomes fertile ground for healing and transformation.

Gurm (2020) provides a framework for culturally competent services to draw from Indigenous knowledge systems, incorporate Indigenous practitioners and elders, repair the fragmented Indigenous identity, and incorporate a connection to spirit and spirituality. Further, the values of respect, wisdom, responsibility, and relationships should all be modeled. Lastly, Gurm (2020) suggests the incorporation of storytelling to facilitate healing when addressing trauma and griefwork, as this is a traditional approach consistently employed by Indigenous peoples.

Social service organizations and agencies play an essential role in setting the standard for culturally competent practice. Pihama et al. (2019) share the approach when developing services for Indigenous Māori from Aotearoa (New Zealand): "Healing must take place on both individual and collective levels to prevent intergenerational transmission of trauma" (p. 1). They further highlight the importance of building services on the Māori cultural and healing paradigms that have eroded as a result of the colonial experience. Lastly, they emphasize the need for services to be developed and implemented by Indigenous peoples for Indigenous peoples. Similarly, Klingspohn (2018) emphasizes the need for the integration of Indigenous ceremonies, language, and traditions into family group counseling. More specifically, First Nation ceremonies such as smudging, the talking circle, and the sweat lodge for Aboriginal men have been effectively incorporated into programs.

Agency policies have the opportunity to shift from traditional approaches to ones that meet the nuanced needs of CHamoru client systems. For example, the employment of personnel whose identities reflect the demographic composition of clients is a key strategy. This effort reaffirms the need to learn about CHamoru culture. Further, when clients are able to see themselves in social service practitioners, they typically feel safer and more comfortable. This culturally competent approach is reassuring to clients—particularly when they have engaged in services that have left them feeling frustrated, disenfranchised, and underserved in the past.

In addition, a social service agency's effort towards language access and proficiency for limited English speakers is necessary. For clients who feel more comfortable speaking in the CHamoru language, working with personnel with fluency in the language facilitates the client engagement process more efficiently and with greater depth. Access to language speakers, translated materials (especially consent forms), and marketing materials in the Native language are efforts that can facilitate trust with potential clients. The late Senator Angel Leon Guerrero Santos, Indigenous rights defender from Guåhan, consistently referenced the Indigenous language as the voice of the Indigenous soul. It is from this level of spirit that healing is facilitated.

Another strategy that agencies can employ is some mechanism for consultation with the mañaina. This is consistent with the primary role mañaina play in CHamoru society in the past and in the present. This can take multiple forms, including a seat on its governing body or board, the creation of a mañaina advisory council, or the hiring of mañaina to play a visible and active role in the delivery of culturally competent interventions to agency client systems—such as utilizing mañaina as a resource in family therapy sessions because their words are highly regarded and respected. Mañaina can also share life lessons through storytelling. Their recommendations and feedback can be solicited in the design and development of new programs as a check for potential efficacy by evaluating the proposed program's cultural alignment. In this case, the influence of the mañaina in the cultural worldview of CHamorus is replicated in the service delivery system.

Similarly, acknowledging ancestors as part of agency protocols serves as another source of empowerment for CHamoru clients. Like other cultures in the Asia-Pacific region, CHamorus traditionally venerated their ancestors. In ancient times, skulls of ancestors or maranan uchan were kept in their homes as an extension of their inclusion of the deceased in the family. CHamorus are highly relational and contextualize other CHamorus through their clan identifications. Upon meeting each other, one usually asks, "What's your last name? What village are you from? Who are your parents?" This is usually followed by asking their relation to notable members of the person's clan. Given this cultural practice, agencies could mirror this protocol as part of engaging new clients. For example, a private, behavioral health clinic in Guåhan dedicated a table to the display of their personnel's ancestors who have died. As part of client engagement, clients were introduced to the provider's clan by sharing the pictures and likewise, clients were given the opportunity to share their lineage. This allows for a deeper sense of connection with social service practitioners.

In specifically examining curriculum content and interventions for working with clients, Duran and Duran (1995) emphasize the need for individual counselors working with Indigenous peoples to shift away from a Eurocentric worldview to embrace one that is consistent with Indigenous beliefs. This includes the reframing of conceptualizations of healing and mental health. The process of unlearning Western treatment models taught in mainstream counseling programs becomes necessary to increase efficacy when working with Indigenous populations. This shift is an initial step towards effectively addressing issues of family violence in the counseling process. An example of this entails placing the focus of treatment in the context of the total family system. This reinforces the development of a strong family group counseling component in services, as opposed to focusing solely on the individual. Practices such as this are associated with the collective values of CHamorus.

Family violence interventions should intentionally incorporate components to decolonize CHamorus' identities and maladaptive coping mechanisms that contradict the very essence of traditional practices. This entails the reeducation process of traditional gender roles, parenting accounts, and the value of the elderly. For example, the development of training curricula that specifically teach CHamorus the traditional value assigned to women will empower them from the context of their cultural identity and re-instill in them a sense of their maga'håga (female chief) qualities. Nonetheless, emphasis should be given to the complementarity in the relationship between women and men in the provision of services and not the domination of one over the other. In addition, notions of toxic masculinity should also be dispelled and rejected as cultural practice.

In an effort to specifically address child abuse, the parenting account described by Juan Pobre can serve as a reference point for parenting skills training and helping CHamorus to decolonize their parenting roles when engaging their children. The account specifically presents parenting strategies such as timeout, role modeling, and the use of praise. These parenting strategies have been found to be universally effective today and are taught in parenting curricula in the social service field. Hence, these strategies should be incorporated into parenting classes because they are consistent with historical accounts of traditional parenting styles and will serve to empower parents by connecting them with practices that reflect their Indigenous identities.

Social service interventions could also analyze traditional CHamoru chants, legends, or proverbs delivered through storytelling. For example, chants in the CHamoru language connect clients and help to give voice and expression to the Indigenous spirit. Chants were traditionally used ritualistically during funerals and special life rites. They tell the stories of our ancestors and traditional ways of life. While the use of chants was not so visible during the Spanish colonial period, a revitalization of chanting has occurred in more recent history and chants are especially used to bless events and to invite ancestors to be present.

Just as the use of traditional chants can serve as an intervention for working with CHamoru clients, so too can the use of traditional legends. The CHamoru legend of Taga is highly illustrative of family violence. Here's the Farrell (2019) rendition of the legend:

> According to CHamoru legend, Taga was born to the *maga'låhi* or chief of Ritidian Village, Guam. In the legend, Taga was a giant. Dissatisfied with his father's rule, the boy challenged his father to a fight. When Taga lost the fight, he moved to Rota, where he challenged the leading *maga'låhi* to a series of contests. Winning these contests, he married a local CHamoru woman and had a daughter. At As Nieves, Rota, he began excavating what would have been the largest latte stones in the Marianas – perhaps he was trying to impress his father. For an unknown reason, however, Taga moved from Rota to Tinian without lifting the stones out of the ground. As he had on Rota, the giant Taga gained power in Tinian and had a son. He then oversaw the construction of his home, the House of Taga, on Sanhalom Bay on the southwest coast of the island. The house consisted of 12 latte stones, with a wooden house built on top of the stones. When

the son of Taga turned five years old, Taga gave him a giant *ayuyu* (coconut crab) as a present. Unfortunately, while the boy was walking the crab, it cut the twine leash and ran under a young coconut tree. The boy ran back to Taga House and asked his father to push over the coconut tree so he could get the crab. Taga refused, explaining that the coconuts were just beginning to bear fruit. The boy became furious. He ran back to the tree and shook it furiously, finally pushing over the tree himself. While the boy was pulling the crab from the hole he had just created, he noticed water. It was fresh water. He gave the well to his half-sister for her to bathe in. When Taga saw his young son perform this great feat of strength, he recognized that the boy might become bigger and stronger than even himself. He remembered fighting his own father. That night, Taga crept into the boy's room and smothered him to death. Taga's daughter saw this. She became so frightened, she ran away to the deep forest and hid. By the time she was returned to her mother, the girl was so weak that she died. Taga buried the girl in a cavity dug in one of the tasa of Taga House. This grieved the mother so much, she too died. This left Taga, the biggest and strongest of all CHamoru *maga'låhi*, shamed. (para. 2–5)

An in-depth analysis of the legend could discuss the impact of family violence on the Taga family system. Specific questions could explore the following: How does intergenerational paternal conflict and violence affect generations to come? How does the perpetrator of hyper-masculine violence feel as a result of his or her actions? How does the emotion of anger play a role in violence? How does fear impact our relationship with others? Do anger and power justify the loss of life? To what extent do you think Taga experienced regret as a result of killing his son? How do you think Taga's grief impacted his life with the loss of his son, daughter, and wife as a result of jealousy and the need to maintain power? How does the experience of shame affect our future behavior? What alternatives to violence could Taga have used to address his feelings of discontent? The use of CHamoru legends provides a relatable reference point for examining the consequences of family violence and helps to empower clients by reconnecting them with traditional stories reflective of their personal identities and by promoting the CHamoru value of inafa'maolek (collective peace).

A final recommendation for social service providers is to have family members affirm their commitment to refrain from engaging in family violence and alternatively to make a pledge to uphold inafa'maolek in their homes and lives. The following pledge is an adaptation from de La Cruz and Natividad's (2017) curriculum for teaching personal well-being:

Inafa'moalek (Collective Peace) Family Pledge

The following pledge is adapted from *Navigating Personal Well-being and Sexuality: A Facilitator's Guide for Working with Chuukese and CHamoru Communities*, by T. de La Cruz & L. Natividad (2017):

> Because I love my *manggåfa* and want only the best for them, I promise to always center *inafa'maolek* in our home. I vow to be peaceful and to listen to others. I will tell them how I feel and not let my anger be a reason to hurt or harm them. I will respect how they feel and try to understand them. I will use my hands only for loving and not for hurting. I will use my words only for saying things to make my family feel good about themselves and I will not say hurtful things. With the guidance of our ancestors, I promise to do the following to practice *inafa'maolek* in my home:
> 1.
> 2.
> 3.
> I make this vow in the spirit of *inafa'maolek* and *guinaiya* (love).

This degree of integration of cultural proficiency in family violence prevention and treatment programs aims to improve outcomes for CHamoru client systems.

Conclusion

This chapter explored the intersectionality of family violence, historical trauma, and CHamoru families living in the Mariana Islands. It introduced the framework of historical trauma and examined traditional concepts of i manggåfa (the family system) as presented in historical accounts, specifically examining the role of gender, the marital relationship, and CHamoru parenting practices. As CHamorus struggle with deconstructing their colonized world, it is strategic to employ the use of historical references to traditional practices as a means of decolonizing their experience and to develop culturally proficient social services. This chapter also offered suggestions for social service practitioners in developing culturally proficient intervention strategies for working with CHamoru families who have experienced family violence. It is from this cultural vantage point that CHamorus will reclaim their personal power and live inafa'maolek (community peace).

References

Braveheart, M., Chase, J., Elkins, J., & Altschul, D. (2011). Historical trauma among indigenous peoples of the Americas: Concepts, research and clinical considerations. *Journal of Psychoactive Drugs, 43*(4), 282–290.

Cheers, B., Binell, M., Coleman, H., Gentle, I., Miller, G., Taylor, J., & Weetra, C. (2006). Family violence: An Australian indigenous community tells its story. *International Social Work, 49*(1), 51–63.

CNMI Department of Commerce/Central Statistics Division. (n.d.). *2015 Commonwealth of the Northern Mariana Islands statistical yearbook.* https://ver1.cnmicommerce.com/wp-content/uploads/2017/11/2015-Yearbook-11222017.pdf

CNMI Office of the Attorney General. (2018). *2018 annual report.* https://www.cnmioag.org/publications/2018-annual-report/

Cunningham, L. J. (1992). *Ancient Chamorro society.* Bess Press.

de La Cruz, T., & Natividad, L. (2017). *Navigating personal well-being and sexuality: A facilitator's guide for working with Chuukese and CHamoru communities.* University of Guam Press.

Driver, M. (1989). *The account of Fray Juan Pobre's residence in the Marinas, 1602.* Miscellaneous Series No. 8. University of Guam Micronesia Area Research Center.

Duran, E., & Duran, B. (1995). *Native American post-colonial psychology.* State University of New York Press.

Encinares, E. (2019, April 5). DYS: 200 reports of child abuse in NMI in FY 2018. *Saipan Tribune.* https://www.saipantribune.com/index.php/dys-200-reports-of-child-abuse-in-nmi-in-fy-2018/

Farrell, D. (2019, November 16). Taga. In *Guampedia.* https://www.guampedia.com/taga/#:~:text=According%20to%20CHamoru%20legend%2C%20Taga,to%20a%20series%20of%20contests.

Fast, E., & Collin-Vezina, D. (2010). Historical trauma, race-based trauma and resilience of indigenous peoples: A literature review. *First Peoples Child & Family Review, 5*(1), 126–136.

Freycinet, L. (2003). *An account of the Corvette L'Uraine's sojourn at the Mariana Islands, 1819.* CNMI Division of Historic Preservation.

Guam Bureau of Adult Protective Services. (2016–2018). *Statistics from 2016–2018* [Unpublished raw data]. Guam Coalition Against Sexual Assault and Family Violence.

Guam Family Violence Act of 1998, 9 Guam Code § 30.10 (1998).

Guam Office of the Governor Bureau of Statistics and Plans. (2018). *Guam statistical yearbook 2017.* http://bsp.guam.gov/wp-bsp-content/uploads/2019/01/2017-GU-STAT-YRBK_Final.pdf

Guam Police Department Domestic Assault Response Team. (2016–2018). *Sexual assault and domestic violence statistics* [Unpublished raw data]. Guam Coalition Against Sexual Assault and Family Violence.

Guam STOP Violence Against Women. (2019). *Primary victim data collection* [Unpublished raw data]. Guam Coalition Against Sexual Assault and Family Violence.

Gurm, B. (2020). Relationship violence in indigenous populations. In B. Gurm, G. Salgado, J. Marchbank, & S. Early (Eds.), *Making sense of a global pandemic: Relationship violence and working together towards a violence-free society.* Kwantlen Polytechnic University. https://kpu.pressbooks.pub/nevr/chapter/chapter-19/

Klingspohn, D. (2018). The importance of culture in addressing domestic violence for First Nation's women. *Frontiers in Psychology, 9*(872), 1–7.

Lirio, L. (2018, October 5). October declared DV Awareness Month. *Guam Daily Post.* https://www.postguam.com/news/cnmi/october-declared-domestic-violence-awareness-month/article_7ad7651e-c796-11e8-991f-db51d8bf350c.html

Lynch, J. (1998). *Pacific languages: An introduction.* University of Hawaii Press.

Marsh, K. (2018, December 18). Division of labor by age, class, gender. In *Guampedia.* https://www.guampedia.com/division-of-labor-by-age-class-gender/

Marshall, M. (1981). Sibling sets as building blocks in greater Trukese society. In M. Marshall (Ed.), *Siblingship in Oceania: Studies in the meaning of kin relations.* (pp. 201-224). University Press of America.

Maurin, I. (2019, October 4). October is DV Awareness Month. *Saipan Tribune.* https://www.saipantribune.com/index.php/oct-is-domestic-violence-awareness-month/#:~:text=These%20sobering%20numbers%20were%20the,In%20signing%20the%20proclamation%2C%20Gov

Mendiola, T. (2019, October 14). Women's roles. In *Guampedia*. https://www.guampedia.com/womens-roles/
National Association of Social Workers. (2015). *Standards and indicators for cultural competency in social work practice*. NASW Press.
Pier, P. T. (1998). *An exploratory study of community trauma and culturally responsive counseling with Chamorro clients* (Publication No. AAI9841910) [Doctoral dissertation, UMass Amherst]. ProQuest. https://scholarworks.umass.edu/dissertations_1/1257
Pihama, L., Cameron, N., & Nana, R. T. (2019). Historical trauma and whānau violence. *New Zealand Family Violence Clearinghouse*. https://www.nzfvc.org.nz/issues-paper-15-historical-trauma.
Rapadas, J. (1997). Perpetrators of family violence. In J. Kiffer (Ed.), *Family violence on Guam*. Superior Court of Guam.
Robago, M. (2018, March 8). Fraud most common crime vs. man'amko. *Saipan Tribune*. https://www.saipantribune.com/index.php/fraud-common-crime-vs-manamko/
Russell, S. (1998). *Tiempon i manmofo'na*. CNMI Division of Historic Preservation.
Twaddle, I., Roberto, P., & Quintanilla, L. (2003). Chamorro perspectives on mental health issues in Guam: Cross currents of indigenous and Western cultural discourses. *South Pacific Journal of Psychology, 14*, 30–59.
Underwood, R. (1992). Families, women and rapid change. *ISLA: A Journal of Micronesian Studies, 1*(2), 169–171.
US Census Bureau. (2014). *2010 census of population and housing, Guam demographic profile summary file: Technical documentation*. https://www.census.gov/prod/cen2010/doc/dpsfgu.pdf
Vickers, P., & Moyer, R. (2020). Healing complex trauma 1: A unity of minds, hearts, and culture. *Journal of Indigenous Wellbeing, 5*(1), 3–15.

Shifts

Ti Siña Ma Funas Ham: Shapes of CHamoru Erasure in Guam

Kenneth Gofigan Kuper

Driving around Guam, one is likely to see "TANO Y CHAMORRO"[20] printed on the bottom half of our license plates. Translated as "Land of the CHamoru," this phrase serves as a reminder that Guam (as part of the Marianas Archipelago) is the homeland of the CHamoru people. Guam is CHamoru land, and this is an unchangeable fact. Yet, this does not deter some from conjuring the dark magic of trying to change what should be unchangeable. In March 2017, District Court of Guam Judge Francis Tydingco-Gatewood ruled in favor of plaintiff Arnold "Dave" Davis in *Davis v. Guam*:

> Davis sued the government of Guam in federal court in hopes of overturning the Guam law limiting the electorate in any future self-determination plebiscite to those falling within the statutory definition of a "native inhabitant of Guam," or those persons who became US citizens by virtue of the passage in Congress of the 1950 Organic Act of Guam (and descendants of those persons). (Aguon, 2014, p. 282)

Gatewood ruled in favor of Davis: "Having found that the classification is racial, this court finds that the Plebiscite statute impermissibly imposed race-based restrictions on the voting rights of non-Native inhabitants of Guam, in violation of the Fifteenth Amendment" (*Davis v. Guam,* 2017). The Government of Guam would appeal this ruling and after the US Supreme Court denied hearing the case, the Government of Guam officially exhausted local and national remedies. Thus, *Davis v. Guam* stands.[21] This ruling demonstrates friction between the colonial US legal system and genuine CHamoru self-determination in Guam when it comes to the political status plebiscite. This case is but one example, I argue, of the unjust treatment of CHamorus as the Indigenous people of the island being erased in favor of a "one amongst many" discourse, or what Kanaka Maoli scholar, Kehaulani Kauanui, (2008) calls "colonialism through equality."

In this chapter, I argue that this logic of erasure is not confined to this example; I use settler colonial theory to elucidate the ways CHamoru erasure can be found in various shapes in Guam. Tracking these shapes is an important and necessary task to help prevent further instances of CHamoru erasure, whether planned or not. I trace these shapes of erasure in Guam from physical militarization to settler colonial logics and discourses enforced by American legal institutions. I am inspired by Dine scholar Glen Coulthard (2014), who argues that in order to maintain its dominance temporally and spatially, colonial power has shape-shifted from being primarily exclusive and assimilationist in structure to more accommodating and engaging. Yet, it is still colonial in its foundation. Thus, I aim to dissect the anatomy of CHamoru erasure with an eye towards understanding the physiology of how these seemingly disparate anatomical parts coalesce to pump the blood of erasure in Guam today.

To accomplish that goal, this chapter is divided into four parts. In the first section, I introduce Guam and engage with settler colonial theory to situate my usage of erasure and show that despite not meeting the typical characteristics of settler colonialism, the logics of settler colonialism still operate in Guam today and can be a useful analytic. The second section then traces the physical history of "destroying and replacing" during and after World War II, which helped create the conditions of possibility for further CHamoru erasure today. I argue that this material transformation of the island set the stage for other forms of erasure. The third section then demonstrates the discursive operationalization of this process of erasure in the present day through the imposition of settler colonial logics, particularly a disguised form of multiculturalism. In this section, I also further explore the legal shape of CHamoru erasure via the lawfare of individual rights to hinder the CHamoru push for self-determination. The final section then outlines paths forward for CHamoru and non-CHamoru relationships that are not predicated on erasure.

Guam and Settler Colonialism

At present, Guam is an organized, unincorporated territory of the United States. Due to this political status, the people of Guam, most being citizens of the United States, have no voting representation in the US House of Representatives, no representation in the US Senate, and no votes in the Electoral College, which elects the President of the United States. Furthermore, as an unincorporated territory, Guam falls under the plenary power or "full and complete legislative authority" of Congress as a result of Article IV, Section III, Clause II of the United States Constitution, also known as the Territorial Clause (Sparrow, 2006). Per the Insular Cases, Guam is considered "foreign in a domestic sense" to the American polity (*Downes v. Bidwell*, 1901). As former Governor of Guam, Joseph Ada (1989), wrote, "Guam is governed exclusively under rules designed at the height of imperial fever, at a time when some legal fiction was needed to justify the maintenance of war booty, to justify the rule of people in a condition similar to serfdom."

Demographically, as of 2010, Guam had a population of 159,358 people with indigenous CHamorus comprising only 37.1% of the total population (US Census Bureau, 2010). Intertwined with this political status and demographic situation, the island is also heavily militarized. The US military currently occupies roughly 27% of the island, which is a mere 32 miles long and 12 miles wide. There is a large air force base in the north (Andersen Air Force Base), a navy base in the south (Naval Base Guam), the continuing development of a new Marine Corps installation, a THAAD anti-missile defense system, and a naval ordnance annex all located on the island. Guam currently serves as a critical piece in US strategy and power-projection in the Indo-Pacific. Guam's role in maintaining American preponderance in this region has remained constant, and this is important to understand not only Guam's place in the world, but also CHamoru erasure. It is the entanglement of Guam's geographical location and political status that serves as the primary reason for US presence in the island. To put it another way, this is the key to erasure.

At first glance, Guam might not seem a good fit for settler colonial analysis. I argue that although not being a "textbook" settler colony, settler colonial theory helps to explain the processes of erasure accompanying political colonization and militarization. Settler colonialism refers to a "historically created system of power that aims to expropriate Indigenous territories and eliminate modes of production in order to replace Indigenous peoples with settlers who are discursively constituted as superior and thus more deserving over these contested lands and resources" (Saranillo, 2015, p. 284). In his article, "Settler Colonialism and the Elimination of the Native," Patrick Wolfe (2006) argues that territoriality is the driving force of settler colonialism and that "settler society required the practical elimination of the Natives in order to establish itself on their territory" (p. 389), thus making settler colonialism inherently eliminatory. Wolfe (2006) dubs this the "logic of elimination." Unlike traditional colonies, labor is not necessarily key in settler colonialism, land is. When looking at settler colonies around the world such as Hawai'i, Australia, the United States, or Canada, Guam has glaring differences. Unlike the situation of Indigenous peoples in the aforementioned examples, CHamorus still make up the largest portion of the population (even if only 37%) and still control the mechanisms of political power at the local territorial level. At the time of writing in 2021, CHamorus make up a majority of the senators in the Guam Legislature, comprise a majority of the Guam Supreme and Superior Court, and serve in the highest positions of the Guam Executive Branch, including the Governor, Lieutenant Governor, and most cabinet positions. Thus, one could argue that CHamorus have not been eliminated.

However, settler colonialism as an analytic is still relevant. As described by Lorenzo Veracini, "settler colonialism as paradigm emphasized circumstances primarily characterized by a determination to erase colonized subjectivities rather than reproduce their subordination" (Cavanagh & Veracini, 2017, p. 3). Furthermore, "The scholars contributing to settler colonial studies have emphasized the continuing operation of an unchanged set of unequal relations. Settler colonialism as a mode of domination, it was often noted, has typically resisted formal decolonization" (Cavanagh & Veracini, 2017, p. 3). Core characteristics of settler colonialism make it relevant to understanding the shape of colonialism in Guam today, such as the drive for territoriality and land, the continued operation of an unchanged set of unequal relations, and a determination to erase colonized subjectivities.

Destroy and Replace

The nature of the United States' relationship to Guam has been evident almost since the moment the former obtained the latter as a spoil of the Spanish-American War in 1898. The US military would subsequently establish a naval presence on the island, thus beginning the drive for territoriality and land that in part characterizes the dynamics of its settler colonialism in the region. During this period, the island was used as a coaling station with the highest-ranking naval officer serving as the governor of the island. Alfred Thayer Mahan, who served as president of the Naval War College, emphasized the importance of a strong naval capability if the United States wanted to scramble for the world's wealth. Mahan (2004) argued that permanent naval bases and coaling stations were crucial to safeguarding the national security of the United States and urged the country to shape a "healthy regional balance of power through forward basing, a strong navy and alignment among the maritime powers" (p. 3). In line with Mahan's strategic thinking, Guam was used as both a coaling station and a naval possession of the US military. While the United States would utilize Guam as a naval possession from 1899 to 1941, World War II and its aftermath served as a turning point in Guam's transformation. I argue that the physical destruction of the island, taking of CHamoru land, and subsequent emigration and immigration constitute three elements of material erasure after the war.

On December 8, 1941, the Japanese bombed Guam just 4 hours after they bombed Pearl Harbor in O'ahu. From December 1941 to July 1944, CHamorus suffered under brutal Japanese occupation that involved intense manual labor, rapes, beheadings, and massacres. In 1944, 3 years into the Japanese occupation, the United States returned to the island, eventually defeating the Japanese and re-establishing control over the island. This reoccupation and its subsequent consequences helped physically transform the island into its current status as a giant military base. As part of the US plan to retake the island from the Japanese, they engaged in heavy bombardment. As a result of this approach and the wider conflict, about 80% of the island's permanent structures were destroyed and the capital of Hagåtña was nearly completely bombarded into concrete rubble (Political Status Education Coordinating Commission, 1994). According to Guam historian Pedro Sanchez (1988), "Not a single dwelling remained in Asan, Piti, Agat, and Sumay, the pre-war hometowns of over 4,000 Chamorros" (p. 254).

During the remainder of the war and during the reconstruction of the island thereafter, the military engaged in rampant land takings. By 1946, over 200,000 military personnel were stationed in Guam, with only one-third of the land remaining in CHamoru hands. By 1947, 1,350 families had lost their lands to the military, with 11,000 of the 20,000 inhabitants in Hagåtña and Sumay alone being displaced and relocated. While CHamorus were not completely resistant to land being "temporarily" taken by the military for bases to finish the war, what angered them was the military taking of land for the construction of recreational facilities. As Anne Perez Hattori (2001) writes, "In Agaña, roughly five hundred people were displaced when eighty-two lots were condemned for a park and in Tamuning, sixty hectares of Tumon Beach were condemned for a military recreational center" (p. 190).

The war and these land takings did not just lead to the dispossession of CHamorus from their land, but also led to non-CHamorus becoming a majority of the population in two ways: CHamoru emigration and non-CHamoru immigration. With a significant amount of the land bombarded during the war, the prevalent pre-war CHamoru subsistence lifestyle was nearly impossible. In 1940, there were an estimated 2,747 CHamoru farmers in Guam, with the number dropping to a mere 311 by 1960 (del Valle, 1979). This violent interruption of CHamoru sustainability led many CHamorus to move to the United States for higher education, economic opportunities, and military service (Untalan, 2015). Furthermore, another impetus for emigration was the lifting of Guam' security clearance in 1962 along with the development of a tourism industry and the subsequent spike in CHamoru land sales as the commercial real estate market boomed. According to the decennial census there were 30,695 CHamorus in the United States in 1980, 49,345 in 1990, and around 97,000 in 2010. This continuous exodus reinforces Patrick Wolfe's (2006) argument that invasion is a structure, not an event. By this he means "elimination is an organizing principle of settler-colonial society rather than a one-off (and superseded) occurrence" (p. 388). Thus, one cannot just point to the battles of World War II to explain Guam's current ontology; one has to understand WWII as a structural condition of possibility for the transformation of the island. In a similar fashion, CHamoru erasure is a result of this entangled structure of postwar militarization and colonialism.

As CHamorus left, postwar Guam also saw the influx of non-CHamorus into the island. A large group of Filipinos was brought into Guam as "H-2 workers" for labor and construction detail. Before the war, there were only a few hundred Filipinos in Guam. However, by 1950, there were around 7,258, and as of 2010, there were 41,944 Filipinos, equivalent to 26% of Guam's population (Quan, 2014). There was also a large White population in Guam during the postwar era, many of them being transient personnel to fill positions in administration and education. In 1950, Whites comprised 39% of the population, though this number has dropped immensely since then. Fellow islanders from the rest of Micronesia also moved to Guam after the Compacts of Free Association, which allowed travel to and from United States soil without a visa, and these immigrants now make up around 12% of the population. This in itself is not problematic, but rather illustrative of the lack of control CHamorus had over what their island would become after the war, producing unequal relations between the Indigenous people of Guam and the US military when it came to subsequently making decisions affecting the island. Yet this lack of control did not mean lack of CHamoru resistance. When it came to the taking of land, for example, CHamorus made their voices heard. When representatives of the US Congress visited Guam in 1949, CHamorus such as Frank Perez testified how unfair the compensation process for the land was. Furthermore, the Guam Congress, which was only an advisory body, did everything within its power to help resolve the land issues, from holding conferences with naval officials, to asking for legal clarification and pushing for US citizenship to gain protection from unbridled power.

Overall, these changes would have lasting ramifications for the island. These events helped set the stage for the island's contemporary status as an American territory with heavy military presence. Changing the material realities of the island enabled other shapes of CHamoru erasure. Dean Saranillo (2015) argues that there is a "mutual relationship between the occupation of contested space and controlling the representation of this occupation" (p. 285). This section explores the former, while the next section explores the latter through an examination of the ways that settler colonialism has instrumentalized multicultural discourse (backed by the US legal system) to normalize the island's current conditions.

Lastly, it is important to note that I am not concerned with intent here. One might argue that the United States had a deliberate plan for CHamoru erasure and wanted to create a *terra nullius*[22] dream. One could also argue that CHamoru erasure was not an intent and that it was a side effect of all the elements of converting the island into a military base. Whether it was the intent of the United States or not, the fact is that the post-World War II militarization of the island helped to create the conditions of success for discursive CHamoru erasure in Guam today.

Erasure through "One Amongst Many"

In this section, I trace the ways that a particular form of multiculturalism has produced a "one amongst many" discourse in Guam. By "one amongst many," I refer to the idea that CHamorus are just like any other group in Guam, and attempts to honor their indigeneity is a threat to the multicultural fabric of Guam's community. In doing this, there is an erasure of their subjectivity as "colonized peoples" in favor of just being another group amongst many in the island. This, in turn, produces unequal relations as any claims towards justice can be thwarted in the US legal system. Multiculturalism, at its most basic level, can be defined as "the coexistence of people with many cultural identities in a common state, society, or community" (Oxford University Press, n.d.). Multiculturalism is often celebrated as a successful achievement of modern society and is presented as a victory against blatant racism. It has made its way into policy and academia, with goals such as multicultural education and keywords such as "diversity" being ubiquitous in corporate models. These basic definitions and concepts are not the cause of consternation in this piece. The presence of a diversity of cultures in Guam is not the cause of CHamoru erasure. CHamorus were able to co-exist with other ethnic groups throughout history without any serious threat to lina'la' CHamoru (CHamoru life). In the current political environment, it is intellectually lazy to conflate Indigenous critiques of multiculturalism with xenophobia or Trump-era anti-immigrant discourse, and it is my hope that this piece will help to distinguish these critiques from such xenophobic discourse. In making this distinction, I hope to underscore how settler colonial logics utilize the discourse of multiculturalism towards erasure that is the onus of concern here, and in doing so seek to erase indigeneity while maintaining unequal relations.

Elizabeth Povinelli (as cited in Saranillo, 2015) argues that "in modern liberal democratic societies, multiculturalism is a characteristic of settler colonialism" that often creates "the conditions under which indigenous peoples are forced into a politics of recognition and authenticity in order for their claims to not be disqualified" (p. 285). To put it another way, in order for Indigenous peoples to actually make claims, they often have to "prove" their authenticity or why they should be treated any differently (similar to how Native American tribes petitioning for federal recognition must submit paperwork showing cultural authenticity and continuity). This consistent requirement of "proving" facilitates projects of erasure: failing to prove authenticity can mean a rejection of either legal or discursive weight to their grievances, thus enforcing unequal relations between the US government and Indigenous peoples.

I argue that this exists in Guam today via a particular form of multiculturalism. As Michael Lujan Bevacqua and I (2016) argue regarding multiculturalism in Guam,

> Despite this emphasis on equality or diversity, in truth all cultures are supposed to respect and adhere to the dominance of a single, oftentimes invisible culture that will act as the mediator, telling each culture what it is allowed to practice and how much of its language should be spoken. This culture is dominant in the way it does not provide particularity to the multicultural matrix, but instead its particularity acts as the universal structure. (p. 262)

Thus, this understanding of multiculturalism is of a specific discourse that acts as an "assimilationist machine" serving the militarized, territorial needs of empire.

The danger of this circumstance is the subsequent minoritization of Indigenous peoples, or in Guam's case, the positioning of CHamorus as just one amongst many. Under this discourse, Indigenous peoples are presented as just another ethnic group or race within the multicultural fabric of society. The condition of possibility of erasure is the conflation of indigeneity with race or ethnicity. One of the most cited definitions of Indigenous peoples can be found in a 1986 U.N. study by Special Rapporteur Jose Martinez Cobo, where he defines Indigenous peoples as

> Indigenous communities, peoples and nations are those which, having a historical continuity with pre-invasion and pre-colonial societies that developed on their territories, consider themselves distinct from other sectors of the societies now prevailing in those territories or parts of them. They form at present non-dominant sectors of society and are determined to preserve, develop and transmit to future generations their ancestral territories, and their ethnic identity, as the basis of their continued existence as peoples, in accordance with their own cultural patterns, social institutions and legal systems.

Per this definition, Indigenous is two-pronged: a long-established deep connection to the land (predating historical displacement by other groups) and the existence of an unjust social relationship usually as a result of colonialism or current state repression—or both. Indigeneity is not race, and to conflate the two is to erase prospects for self-determination and sovereignty.

As Choctaw scholar Jodi Byrd (2011) writes on the role of minoritization, "Under this paradigm, American Indian national assertions of sovereignty, self-determination, and land rights disappear into US territoriality as indigenous identity becomes a racial identity and citizens of colonized indigenous nations become internal ethnic minorities within the colonizing nation-state" (p. xxvi). Byrd argues that when indigeneity becomes erased and Indigenous peoples are simply considered ethnic minorities, their claims to self-determination are essentially erased. In this framework, Indigenous peoples become just "one amongst many" ethnic groups in a particular place. Indigenous struggles for sovereignty and rights are too easily dismissed as either affirmative action policies or illegal, unfair practices.[23]

In Guam, one can find examples of this "one amongst many" discourse in which CHamorus are represented as just another ethnic group in the island. I provide two here. First, Dave Davis, introduced earlier, previously had a weekly column in the *Marianas Variety*, a newspaper he used as a platform for anti-CHamoru sentiments. In his anti-CHamoru writings, one catchphrase stands out: "Our Guam license plates carry a logo translated as 'Land of the Chamorro,' home to the ancient Chamorro it certainly was, but that was then and this is now" (Davis, 2011). While not directly stating "multiculturalism," his words would later come to life when he sued the Government of Guam due to what he considered to be CHamorus discriminating against non-CHamorus on the issue of the political status plebiscite.

Second, in March of 2015, fellow CHamoru scholar Michael Lujan Bevacqua and I organized "Ha'ånen Fino' Chamoru Ha'," a day in which we encouraged everyone to speak in the CHamoru language as much as possible regardless of where they were or what they were doing. There were close to 100 people who actively participated and wrote about their experiences. While this event was a great push for CHamoru language revitalization and led to many taking first steps to learn the language, the discursive power of the logics of erasure were still inescapable. In reflecting on their experiences of this event, some participants said they were harassed by non-CHamorus for speaking CHamoru to them. In one particular instance, a non-CHamoru waitress asked a CHamoru speaker ordering food, "Why are you speaking that language? I don't understand, this is America" (M. Bevacqua, personal communication, 2015). These examples display the friction and dissenting views on where the CHamoru people, language, and culture fit within Guam in this "modern time."

This discursive force of CHamoru erasure does not just stay in the realm of discourse. It also manifests itself through legal institutions and most recently in the *Davis v. Guam* lawsuit through the *instrumentalizing of individual voting rights and the invocation of civil rights*. Arnold "Dave" Davis is a White settler and retired Air Force officer. He attempted to register for the Decolonization Registry, which was a registry established by Guam Law 25-106, yet he was turned away because he did not meet the criteria of being a native inhabitant (Leon Guerrero, 2014). In 2011, Davis sued the Government of Guam, the Guam Election Commission and other related parties, reasoning that he was being discriminated against because of his inability to register for the Decolonization Registry and subsequently vote in the political status plebiscite. His attorneys argued that this was a violation of the Voting Rights Act, the Organic Act of Guam, and his Fifth, Fourteenth, and Fifteenth Amendment rights.

Breitbart, the news hub of the alt-right movement, ran a piece on the Davis case that stated, "Many of the territory's elected officials and anti-American activists are starting to resemble the unabashed segregationists of the Old South of the 1950s. Think of it as a Pacific Islander version of *Plessy vs. Ferguson*" (von Spakovsky & Clegg, 2017). The same lead author, in the conservative publication *National Review*, writes,

> To base decisions on your ancestry when parceling out political power is anathema to the 15th Amendment. It is the sort of vile evil that the Voting Rights Act of 1965 rooted out. But it is alive and well on Guam and will continue unless a federal judge finally acts to stop this modern, progressive "identity politics" version of Jim Crow discrimination. (von Spakovsky, 2016)

One can see settler colonial logics at work here in aiming to preserve unequal relations as a method of ensuring access to land (even if not the intention), in the form of retaining Guam's political status quo and the consequent military presence in the island. This is a completely dehistoricized argument that does not take into account Guam's complicated history, including the complete transformation of the island after the war and the lack of CHamoru sovereignty. Further, by enforcing settler colonial logics, CHamorus are positioned as "one amongst many" who want to disenfranchise others. CHamoru subjectivity as colonized people is erased in these narratives.

In laying bare the agenda of this lawsuit and countering this "Jim Crow" discourse, we find that *Davis v. Guam* fits within a history of "reverse discrimination" that is being used to thwart movements for Native, Black, and Latinx liberation. The boilerplate complaint is that White Americans are being discriminated against by any program that seeks to serve non-White communities (even if these programs are meant to right historical wrongs). This argument is strengthened when one looks at Davis' legal representation, most especially the Center for Individual Rights, which has helped dismantle affirmative action programs throughout US universities. For example, in 1999, "the Center for Individual Rights launched a national campaign urging students to sue their colleges for racial discrimination" (Flanders, 1999). Furthermore, according to the Center for Individual Rights (n.d.), they have "brought a series of high-profile cases designed to get the government out of the business of classifying citizens by race." The group calls this color-blindness. Color-blindness, often seen as the antithesis to multiculturalism, attempts to erase racial differences or celebration of these differences in favor of what advocates purport to be neutral treatment of all. Thus, both multiculturalism and color-blindness can be used towards Indigenous erasure, especially in the US legal system. The ties that bind them is the conflation of CHamoru indigeneity with a simple racial designation.

Judi Rohrer (2016) describes this particular use of the US legal system as a one-two punch against Indigenous peoples. The first punch is to problematize collective Native identity and the second punch is to naturalize White settler subjectivity via a color-blind ideology (Rohrer, 2016). Lawsuits such as Davis' serve as camouflaged attempts at usurping CHamoru self-determination. They present themselves as advocating for justice and equality while supporting the existence of colonial structures. As argued by Serrano (2018),

> This co-optation of civil rights tightly constrains the rights of Indigenous peoples. It does so in part by discounting the history of colonization—the confiscation of land, barring of language, suppression of identity, and loss of self-governance—and its harsh present-day consequences. Once stripped of this historical and modern-day context, "programs to uplift indigenous people in their homeland [are] recast as simply wrong-headed 'racial preferences.'"

> Politically, the success of these coordinated reverse-discrimination legal challenges ... threaten Indigenous efforts to restore a measure of self-determination and self-government. (p. 510)

This is by far the scariest component of the picture. When self-determination is wrongfully recast as just selfish racial preference, it can affect how others view the issue and lead to the continuation of unequal relations between CHamorus and the US military (via the US federal government) regarding the island's destiny. If CHamoru self-determination is wrongfully recast as an inherently "exclusionary" process, then the project of CHamoru erasure is easier to complete. Lastly, if this thought process and discourse is enforced via the power of the colonial legal system, then CHamoru erasure reaches a new pinnacle. Erasure can occur through the institutionalization of "equality" as seen in the Davis case. Davis would eventually go on to win his case, and sadly many in Guam were not surprised. We know that the US legal system is skewed against Indigenous peoples and unincorporated territories. This form of CHamoru erasure is perhaps the most expected.

The idea for this chapter came from asking myself two questions, "How does the inability of a White settler, retired Air Force officer, to participate in a vote meant to right the colonial wrongs of 400 years become conflated with the massive push by African Americans to rid the shackles of slavery and participate fully in the society they were forced to enter?" and "How does Guam history simply get erased to the point where CHamorus can be viewed as just another ethnic group in the island?" I use the guises of CHamoru erasure to better understand this. This erasure was built on a material, physical transformation after the war and gains its strength via a discourse of "one amongst many" which conflates indigeneity with race and enforced via lawfare in US legal institutions. Settler colonial theory is a useful analytical frame in understanding all this physiology of erasure. Ending here, however, leaves one unfulfilled and uncertain about the future. I turn to the final section for a glimpse of something different.

Paving Other Paths (Warning Beacons and New Relationalities)

It is my hope that this piece has two lasting effects. The first is to serve as a warning beacon to other Indigenous peoples. CHamoru erasure was not the result of a single event or policy. Erasure takes many forms including physical, discursive, and legal shapes, and many forms co-exist simultaneously. Thus, it is impossible to place blame on any single factor, and not every factor was deliberately deployed to erase CHamorus. In this chapter, I navigated the historical landscape from land-taking to community discourse to lawsuits. My experience is indicative of the multi-faceted work of tracking the elements of Indigenous erasure. Yet, the ramifications of failing to track the emerging shapes of erasure are too great for us to fail. Indigenous peoples must continue to work together on a multiscalar level (local, national, regional, and international level) to share their stories and warn others of the forms erasure took in their respective experiences, locales, and stories. Kanaka Maoli scholar, Noelani Goodyear Kaʻōpua (2013) describes Indigenous as a category of alliance. This alliance is critical, and I hope that the story of CHamoru erasure outlined here can strengthen these intra-Indigenous alliances.

The second hope I have for this piece is for it to serve as a discussion point for alternative forms of relationalities between CHamorus and non-CHamorus in Guam. *Davis v. Guam* has shown how there are some in Guam who look at CHamoru self-determination as a zero-sum endeavor. For them, for CHamorus to self-determine or for Guam to be decolonized, non-CHamorus must pay the costs. This manifests in various ways, with non-CHamorus arguing that decolonization leads to marginalization of non-CHamorus, or non-CHamorus being kicked off the island if Guam were to decolonize. There are ways to move beyond this zero-sum depiction of CHamoru self-determination, and I hope this piece becomes a part of that conversation. So, even if it will be hard to change the legal elements or overcome the physical transformation, I ponder what courses of action the community can take. To put it another way, is there a future for Guam in which CHamorus and non-CHamorus co-exist in an affirmative way that holds the unfinished quest of CHamoru self-determination as important? In many ways, this work has already begun.

On June 28, 2013, "Beyond the Fence," the local Public Radio Guam (KPRG) show, aired a very interesting episode. It was entitled, "Ep. 151 Guam Filipinos in Support of Chamorro Self-Determination." According to the program host, the goal of this particular show was to give airtime to those Filipinos who acknowledge they are not eligible to vote in a possible political status plebiscite in Guam, and yet are still supportive of Chamorro self-determination. The impetus for the show was the celebration of Araw ng Kasarinlan, or "Day of Freedom," where Filipinos celebrate the Philippine Declaration of Independence from Spain. This day is celebrated in Guam with various events held throughout the month allowing Filipinos to acknowledge their political independence. The program hosts wanted Filipinos to think of their role in relation to the CHamoru people and the CHamoru decolonization movements. When I first heard this particular program, I knew there was something special about it. The basic premise of this episode shows non-CHamorus being completely comfortable imagining a future for the island that does not neatly fit within the political family of "America." Furthermore, the guests were unabashedly vocal that as non-CHamorus they would not be voting in the political status plebiscite and that they completely understood why. They were the antidote to the Davis poison.

Critical conversations between CHamorus and non-CHamorus on their respectful responsibilities need to continue, and to be amplified and multiplied. Now more than ever, we need new ways of connecting to one another. As Dean Saranillo (2015) notes,

> By taking seriously Indigenous knowledges and economies, we can create another future, and in the creation of an alternative future, more space for mutual respect can occur. Settler states have no interests in non-Natives identifying with Native movements, as such identification opens our world to alternatives that the settler state denies are possible. (p. 204)

As CHamoru self-determination still needs to be exercised, we have two futures ahead of us. The first is a continuation and exacerbation of CHamoru erasure; the second is a decolonial future of new relations amongst CHamorus and non-CHamorus in Guam. May this piece serve as one push towards the latter. Erasure is not an acceptable outcome in the land of the CHamoru people. I write this piece as one instrument of my resistance. As the visual expression of an aggressive call from a mountaintop. A voice yelling, Ti Siña Ma Funas Ham. "They Cannot Erase Us."

References

Ada, J. F. (1989). Statement of Gov. Joseph F. Ada, Chairman, Guam Commission on Self-Determination. In *H.R. 98 Guam Commonwealth Act. Hearing before the US House of Representatives Committee on Interior and Insular Affairs.* (p. 85). 101st Congress, Honolulu, December 11, 1989.

Aguon, J. (2014). Our stories are maps larger than can be held: Self-determination and the normative force of law at the periphery of American expansionism. In A. Goldstein (Ed.), *Formations of United States colonialism* (pp. 265–288). Duke University Press.

Bevacqua, M. L., & Kuper, K. (2016). Gefpa'go na dinagi: Decolonization and the CHamoru language of Guam. In M. Ishihara, E. Hoshino, & Y. Fujita (Eds.), *Self-determinable development of small islands* (pp. 253–267). Springer Press.

Byrd, J. (2011). *The transit of empire: Indigenous critiques of colonialism.* University of Minnesota Press.

Cavanagh, E., & Veracini, L. (2017). *The Routledge handbook of the history of settler colonialism.* Routledge Handbooks.

Center for Individual Rights. (n.d.). *Mission.* https://www.cir-usa.org/mission/

Cobo, J. (1986). "Study on the problem of discrimination against Indigenous populations." United Nations. https://digitallibrary.un.org/record/133666?ln=en

Coulthard, G. (2014). *Red skin, white masks: Rejecting the colonial politics of recognition.* University of Minnesota Press.

Davis, D. (2011, November 29). Letter to the editor: The winds of change on Guam. *Marianas Variety.* https://mvariety.com/views/letters_to_editor/letter-to-the-editor-the-winds-of-change-on-guam/article_00efe01d-4ec7-55d6-b7e3-73c402b0231c.html

Davis v. Guam, No. 1:2011cv00035 (D. Gu. 2017). https://law.justia.com/cases/federal/district-courts/guam/gudce/1:2011cv00035/8773/149/

del Valle, T. (1979). *Social and cultural change in the community of Umatac, southern Guam.* Micronesian Area Research Center.

Downes v. Bidwell, 182 US 244 (1901). https://supreme.justia.com/cases/federal/us/182/244/

Flanders, L. (1999). Affirmative racism. *The Nation.* https://www.thenation.com/article/archive/affirmative-racism/

Goodyear Ka'ōpua, N. (2013). *The seeds we planted: Portraits of a native Hawaiian charter school.* University of Minnesota Press.

Hattori, A. (2001). Guardians of our soil: Indigenous responses to Post-World War II military land appropriation in Guam. In L. E. Armentraut Ma (Ed.), *Farms, firms, & runways: Perspectives on US military bases in the Western Pacific* (pp. 186–202). Imprint Publications.

Kauanui, K. (2008). Colonialism in equality: Hawaiian sovereignty and the question of US civil rights. *South Atlantic Quarterly, 107*(4), 635–650.

Leon Guerrero, V. (2014). CHamoru registry and the decolonization registry. In *Guampedia.* https://www.guampedia.com/chamorro-registry-and-the-decolonization-registry/

Mahan, A. (2004). *The influence of sea power upon history 1660–1783.* Little Brown.

Oxford University Press. (n.d.). Multiculturalism. In *Oxford Reference.* https://www.oxfordreference.com/view/10.1093/oi/authority.20110810105436897

Political Status Education Coordination Commission. (1994). *Hale'-ta: I ma gobetna-ña Guam*, Political Status Education Coordination Commission.

Quan, C. (2014). Filipinos on Guam. In *Guampedia.* http://www.guampedia.com/filipinos-on-guam/

Rohrer, J. (2016). *Staking claim: Settler colonialism and racialization in Hawai'i.* University of Arizona Press.

Sanchez, P. (1988). *Guahan Guam: The history of our island.* Sanchez Publishing House.

Sarantillo, D. (2015). Settler colonialism. In S. N. Teves, A. Smith, & M. Raheja (Eds.), *Native studies keywords* (pp. 284–300). University of Arizona Press.

Serrano, S. (2018). A reparative justice approach to assessing ancestral classifications aimed at colonization's harms. *William & Mary Bill of Rights Journal, 27*(2), 501–537. https://scholarship.law.wm.edu/wmborj/vol27/iss2/6

Sparrow, B. (2006). *The insular cases and the emergence of American empire.* University Press of Kansas.

Untalan, F. (2015). CHamoru migration to the US. In *Guampedia.* https://www.guampedia.com/chamorro-migration-to-the-u-s/

US Census Bureau. (2010). *2010 island areas—Guam data set*. https://www.census.gov/data/datasets/2010/dec/guam.html

Von Spakovsky, H. (2016). Jim Crow rears its ugly head in guam. *National Review*. http://www.nationalreview.com/article/439477/guam-voters-face-race-based-discrimination-reminiscent-jim-crow

Von Spakovsky, H., & Clegg, R. (2017). Guam is recreating the old segregationist South. *Breitbart*. http://www.breitbart.com/national-security/2017/03/27/guam-recreating-old-segregationist-south/

Wolfe, P. (2006.) Settler colonialism and the elimination of the native. *Journal of Genocide Research, 8*(4), 387–409.

Language Change in Saipan: Attitudes and Visions

Dominique B. Hess

Saipan has experienced several foreign administrations over the past centuries: the Spanish, German, Japanese, and finally the United States after World War II. Amongst the many consequences of these political changes, these administrations brought their own language to Saipan so that the island has been in close contact with different languages for almost 350 years. Each of these foreign languages has left its mark on the local languages at different linguistic and social levels. Here we examine the influence of English on the local community in Saipan and its emergence as the dominant language on the island. Moreover, local Chamorro and Carolinian speakers contribute their own perspectives towards the current language situation and their visions for Saipan's linguistic future. The data used for this chapter are taken from recorded conversations with the local community—a linguistic corpus (a collection of written and spoken texts) collected in June-August 2015 containing 95 sociolinguistic interviews with Indigenous Chamorros and Carolinians ranging in age from 12-79 years.[24]

Although different dialects of English were used by whalers, beachcombers, traders and missionaries in the 19th century, the first significant incursion of English into the Saipan community was when the Americans started administering the Northern Mariana Islands in 1944. English started to be taught in school and was, and often still is, seen as the language of educational possibilities, success, Westernization, and access to a "New World." According to a middle-aged male Chamorro speaker, Sa47m34[25], "[t]he English language is the most important around the world. It's the first language that people should [use to] communicate around the world because if we don't communicate [in] English … how can we communicate?" Parents believe that English is the key to giving their children the best possible future, and thus often speak English at home and use the local languages less frequently. Consequently, the emergence of English as a first language has been observed over the years. A generational shift has been taking place, which has resulted in the younger generation speaking mostly in English with only a few of the younger population in Saipan still speaking in their Native tongue. In fact, English is used equally or more often than other languages at home by 59% of the population, whereas only 22% of the population speak Chamorro and 5.6% Carolinian at home (CNMI Department of Commerce, 2010, pp. 181–86).[26] Other intertwined and complex factors influence the use of the English language: in particular, global movement has had a great impact on the language situation in Saipan.

Global Movement and Saipan

Global movement, in this chapter, is understood as human mobility into and out of Saipan. Immigration—inward mobility—occurred as many guest workers entered Saipan during the economic boom in the 1980s and 1990s when the garment factories flourished (Farrell, 1991, pp. 648–649). Saipan turned into a multicultural island. Japanese investors realized the opportunity for a holiday destination and invested in tourism, resulting in the construction of hotels, restaurants, golf courses, scuba-diving shops, and nightclubs, among many other recreational facilities. According to Quimby (2016), 75% of the tourists (736,177) were Japanese. Due to the lax immigration and labor regulations, as well as the business-friendly wage laws in the CNMI, many guest workers made Saipan their home: Chinese workers were primarily employed in the garment industry, Filipino workers in the tourism sector, and only a small number of Chinese and Filipinos were employed in the construction sector and private households (Farrell, 1991, pp. 648–649; Quimby, 2016). Even as

Saipan experienced an economic and tourism decline after 2000 and many immigrants returned to their homelands, many long-term guest workers stayed in Saipan. Moreover, due to new visa (Guam-CNMI Visa Waiver Program 2009) and airline agreements (direct flights from Seoul as of 2006), tourism from Russia and South Korea has been increasing, with Korea now one of the leading source markets for the CNMI today (Camacho, 2015; US Customs and Border Protection, 2012; Horwath HTL, 2017). Since 2012, there has also been a large increase in Chinese tourists and immigrants. According to Horwath HTL (2017), "[a]s of the end of 2014, China took over as the largest source market for the CNMI, accounting for 37% of total arrivals, replacing the historically dominant player, Japan" (p. 9).

Today, only 27% of the Saipan population are Indigenous Chamorros and Carolinians, and the rest (73%) of the population are non-local: 36% Filipinos, 7% Chinese, 5% Koreans, and 12% who have two or more ethnic origins, among many other ethnicities that are represented in the CNMI to a smaller extent (CNMI Department of Commerce, 2010, p. 41). The considerable number of immigrants and tourists in the CNMI has had a significant impact on contemporary language use. The increase in multiculturalism in Saipan has resulted in English being used more and more as the lingua franca.[27] Topping (2003) nicely describes the language contact situation as follows:

> In the Marianas, Chamorros talk to their Filipina maids in English. The maids talk to the children in English. The children talk to the Korean or Chinese shopkeepers in English. Japanese hotel managers on Guam and Saipan talk to Palauan desk clerks in English. And so on. (p. 523)

Due to the economic downturn, starting in the late 1990s and lasting for about a decade, many foreign workers and permanent residents left the island, and the population of the CNMI fell by 22% between 2002 and 2010 (Quimby, 2016). Despite this mass emigration, the language situation did not change: children who had grown accustomed to using English at home continue this practice today.

Outward mobility surged, as many local people took the opportunity to go to the US mainland. People mostly left for educational and work reasons, but also because of family responsibilities or medical treatment. People who have spent several years abroad, quite naturally, have accommodated[28] their English to the English varieties spoken in North America and often speak English as a first language. McPhetres (1992) comments thus on the outward mobility and its effect on the languages:

> Perhaps as many Chamorros are living in the US mainland as in the islands. This out migration, particularly to Southern California, is fast assimilating Chamorros into American culture. In fact, most educated (high school and college) Chamorros speak English to their children at home because this will help them to get ahead. In many cases, Chamorro is spoken only in anger or chastisement of the children. This is happening in the Marianas as well. A growing number of local children are growing up with the idea that English is their first language and Chamorro is something to swear in. (p. 263)

Clearly, people who have spent time in the US mainland are influenced by the English dialects spoken there and are most likely to use English as their first language. In some, if not most, cases this also holds true for families in the CNMI. A middle-aged female Carolinian speaker, Sa54f43, confirms the language change in the CNMI after returning from Hawai'i, where she lived for 9 years: "Saipan has changed quite a lot. It's more Americanized than when I first left. It may be a Carolinian house, a Chamorro house or even a Filipino or Chinese house, and they speak English."

Furthermore, the influx of modern technology has also augmented the dominant status of English on the island. Topping (1985) notes that "English is used in all radio and TV broadcasting, local newspapers, and government publications" in the CNMI (p. 128). Studies have demonstrated that media exposure leads to incidental foreign language acquisition (Kuppens, 2010), an important consideration in the case of Saipan when initially media only existed in the English language. Media, including TV programs and commercials, are one of the strongest influences on the dominance of English (Topping, 2003, p. 523). A young Chamorro speaker, Sa18m22, explains the supremacy of English in the media: "kids are not going to sit there and watch the older local figures speak about politics in a language that they don't completely understand ... they're going to gravitate towards what's funny what's more interesting and ... that's Western culture." Shigemoto (1997) was concerned about the decline of the use of local languages and argued that the impact of American mass media is noticeable on the island and that elements of the Western culture advance into local culture: "[M]ass media are damaging to local languages because they have displaced traditional pastimes, such as engaging in local crafts like canoe-building or listening to stories, which are transmitted through the indigenous languages" (p. 5). Her concern is still valid today as the use of English has gained even greater popularity. Since 2014, a 3G network has been available in Saipan and connects the island to the rest of the world (Bagnol, 2014). The use of English has expanded via the internet, including social media like Facebook, YouTube, Twitter, Instagram, and Netflix, and dominates all other languages. A 17-year-old teenage Carolinian girl, Sa09f17, confirmed the predominant usage of English. When I asked her "what about on Facebook, is it all in English or do you use Carolinian?" she answered, "no, it's all in English." Hence, even people who have not been physically mobile in their lives now have a high exposure to English spoken as a native language through various types of media, which impacts their English language use remarkably.

Due to this constant exposure to English over time, and especially since the late 1960s when the Peace Corps[29] started to arrive in Micronesia and the contact possibilities between the local community and Americans increased (cf. Farrell, 1991, pp. 556–557), English is spoken in everyday life on the island.

Consequences of Globalization & the Emergence of English as a Dominant Language
The consequences of globalization, and especially global movement to and away from Saipan, as well as the emergence of English as a dominant language, have led to social changes on the island. With the many long-term contract workers residing in Saipan, the island society is increasingly multicultural. People of different ethnic backgrounds live alongside each other and communicate, most typically through English. The tension of *diversity versus unity* emerges and the question arises of how traditional cultures and languages can survive in the future in such a context. An elderly Chamorro woman, Sa62f73, clearly advocates cultural diversity and uses the beautiful metaphor of a salad to describe the multicultural situation in Saipan:

> I look at it more of a salad. Yeah, that each of us, I'm a Chamorro, you are from Switzerland, but we're all islanders, you know, we're all Saipanese, we're all here trying to make this island the best island. We're not here to make it a little Philippine and we're not here to make it a little Korea, we're not here to make it a little China and a little, you know, we're here to make a nice island, yeah. But see being a salad, I don't like to make it a melting pot because you lose your identity. I don't want you to lose your identity. You should have them because that's what brings the richness and when you eat a salad each of them has some different taste.

This attitude of celebrating the existing cultural diversity in Saipan clearly is in place and was observed for example during the Liberation Day Festivities in 2015 with the slogan "Peace in Diversity." Nevertheless, the population of Saipan presents a unity towards the outside and manages to overcome cultural tensions with a united language—the English language.

Some speakers are aware of the fact that for them English is more easily accessible than their local language. Sa79f24 states, "I mean sometimes like, I would tell them like I am proud of who I am but sometimes it's easier for me to communicate in English than it is to communicate in Carolinian." The younger generation especially faces the challenge of being bilingual if not trilingual in Saipan and trying to remain conversant in their local language. Sometimes if they do, however, they are made fun of by their parents, as this young Carolinian girl, Sa09f17, stated: "[Y]eah [my parents] would just look at me and give me some weird look where they're like, 'why you speaking to me like that [in Carolinian]?'" Not surprisingly, the younger generation, conversely, do ridicule their parents too when speaking in the local language, as this middle-aged woman, Sa74f35, revealed: "[M]y kids make fun of my language, it's mostly English." The young Carolinian confirms that the language most often used at home is English and is no longer the local language, as already discussed above. Clearly, this issue of choosing English over the local languages is unidirectional. Whatever reasons exist, English is the more frequently spoken language inside and outside the home in local families, and consequently, it has become the easier language to communicate in for some, and thus has emerged and been accepted as the lingua franca in the community. Therefore, the question arises of what the future of Saipan's multilingual language situation might hold and what visions the local people of Saipan have for their island.

Language Vision

The future of the language situation in Saipan is uncertain. According to Jourdan and Salaün (2013), "[t]wo levels of linguistic tensions appear. First that which opposes language unity vs. language diversity; young multilingual countries need language unity to build a country out of diversity. Second that which opposes powerful international languages vs. small local languages" (p. 214). Good reasons clearly exist why English as a shared language has emerged in the CNMI. As discussed earlier, some local people strongly believe that English is going to be the only language spoken on the island in the future. "I think in their [the younger] generation Carolinian is going to erase. Everything is all English," said Sa74f35.³⁰

On the other hand, there are people who have a vision of a multilingual Saipan. They advocate for diversity and support the local languages with school and cultural programs. Children attend Chamorro or Carolinian Language Heritage Studies (CCLHS) during school; to celebrate, recognize, and promote Chamorro and Saipan Carolinian heritage, the month of September is the annual Cultural Heritage Month in Saipan, that promotes traditional dances, art, and cooking among much more (cf. Encinares, 2016). People want, furthermore, to promote Saipan's cultural and linguistic diversity in the education system. Sa62f73 said, "On Saipan I'm not so sure a bilingual approach is appropriate at this time; I think it's more of a multicultural and a multilingual approach—not [a] bilingual anymore." This is demonstrated in the offer of various clubs in schools that promote cultural diversity, such as the Polksai Chamorro Club, the Refaluwasch Culture Club³¹, the Filipino Club, or the Japanese Club (Marianas High School, 2021).

These tensions between language unity vs. diversity and global vs. local languages contribute to language maintenance or language shift. Principal factors for language maintenance or shift include "individual, family, community, and broader societal factors" (Potowski, 2013, p. 322). On an individual level, if an intrinsic motivation for learning and speaking the local languages by young speakers exists, such as by this young Chamorro girl, Sa40f14, who stated "English is the main language here especially in public but I like speaking Chamorro, it's fun," then the survival of the local languages being spoken on the island may be prolonged. Favoring bilingualism or multilingualism and having a positive attitude towards the heritage language is one step in the direction of language maintenance. For language maintenance to succeed, however, more is needed than a positive attitude (Potowski, 2013, p. 323). Fishman (2013) insists on the importance of transmitting a language from one generation to the next and understanding how this transmission is shaped socioculturally, as a result of social, economic, and political experiences (pp. 468–469).

The Indigenous languages spoken in Saipan are currently in a transitional phase and are experiencing language shift. Ellis (2012) mentions two developments and suggests that Chamorro and Carolinian are evolving into contemporary forms of the local languages or a local variety of English, or both:

> A document prepared for the CNMI State Education Agency Program (Buckley 1991) arrived at the conclusion that many indigenous children on Saipan were, or were soon becoming, "semi-lingual" — they were not fluent in any language. ... The following year I suggested in a research proposal to the Public School System (Ellis 1992) that Saipan children were not "semi-lingual." Rather, they were speaking a "transitional" form of Chamorro or SpnCRL [Saipan Carolinian] moving towards either "a contemporary form of Chamorro/Carolinian" or "a localized style of English," and sometimes both. (pp. 352–353)

Which direction the Indigenous languages will be taking, however, is still uncertain. From the conversations I had with members of the local community during my fieldwork and from the perspective of my research, I can only comment on the emergence of a local variety of English (cf. Hess, in press). The English spoken in Saipan is indeed developing its own character. The localized style of English, however, is socially conditioned by, for example, whether local speakers have positive attitudes towards the English language, have spent several years abroad in the US mainland, what educational background speakers have had, or their level of exposure to English media. One possible vision for the language outcome is the mixing of English and the Native languages. This mixing of languages is slowly but surely occurring among the younger generation, as a middle-aged female speaker, Sa54f43, explains that "The English language also is added into the speech of our young ones. It's really, really funny sometimes when you, when you're talking to them because they're using Chamorro, English and Carolinian in one sentence, you know. Yeah, they're mixing it all up." A young Carolinian girl, Sa79f24, also commented on the mixing of the languages and called it the "Saipanese way." She states,

> I have some co-workers you know they're like local too so like we speak this, uhm, local English and I don't know if you ever heard of it. It's like where we mix like our local words and English like I don't know it's confusing ... It's English but then it's just like the local way of talking English that's how I'd say it the Saipanese way.

In this sense, the people of Saipan try to make the English language their own and adapt it into their specific culture to fit its purpose for the local community. The English spoken in Saipan is "Saipanese English" and has its own distinctive local "flavor" to it.

Clearly, languages are dynamic and ever-changing. Saipan has been in close contact with different languages since the Spanish first set foot on the island, and its languages continued to be impacted by the languages of the different administrations, by the languages chosen for education, by globalization and especially global movement into and out of Saipan, as well as media exposure nowadays. This has had a considerable effect on the language situation in Saipan, whereby the English language has become more and more the dominant language both inside and outside of the home. Linguistic visions of English being the dominant language exist alongside efforts at promoting the local languages. Currently, the local languages and English are in a transitional phase and are undergoing language change. It is hard to predict what path a language, or in this case languages, is taking; however, the vision of a "Saipanese way" of speaking English, a localized variety of English, may be a reality very soon. Languages are what people make of them, shaping them in a way that reflects their history and their identity. We can only speculate on the future of the languages spoken in Saipan, their ongoing development, their maintenance, shift or loss, or their spread to speakers of other ethnicities and, thus, who will be speaking them in the future.

References

Bagnol, R. C. (2014, July 10). Docomo Pacific launches 3G network on Saipan. *Marianas Variety*. http://www.mvariety.com/advertising/special-advertising-feature-2/67125-docomo-pacific-launches-3g-network-on-saipan

Buckley, D. (1991). *SEA program director report, ms*. CNMI Public School System.

Camacho, J. (2015, February 27). MVA looks to Russia market's rebound. *Saipan Tribune*. http://www.saipantribune.com/index.php/mva-looks-russia-markets-rebound/

CNMI Department of Commerce. (2010). *2010 census demographics profile summary Saipan village tables*. http://i2i042u7ucg3bwn5b3lofquc.wpengine.netdna-cdn.com/wp-content/uploads/2012/12/2010-Census-Demographics-Profile-Summary-Saipan-Village-Tables.pdf

Ellis, J. S. (1992). *Proposal for CNMI PSS language research*. CNMI Public School System.

Ellis, J. S. (2012). *Saipan Carolinian, one Chuukic language blended from many* [Doctoral dissertation, University of Hawaii at Manoa]. http://www.ling.hawaii.edu/graduate/Dissertations/JimEllisFinal.pdf

Ellis, J. S. (2016). The brief existence of Saipan Carolinian: A study of a vanishing language storing valuable linguistic and historical insights on the tongue of its speakers. In L. Filipović, & M. Pütz (Eds.), *Endangered languages and languages in danger* (pp. 171–202). John Benjamins Publishing Company.

Encinares, E. (2016, August 30). September proclaimed cultural heritage month. *Saipan Tribune*. http://www.saipantribune.com/index.php/september-proclaimed-cultural-heritage-month/

Farrell, D. A. (1991). *History of the Northern Mariana Islands*. CNMI Public School System.

Firth, A. (1996). The discursive accomplishment of normality: On 'lingua franca' English and conversational analysis. *Journal of Pragmatics, 26*(2), 237–59.

Fishman, J. A. (2013). Language maintenance, language shift, and reversing language shift. In T. K. Bhatia, & W. C. Richtie (Eds.), *The handbook of bilingualism and multilingualism* (3rd ed., pp. 466–94). Blackwell Publishing Ltd.

Hess, D. B. (in press). *Saipanese English: Local and global sociolinguistic trends*. Manuscript submitted for publication. John Benjamins Publishing Company.

Horwath HTL. (2017). Tourism development in the US Commonwealth of the Northern Mariana Islands. https://drive.google.com/file/d/1WBM9XQtTyqSm_2VvCp5T8CyxT_IHhQkz/view

Jourdan, C., & Salaün, M. (2013). Vernacular and culturally based education in Oceania today: Articulating global, national and local agendas. *Current Issues in Language Planning, 14*(2), 205–16.

Kuehling, S. (2012). Carolinians in Saipan: Shared sensations and subtle voices. *Pacific Studies, 35*(1–2), 44–89.

Kuppens, A. H. (2010). Incidental foreign language acquisition from media exposure. *Learning, Media and Technology, 35*(1), 65–85.

Marianas High School. (2021). *Student council: Marianas High School, school year 2021-2022 clubs*. https://www.marianashighschool.com/stuco-page

McPhetres, S. F. (1992). Elements of social change in the contemporary Northern Mariana Islands. In A.B. Robillard (Ed.), *Social change in the Pacific Islands* (pp. 241–63). Kegan Paul International.

Potowski, K. (2013). Language maintenance and shift. In R. Bayley, R. Cameron, & C. Lucas (Eds.), *The Oxford handbook of sociolinguistics* (pp. 321–339). Oxford University Press.

Quimby, F. (2016). Northern Mariana Islands. In S. Levine (Ed.), *Pacific ways: Government and politics in the Pacific Islands* (2nd ed.). Victoria University Press.

Shigemoto, J. (1997). *Language change and language planning and policy*. Pacific Resources for Education and Learning (PREL Briefing Paper). http://prel.org/

Topping, D. M. (1985). Review of US language policy in the TTPI. In K. Knudsen (Ed.), *History of the Trust Territory of the Pacific Islands: Proceedings of the ninth annual Pacific Islands conference* (pp. 105–32). Pacific Islands Studies Program, Center for Asian and Pacific Studies, University of Hawaii at Manoa.

Topping, D. M. (2003). Saviors of languages: Who will be the real messiah? *Oceanic Linguistics, 42*(2), 522–27.

US Customs and Border Protection. (2012, January 26). *Russian citizens now eligible to travel to Guam visa-free*. https://www.cbp.gov/newsroom/national-media-release/russian-citizens-now-eligible-travel-guam-visa-free

What Saved Me

Victoria-Lola M. Leon Guerrero

Author Note: While this essay is based on real events, some names were changed.

When I was five, I would venture outside every evening at six. We had a big kamachili tree in our front yard, and I would run to it, excited to play with my "friends" as I had called them. I remember the scene—the red-orange hue of the sky as the last rays of sun peaked through the tree's canopy and the mystic glow around me. It was magical. My favorite time of day. Until my mom realized what I had been doing.

"Toya, come back inside. It's after six," she said quietly, bending down to take my hands and pull me up. "You know the taotaomo'na come out at six. You're not supposed to be out here."

I quietly followed her into the house, feeling a deep sadness as I looked back to the tree. The next day, ignoring what my mom had said, I made for the door at sunset, but this time, my mom followed quickly.

"Where are you going, Toya? It's six. It's time to stay inside. Come help me in the kitchen."
"But Mama, my friends are going to miss me."
"What friends?"
"My friends at the kamachili tree. They're calling me outside to play."
"No, Toya, it's not time to play anymore. Let's go finish making dinner."

As I followed my mom to the kitchen, my ears started ringing and an intense heat coursed through my body. I stopped walking. "Mama," I said, "I don't feel good."

"Oh Toya, you're so pale!" my mom exclaimed when she turned to look at me. She felt my forehead and said I was burning up. She carried me into my room, placed me on my bed and told me to rest while she got me some water and medicine. I fell into a deep sleep. The next morning, my fever was gone, but my mom kept me home from school. She watched me closely all day, but I was perfectly healthy.

"Mama, can I go outside?" I asked while standing at the screen door staring at the kamachili tree.
"No, Toya, it's getting late."
"Please mama," I pleaded.
"No."

I made my way to the living room, and my ears started to ring again. I collapsed onto the couch and began to sob.

"What's wrong?" My mom asked, rushing over.
"I don't feel good, mama."
"Oh, baby, you're burning up again. I'm going to take you to the doctor."

When we got to the clinic, the doctor in urgent care could not figure out why my fever was so high. He sent us back home and told me to rest and drink a lot of water. My mom called my grandma, and she instantly knew what was wrong.

"They're making her sick," she told my mom, "because you're keeping her away from them. I'll call Maman Rosa."

Grandma Chilang's cousin Maman Rosa was a suruhåna, a traditional healer, and grandma always called her when she was sick. She would bring åmot—dark brown teas, leaves, roots, bottles of oil, whatever the sickness called for. Grandma told her what was happening to me, and she said she would meet us the next day at 6 p.m. under the kamachili tree.

I stayed home from school again and was feeling well the entire day. At 5:45 that evening, my mom and I went outside to sit with grandma in front of the house and wait for Maman Rosa. She arrived just before six with a bottle of oil and a bundle of dried palm leaves that had been blessed at the church on Palm Sunday. We all headed to the tree. Feeling free again, I started to run ahead of them.

"Slow down, Toya. Come back," my mom called after me.
"Polu ha'," Maman Rosa said, telling my mom to let me go.

Maman Rosa placed a woven mat on the earth beneath the tree and called me to lie down. She placed my head in her lap and gently massaged oil into my temples and between my eyes. Then she softly closed my eyes, removed my head from her lap and placed it on the mat. I felt a stillness in the air, and the evening bustle of the chickens and dogs in our yard started to fade. First I could smell flowers. Musky ylang ylang wafted above me followed by the thick scent of smoke coming in and out of my nostrils. I opened my eyes to see Maman Rosa walking around me. She had lit the tips of the palm leaves with fire and held the bundle together like a wand that she moved in circular motions above my body and up toward the tree, creating patterns of smoke. Her lips moved quickly as she chanted prayers in CHamoru. I closed my eyes again and must have drifted off to sleep, because the next thing I remember was being lifted to sit up and Maman Rosa placing the crucifix at the end of her rosary beads in between my eyes, to my lips for me to kiss and then to my heart.

"Maolek," she said. "Sen malak na palao'an hao."

She pulled me into a deep embrace and sniffed the top of my head. My mom also gave me a hug, and my grandma told me that everything was going to be OK. Maman Rosa started talking to them in CHamoru, explaining that there were spirits in the tree who had taken a liking to me. Some of them were children themselves, and they had just wanted to play. She said I was a very bright child, and they had been calling me to them for a while. It was only because my mom had been keeping me from them that they were making me sick. She had used the palm leaves to bless the area and said I would not be bothered anymore.

"They're not bad spirits," I remember my grandma saying. "They just really like you. But you cannot live in their world, because we need you here."

I never had a sense that the taotaomo'na were bad. I knew they were the spirits of my ancestors. Like me, they enjoyed the beauty of our island, and they liked to have fun outside. But after getting sick, I was more cautious. When I would go outside at night, I would be very quick and quiet. If I had to throw out the trash or take clothes from the line and the sun was already down, I would rush to complete my chore and dash back into the house. It was not exactly fear, as much as respect for their time and space. I did not want to intrude. As I got older, I learned how to recognize their presence and show respect without having to flee. When a sudden wind would rustle the dried leaves in the jungle, or the scent of ylang ylang would waft by my nose at night, or a feeling deep in the pit of my stomach would stop me in my tracks as I crossed certain trees, I knew they were there. And I would just offer a little prayer, send them love and carry on.

In my family there are many taotaomo'na stories, and often when someone falls ill or is the victim of an unexpected or early death, there is always a theory that connects their misfortune to having been disrespectful to the taotaomo'na. In one of the worst accidents of our family's history, my Uncle Billy fell from the second story balcony of his home while peeing over the ledge in the middle of the night. My grandpa's sister strongly believes that he was knocked over by a taotaomo'na, who had been passing through the jungle surrounding the house at that very moment. She said the house was on the path that the spirits traveled to get from the jungle to the ocean and back, and that as they were returning to the jungle, he must have accidentally peed on one of them, upsetting the taotaomo'na enough to push him off. My beloved uncle did not survive that fall, and after his death the house had to be blessed with holy water from the Catholic Church to ensure his spirit would be set free. Just a few feet away from where he landed, there is a shrine to the Virgin Mary.

This juxtaposition of faith—our Indigenous belief in ancestral veneration and our Catholic belief in God and Mother Mary—was how I had come to know spirituality. I was taught to ask permission from my ancestors before entering the jungle, and told to wear religious medals to keep bad spirits away. But as I grew older, I often found myself caught in the middle of these two worlds, trying to find exactly where I fit and wondering what to believe.

When I was pregnant with my first child, my family scolded me because I broke all the rules. Pregnant women are not supposed to go into the jungle or areas where there is a high concentration of taotaomo'na. But I had gone hiking to the ancient village of Pågat and walked in the jungles of Luta, singing love songs and visiting latte. My friends in Luta taught me how to protect my womb with lada' leaves from the noni tree. I had always asked for permission and followed my instincts, but it did not matter. I should not have been there in the first place, my parents would tell me. They said I traveled too much while I was pregnant. I flew to Saipan and Tinian, to Japan and Okinawa. My cousin said I was "too active" and should not have raised my voice so passionately when I was protesting the prospect of a firing range at Pågat. Driven by the life growing inside of me, I believed that I could not be silent about injustice, because I was becoming a mother.

I carried my son safely in my womb until he was born, but when he entered this world, I could not protect him any longer. He was born with a birth defect and was rushed away from me and into an operating room. After surviving four hours of surgery and then four more hours fighting for his life, Sai died in my arms. It was by far the worst tragedy of my life. I had never felt so lost. So trapped in my fears. So guilty. I had become unrecognizable in my grief, and my family was deeply worried. They feared I had upset a taotaomo'na while I was pregnant and that I might still be sick.

My husband Josh and I went from being the couple dancing in the front row of a concert to people who went grocery shopping in the middle of the night to avoid running into people we knew. Even though we had been showered with love and support in our loss, we really wanted to be alone. And more than anything, we became desperate for answers. One day, a couple of months after we lost Sai, my Auntie Cil called from Saipan and asked if I wanted to visit a suruhånu that she really trusted to help me figure out what had happened.

"He's the best, Nen," she said. "He can communicate with taotaomo'na from all of our islands. Since you went to Luta and Tinian, he may be able to tell you if something happened there and that way if you need to go back to apologize, you can."

"OK, Auntie Cil, can we come next week?"

"Of course, Nen, any time. You can come stay with us. I will bring you to him."

Josh and I booked a ticket to Saipan right away, certain that this was the right thing to do. When we got there, we spent our first day reconnecting with family and visiting the graves of my grandparents and Uncle Billy. We had dinner at Auntie Mel's house, and it was so comforting to be around her. Auntie Mel had come to Guam for Sai's funeral and was there for me in a way no one else could be. She had lost two of her own babies and talked me through the motions of burying mine—something I had never imagined having to do.

"You have to be the one to dress him," she had encouraged me on the day of the funeral. "This is your only chance to dress your son. Take your time. Look at his body. Kiss him. Love him. You don't ever want to look back on this day and wish you had taken more time to look at him. Study his face, so you'll never forget it." And she had stood by my side the entire time as I put on his tiny, white clothes. Seeing her in Saipan for the first time since that day made me feel safe. I did not have to tell her what the last few months had been like. She already knew. I did not have to ask her about what to expect with the suruhånu the next day, she dove right into the conversation. "I know you might be worried about what Harold's going to say to you tomorrow, but it's OK. You have to trust him. You need to know what happened. It's time you found out. And Harold, he'll be able to tell you. You won't even have to tell him why you're there. He'll already know."

She then shared a story I had never been told about Uncle Billy. One time, he had gotten really sick after fishing at night. An animan tåsi had followed him home. These spirits of the ocean are known to be the most powerful spirits. That night when he was sleeping, his entire body went numb. He lost feeling from his toes all the way up to his head. He could not move at all. He said he felt like someone was choking him, but he could not lift his arms to stop it. He tried to scream for help, but no sound would escape his mouth. He had to just lay there for hours until it went away. This happened to him every night after that, and our family members kept telling him to go see Harold, but he was too proud. He said the taotaomo'na liked him. They had always led him to the best fish at night. He did not need anyone's help, he said. But one night, when he was playing cards at my cousin Sus's apartment, his legs started to go numb. Sus asked him why he had not gone to see Harold yet, and Uncle Billy joked that if Harold was so good at reading minds, why had he not come to see him yet. A few minutes later, they saw a shadow passing the window and then heard a knock at the door. "Håfa, Billy-Bert, you called me?" Harold said through the door, and Uncle Billy nearly lost it. He rushed to the door and let Harold in. It took three days, but Harold made the animan tåsi go away.

Auntie Mel and I talked at the kitchen table for a few hours like this, sharing taotaomo'na stories, memories of Uncle Billy, whose loss was still so fresh in our family (it had only been a year since his unexpected death), and catching up on news of all of our relatives in Saipan and Guam. I was feeling much more like myself and was ready to meet Harold the next morning.

Auntie Cil drove us to a mint-green house with a vibrant garden in front of it. Hibiscus of every hue, puti tai nobiu, plumeria and orchids bloomed colorfully. Harold was waiting for us at the front of the house. "Maila," he called to us in CHamoru. "Come in." I took his hand to ningnge' him, and Josh did the same. He felt like an old friend. Like I had known him in my childhood, and we could just pick up where we had left off despite not having seen each other in a long time. His brown skin was tight and youthful. His eyes were those of a man in his 40s, but his hair was completely white like a chungi bird. It was still shiny and thick, but all white. And his hands were wrinkled with an age beyond this lifetime. I could tell that Harold's hands had absorbed the sickness and pain of countless people, my relatives included.

There were a lot of roosters around the house. Some were in the back yard, tied at the ankle to a leash rooted in the earth; others were in cages. "Are those your birds?" I asked.

"No, my brother's. Let's go over here." He motioned us toward a bench on the side of the house shaded by an ylang ylang tree. Josh and I sat on the bench, and Auntie Cil stayed at the front of the house. I could smell the ylang ylang. The scent shot to my gut, and it was wrenching. Did I want to know what he was going to tell me? Would he tell me that I had done something wrong? That I had hurt my baby? Josh held my hand, and Harold stood in front of me with a bottle of oil. I closed my eyes sensing this was what he wanted me to do and tried to listen to him, but all I could hear were the roosters and my fears playing over and over in my mind. Harold rubbed the oil on my forehead and rested his palm over my third eye—the space of inner vision between my eyes. The roosters faded to silence, and the scent of ylang ylang grew stronger. The silence was absolute and lasted for several minutes. It filled me with the same calm I had felt with Maman Rosa at the kamachili tree. Just as I started to remember her, Harold spoke.

"A spirit wanted your baby," he told me. "She is a woman, not much older than you. I can see you through her eyes. You are at the University of Guam, and you are rushing. You go from the parking lot to the Field House. You cross the street diagonally, do you remember this? There is a big tree there, do you know which one I am talking about? The trongkon nunu?"

"Hunggan. I know exactly which one you are talking about. I remember that day. I teach there, and I was going to turn in my grades. I was so excited the semester was over that I practically ran into the records office in the Field House."

"As you pass the tree, you bump into her, the spirit. She is very sad, but when she sees you and your baby inside you, she feels happy. She wants your baby ... she says your baby is beautiful, so beautiful. Was she a girl?"

"No, a boy."

"He is a beautiful boy. Has very feminine features, a ... a woman's energy. She sees your baby, and she sees you, how happy you are, and she wants what you have. She could never have children. Her whole life all she wanted was a child, and she couldn't have one. She doesn't mean to hurt you, but when she sees you, she thinks this is her chance. She tries to enter you, to take your child. You felt it ... when she bumped into you, she says you felt it. Do you remember?"

"I do. I ... felt something that day. I even stopped and said, 'Dispensa yu',' because I didn't ask permission to pass under the trongkon nunu. I felt something brush me, like a strong wind. I got cold, fugu', and just stopped in the middle of the street."

"Your baby felt it, too. The lady tried to take him, but she couldn't. And that struggle is why your baby didn't form all the way. But God won. He let you have your baby. You got to see him, right? You got to meet him, and hold him? God let you have that."

I was silent, but my thoughts were racing. God won? God and a spirit woman went to battle for my baby? Why did I not know about it? Why was I not allowed to fight for his life? It all sounded so crazy. So unfair.

Harold's hand was still on my forehead. My eyes were still closed, and I was floating somewhere between his bench and that trongkon nunu. For a moment, I was there, at the trongkon nunu on that day. I remembered what it felt like to be pregnant. How that morning I had looked in the mirror and saw a pregnant me staring back with a newly stretched belly and fuller breasts. She was the most beautiful me I had ever seen. And I really was happy. I wanted to stay there, in the memory of that day, and slow down. Take the front entrance to the Field House and not the one next to the trongkon nunu. Would that have changed Sai's fate?

"It was not your fault," Harold said, bringing me back to the bench.
"But I shouldn't have walked that way."

"There's nothing you could have done. Your baby was not meant to be part of this world. I know you have heard this before, and you think it's just what people say, but it's true. When I look at your baby now, I can see that he was meant for something greater. He was not really a boy or a girl, but something more. I just see brightness. God won."

Fuck God, I thought, but could not say it out loud.

Harold removed his hand from my forehead. The oil traveled slowly down the bridge of my nose, over my lips, and dripped into my shirt. My breasts, still full of milk for Sai, felt the cold tingle as the oil settled between them. If he was not meant for this life, why had they still been so full?

"Harold, I'm scared of what you saw. I'm angry with God. I ... I don't know if I believe in God anymore. I believe in what you saw. You had no way of knowing that

I walked into the Field House that day, or how I crossed the street, so I believe you, but I am struggling to accept this idea that God won and that I am supposed to be happy with that."

"You can believe whatever you want to believe. I am just telling you what they're telling me."

"Saina ma'åse, Harold, I appreciate everything you have done for me today."

"It's Si Yu'os ma'åse, hagå-hu. Why do you people from Guam always like to change things?"

"Ai, dispensa yu'. Si Yu'os ma'åse, Harold."

"You have a gift, too. I can tell. If you listened, if you really listened, you could hear them, too. They like you."

"I've been told that before, that the taotaomo'na like me. Why?"

"There's something about you ... you just need to listen, and you'll hear them. Don't wipe the oil off your body, OK? Leave it on until you wake up tomorrow."

"OK."

We said good-bye, and the next day Josh and I flew back to Guam. I struggled for truth, for meaning in Harold's vision, and it made me frantic. Obsessive. I replayed both the moment I had crossed the street that day and my visit with Harold over and over again. I did not feel at peace, knowing that my baby was now with God. Instead, I kept digging for more answers. Josh and I looked up what was happening in my womb on the day I had passed that trongkon nunu. I looked in my email, saw that grades were due the third week of May. I started counting weeks in my mind. I would have been thirteen weeks pregnant. I typed "when does a baby's intestines form?" into a search engine. According to the Mayo Clinic, "Thirteen weeks into your pregnancy, or 11 weeks after conception, your baby's intestines have returned to his or her abdomen from the umbilical cord ... "

Sai's intestines had never returned to his abdomen. That was what went wrong, biologically. His intestines had grown outside of his body in a sac called an omphalocele. I was speechless. This spirit's struggle to take my baby could really have done this, metaphysically. It was the exact week. I looked over at Josh, who was reading with me, and his furrowed brow suggested that he, too, was teetering between reality and fantasy in his mind. We had genuinely believed that our baby would survive. Even when I felt his breath leave his body, I could not accept that it was real. I held on to him for nearly two hours afterwards. Carrying him close to my chest, hoping that my heart would wake him. But he never came back, and I could not understand why. After months of searching for a reason, we finally had one, and I didn't know how to believe it, even though everything I had learned from my elders told me that I should.

In our culture, we do not question our elders or their beliefs. We listen to them and respect them, like we have always been taught to respect the taotaomo'na, our first elders. It was easy for me to understand the woman who wanted Sai. To comprehend her desire for a baby, because after losing him, it was all I wanted, too. But to accept that this was God's plan, as my elders were telling me, was a challenge. Why would God cause us such pain? Why would God give us a baby we could not keep? Just as I was raised not to question my elders, they were raised not to question God. Even though they had deep respect for the taotaomo'na, their ultimate faith was always their belief in God and the teachings of the Church. But I could not reconcile with God no matter how hard I tried. Not even for my mom, who kept inviting me to church even though I would not go.

The turning point in my faith was not just about what had happened to Sai. It had been coming for a while. I had been a devout Catholic growing up—I had received my sacraments and attended eskuelan påle', or Sunday school, every year until I was confirmed. I looked forward to Mass and seeing everyone from my village there. But as I became an adult, I dug more deeply into my history as a CHamoru woman. I read about the CHamoru-Spanish Wars and the violence and manipulation that were used to convert and colonize my ancestors. I felt one of my best friend's pain when her mother turned her away and disowned her for loving a woman, because as a Catholic, she truly believed her daughter was going to hell. I cringed every time I read about a child who had trusted a priest and was abused by him and then abandoned, left to suffer with this wound in silence. Over time, I found it harder to attend Mass without questioning the prayers or struggling through the priest's homily. I would leave the church feeling very sad. Thus, instead of turning to the Catholic faith during my time of need, I turned away from it.

I have never stopped praying, but my prayers are no longer the rote prayers of my childhood. Instead, they have become very personal and conversational, full of gratitude to our Creator, acceptance for all of life's lessons and praise to the ancestors who carved a trail for me to follow. My spiritual life has become very personal. I find myself in the jungle more, wanting to feel connected to the spirits there. I listen to them more deeply, as Harold had advised, and I can hear them in ways I had not before. Tracing their footsteps deeper into the halom tåno, I have found the freedom I had felt as a child running to the kamachili tree. And that is truly what saved me.

Contemporary Dynamics of Traditional Healing in Guam and the Commonwealth of the Northern Mariana Islands

Tricia Lizama

In 2008 or thereabouts, I was faced with the daunting task of choosing a dissertation topic. Critical to this reflection process was selecting a topic that would contribute to the literature on the CHamoru people. As a young child, I grew up with a grandma who always had a type of tea or chå brewing on the stove top and then later stored in the refrigerator. Her brews served as a remedy for colds, congestion, and the flu, but the "why" or "what was in the chå" was never understood. Nånan Biha (Grandma) said that those who were born breech were recognized as "having good hands." My grandma gave me directions for massaging young babies and children due to my "having good hands," but no other explanation as to "why" was offered.

When my aunt became ill, she was taken to a healer and "diagnosed" with having a spiritual sickness. Many of these experiences and the unanswered "whys" became the impetus for choosing a dissertation topic. The dissertation became the means of resolving these unanswered questions. On this journey, I met many healers and interviewed at least 40 healers in Guam, Saipan, Rota, and Tinian. The interviews lasted between 2 and 4 hours each, and many of the healers had such a wealth of information that subsequent visits with them were arranged. Through these interviews and the relationships established with the healers, many of the "whys," along with the whom, what, and when, were answered. I share a glimpse of the worldview of the Mariana Islands healer in this chapter. In addition, I provide an exploratory overview of the current state of traditional healing in the Marianas. The chapter concludes with a consideration of the future of traditional healing in the region.

Literature Review

Many studies have documented traditional healing in the Commonwealth of the Northern Marianas (CNMI) and Guam. Although Guam and the Mariana Islands have varied colonial histories, they share the same cultural history and practices. The main function of the Native healers of the CHamoru and Carolinian people, the suruhåna or suruhånu, was (and still is) to promote good health within the community, which will in turn enhance the survival potential of the population (McMakin, 1978). The assumption driving the promotion of good health is that without good health, other forms of cultural activities will be affected. Many of the statements below are examples of how important and valued the role of a traditional healer was and still is. Thompson (1947), writing about the art of being a suruhåna or suruhånu, stated that due to colonization,

> already much has disappeared, and if the remainder is not recorded before the present generation of herb specialists dies out, an important survival of ancient Chamorro culture will probably be lost—a survival which, upon scientific investigation, may yield results valuable to modern medicine. (p. 198)

McMakin (1978) noted in his anthropological study of the suruhåna/u that the craft of being a suruhåna/u was "the most intact survival of a cultural activity of the pre-contact Chamorro" (p. 14). McMakin (1978) further stated that the use of traditional medicine in Guam has persisted through time due to the continued demand for the practice. Workman, Cruz-Ortiz, and Kamminga-Quinata (1994) also confirmed through their interviews of 33 people that the Indigenous practice of healing and curing with herbs has survived. Lizama (2011) conducted her dissertation on preserving and perpetuating traditional healing practices in modern Guam. Lizama conducted a qualitative study and interviewed 11 traditional healers. In her findings, all of the healers were practicing and valued the importance of their knowledge and passing it on. These authors show that throughout Guam's history, traditional healers have been an important component to health care in Guam. This statement is also true for the CNMI.

In order to recognize the practice of traditional healers in the CNMI, Borja and Roppul (2009) published the *Directory of Traditional Healers and Medicinal Plants in the Commonwealth of the Northern Mariana Islands*. Borja and Roppul were able to interview and document 45 CHamoru and Carolinian healers. They noted in the biography compiled for each of these 45 healers that each was able to apprentice with another healer before practicing on their own. Borja and Roppul's compilation of the 45 healers into a directory is significant as it is a way of preserving and perpetuating the knowledge that these healers have, and this effort of compiling a directory was the first of its kind. Furthermore, Demapan (2011) conducted an ethnographic study focusing on exploring the contemporary medical practices of traditional healers in the CNMI. Demapan used the healers from the *Directory of Traditional Healers and Medicinal Plants in the Commonwealth of the Northern Marianas* to find her study subjects. Although only 12 of the healers met the criteria for her study, Demapan was able to conclude the following: 1) traditional healer candidates have to be interested and have to be recognized as being a potential healer; 2) most traditional healers said they treated a range of sicknesses including physical, psychological, and spiritual sickness; and 3) the primary role as a *suruhånu* and *suruhåna* is to treat the sick and to be a helping member of the community. In addition, a qualitative study by J.E.H. Arriola (2009) focused on exploring and constructing the CHamoru epistemology of mental health. Arriola constructed the CHamoru epistemology of cultural values and developed a theoretical model called "I Sisteman Nuebo yan I Tiempon Antes" (The New System and Old Times), to explain the CHamoru epistemology of mental health. Through his model, Arriola was able to identify the suruhånu and suruhåna as cultural figures who have a very important role in preventing and treating the dysfunctional imbalances of a person. M. Arriola (2015) conducted a study entitled "Patients' Perspectives on Indigenous Health Care Received from *Suruhånas* and *Suruhånus* on the Pacific Island of Saipan." One of her conclusions from this study was that traditional healing is still being used by many people in Saipan. In addition, another conclusion via her participant interviews was that traditional healers are perceived as prominent cultural figures who continue to play a vital role as helpers and healers in the community. We can conclude from this literature that the role of traditional healers in Guam and in the CNMI is a very important one and is being preserved and documented (J. E. H. Arriola, 2009; M. Arriola, 2015; Borja & Roppul, 2009; Demapan, 2011; Lizama, 2011; McMakin, 1978; Thompson, 1947; Workman et al., 1994). These various studies have documented that the people of the CNMI and Guam continue to seek out services from suruhånu or suruhåna for the diagnosis and treatment of minor ailments, spiritual ailments, and chronic disease.

History of Traditional Healing

Traditional healing practices, particularly the use of herbal medicine, have been used in the and Guam for centuries. In the CNMI, the traditional healer is known as the suruhånu (male healer) or the suruhåna (female healer). In Guam, the first healers were known as makåhna and kakåhna (shamans who were believed to have magical powers). With the impact of Spanish colonization and the introduction of Christianity, the makåhna and kakåhna no longer practiced. However, others believe that the makåhna and kakåhna continued practicing but identified themselves as suruhånu and suruhåna (derived from *cirujano*, the Spanish loanword for "surgeon"). Today in the CNMI, the healer is still commonly called a suruhånu or suruhåna, and sometimes called a yo'åmte, while in Guam the healer is identified as a yo'åmte (meaning "a deeper type of healer"). The terms suruhånu and suruhåna are still used in Guam, but people are starting to use the term yo'åmte more frequently.

Types of Healing

Suruhånu, suruhåna, and yo'åmte use different kinds of herbs and plants to make remedies for sickness. Sickness can be defined as physical, spiritual, and emotional illness. In both the CNMI and Guam, each healer is capable of performing a variety of healing in addition to practicing a particular specialty. For example, a healer can make åmot (medicine), and provide lasa (massage) and suffe' (working with the spirits or taotaomo'na). Some healers can do all three types of healing (åmot, lasa, and såffe), and some can do a combination of two types of healing. It is more common to find healers doing the åmot and the lasa. Due to the nature of the healing with the spirits, only some healers choose to do this type. Many healers have commented that spiritual healing requires greater energy, because the healer must be stronger than the spirit. If the spirit is stronger, the healer can get sick or be affected negatively by the spirit. As a result, healers are more cautious about working with spirits. Based on what the patient tells them, they can assess the strength of the spirit. At that point, they must decide whether to treat the patient or refer the patient to another healer who specializes in spiritual healing. Another important concept that was noted in interviews conducted by Borja and Roppul (2009) concerning treatment of patients, is the concept of hiningok ("to be heard"). This concept implies that the medicine must be meant for that person being treated if it is to work. If it is not meant to be, ti hiningok, then the medicine or treatment will not work on the patient. A physical sign of ti hiningok is if the åmot wilts in the hands of the healer. If this happens, the understanding is that the åmot will not work or the patient will not come for treatment (Borja & Roppul, 2009). This implies that åmot also has a spirit nature. This is also probably why many of the healers explained that it is always important to pray to the spirits before and during the administration of the åmot (J. E. H. Arriola, 2009; M. Arriola, 2015; Borja & Roppul, 2009; Demapan, 2011; Lizama, 2011, 2014).

Healers treat a variety of ailments, such as fevers, mouth sores, rashes, toothaches, cuts and burns, sprained ankles, female issues, and congestion. Just as healers have a specialty, they also have sub-specialties with the type of patients and ailments they treat. For example, there are healers who specialize in treating illness of babies and congestion. Others help with female problems such as heavy bleeding, menopause, or fertility issues. These healers can address other issues, but most have a specialty. If a patient comes to the healer for a problem that the healer is not able to help with, the healer refers the patient to another healer in the community who can help. This concept is very similar to Western medicine in that a doctor trains for a specific field. All doctors basically have the same initial training. After several years of training, the doctor identifies a specialty such as internal medicine, obstetrics, psychiatry, or pediatrics. Among healers, a specialty is chosen for them based on what was passed on to them from previous generations. An example is a female healer in Rota who knows many of the herbal plants, but patients seek her out primarily for one illness, shingles, Tininun San Antonio in CHamoru. Her mother was the expert in treating Tininun San Antonio, and her mother passed her knowledge on to this healer. Although this healer has knowledge of many herbal plants, her primary specialty is treating shingles. According to Borja and Roppul (2009) and Demapan (2011), healers have specialties and can be classified into the following categories: physical, psychological, and spiritual.

The Process of Becoming a Healer
Knowledge of traditional healing is generally kept within families and passed on

from one generation to another. Healers usually learn their craft from their mother, grandmother, father, grandfather, or another close relative. As young children, some at only 2 or 3 years of age, they begin to accompany their relative to identify, pick, and gather medicine. Actual training to be a healer starts at a very young age. After the child is proficient in identifying the plant, herbs, and roots, they are sent off to identify and pick herbs on their own. This training continues when the child observes how the herbs are cleaned and prepared. Youth can spend years of observing until they are deemed ready to practice. At that point, they are given more responsibility for preparing the åmot with the assistance of the healer until the healer is confident that the "apprentice" is ready to prepare the åmot independently.

Although being able to identify and prepare the åmot are very important in the training process, there are many more important "rules" that the "apprentice" has to learn. There are rules about respect and entering the jungle as well as rules about the relationship that one has with the environment, the spirit world, and God. For example, before anyone enters the jungle, the person must ask the spirits of the jungle for permission to enter. CHamorus believe that spirits exist everywhere. If someone were to enter the jungle without asking permission, negative consequences might ensue. Some people claim that a part of their body became swollen, or a purple bruise appeared on their arm or leg as if someone "pinched" them. In Rota, a healer was observed who not only asked permission to enter the jungle but also asked permission from the plants that she was taking as part of her åmot. She chanted to the plants to ask permission to take only a few of the leaves because that was what she needed at the time. She also assured the plants that she was very appreciative of them because they helped her to heal someone who needed help. In addition to asking permission, healers observe rules that regulate when the åmot can be picked and under what conditions. Many healers suggest that the åmot be picked early in the morning. Also, the consensus is that as long as it is not raining, the åmot can be picked before 3 p.m. They discourage picking after 3 p.m. because that is when the "not so nice" spirits roam and can "intercept" the åmot. The mean spirits can cause the åmot to become bad, making it useless or ineffective.

The last set of rules for healers involves learning what time of day they can treat people and what is acceptable and unacceptable for "payment." The rules of when not to treat people are very similar to the rules of when to pick åmot. Healers can treat people during most of the day but will stop at around 3 p.m. This is in line with the belief that the mean spirits are more prone to roam after 3 p.m. Healers believe that people should never be treated and åmot should never be picked or transported between 5 to 6 p.m. This is the time that many of the mean spirits roam. Due to the long training time and the intricacies of being a healer, the process of learning how to be a traditional healer takes years and is safeguarded within the family.

Training goes beyond learning about the medicine; the child is also taught about massage or lasa. CHamorus believe that a child with "good hands" is born breech (bottom or feet first) and has the gift of massaging. Healers believe that, if a child has the gift, then it should be nurtured. However, children do not perform massage at an early age because they do not have the strength. They probably just massage babies and people within their own family. There are certain rules that govern the act of massaging. A woman should never massage when she is experiencing menstruation. A male healer who massages should not massage a woman for fertility issues because that involves having to touch the woman's vagina, which may not be acceptable to her husband. The healer may also experience fear of being accused of sexual assault.

Many of the rules regarding traditional healing are still very much intact in modern times. The jungle is still respected, permission is sought, and rules for picking plants and propagating them are followed. All of these rules are based on CHamoru values and culture. J. E. H. Arriola (2009) constructed the epistemology of CHamoru values as follows: (1) Yu'os Tåta (God the Father), who is believed to be the ultimate authority in the lives of the CHamoru people; (2) familia (family) life, which revolves around the family unit; (3) tano' (land), which is understood to be the roots of cultural identity; (4) inafa'maolek (interdependence), understood as a cultural practice that promotes the value of respetu (respect) and fosters harmonious interaction among the people, as well as between the people and the land; (5) chenchule' (gifted reciprocity), understood as an unspoken obligation done out of respect and gratitude to assist a family in need; (6) mamåhlao (shame), to be respectful and humble in the presence of other people; (7) manayuda (assistance), the act of helping family and friends; (8) manåmko' (elderly), people of age who are given the utmost respect; and (9) taotaomo'na (ancestral spirits), who are worshiped and thought of as spiritual forces that help with the harmonious flow of inafa'maolek between the people, land, and the universe (p. 21).

Currently, there are an estimated 80 to 90 healers in the CNMI and Guam. The *Directory of Traditional Healers and Medicinal Plants in the Commonwealth of the Northern Marianas* (Borja & Roppul, 2009) identifies 45 healers who were interviewed in the CNMI; however, not all the healers were interviewed, out of respect for traditional practices. Generally, healers do not advertise. Accessing a healer is via word of mouth. One would never see an advertisement of a healer promoting their services. Being interviewed and listed in the directory can be seen as a very public act and may be perceived by some healers as advertisement. However, Borja and Roppul (2009) argued that documenting the identity and knowledge of the traditional healers will support the preservation of the Indigenous knowledge and provides a resource to the community, by means of a directory which will help others gain access to traditional healers instead of just by word of mouth. Typically, healers work out of their home. Currently, there are no partnerships between the hospitals in the CNMI or Guam and the healers. Many doctors in the CNMI and some doctors in Guam, mostly CHamoru, are aware of the existence of the healers. In an informal conversation with a pediatrician in Guam, he said that if a baby were heavily congested or had a bad cold, he would refer the child to a healer. He added that he grew up knowing about the traditional healers and was treated by one as a child.

Among the 80 to 90 healers in the CNMI and Guam, approximately 15 to 20 of them have died during the past 5 years. There will be a shortage of healers if the knowledge is not preserved or perpetuated as healers are dying.

Perpetuation of Healing Tradition
Many healers spoke of their difficulties in identifying a family member to whom they would like to pass their knowledge and tradition. According to Demapan (2011), the traditional healer aspirant must show interest and be recognized as wanting to be a healer. However, finding these potential healers and future apprentices has been challenging. Lizama (2014) conducted an interview with a Saipan healer, who explained that he did not have children, and although his siblings had children, they were still very young and did not show an interest. He observed that the children were too consumed with TV, their iPad, and technology overall. He was disheartened that they did not express an interest to learn. His mother told him that he could only pass on the knowledge to another family member. He expressed deep hurt because without another family member to pass on his knowledge to,

his valuable knowledge would die with him. The sentiment of this healer has been a common theme of healers in Guam and in the CNMI. Many healers lament that their children are consumed with other things or too busy to learn. A consequence of this situation is that the healers no longer try to teach their children or grandchildren if their attempts have been rejected. Although many of the "rules" are honored and are continued by the healers, identifying someone at a young age to start learning has been very difficult. If healers are not able to pass on the tradition to a family member, then to whom will they pass on their knowledge? Technology and modernization are obstacles in the way of recruiting and training young children and family members. The impact of technology and modernization on the younger generation as it affects traditional healing is significant. As a response to this impact in Guam, an apprenticeship program has been developed. In Saipan and in Rota, traditional healing is taught in the school system, and community gardens have been established. These gardens contain medicinal plants that are used to teach children at a young age and have been introduced into the school curriculum. This instructional method differs from the traditional ways, as the learning of traditional healing was previously done in the home. Now, the exposure to plants and healing is done through the school curriculum.

Although a formal apprenticeship program exists in Guam, recruitment to be an apprentice has been very difficult. In the past 5 years, there have been three apprentices and in 2021 the Guma Yo'åmte (House of Healers) has one apprentice. Much time and commitment are required of an apprentice. The apprentice accompanies the healer picking åmot and trains at the healing center, observing and being observed. This requires the apprentice to be there at all times. The traditional healer apprenticeship is very different from an internship or a practicum placement. An internship has a set requirement of hours for completion. The current model of apprenticeship in the healing center does not have a set number of hours; instead, the healers will assess when the apprentice is ready. This can be a difficult time commitment for many, as well as an economic hardship, as apprentices are not paid.

A cultural and social shift has begun, as some healers are now passing on their knowledge to an "apprentice" outside of their family. However, not all healers agree with this shift. Organized groups such as the Åmot Natibu in Saipan and the Håya Foundation and Åmot Farm in Guam have joined together to support the healers, hear their concerns, and help with the preservation and perpetuation of the traditional healing practices. The Inetnon Åmot Natibu/Ammwelil Safeyal Faluwasch (IÅN/ASF) is a nonprofit organization formed in 2007 that advocates for, recognizes, and supports traditional healers in the Marianas. Another goal of the IÅN/ASF is to aid in the protection of medicinal plants and to document the healing tradition, as much knowledge is passed on orally. One of the IÅN/ASF's first major projects was to provide the community with a comprehensive trilingual directory (English, CHamoru, and Carolinian) of Indigenous traditional healers in the CNMI. This project was the first documented directory and listed at least 45 traditional healers who are living and currently practicing (although some may have passed since the publication of the directory) in the CNMI. The healers were able to provide a brief description of themselves, how they learned their craft, what their specialties are, and even some recipes for certain ailments. The 700-page directory documents the stories of 45 traditional healers in Saipan, Rota, and Tinian, who chose to be included. This publication is significant in many ways because one of the rules for healers is that they not publicize what they do, and this rule likely prevented many healers from contributing to the publication. The Guam Council on the Arts and Humanities Agency (CAHA) has been trying to establish a similar directory of healers, yet for years they have not been successful, possibly due to the traditional rule prohibiting healers from advertising.

The Håya Foundation (2018) was established in Guam in 2005 to "enhance the well-being of our people," and in support of that mission they have worked on preserving, promoting, and perpetuating our traditional healing practices. The Åmot Farm is a preservation farm of medicinal native and introduced plants grown and tended using organic methods. In addition, the Åmot Farm promotes and perpetuates the healing practices by providing edu-tourism and ecotourism via farm tours. Although the Håya Foundation and the Åmot Farm are two separate non-profit entities, they work together with a common mission of preserving and perpetuating traditional healing practices.

The Håya Foundation and the Inetnon Åmot Natibu/Ammwelil Safeyal Faluwasch have worked together to address challenges facing our traditional healers. Three Konfrensian Åmot [Conference for Medicinal Herbs] have been held and were very successful. The primary role of these conferences is to bring together the healers so that they can advocate for what they need help with and to educate others about the state of traditional medicine.

There are many obstacles to the preservation and perpetuation of the traditional healing practices. As mentioned earlier, the knowledge was passed on from generation to generation and yet today many of the children of the healers do not want to perpetuate the tradition. Other obstacles include difficulty accessing medicinal plants and herbs, economic hardship, fear of being exploited, and conflicting CHamoru values, such as that between mamåhlao (humility) and banidosu/a (self-promotion).

In Guam and Saipan, new construction projects, such as hotels and other establishments have involved the clearing of jungle areas, the natural habitat of many of the medicinal plants. Consequently, finding herbs and plants has become increasingly difficult. In Saipan, plants that grew in locations close to a healer are no longer available, resulting in healers having to do more traveling or hiking through rough terrain to gain access to the herbs they need to treat patients. A problem that directly impacts Guam is that many of the herbs grow in lush environments controlled by the military. Some of these lands cannot be accessed by healers, and those who do have access need to provide a reason for entry and must produce the appropriate paperwork. A healer from Saipan who was living in Guam shared his story of how he was told that he could get all the medicinal herbs that he needed at Ritidian (a wildlife refuge). He made his way to Ritidian and saw the herbs he needed to treat a patient. He started to collect them but was confronted by a preservation officer who told him that he could not just pick whatever he wanted and that he must get a pass. The healer argued with the preservation officer, declaring that this land belongs to the people and that he needs the medicine to treat a person. He was almost arrested, and by the time the issue was resolved, it was too late to pick the herbs he needed (according to the rules of when to pick medicine). Feeling sad, the healer left knowing that he could not help the patient until the next day. He also felt angry that he could not access the jungle. He did not experience such obstacles accessing restricted lands in Saipan.

Healers in Rota and Tinian, when asked if they had problems collecting the åmot or having access, stated that they generally did not have any difficulties gathering the medicine. They complained, however, that many young people do not recognize the difference between medicinal plants/herbs and weeds, so when doing yard work or bush cutting, they inadvertently kill the plants. The older healers explained that some plants flourish in their natural habitats in the valley, near water, or near rocky environments and can be difficult to access, as the healers are not as fit as they used to be. Thus, while access to traditional plants in Saipan is not quite as obstructed as in Guam, in general, access has become constrained by various means and to various degrees in all the islands in the Marianas.

Additional Dynamics at Work Today
When asked where they obtained their healing power, many of the healers responded that it was a gift from God. Some said that the spirits also guided them. As mentioned earlier, a healer must adhere to traditional rules; one in particular stipulates that a healer should never take money as a form of payment. Demapan's (2011) interviews with healers revealed that most do not charge for treatment. Traditionally, in gratitude for the healer's help, an individual or family will leave gifts of appreciation. These gifts can take the form of a case of frozen chicken, a sack of rice, or fresh fruits, vegetables, or fish. Whatever the patient gives out of the kindness of the heart should be accepted.

When I asked healers about accepting money as payment, there were several differing opinions. Many healers said they accepted anything but money. Some explained that instead of money, they tell the patient to take the money and offer Mass intentions at church. One healer questioned the difference between taking a case of spareribs versus accepting money. Why could he not take the money and buy what is needed? He noted that in the past, there may not have been a need for money, but in modern times, the need exists.

A commonality among the healers in the CNMI and Guam is that healers will accept whatever a patient gives. If the patient cannot give anything, that is also fine. The healers feel that they received the healing gift from God and that they should not charge. Many believe that if they charge, the healing would not work, and the patient would not be helped. For healers who were open to accepting money, they had one rule: the money could not be given directly to them and either had to be left on the table or on another object. These healers also believe that a healer could not name a price or have a set price list, unlike massage establishments, which post price lists for a 30-minute massage, a 60-minute massage, etc. These healers feel that if a person wants to pay in cash, it is up to the individual to determine how much they want to give, so long as it is from the kindness of their heart.

Another change that has been observed is that for centuries, healers have practiced out of their homes, their natural habitat. This is still very true for the CNMI, but there have been some changes in Guam. For example, in May 2016, the Guma Yo'åmte was established because many in the community wanted access to a healer, but did not know where to find one. Traditionally, healers do not advertise and are located by word of mouth. Today, there are three healers who practice full-time at the Guma Yo'åmte and two who practice part-time in addition to conducting home visits.

This shift marks a change, since healers did not usually go to patients' homes unless it was a spiritual issue that required them to såffe the person's home and other belongings. The two healers who conduct home visits receive many requests from those who have had strokes or more serious health conditions that prevent them from being transported by car to Guma Yo'åmte. Having a house of healers and healers who do home visits is different from what has been practiced in the past. However, these practices are necessary to improve access to care provided by traditional healers. Now that some healers are conducting home visits, concerns over the need and cost of gas have emerged, leading to questions of whether these healers should charge a fee for costs incurred when conducting home visits. When asked about charging for gas, the healers responded by saying, "Whatever people want to give." With further inquiry, one of the healers commented, "It always works out. For example, someone will give $20, someone will give $0, and then someone gives $100. I don't worry about it because it always works out."

The popularity of a centralized healing center, the Guma Yo'åmte, is represented in several charts below, which show the utilization of the services that the Guma Yo'åmte provided from May 2016 until June 2017. Originally the Guma Yo'åmte was only open Mondays, Wednesdays, Fridays, and half day on Saturdays. However, the response from the community has been phenomenal. Due the demand, as of September 2017, they are open every day except Sunday. The chart below (Figure 1) shows that the Guma Yo'åmte has had about 1,999 visitors between May 2016 when it opened, and June 2017, averaging about 143 visitors a month. Some are repeat visitors because most treatments require that patients be tended to for 3 days in a row.

Figure 1

Monthly Visitors to the Guma Yo'åmte in Guam.

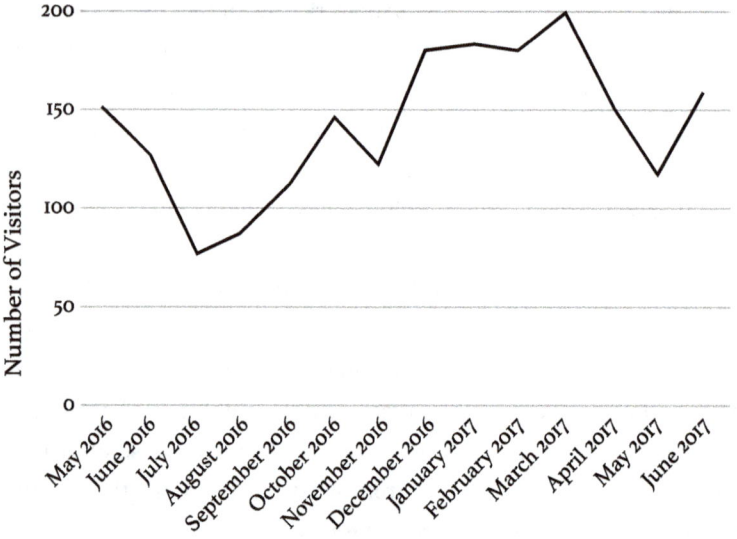

Note. Data comes from the visitor's log. Total number of visitors is 1,999. Average monthly number of visitors is 143.

The chart below (Figure 2) displays the age of female visitors and the problems for which they sought treatment at the Guma Yo'åmte within a particular month. The healers were sought out for the following: såffe, massage, chotge, and there were two other categories for unspecified and other problems. It should be noted that the demographic information is limited. Although the Guma Yo'åmte had the forms available, no one was ensuring that patients were filling out the forms completely. If a patient completed a form, it was appreciated, but it was not of great concern if they did not. Greater efforts are now being taken to encourage the completion of forms by patients.

Figure 2

Age and Requested Service of a Selection of Female Visitors to Guma Yo'åmte

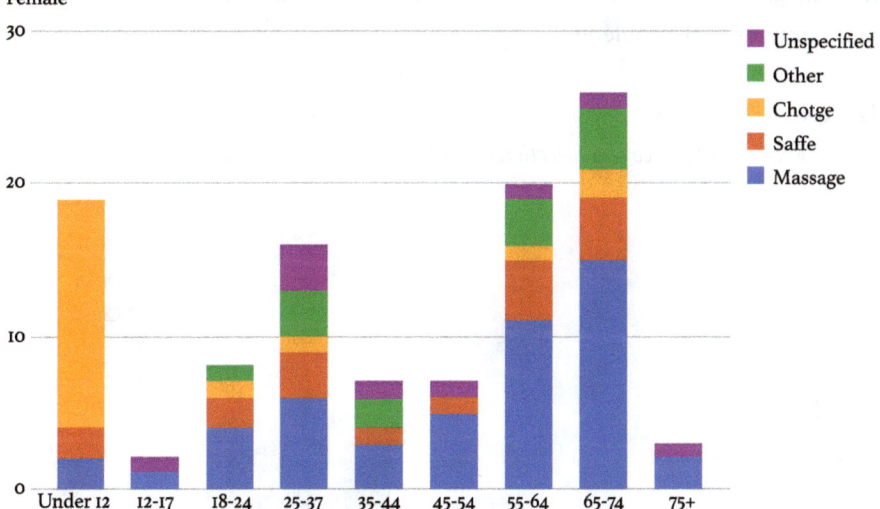

Note: Data comes from intake forms. Total number of female visitors in this particular month was 108.

From the information collected, 108 females filled out the intake form. These females ranged in age from under 12 to over 75. The majority of patients were seen for massage, with the exception of those under the age of 12, who were seen for chotge. Chotge is a method used for newborns, infants, and young children where the åmot is put into a cloth and squeezed into the child's mouth. This type of åmot and method is used for children who have a lot of congestion, a bad cold, or are coughing. The method is commonly used for newborns who may have ingested amniotic fluid, or who may need to clear their system of any food or toxins from the mother. For example, if a child has skin problems, the healer may tell the mother that she might have consumed too many spicy foods while pregnant, which may have caused the child's skin problems. The unspecified or other categories could mean that patients came for reasons such as the flu, pneumonia, fertility concerns, menstruation, or menopause.

The results were very similar for the male patients (Figure 3). There were 70 male patients who filled out the demographic form. These patients also ranged in age from under 12 to over 75. Many of the patients came for a massage, with the exception of patients under the age of 12, who came for chotge and massage. There were also many patients who came for other ailments such as the såffe. The unspecified or other categories could mean that they came for conditions such as the flu, pneumonia, sprains, or back problems.

Figure 3

Age and Requested Service of a Selection of Male Visitors to Guma Yo'åmte

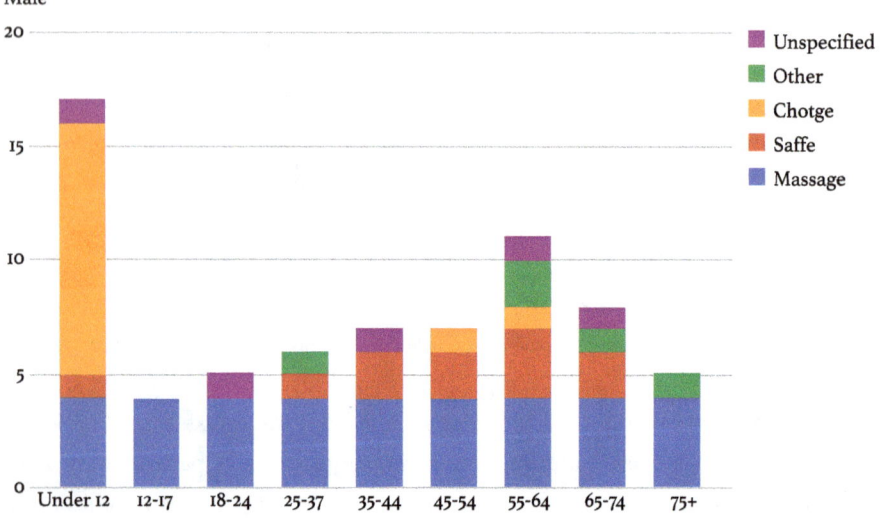

Note. Data comes from intake forms. Total number of male visitors in this particular month was 70.

Five patients did not fill out the gender portion of the form. One person between the ages of 35 to 44 sought help for såffe, and another between the ages of 45 to 54 sought massage. Two visitors under the age of 12 and another patient between 12-and 17-years-old indicated "other." Although there have not been many demographic forms completed by this particular group, it is clear that overall, many people are seeking the services of a traditional healer. The demand for traditional healing services is quite high. Based on observations by healers and conversations with them, all age groups are utilizing the services of the healers.

Conclusions

The practice of traditional healing has continued in the Marianas despite struggles with preservation and perpetuation. However, in order for traditional healing practices to survive, a new model of practice has been developed. This new model involves a centralized location where healers can practice, as well as the development of an apprenticeship system for those interested in learning but who may not be from a family of traditional healers. Some healers still practice out of their homes, and most healers—both in the home and at the Guma Yo'åmte—still honor the traditional rules of picking åmot and respect. Another change has been the communication between healers within formal settings, such as within meetings and at conferences. Healers have redefined what "advertising" or "publicizing" their services mean; they now speak publicly at school sites, are present at fairs, and conduct demonstrations at public events. They also attend conferences that deal with healing and have increased their public presence. The examples above are changes that are being made among Guam healers. In January 2018, at the Third Konfrensian Åmot, healers from the CNMI echoed the sentiments of healers from Guam and expressed their desire for the establishment of a healing center. Healers from Saipan and Rota have sought assistance from the Håya Foundation to open healing centers in Saipan and Rota. The Håya Foundation will work closely with the Inetnon Åmot Natibu/Ammwelil Safeyal Faluwasch to help develop healing centers in Saipan, Rota, and eventually, Tinian. The island groups have agreed to tackle the threat of extinction of traditional healing practices if there is not a mechanism in place for preservation. The Saipan healers would like to be next in opening a healing center in collaboration with healers from Rota. As an additional collaborative effort, the healers facilitated a CHamoru immersion camp in the summer of 2017 to teach 40 youths ages 14 and up about traditional CHamoru practices, including, but not limited to, fishing, weaving, and storytelling. While there are still distinct differences among the Mariana Islands and some debate over how the practice should be passed on, it is universally agreed that the practice is deeply embedded in the CHamoru culture and must be passed on. If the methods described above do not continue and apprentices are not trained, a crisis will occur as at least 25% of the healers interviewed have already passed away from 2014 to 2020.

References

Arriola, J. E. H. (2009). *"I hinenggen chamorro yan i salut hinasso" The battle for sanity: De(constructing) mental health through a Chamorro epistemological framework* [Unpublished master's thesis]. University of Hawai'i, Mānoa.

Arriola, M. (2015). *Patients' perspectives on Indigenous health care received from suruhånus and suruhånas on the Pacific island of Saipan* [Unpublished master's thesis]. University of Guam.

Borja, M., & Roppul, J. S. (2009). *Directory of traditional healers and medicinal plants in the Commonwealth of the Northern Mariana Islands*. Inetnon Åmot Natibu/Ammwelil Safeyel Faluwasch.

Demapan, I. (2011). *Traditional healers of the Commonwealth of the Northern Mariana Islands and their medical practices*. [Unpublished doctoral dissertation]. Saybrook University.

Håya Foundation (2018). *Håya Foundation.* www.hayafoundation.com.

Lizama, T. A. (2011). *How are traditional Chamoru healing practices being perpetuated and preserved in modern Guam: A phenomenological study* (Publication No. 3444162) [Doctoral dissertation, Capella University]. ProQuest Dissertations Publishing.

Lizama, T. A. (2014). Yóåmte: A deeper type of healing exploring the state of indigenous Chamorro healing practices. *Pacific Asia Inquiry, 5*(1), 97–106.

McMakin, P. (1978). The suruhanos: Traditional curers on the island of Guam in Micronesia. *Micronesica, 14*(1), 13–67.

Thompson, L. (1947). *Guam and its people*. Princeton University Press.

Workman, A., Cruz-Ortiz, L., & Kaminga-Quinata, D. (1994). Use of traditional healers on Guam. In J. Morrison, P. Geraghty, & L. Crowl (Eds.) *Science of Pacific Island people: Fauna, flora, food and medicine.* (Vol. III, pp. 201–233). Institute of Pacific Studies, University of the South Pacific.

Fanachu Famalåo'an: Women are Emerging as Leaders in the Community-wide Resistance to Militarization in the Commonwealth of the Northern Mariana Islands

Sylvia C. Frain

Digital, legal, political, and spiritual resistance to escalating militarization in the Commonwealth of the Northern Mariana Islands (hereafter CNMI) is currently unfolding across the archipelago.[32] Chamorro and Refaluwasch (Carolinian) women and women-led organizations are resisting through online petitions, solidarity videos, and federal lawsuits. The context of the resistance relates directly to the United States Department of Defense's (hereafter DOD) latest Draft/Overseas Environmental Impact Statement released in April 2015, *The Commonwealth of the Northern Mariana Islands Joint Military Training*.

The Commonwealth of the Northern Mariana Islands Joint Military Training
In April 2015, *The Commonwealth of the Northern Mariana Islands Joint Military Training* (CJMT) Draft Environmental Impact Statement (DEIS) / Overseas Environmental Impact Statement (OEIS) document was released. This 1,400-page document proposes the creation of Live-Fire Training Range Complexes (LFTRCs) on Pågan and Tinian islands, the use of the beaches for amphibious landings, and the sea around

the islands for war exercises and sonar testing.[33] The US Navy wants Tinian for 20 weeks of live-fire training and 22 weeks a year of non-live activity, including munitions storage, danger zones, and airspace and seaspace restrictions (Figure 1). The military wants to employ the island of Pågan as a high-level bombing range for exercises from the land, air, and sea, including "guns-blazing war games" for at least 16 weeks a year (Cloud, 2015). However, the CJMT document includes the possibility of such activity for 40 weeks per year in Pågan and 45 weeks in Tinian (Hofschneider, 2016b). The current surge in women's resistance to these plans is evident through online petitions, solidarity videos, and court cases (Frain, 2017).

Figure 1

Map from the Draft Environmental Impact Statement/Overseas Environmental Impact Statement for Commonwealth of the Northern Mariana Islands Joint Military Training

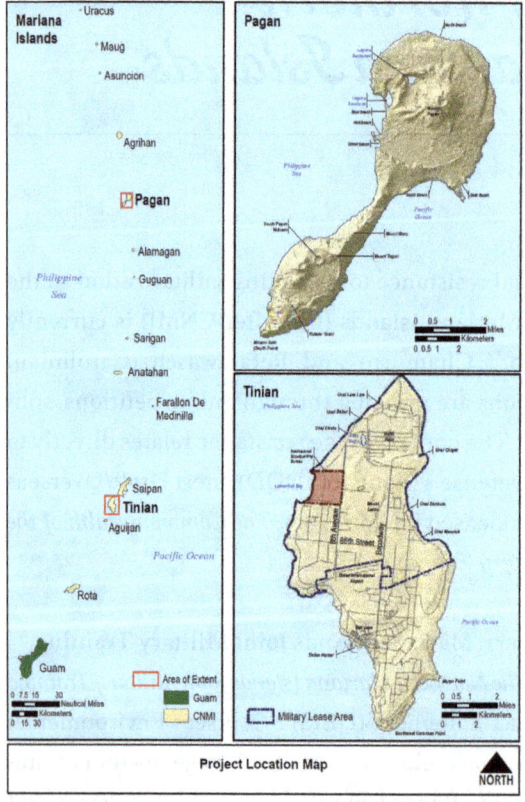

Note. From *CNMI Joint Military Training EIS/OEIS*, by US Marine Corps Forces Pacific, 2015. (http://www.cnmi-jointmilitarytrainingeis.com/documents). Copyright 2015 by Naval Facilities Engineering Command, Pacific.

During the negotiations that began in 1972 for the "Covenant to Establish a Commonwealth of the Northern Mariana Islands in Political Union with the United States," the US Navy announced it needed to establish a $300 million joint Air Force-Navy airfield, a multi-service airbase, a logistics supply depot, a marine amphibious training center, and an over-the-horizon radar facility in Tinian. The DOD wanted to "lease" the entire island of Tinian. The residents were promised US military base jobs, education for their children in base schools, use of the hospital, and other benefits. But the promises relating to the benefits for the community never came to fruition. The joint-base plan was never implemented, nor was the school or hospital (Hofschneider, 2016b). Many saw this not as true self-determination; rather, the "United States, needing to ensure their military objectives, rigged the Commonwealth Covenant plebiscite" (Dé Ishtar, 1994, p. 93).

The Covenant Agreement offers two sections for interaction between local CNMI political leaders on the one hand, and the DOD and the US federal government on the other. Both the Military Technical Agreement (MTA) relating to the military lease for Tinian and "Section 902" permit consultations and discussions between the CNMI leadership and the US DOI to (re)assess "all matters affecting the relationship between them" (Villahermosa, 2016a). In June 2016, Governor Ralph Deleon Guerrero Torres traveled to Washington, DC for the Covenant 902 talks with the Department of the Interior (DOI) and the DOD (Hofschneider, 2016b). Speaking to the DOD personally regarding the proposed CJMT document, he stated, "We have an existing contract. That needs to be fulfilled before you start proposing anything else. That's what we want. Nothing more, nothing else" (Chan, 2016). Torres referred to the MTA as the "existing contract." In addition, Torres wrote in a letter to Lt. Gen. Anthony Crutchfield, the DOD's current point of contact, in which he asserted that prior programmatic agreements "with the military should move forward first before another agreement is signed" (Villahermosa, 2016b).

Today's resistance to the militarization of the islands is met with the DOD response that the residents "knew about their military obligations when they voted for the Marianas Commonwealth Covenant." When challenged about past "unfulfilled promises" made by the DOD and previous agreements, the (now former) Marine Forces Pacific Executive Director, Craig B. Whelden, claims that he "does not know what happened 30 or 40 years ago" (Zotomayor, 2015c, p. 4). The contemporary situation is further complicated because the LFTRC plans for Tinian and Pågan islands are contingent on the relocation of the 5,000 Marines and their dependents to Andersen Air Force Base in Guam. Tinian and Pågan islands become LFTRCs, while Guam provides the housing and an additional LFTRC.

The resistance is complex, especially as the population of the CNMI serves in the US military at extremely high rates. The forms of resistance demonstrate an understanding that the "US military" is not one monolithic organization, but it is diverse. Indigenous residents proudly serve in the US Armed Forces, while at the same time they want to "protect and defend" their sacred lands and seas from becoming Live Fire Training Range Complexes: "We definitely support our military's needs to train and be ready, but please do not destroy our homes in [the] process" (Hofschneider, 2016a). The women leading the resistance also reiterate how they are not "anti-military," but demand that the DOD explain unfulfilled commitments and uphold previous agreements, before drafting *new* agreements and making additional promises to the community (T. Sablan, personal communication, July 9, 2016).

Although the projects are interconnected and interdependent, the DOD has released six Environmental Impact Statement (EIS) documents at various stages as if they are *separate* projects. This tactic of "unbundling" and detaching is the focus of a lawsuit recently filed in the federal court in Saipan and discussed in the final section of this chapter (Ngata, 2016). While the CNMI is considered "America's best-kept secret" by the tourism industry, it is also considered US "soil" by the DOD, which can potentially exercise eminent domain in the name of "national security" to use the land, sea, and air for military purposes (Ortigas, 2016; Villahermosa, 2016c).

The Community Responds During the Public Comment Period 2015
After the release of this large and highly technical CJMT document, and as required by the National Environmental Policy Act (NEPA), the US military provided only 30 to 90 days for the public to submit written or verbal comments from elected officials, governmental agencies, private-sector institutions, businesses, community organizations and the general public (Zotomayor, 2015a).[34] During this period, the DOD held (and controlled) "culturally inappropriate open-house style public meetings" at schools in Saipan and Tinian, some of which were poorly attended. Four Chamorro and Refaluwasch scholars and residents outlined how the EIS "public meeting"

forum is culturally incompatible with Chamorro and Refaluwasch methods of gathering community input and feedback.[35] They discuss how reciprocal culture creates generous hosts, but there are "obligations and proper etiquette for the guests," for example, a US government agency like the military (Cabrera et al., 2015). Within the framework of being a "good guest," the authors discuss how to properly and respectfully gather input from the community and the importance of oral culture. "Good Guests" do not ask for "more than they should receive given the relationship history and the reciprocal obligations tied to that request" (Cabrera et al., 2015).

Numerous residents are also US Armed Forces veterans, and they spoke at these meetings of their experience of "protecting and defending" US interests abroad, and how they are now resisting the destruction of their homeland. Veteran Francella Kaipat Reyes delivered her testimony with her daughter Natasha by her side. As described by her auntie:

> When she raised her right hand and swore to protect and defend her country and her people, she did so with no questions asked. And she endured the painful sacrifice of leaving her daughter motherless for 13 months while she was deployed overseas. She told us her feet touched the sands (and grounds) of Iraq, Afghanistan, and other remote places that's [sic] hard for us to pronounce, let alone spell. Through it all, she gave her all and served as a loyal, patriotic daughter of the CNMI, serving her people and country. Today, she adds her plea to the chorus of voices asking for Uncle Sam not to destroy Pågan. (Kaipat, 2015)

Peace activist, Director of Community Building with the Micronesian Climate Change Alliance, teacher, and mother, Moñeka De Oro provided testimony at the CJMT Public Meeting held at Tinian Junior Senior High School on April 30, 2015 (on the same date as the popular Tinian Fiesta, a community event that nearly all 3,500 residents attend). In a video of her testimony posted on Alternative Zero Coalition's (2015) Facebook page, De Oro proclaimed,

> As a Chamoru, I would be remiss if I didn't teach my students about the 4,000-year-old history and how our ancestors have fought hard over the last 500 years against foreign domination to keep our islands, our language, and our culture alive. We need to still honor them here today. As a Peace Activist, I would be remiss if I didn't teach my students that in the 239 years of American history, 222 of those years have been fighting wars and in conflicts all over the world. And Chamorros, Carolinians [Refaluwasch], and Micronesians have

been fighting, suffering and dying in these wars. And we STILL can't vote for a president! Enough is enough! Not one bomb, not one bullet in our islands! I would be remiss if I didn't tell my students that there is a better way. Our ancestors knew a better way. They knew something that the American forefathers never knew. Something that the American consume-and-waste economy does not know. That we are all one!

At the EIS meetings, these women (one a soldier, the other a teacher, and both mothers) highlighted "protecting" and "defending," while honoring the ancestors and the genealogy of resistance to keep the islands, language, and culture alive. The soldier vowed to protect and defend her people and country and served in the US military overseas. However, when she returned, "Uncle Sam" wanted to destroy her homeland. The teacher alluded to honoring the ancestors, whose knowledge is 4,000 years old—much older than the US "ideals" of democracy and freedom that come at the expense of the people of the Marianas and that are required parts of the curriculum in the local schools.

Despite the recurring release of numerous "lengthy, technical, complex American English-language documents that refer to one another, which have been 11,000, 4,000, and 1,500 pages long," CNMI residents, including politicians, and even US federal agencies, have expressed strong opposition to the expanding militarization (Cabrera et al., 2015). A record number of nearly 30,000 written comments opposing the project were submitted during the public response period, closing on October 2, 2015 (Hofschneider, 2016d). Residents and their supporters continue to voice their concerns through letters to the editors of the local newspapers, the *Marianas Variety* and the *Saipan Tribune* (Dayao, 2015a; Dayao, 2015b; Frain, 2015; Zotomayor, 2015b). Local residents question the necessity of using their limited landmass and waters for high impact, live-fire training purposes. Cinta M. Kaipat (2015), a Chamorro and Refaluwasch attorney who was born on Agrigan, an island north of her childhood home of Pågan, and who currently resides in Saipan, asked, "how would they [the military] like it if this was done in their backyard? If they need to do this training so badly, why not in California, Washington [State], or Texas?"

Legal Response by Dentons Environmental Science Associates
In addition to the public hearings and a record number of written comments submitted, many CNMI politicians have also voiced opposition to the further militarization

of the archipelago. In April 2015, shortly after the release of the CJMT proposal, the Federal and Foreign Affairs Committee in the Marianas House voted 19-0 in favor of a resolution introduced by the late Governor Inos to "oppose any and all proposed military use of Pågan" (Cloud, 2015). The House Committee on Federal and Foreign Affairs Chair, Representative Angel Demapan, referred to Guam's experience with the DOD and to a successful lawsuit, which saved the sacred Pågat village from becoming an LFTRC. Representative Demapan stated,

> The [US] military used the same tactics with the people of Guam when they tried to build a base in a Chamorro village which the people of Guam opposed. You would think after the military's experience with Guam that they would learn, but it appears that they didn't learn and they are treating us the same way and with the same tactics that they imposed on the people of Guam. But we will remain vigilant and we will fight for our position. (Villahermosa, 2015)

In support of this stance, the CNMI administration hired a team of legal experts, Dentons Environmental Science Associates (hereafter Dentons), to review the "legal adequacy" of the CJMT proposal on behalf of the CNMI government. They found it "fails to meet even the most basic requirements ... and the limited evidence presented in the document suggests that the CJMT would violate both federal and CNMI law" (Dentons US LLP Environmental Science Associates, 2015). Attorney Nicholas Yost of Dentons reassured the CNMI that "no one is above the law and that includes the military." Attorney Matthew Adams, also with Dentons, added that the DEIS lacks "alternatives, impact analysis, mitigation, and public input" and concluded, based on these initial findings, that the CJMT is "non-compliant with the basic principles of the NEPA" (Kedi & Scaliem, 2015, p. 3).[36]

An Environmental Commitment Example: Chiget Mortar Range

For the past 5 years, Tinian mayors, CNMI governors, and local historians have issued numerous requests for the DOD to clean up the Chiget Mortar Range. Tinian Mayor, Joey P. San Nicolas, continuously demands this must happen before Tinian considers the construction of additional LFTRCs (Chan, 2015a; Chan 2015b; Zotomayor, 2015c). The 97.5-acre Chiget Mortar artillery range was used or live-fire training from 1945-1994 and remains a military "scar" and a "dudded impact area." It is contaminated with chromium and iron, exceeding the 2008 Guam Environmental Protection Agency Pacific Basin Environment Screening Levels for groundwater that is a current or potential source of drinking water (Chan, 2015b). Located next to the popular tourist site, the Tinian Blow Hole, the range has remained closed. This serves as an example of what happens to a "high-impact area," such as those outlined in the CJMT. For those resisting militarization, it demonstrates an additional unfulfilled commitment by the DOD. Women's resistance in Tinian maintains that they are not "unpatriotic" or "un-American," and in fact, "We believed in America," but historical (in)actions by both the US federal government and the DOD show otherwise (Hofschneider, 2016d).[37] The ongoing environmental degradation is an everyday aspect of militarization that fuels the women's legal, political, and spiritual resistance.

Military Technical Agreement, Section 802
Commonly referred to as the "MTA," the Military Technical Agreement Article 8: Property, Section 802, Id.§104, states that, "property will be made available to the Government of the United States by lease to enable it to carry out its defense responsibilities" (Willens & Siemer, 2002). In addition, the MTA outlines the perimeters of the military lease and use of land in Saipan, Tinian, and No'os (Farrallon de Medinilla, FDM) islands. The 1970s lease value of the land and waters immediately adjacent to Tinian was determined at $17.5 million US (approximately $74 million today), while the entire island and waters surrounding No'os (Farrallon de Medinilla, FDM) were valued at $20,600 US (approximately $86,000 today) (Farrell, 1991, p. 595). The MTA instructs the US to "recognize" and "respect" that the people "need, depend upon and cherish their very limited land," of 184 square miles (Taitano, 2015). However, the extent of this recognition is unclear, and many are concerned that the US military may still use the principle of eminent domain and claim "national security" to push the militarization plans, while disregarding the Covenant Agreement.

Save Tinian #SaveTinian
While the MTA outlines the structure of the lease, including the acreage, price, and activities the military may conduct, the exploitation of Tinian for an LFTRC and the use of live fire are in direct violation of the Covenant Agreement. The planned construction of an LFTRC will degrade land, destroy acres of coral, and put residents at risk of death and injury from stray ordnance. Furthermore, the Environmental Protection Agency (EPA) is concerned that the planned construction will pollute the Tinian aquifer, the only groundwater source for its 3,100 residents (Hofschneider, 2016b).[38] The late Eloy Inos, the 8th Governor of the CNMI, stated it would "violate the terms and spirit of the original Tinian land lease agreement" (Chan, 2015a).

Members of the Tinian Women's Association (hereafter TWA), a non-profit group dedicated to preserving the Chamorro culture and advocating for Tinian women and children, submitted comments to the Navy's environmental review and passed out informational flyers to inform local residents. Deborah Fleming, who was a child during the formation of the Covenant and is now a spokeswoman for TWA, said that when two-thirds of Tinian was leased by the US military in the 1970s, "use of the island as a firing range was never discussed, and elders would not have agreed to this. It is as far beyond" what local communities agreed to when they participated in the political status plebiscite. Fleming continued, "Now we're presented with a totally different picture of using our island as a bombing range which we oppose because the plan fails to identify what those effects are, so that our people are aware about exactly what is happening" (Radio New Zealand, 2016). TWA member Florine Hofschneider said in a media statement, "We refuse to accept the Navy's plan to subject our children to nearly constant bombardment" (Jones, 2016).[39] The women's legal resistance is based on the MTA, while their political resistance is interwoven with the local politicians' efforts and abilities as structured through the Covenant 902 talks. As Ms. Fleming stated, "We believed in America. Instead what they want to do is destroy our island" (Hofschneider, 2016d).

While maintaining that they are not "anti-military" or "anti-American," local residents assert that the military must *at least* fulfill past promises. They believe that neither live-fire bombing in Tinian nor the use of Pågan were included in the Covenant Agreement. They question the necessity of using their limited landmass and waters for high impact, live-fire training purposes.

Save Pågan #SavePagan
The MTA outlined the lease for two-thirds of Tinian, and all of No'os; however, it never mentioned any additional islands, including Pågan island. The US Navy considers Pågan the "perfect" diverse training location. Its aim includes "tank maneuvers, amphibious landings, land mines, grenade launchers, rockets, mortars, missiles, shells, and air-dropped bombs up to 1000 pounds" from B-52s, drones, helicopters, and fighter jets (Chamorro.com, 2016). The black sand beaches are large enough for "amphibious landings and trainings" with fleets of warships (US Marine Corps Forces Pacific, 2015). The former executive director of Marine Corps forces in the Pacific claims that "We would protect it like it was our own" (Cloud, 2015).

Homestead Program

According to the late Northern Islands Mayor, Jerome Kaipat Aldan, the Chamorro people's history on Pågan goes back to the 1300s, and despite forced relocation by Spanish, German, Japanese, and US colonizers, the ancestral connections remain strong to the volcanic and resource-rich island and waters surrounding it (Hofschneider, 2016c).[40] For over 30 years, more than 50 families who consider Pågan home have planned and are eager to return to the homesteads (Cave, 2015). It is this community of residents, led by women, who are instrumental in the digital, legal, political, and spiritual resistance. The former residents who remain in Saipan have formed coalitions and consistently advocate for the implementation of a homestead program, which will grant homestead lots to former residents (Todiño, 2014).

Women's Resistance

Three women-led organizations based in the CNMI are involved in the resistance, each with varying focuses and goals. The community group, Tinian Women's Association, cites the DOD's unfulfilled past commitments and previous agreements as the source of their legal and political resistance. The Guardians of Gani' spiritually resist militarization to protect the sensitive and unique environments of the Northern Mariana Islands, and honor the genealogical connection to the archipelago. Digital resistance by Alternative Zero Coalition employs new media technologies to foster fluidarity and seek to control the future development of Pågan, as former residents express their desire to return home (Figure 2).

Figure 2

Logo for Alternative Zero Coalition, Based on Sa'ipan in the Commonwealth of the Northern Mariana Islands (CNMI)

Note. From *Alternative Zero Coalition*, by Alternative Zero Coalition, n.d. (https://www.facebook.com/AlternativeZeroMarianas/photos/a.837916642956746/840271059387971/?type=1&theater).

Through similar avenues used in Guam to counter the initial military "build-up" announcement, CNMI women are employing digital, legal, political, and spiritual forms of resistance. First, an online petition gathered international support with over 120,000 signatures and (inter)national media coverage. Second, the young women in Guam filmed and shared a solidary YouTube video, encouraging others to #jointhemovement. Third, a lawsuit was filed in July 2016 accusing the DOD of failing to create one complete EIS document or explore potential alternative locations. Finally, the resistance efforts are grounded in the spiritual connection to the seascape, supported by matriarchal principles, and shared on digital platforms through hashtags such as #SaveTinian #SavePagan and #JoinTheMovement.

As the community waits for additional EIS documents to be released by the DOD, women-led community organizations, along with a woman attorney from Tinian working with Earthjustice, filed a lawsuit against the DOD with the federal court in Saipan. The Northern Islands Mayor's Office created a CNMI Northern Islands Facebook page to highlight the beauty of the islands, and for other users to share their stories and visualize the connection. Arley Long from Tinian created the letter,"DO NOT use the inhabited US islands of Tinian and Pågan as a HIGH IMPACT bombing range" on the online petitioning platform, Change.org (Figure 3). Long's letter petitioned the legal and political "decision makers," including the DOD, in which the islanders have no input; the President of the United States, who they cannot vote for; the United States House of Representatives, in which they have a nonvoting delegate; and the United States Senate, in which they are without representation. Within a number of weeks, the petition gathered 121,454 signatures from across the globe, and stories were featured in *The Guardian* and in the US military publication, *Stars and Stripes* (McCurry, 2015; Olson, 2015).[41] Garnering this much overseas attention reveals that is not due to lack of *interest* that people beyond the archipelago are not involved, but rather that their political representatives and the (inter)national media fail to inform them.

Figure 3

"Don't Drop Bombs in my Backyard!" Screenshot from a Change.org Petition Created by Arley Long of Tini'an, May 2015

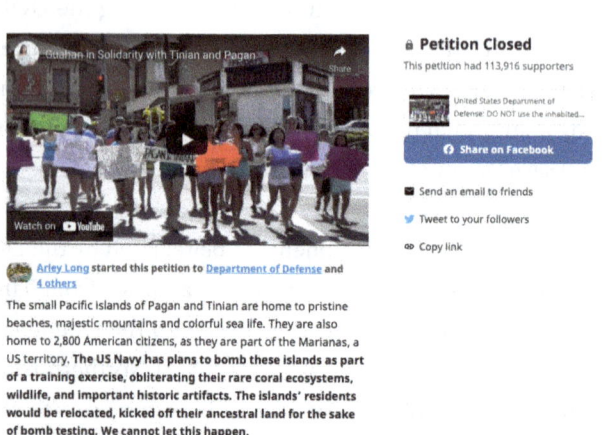

Note. Adapted from Change.org, by Arley Long, 2015, May (https://www.change.org/p/united-states-department-of-defense-do-not-use-the-inhabited-us-islands-of-tinian-pagan-as-a-high-impact-bombing-range).

As an online petition platform, Change.org allows for "petition updates" to provide up-to-date information regarding a cause, as well as comments from those virtually signing a petition.[42] There are debates regarding the "success" of online petitions, with some scholars criticizing "clicktivism" for not translating into real political or social action or movements beyond the digital realm (Johnson, 2011). Others maintain that "hashtag activism" and "digital technologies have imbued everyday citizenship with more power than ever before" (Karpf, 2015, p. 61). In this case, the online petition did lead to real action and inspired the people of the Mariana Islands to know that thousands of people *beyond* the archipelago signed on in solidarity.[43] The "one response" from the decision makers came from Representative Mike Honda of California, who is Chair Emeritus of the Congressional Asian Pacific American Caucus. Representative Honda expressed his support for the digital petition, and he commented on how the House of Representatives considered the National Defense Authorization Act in June of 2015:

My good friend Delegate Gregorio Kilili Sablan from CNMI offered an amendment that would have required the Department of Defense to reach an agreement with the Government of the Northern Marianas on the nature and scope of activities before any funds could be expended for expanded military activities in the Northern Mariana Islands ... I voted in support of the amendment. Unfortunately, it was defeated by a vote of 173-256. (Honda, 2015)

Although the online petition has since closed, the site contains comments from signatories, media updates, and links to share on new media platforms. The women protectors and defenders believe that the more people know about the Marianas archipelago, the more likely the resistance will result in stopping the Pacific pivot in the Marianas. This is an era of Indigenous resistance, such as defenders of Mauna Kea, the 4,200-meter-high volcano on the Big Island of Hawai'i and digitalized as #WeAreMaunaKea, which (so far) has halted the construction of an additional telescope, and the water protectors at Standing Rock, North Dakota, resisting the "black snake" of oil pipelines with #NoDAPL and #WaterIsLife (Ngata, 2016; NYC Stands with Standing Rock Collective, 2016). Sharing and honoring sacred rights in one place helps to inspire solidarity with others struggling elsewhere. Digitally, the protectors in Oceania and the continental US embody the reciprocal connection between the sacred environment and themselves.

In 2015, the History and Culture of Guam class at the Academy of Our Lady of Guam, launched a "video campaign in solidarity with the rest of the Marianas [sic] Islands" to support their sisters in the north. The students created the three-minute video, *Guahan in Solidarity with Tinian and Pågan*, stating, "The United States military has made plans to use our islands as live-fire ranges without consenting [sic] the Indigenous people that inhabit these precious islands." The short video opens with dramatic music and beautiful imagery of Tinian and Pågan islands, and then abruptly cuts to President Obama giving a speech, representing the 2011 "Asia Pacific Pivot" announcement he gave in Australia. The first minute includes archival footage of US flags and soldiers marching, as well as explosive live-fire military bombings and amphibious landings, analogous to those proposed for Tinian and Pågan. A news correspondent with a non-American accent narrates, stating, "the US military has not taken Indigenous and cultural factors into account. The military plans to lease the 'uninhibited island' in its entirety so the Navy, Army, Air Force, and Marines can carry out live-fire trainings." They contrast the colonial-military imagery with a young woman on the beach waving the Guam flag.

The juxtaposition of imagery is understood as the imperial ideologies pushed by the US federal government and the DOD. Framed as "national defense," the imagery includes symbols of empire—flags, military weapons, and troops. As the music shifts to relaxing instrumental, a dozen young women line up on the beach, representing a more sacred and Indigenous approach to social systems. Joining hands, the women express unity and solidarity with their sisters in the islands to the north. They display the signs: "🌺 Pågan," "Prutehi yan Difendi," and "Protect and Defend Pågan and Tinian," "Our Islands Are Sacred," and "We Stand with Pågan and Tinian." The final scene shows the young women all coming together at the main intersection in downtown Tumon Bay, the tourist district. They include the hashtag #WeStandWithPåganandTinian. The video ends with the hashtag #OurIslandsAreSacred and encourages the viewers to "Join the Movement" to protect Pågan and Tinian (see Figure 4). As of October 2021, the video has over 14,448 views and has gained support globally.[44]

Figure 4

"Guahan in Solidarity with Tinian and Pagan" Video Posted on YouTube by High School Seniors in Guåhan

Note. Adapted from *Guahan in Solidarity with Tinian and Pagan* [Video], by Tasi Yanger, 2015, May 6, (https://www.youtube.com/watch?v=bL5yDV0IZtQ)

Similar themes from the resistance in Guam are shared throughout the archipelago. Such resistance often references the Inifresi, the Chamorro pledge, through the phrase "prutehi yan difendi." The symbols of solidarity included in the #OurIslandsAreSacred #WeStandWithPaganandTinian hashtags, link the movements across the archipelago, both digitally and culturally. Arley Long, the mother who created the online petition in Tinian, included the link to the YouTube video under "updates" on the Change.org online petition as well.

It is through digital and community resistance that Chamorro and Refaluwasch women of the Mariana Islands foster transoceanic fluidity and visualize an alternative decolonized and demilitarized future for themselves and generations to come. The resistance in the Mariana archipelago navigates within Indigenous collective cultural frameworks and adapts digital technologies and new media platforms.

Legal Resistance: Suing the US Department of Defense
The final section of this chapter analyzes future possibilities, as women-led community groups filed a lawsuit against the DOD in the United States District Court for the CNMI in Saipan in July 2016 (Figure 5). Kimberlyn King-Hinds is the local attorney working with the environmental law organization, Earthjustice. In addition to gathering community support, King-Hinds has the support of CNMI elected officials, including the Mayor of Tinian, the Governor of the CNMI, and the late Mayor Aldan of the CNMI, who was the first to oppose the live-fire training (Perez, 2016). The women-led legal resistance and the filing of a lawsuit against the US Navy and DOD in the federal court in Saipan are specifically related to the ten years of EIS documents released since The United States-Japan Roadmap for Realignment Implementation Agreement announcement of 2006, culminating with the CJMT document released in 2015.

Figure 5

Women from the Commonwealth of the Northern Mariana Islands who are Leading the Lawsuit Against the Department of Defense

Note. Earthjustice lawyer David Henkin with local attorney Kimberlyn King-Hinds and the representatives of the Tinian Women's Association, the Guardians of Gani, Pagan Watch and the Center for Biological Diversity are pictured Thursday, Aug. 9, 2018, outside the Horiguchi Building in Garapan, Saipan. From *The Guam Daily Post,* by B. Manabat, 2022. https://www.postguam.com/news/cnmi/court-affirms-dismissal-of-lawsuit-against-dod-navy/article_112e0caa-fbdb-11ea-8a3f-df0ce44bc0b1.html

The lawsuit accuses the US Navy and the DOD of failing to produce one concise EIS report, a violation of the National Environmental Policy Act (NEPA). The second complaint is similar to the 2010 case in Guam in which residents successfully sued. The DOD has not considered *any* alternative locations for high-impact LFTRCs, which could potentially cause less harm (Hofschneider, 2016b).

The Law Office of Kimberlyn King-Hinds (F0495) of San Jose Village, Tinian, filed Civil No. 16-00022 in the United States District Court for the CNMI in Saipan on behalf of the following organizations: the Tinian Women's Association, Guardians of Gani', PaganWatch, and the Center for Biological Diversity. The listed defendants include: the United States Department of the Navy; Ray Mabus, Secretary of the Navy; the United States Department of Defense; and Ashton Carter, Secretary of Defense. The plaintiffs are claiming that the Navy violated the National Environmental Policy Act (NEPA), 42 USC. §§ 4321 et seq., when it failed to evaluate the environmental effects of military tests in an initial Environmental Impact Statement (EIS) relating to the permanent stationing of thousands of United States Marines on the island of Guåhan and the proposal to conduct live-fire training for those Marines on the islands of Tinian and Pågan in the Commonwealth of the Northern Mariana Islands (CNMI), as related to the Pacific pivot foreign policy. According to the complaint, the Navy failed to

> Evaluate in a single environmental impact statement (EIS) the impacts of both permanent stationing of Marines on Guam and the training on Tinian and Pågan the Navy claims those Marines will need to perform their national security mission. In addition to segmenting illegally the environmental review of its Guam and CNMI Military Relocation project, the Navy further violated its NEPA duties when it refused to consider alternative locations outside of the Mariana Islands where the Marines could accomplish their mission with fewer adverse impacts. (King-Hinds, 2016)

The Navy is in violation of the NEPA by failing to evaluate the "connected actions" between the build-up in Guam and the training in the CNMI or to evaluate the impacts of the proposed training at the same time into a single EIS. Therefore, the plaintiffs asked the court to have the 2010 and 2015 Records of Decision (hereafter ROD) regarding the Marine relocation from Okinawa to the Mariana Islands vacated and set aside. Earthjustice attorney, David Henkin, who, along with Tinian-based attorney Kimberlyn King-Hinds, represents the plaintiffs, reminded the media that the "Navy has made a decision to move 5,000 Marines and their families to Guam without considering all the alternatives or whether Guam can absorb that many people in such a short time" (Pang, 2016).[45]

If the ROD were removed, it would halt the build-up on Guåhan as well, since the projects are in fact dependent on each other, despite the DOD sidestepping that claim (Dumat-ol Daleno, 2016). Craig Whelden, formerly of Marine Corps Forces Pacific, said the plans to boost the presence of Marines in Guam and increase training in the CNMI were separate. "They are not directly related, they are indirectly related," he said. "Marines stationed on Guam need a place to train" (Hofschneider, 2016a). However, the attorney Henkin stated,

> The Navy blatantly violated those mandatory legal duties when it decided to station Marines on Guam without any consideration of the destruction from live-fire training the Navy claims those Marines will need or of other places those Marines could be trained with far fewer impacts (Pang, 2016).

Delegate Gregorio "Kilili" S. Sablan, the CNMI nonvoting representative in the US Congress, supports the "right of concerned citizens and community groups in the

Marianas to raise grievances" through the NEPA. He also recognizes that the islands play an important role for "national defense" of the US and that is "why two-thirds of Tinian, major portions of land in Saipan, and the entire island of Farallon de Medinilla (FDM) have been leased to the federal government for military purposes" (Dumat-ol Daleno, 2016).

Florine Hofschneider of the TWA said that, "when the Northern Marianas agreed to remain part of the United States [entering into the Covenant to Establish a Commonwealth of the Northern Mariana Islands in Political Union with the United States of America in 1975], destroying the northern two-thirds of our island [Tinian] with live-fire training and bombing was never part of the deal" (Jones, 2016). Her protection and defense resist the proposed high-impact training involving rockets and grenades planned for 20 weeks per year and "non-live-fire" activities for 22 weeks a year because of their impact on future generations.

The Indigenous Chamorro and Refaluwasch families who once called Pågan home will be prevented from returning if Pågan becomes a target for bombing practice 4 months a year. Whelden claimed that high-explosive munitions would "only be used on the volcanic hull area of Pågan," while the wide beaches are perfect for amphibious exercises (Hofschneider, 2016a). The groups state in a complaint that such military training poses "existential threat" for the Guardians of Gani' and others who advocate a return to "a more traditional, productive and fulfilling lifestyle." The Guardians and their members view Gani', the islands north of Saipan, as the "last frontier to revive their traditions and culture" (Sputnik News, 2016).

While the issues of high-impact and live-fire training are beyond the scope of the Covenant, and the military already uses two-thirds of Tinian and all of No'os, the women are adamant in resisting the additional acquisition of Pågan. Attorney King-Hinds is determined to use her Indigenous knowledge(s) and honor of cultural frameworks, as well as her legal power and Western education, to protect and defend the Mariana Islands.

In May 2017, the *Pacific Daily News* reported that the lawsuit "threatens training operations in the CNMI" (Limtiaco, 2017). Marine General Robert B. Neller said it would be a "problem" if the lawsuit ultimately killed the firing range plan for Guam

Marines" (Olson, 2017). Now is the waiting period for the next EIS document to be released since the DOD has "agreed to perform an additional analysis of the potential environmental impacts," (Hofschneider, 2016a). A new document is expected "later this year" [2017] according to Marine General Neller, and a Record of Decision is expected in summer 2018 (Limtiaco, 2017; Hofschneider, 2016b). The current military activity along the Korean Peninsula also complicates the build-up plans, perhaps postponing them for years to come (Radio New Zealand, 2017).

Conclusion of Fanachu Famalåo'an:
Women's Resistance to Militarization in the Northern Mariana Islands

This chapter analyzed three women-led written and visual resistance efforts encompassing digital, legal, political, and spiritual elements. The Change.org petition, a form of written and digital resistance addressed to Washington DC politicians, was "signed" by over 120,000 people beyond the archipelago and picked up by the (inter)national media (see Figure 3). The YouTube solidarity video, a form of visual resistance portraying political, legal, and spiritual messages, was created by a Guam high school girls' class and was linked on digital sites through hashtags (see Figure 4). The third example, the community lawsuit against the DOD, is the most recent form of written legal and political resistance to militaristic expansion in the Marianas archipelago (see Figure 5). The combination of digital and legal organizing is growing the nonviolent and organized resistance. The strategy is to continue to follow the lawsuit, and prepare for the release of additional DOD plans and EIS documents.

Women are honoring their ancestral knowledge(s) to protect their communities and defend their sacred and scarce land and seascapes from further US militarization. Their resistance combines digital technologies and new media platforms to foster fluidity (solidarity) and unity between Guam, Tinian, Saipan, and the Gani' islands (the Northern Mariana Islands). Through digital, political, and legal resistance, they are visualizing and imagining alternative futures for the Mariana Islands as places to re-establish spiritual practices with eco-tourism possibilities. This is part of the long-term and continuous involvement of many dedicated mothers, sisters, aunties, grandmothers, educators, politicians, and friends in the Marianas. Because militarization is a step-by-step process, so is demilitarization. These women understand that refusing any form of the military is not possible (just yet), but they apply legal pressure to enforce previous promises and agreements. The pending lawsuit is the most effective form of contemporary resistance.

Chamorro and Refaluwasch women's approaches of honoring their matrilineal heritage, respecting family genealogy, and cultivating the connection to the land and seas provide strength. It is through Chamorro and Refaluwasch epistemologies that they resist the devastation of US militarized security protection.

References

Alternative Zero Coalition. (n.d.). *Home* [Facebook page]. Facebook. Retrieved December 11, 2018, from https://www.facebook.com/AlternativeZeroMarianas/photos/a.837916642956746/840271059387971/?type=1&theater

Alternative Zero Coalition. (2015, May 15). *Tinian youth came out in full force to voice their concerns.* [Video]. Facebook. https://www.facebook.com/pg/AlternativeZeroMarianas/videos/?ref=page_internal

Cabrera, G. S., Kaipat, C. M., Marsh-Taitano K. G., & Perez, R. (2015, June 16). Facts you need to know about gathering community input. *Saipan Tribune.* http://www.saipantribune.com/index.php/facts-you-need-to-know-about-gathering-community-input/

Cave, J. (2015, June 13). The Pentagon wants to bomb the hell out of this tiny Pacific island. *Huff Post.* http://www.huffingtonpost.com/2015/05/29/pagan-island-marines-military_n_7342168.html

Chamorro.com. (2016). *Fanohge Chamorro put i tano'-ta!.* http://www.chamorro.com/

Chan, D. B. (2015a, June 29). Public hearing set for clean up of Chiget mortar range. *Saipan Tribune.* http://www.saipantribune.com/index.php/public-hearing-set-for-clean-up-of-chiget-mortar-range/

Chan, D. B. (2015b, August 19). Tinian hearing on Chiget Range today. *Saipan Tribune.* http://www.saipantribune.com/index.php/tinian-hearing-on-chiget-range-today/

Chan, D. B. (2016, June 16). '902 military talks not a matter of give-and-take' Torres: Live-fire bombing and training 'incompatible' with Covenant and technical agreements. *Saipan Tribune.* http://www.saipantribune.com/index.php/902-military-talks-not-matter-give-take/

Cloud, D. S. (2015, May 17). *Island of Pagan opposes plan to use it for Marine invasion training.* Los Angeles Times. http://www.latimes.com/world/asia/la-fg-marines-invade-20150517-story.html - page=1

Dayao, J. (2015a, May 22). DEIS inconsistencies: Tinian and Pagan. *Saipan Tribune.* http://www.saipantribune.com/index.php/deis-inconsistencies-tinian-and-pagan/

Dayao, J. (2015b, May 29). A growing momentum to protect sacred lands. *Saipan Tribune.* http://www.saipantribune.com/index.php/a-growing-momentum-to-protect-scared-lands/

Dé Ishtar, Z. (1994). *Daughters of the Pacific.* Spinifex Press.

Dentons US LLP Environmental Science Associates. (2015). Memorandum: Brief summary of findings regarding legal adequacy of draft environmental impact statement for the commonwealth of the northern mariana islands joint military training project. Dentons.

Dumat-ol Daleno, G. (2016, August 2). CNMI suit could halt Guam buildup. *Pacific Daily News.* http://www.guampdn.com/story/news/2016/08/02/cnmi-suit-could-halt-guam-buildup/87943268/

Farrell, D. A. (1991). *History of the Northern Mariana Islands.* CNMI Public School System.

Frain, S. (2015, May 29). People of the Marianas, you are not alone. *Marianas Variety.* http://www.mvariety.com/cnmi/cnmi-news/editorials/77356-people-of-the-marianas-you-are-not-alone

Frain, S. C. (2016). Resisting political colonization and American militarization in the Marianas Archipelago. *AlterNative: An International Journal of Indigenous Peoples, 12*(3), 298–315.

Frain, S. C. (2017). Women's resistance in the Marianas Archipelago: A US colonial homefront & militarized frontline. *Feminist Formations, 29*(1), 97–135.

Hofschneider, A. (2016a, July 27). Suit challenges US Military plans to bomb islands in Marianas. *Honolulu Civil Beat.* http://www.civilbeat.org/2016/07/suit-challenges-us-military-plans-to-bomb-islands-in-marianas/

Hofschneider, A. (2016b, December 12). Chapter 1: Can these islands survive America's military pivot to Asia? *Honolulu Civil Beat.* http://www.civilbeat.org/2016/12/can-these-islands-survive-americas-military-pivot-to-asia/

Hofschneider, A. (2016c, December 13). Chapter 2: The fight to save Pagan Island from US bombs. *Honolulu Civil Beat.* http://www.civilbeat.org/2016/12/the-fight-to-save-pagan-island-from-us-bombs/

Hofschneider, A. (2016d, December 14). Chapter 3: Tinian: 'we believed in America'. *Honolulu Civil Beat.* http://www.civilbeat.org/2016/12/tinian-we-believed-in-america/

Honda, M. (2015, 2 July). *Honda Motor Company's response.* Change.org. https://www.change.org/p/united-states-department-of-defense-do-not-use-the-inhabited-us-islands-of-tinian-pagan-as-a-high-impact-bombing-range/responses/28935

Johnson, H. L. (2011). Click to donate: Visual images, constructing victims and imagining the female refugee. *Third World Quarterly, 32*(6), 1015–1037. https://doi.org/10.1080/01436597.2011.586235

Jones, C. (2016, July 27). US Navy sued over live-fire training plan in Pacific Ocean. *Navy Times*. https://www.navytimes.com/story/military/2016/07/27/us-navy-sued-over-live-fire-training-plan-pacific-ocean/87613322/

Kaipat, C. M. (2015, May 1). Pagan. *Saipan Tribune*. http://www.saipantribune.com/index.php/pagan/

Karpf, D. (2015). Look at the man behind the curtain: Computational management in "spontaneous" citizen political campaigning. In, G. Elmer, G. Langlois, & J. Redden (Eds.), *Compromised data from social media to big data* (pp. 61–90). Bloomsbury Publishing.

Kedi, K. A., & Scaliem, F. (2015). Relative to expressing opposition to any and all proposed military use of the Northern Mariana Islands of Pågan and any increase in military activities on Tinian, Commonwealth of the Northern Mariana Islands. Resolution No. 34-GA-16, CD1 by Association of Pacific Island Legislatures (APIL). Island of Pohnpei, Federated States of Micronesia.

King-Hinds, K. (2016, July 27). *Complaint for Declaratory and Injunctive Relief*. Edited by United States District Court for the Northern Mariana Islands. Vol. Civil No. 16-00022. District Court for the Northern Mariana Islands: Law Office of Kimberlyn King-Hinds.

Limtiaco, S. (2017, May 25). Marine commander says lawsuit threatens training operations in the CNMI. *Pacific Daily News*. http://www.guampdn.com/story/news/2017/05/26/marine-commander-says-lawsuit-threatens-training-operations-cnmi/347967001/

Long, A. (2015, May). *Don't drop bombs in my backyard!* Change.org. https://www.change.org/p/united-states-department-of-defense-do-not-use-the-inhabited-us-islands-of-tinian-pagan-as-a-high-impact-bombing-range

Manabat, B. (2016, December 5). Navy asks court to dismiss environmental groups' lawsuit. *The Marianas Variety*. http://www.mvariety.com/cnmi/cnmi-news/local/91172-navy-asks-court-to-dismiss-environmental-groups-lawsuit

Manabat, B. (2020, September 23). Court affirms dismissal of lawsuit against DOD, Navy. *Guam Daily Post*. https://www.postguam.com/news/cnmi/court-affirms-dismissal-of-lawsuit-against-dod-navy/article_112e0caa-fbdb-11ea-8a3f-dfoce44bc0b1.html

Martinez, K. (2015, April 1). Court rules navy war games violate law protecting whales and dolphins. Press Release by National Resource Defense Council. https://www.nrdc.org/media/2015/150331-0

McCurry, J. (2015, June 15). Pacific Islands try to stop US military's plans for a simulated war zone. *The Guardian*. http://www.theguardian.com/world/2015/jun/11/bid-block-us-military-plans-pacific-islands-simulated-war-zone-pagan-tinian

Ngata, T. (2016, October 18). Stone in our shoe: The military co-option of indigineity [sic] and protection exposed. *Tina Ngata*. https://thenonplasticmaori.wordpress.com/2016/10/18/stone-in-our-shoe-the-military-co-option-of-indigineity-and-protection-exposed/

NYC Stands with Standing Rock Collective. (2016). *#StandingRockSyllabus*. NYC Stands with Standing Rock. https://nycstandswithstandingrock.wordpress.com/standingrocksyllabus/

Olson, W. (2015, April 17). Mariana officials bristle at US military's live-fire plans for Pagan, Tinian. *Stars and Stripes*. http://www.stripes.com/news/pacific/mariana-officials-bristle-at-us-militarys-live-fire-plans-for-pagan-tinian-1.340648

Olson, W. (2017, May 26). North Korea threat could slow Marines' relocation, commandant says. *Stars and Stripes*. https://www.stripes.com/news/north-korea-threat-could-slow-marines-relocation-commandant-says-1.470332 - .WSyG6VLMxL9

Ortigas, M. (2016, September 1). Voices from the Northern Mariana Islands: Resident of Northern Mariana Islands, "America's best kept secret," recount their woes far from the world's attention. *Al Jazeera*. http://www.aljazeera.com/blogs/asia/2016/08/voices-northern-mariana-islands-160831152622901.html

Pagarao, D. S. (2017, February 20). Aldan succumbs to heart attack. *Saipan Tribune*. https://www.saipantribune.com/index.php/aldan-succumbs-heart-attack/

Paik, K. (2014, June 21). The Pacific Pivot. *Island Breath*. http://islandbreath.blogspot.co.nz/2014/06/the-pacific-pivot.html

Pang, N. (2016, August 10). Implications for Guam in NMI military buildup lawsuit. *Marianas Variety*. http://www.mvariety.com/cnmi/cnmi-news/local/88301-implications-for-guam-in-nmi-military-buildup-lawsuit

Perez, J. (2016, September 12). Aldan: I'm no longer alone opposing live-firing range. *Saipan Tribune*. http://www.saipantribune.com/index.php/aldan-im-no-longer-alone-opposing-live-firing-range/

Radio New Zealand. (2016, July 29). *CNMI lawsuit probes difference in take on islands' use* [Radio broadcast]. Radio New Zealand. http://www.radionz.co.nz/international/pacific-news/309677/cnmi-lawsuit-probes-difference-in-take-on-islands'-use

Radio New Zealand. (2017, May 29). *US moving troops from Japan to Guam could be delayed* [Radio broadcast]. Radio New Zealand. http://www.radionz.co.nz/international/pacific-news/331803/us-moving-troops-from-japan-to-guam-could-be-delayed

Sputnik News. (2016). 'Militarized wasteland': US Navy, Defense Department sued over Marianas training. *Sputnik News*. https://sputniknews.com/military/201608051043954550-marianas-activists-fight-navy-testing/

Taitano, F. (2015). *US Department of the Interior. Office of Insular Affairs. Commonwealth of the Northern Mariana Islands*. https://www.doi.gov/oia/islands/cnmi

Todiño, J. B. (2014, March 30). Northern Island residents want homestead program implemented. *Marianas Variety*. http://www.mvariety.com/cnmi/cnmi-news/local/64163-northern-island-residents-want-homestead-program-implemented

Torre, F. D. L. (2017, January 9). Groups insist on standing to sue Navy over live-fire plan. *Saipan Tribune*. http://www.saipantribune.com/index.php/groups-insist-standing-sue-navy-live-fire-plan/

US Marine Corps Forces Pacific. (2015). *Draft environmental impact statement/overseas environmental impact statement for Commonwealth of the Northern Marianas Islands joint military training*. United States Department of the Navy. Naval Facilities Engineering Command, Pacific. http://www.cnmijointmilitarytrainingeis.com/documents.

Villahermosa, C. A. E. (2015, July 1). NMI consultants: Military not above the law; draft EIS not in compliance with law. *Marianas Variety*. http://www.mvariety.com/cnmi/cnmi-news/local/78375-nmi-consultants-military-not-above-the-law-draft-eis-not-in-compliance-with-law

Villahermosa, C. A. E. (2016a, January 13). Interior official: White House considering NMI's request for 902 talks. *Marianas Variety*. http://www.mvariety.com/cnmi/cnmi-news/local/83009-interior-official-white-house-considering-nmi-s-request-for-902-talks

Villahermosa, C. A. E. (2016b, March 18). Torres wants prior agreements with military to move forward. *Marianas Variety*. http://www.mvariety.com/cnmi/cnmi-news/local/84650-torres-wants-prior-agreements-with-military-to-move-forward

Villahermosa, C. A. E. (2016c, May 11). House passes measure barring DPL from leasing public land for live-fire or bombing activity. *Marianas Variety*. http://www.mvariety.com/cnmi/cnmi-news/local/86069-house-passes-measure-barring-dpl-from-leasing-public-land-for-live-fire-or-bombing-activity

Villahermosa, C. A. E. (2017, April 26). Rep. Angel Demapan questions CJMT meetings. *Marianas Variety*. http://www.mvariety.com/cnmi/cnmi-news/local/94776-rep-angel-demapan-questions-cjmt-meetings

Willens, H. P., & Siemer, D. C. (2002). *An honorable accord: The Covenant between the Northern Mariana Islands and the United States, Pacific Islands monograph series 18*. University of Hawai'i, Honolulu.

Yanger, Tasi. (2015, May 6). *Guahan in solidarity with Tinian and Pagan* [Video]. YouTube. https://www.youtube.com/watch?v=bL5yDV0IZtQ

Zotomayor, A. V. (2015a, May 1). Saipan residents say 'no' to Tinian, Pagan military training. *Marianas Variety*. http://www.mvariety.com/cnmi/cnmi-news/local/76415-saipan-residents-say-no-to-tinian-pagan-military-training

Zotomayor, A. V. (2015b, May 4). Tinian residents emphatically oppose military exercises. *Marianas Variety*. http://www.pireport.org/articles/2015/05/04/tinian-residents-emphatically-oppose-military-exercises

Zotomayor, A. V. (2015c, May 5). Marianas to play key role in national, regional security: Expert. *Marianas Variety*. http://pidp.eastwestcenter.org/pireport/2015/May/05-05-02.html

May I Borrow Some Soy Sauce? The Changing Dynamics of Neighborly Interactions in Rota

Ajani Burrell

The story of Rota is, in many ways, the story of the Commonwealth of the Northern Mariana Islands (CNMI), and in a broader sense, the story of colonial territories in modernity. After the first European visitor to the Marianas in 1521 (Russell, 2002, p. 23)—a brief stopover by Ferdinand Magellan as he attempted to circumnavigate the globe—the people of the region experienced over 400 years of colonial occupation. For the last half century, life has also been dominated by an external power, the United States. Today, the CNMI is a US territory, affected as much by globalization and the technical revolution as any other place on Earth. And yet, the story of Rota—and that of the CNMI—has its own inimitable threads.

The main road from the airport to the historical population center of the island, Songsong village, runs along the northern coastline. On one side, jagged rocks jut from turquoise water. Fronted by foliage—coconut, palm, papaya, noni—and foregrounded by the expansive blue of the Pacific, the shoreline is pockmarked by rocky beaches. On some of the beaches stand thatched or concrete canopies covering picnic tables and barbeque grills. Both the beaches and the gathering areas are almost always empty. On the other side, the land rises in a series of raised limestone plateaus overrun by more emerald foliage. Perhaps most notable along this drive, apart from the tranquil beauty, are the hand-painted signs welcoming everyone—residents and visitors alike. One such sign admonishes passersby of the "Aluf Luta" (the Rota Wave), which helps explain why the drivers of the two or three cars that pass wave as they go by, and why, as one quickly observes, nearly everyone in Rota, whether driver or pedestrian, does the same. Recently designated its own two-week celebration period in August, the Rota Wave is a celebrated part of the island's culture and emblematic of the people's hospitable disposition.

This hospitable disposition was on full display as I went around speaking with people during my two visits to the island. I asked them what they thought about life today, or whether they had noticed any changes in the past few years. Common themes abounded. Most people lamented the loss of some of the more traditional elements of the island's culture. In this case, the traditional culture is best understood as the customs and practices of the local population, which is still overwhelmingly Chamorro and infused with some of the traditions wrought by several centuries of colonial influence, most notably Spanish. The traditional culture, many fear, is dying out. The Chamorro language is spoken less and less with each subsequent generation—its place usurped by English. Notions of respect (respetu) are being supplanted by Western ideals. Manngingi', the practice of taking an elder's hand and sniffing it in a show of respect, is decreasing in prevalence. Instead of manngingi', if there is any display at all, a simple kiss on the cheek (casually referred to as åmen) often suffices. The cultivation and consumption of traditional foods has also been waning, as have other practices such as traditional healing, and skills including basket weaving, fishing, and canoe building.

These circumstances, however, are not unique to Rota. Similar developments have taken place across the Marianas (and other parts of Micronesia) to varying degrees. They are also, in some way, the more notable aspects of cultural loss. It is easy to understand and appreciate that a language is dying, or that certain skills are no longer being widely transmitted from generation to generation. I had come to Rota in hopes of identifying some aspect of the contemporary culture that is quintessentially and ineffably Rota. On my second trip, I stumbled across a potential subject.

For many people in the CNMI, Rota occupies a special place in the culture of the region. As more than one person has said to me, Rota is home to the purest form of Chamorro culture left in the Marianas. The reasons for this can, in part, be traced back over hundreds of years. The divergence between Chamorros of Rota and those of the other inhabited southern islands in the Mariana chain—Saipan, Tinian, and Guam—originates in their different fates under the so-called Spanish period (1521–1899), which Russell (1994; 2002, p. 23) breaks up into an "alternate historic chronology for Rota" that includes three shorter periods: Protohistoric (1521–1668); Reducción (1668–1700); and Isolated Spanish Outpost (1700–1899). The Roman Catholic Church created a lasting foothold in Rota and the rest of the Marianas during the Reducción period, bringing with it the decline or disappearance of many traditional Chamorro practices (Russell, 1998, p. 318). The reducción included the forced relocation of the Indigenous people from the northern islands to Guam. In this, only Rota was spared, and by 1722, when the last of the Chamorro families from Saipan were relocated to Guam, Rota was the only other inhabited island of the Marianas (Farrell, 2011, p. 75). The reducción also included the forced relocation of Chamorros "from traditional settlements to mission villages," which also served to undermine Indigenous culture by upending "traditional land-use practices" and ensuring "that non-Christian practices were efficiently stamped out" (Russell, 1998, p. 317).

Nevertheless, evidence suggests that the impacts of the reducción and subsequent historical eras were not quite as disruptive in Rota as in Guam. Though Rota continued to have a regular missionary presence, reports from those missionaries suggest infrequent visits from outsiders, whether Spanish delegations from Guam or vessels from other nations (Russell, 2002, p. 38). Carlos Madrid (2014), in his case study of Rota's Casa Real, presents evidence that the inhabitants of Rota publicly voiced their displeasure over abusive practices by the Spanish Governor of the region, and suggests that "Christian names were not used on a daily basis, at least not by the people of Rota" (pp. 49-50). Other, later evidence also suggests a minimal Spanish presence in Rota during the Isolated Spanish Outpost period. Census figures from 1758 indicate 244 "Native Indians" living in Rota, but register no "Soldiers" or "Spanish & Filipinos." By comparison, the figures for Guam are 1467, 170, and 830, respectively (Lévesque, 1999, p. 265). Madrid (2014) also reports that over a century later, the people of Rota continued to resist attempts by government officials to relocate the Indigenous population to Guam (p. 50). Rota's isolation was such that for much of this time the island was a refuge for Chamorros fleeing Spanish oppression elsewhere in the chain (Russell, 2002, p. 33). This isolation seems to have continued through the German administration as well (Russell, 2002, p. 39), with the "German administrative presences as exercised by German nationals" limited to Saipan, except for a brief period from 1904-1906, and on average roughly just one official visit to Rota per year on behalf of the administration (Spennemann, 2008, pp. 6–8).

For a number of reasons, the relative isolation of Rota has continued to the present. This is not to say that the island was without dramatic cultural shifts and influences. Rather, given its relative inaccessibility and smaller population, it seems Rota experienced comparatively less impact on its culture than the other islands. One metric that helps underscore this comes from recent demographic data. The 2010 US Census indicates that Rota is the only island in the chain that, as of that year, had a population that was majority Chamorro (CNMI Department of Commerce/Central Statistic Division, 2012, p. 8). In 2010, approximately 37% of the population of Guam were of Chamorro origin (Guam State Data Center Bureau of Statistics and Plans, 2012, p. 24). In Tinian, that figure is about 38%. In Saipan, only 22% of the population were of Chamorro origin (and 26% overall were of Northern Marianas descent—either Carolinian or Chamorro), but in Rota, nearly 52% of the population were of Chamorro origin, more than double that in Saipan (CNMI Department of Commerce/Central Statistic Division, 2012, p. 8). Another metric that helps characterize this unique place in the region comes from the 2016 CNMI Household Income and Expenditure Survey Report (HIESR), which indicates that in both 2005 and 2016 Rota had the second highest percentage of households speaking Chamorro at home (43.8% and 37.8%, respectively) of all the districts in the CNMI. Rota's rates are about double those for the CNMI as a whole (21.5% and 18.6%, respectively). Rota is also the only island of the three inhabited islands in the CNMI where a plurality of the households spoke Chamorro in both 2005 and 2016 (CNMI Department of Commerce/Central Statistic Division, 2017, pp. 21–22). These figures suggest that Rota has been able to retain a more Chamorro identity than its neighbors have been able to.

Despite seeming to retain a stronger Chamorro identity than the other Mariana islands, Rota has still undergone cultural changes, both big and small. During one of my visits, I spoke with Magdalena Mesgon, the Director of the Department of Community and Cultural Affairs (DCCA). She revealed a more nuanced dynamic than many others I had heard, but one perhaps no less telling about the culture today. We were in her air-conditioned office, in what used to be the island's high school, a far cry from the hot, humid weather outside. We had been chatting for a while, when I asked her, again, whether there was anything different about Rota between today and the recent past. She paused for a few moments. "People today," she eventually said, "don't go and ask their neighbors for favors anymore" (M. Mesgon, personal communication, December 12, 2017).

I asked her what she meant. She explained that in the past, if you ran out of salt or soy sauce or eggs and needed it at that moment, you could just go over to the neighbors or send one of the kids to borrow what you needed. But today, people did not do that anymore. "Do you still do this?" I asked. "No," she said, a sad smile on her face.

I was surprised. Shocked even. I almost did not believe it, given what I had learned of the people and customs of Rota. Surely, an island with less than 3,000 inhabitants, a place where everyone professed to know pretty much everyone else, where one way or another you were related to half the island, including many of your neighbors, a place as welcoming and friendly as Rota, where you wave to everyone you pass on the street, such a place would not have lost the practice of asking a neighbor for a small favor in a pinch? Surely that could not be the case, could it? It must just be her, right? "I think most people don't do this anymore," she replied. I decided to find out.

To standardize the exchanges, I simply told people that I was researching present-day culture in Rota and asked if I could pose a few questions. I would start with a hypothetical, based on the dynamic Magdalena shared: you're at home cooking and you realize you've run out of something essential—soy sauce or salt or eggs; would you go to your neighbors to borrow the item? Of the dozen people I spoke with, only one answered unequivocally in the affirmative. For everyone else, the answer was usually a "no" or a qualified "no."

The negative responses I received fell along a spectrum. A few people indicated that the decision to borrow a missing item "depended on the neighbor." If a neighbor was a close family member, they were more comfortable asking for a favor, but they would not ask a more distant relative or neighbors without a relationship to the family. For many others, the answer was an outright and often emphatic "no." A few people I encountered at the airport before leaving Rota said, pointedly, that they do not ask their neighbors for favors. Two women I interviewed at the DCCA offices assumed they had misunderstood what I was asking, leading to the following exchange:

Woman 1: "I thought you were going to say about asking for soy sauce or what in the neighborhood."
Me: "Yes, literally."
Both women laugh.
Woman 1 (with look of mild horror on her face): "Oh-oh-oh, okay."
Woman 2 (shaking her head): "No, we don't do that now."
Me: "So, that is a thing?"
Woman 1: "Back then, yes. Now, no."

A local man in his early 20s, whom I had met at the Chenchon Park Bird Sanctuary, was even more blunt. The sanctuary encompasses a rocky coastline and dense foliage that stretches to the ocean. Birds soared and dipped on a brisk breeze, but otherwise, the park was tranquil in the bright midday sun. Under a gazebo perched atop the cliffline, I posed the hypothetical to him: would he borrow some small item from a neighbor? "Fuck no," he said, shaking his head. "No way."

As people shared their thoughts with me on this issue, I would, as a follow-up, ask why they (and people in general) would not ask a neighbor to borrow some small kitchen item. Almost every person indicated that the reluctance came from a sense of pride or shame. As I reflected on my exchange with the young man at the bird sanctuary, and on my conversations with other people on the subject up to that point, it was difficult for me to understand how this practice could be associated with pride and shame. I also struggled to understand the strength behind the reactions shared by people I spoke with. Often, I could see the discomfort in their faces or in their body language. It was as though even being asked the question subjected them to some sort of shame. The young man was visibly distraught by the suggestion that he might need to ask his neighbor for a favor.

Perhaps the most confounding aspect of this phenomenon was how at odds it was with historical and even current perspectives of the people living in Rota. As an extremely isolated outpost for much of its history, including the post-WWII period, the Rotanese as a group were almost entirely self-reliant. Their survival depended on communal sharing. As one Chamorro manåmku' (elderly person) told me, up until a couple of decades ago, it did not matter if supply ships came or if there was food in the stores or not. The people grew and caught the food they needed. Today, if the ships did not come, people would starve, but historically, the self-reliance and sharing culture of the island was sufficient for survival. Another Chamorro manåmku' I spoke with, named Tony, said much of the same thing. Interestingly, one of the first things Tony shared before I could even pose the standard hypothetical, was that in the past "you can just go to your neighbor and ask for salt or sugar or whatever you need ... but now no more." She explained it this way:

> Before we don't really need money because we don't have money them days, but we work and share things so if you need something then I can share it with you if I have it ... but nowadays if you don't have anything, you don't have money, you're going to die because nobody provide you ... When I was growing up that how I know how people live. In the morning, they don't have, you know, not too many people have matches to make fire, so we usually use wooden stove and we use fire, we have to make fire, so whoever first make fire, on the neighbor, then the next neighbor will come over and ask for fire, even the fire they ask, so they go there and get the coconut shells and make fire, and the next one that sees you smoking then they will come over and get fire, but those are the difference. Now no more.

Given this background, it seems strange then, that in a couple decades, a practice once considered normal, commonplace—necessary even—would become a near-anathema riven with shame.

This circumstance becomes even more confounding in light of other, related practices still evident today. Several people, as we discussed this particular development, also indicated that key components of the sharing culture still exist. The earnest young man I spoke with at the sanctuary told me that if he goes fishing or hunting and comes home with a good catch, he will keep some for himself and his immediate family then divvy up the rest to share. With whom? His neighbors. He said he would take a few pounds to each of his neighbors. And his neighbors would, in turn, do the same with their fish, meat, fruit, or vegetables. But would he, in light of this fact, go to the neighbors for some salt or soy sauce, I asked. "Never," he replied. He was not the only person to mention this dynamic, as several people I spoke with said they too regularly shared excess food from harvests or catches with their neighbors, and their neighbors with them. Similarly, the people of Rota, perhaps because the community is so small and most people are acquainted, have a strong sense of communal trust. I had noticed as I was driving around that there is a nearly complete absence of "Private Property" or "No Trespassing" signs posted on people's land. Coming from Saipan, a larger island where it sometimes seems every other property posts such signs, this struck me as interesting. I asked people about it, and they said no one uses those signs because everyone knows everyone, and more importantly, they *trust* one another. The reluctance, then, to borrow from one's neighbor from time to time is difficult to reconcile in light of such dynamics.

Another interesting aspect of this phenomenon is the relative speed with which it has become ubiquitous. While responses differed among people regarding when this practice changed for them, almost everyone I spoke with indicated that the change had come within the last generation. Most of the people I interviewed were middle-aged, and most told me that they could definitely remember times as a child or adolescent when their parents or grandparents sent them to the neighbors for some missing cooking item. But this was not just limited to those who were middle-aged. The young man at the bird sanctuary could also remember times in his youth when his parents or grandparents sent him on similar errands. For others, the conversion was even more recent, and occasionally they could pinpoint the exact time at which they realized the change was upon them. Magdalena, the Director of DCCA, recounted a conversation with her son from a few years earlier. She had asked him, one day before he left for the military if he could "go to the neighbor and ask … for some foil because I'm wrapping something for my potluck." He turned around, shocked, and said "Mom, are you not ashamed?" Surprised, she said no, she was not ashamed, and called the neighbor and asked about the foil. The neighbor was perfectly happy to share and said to send over the boy to pick it up. Her son refused and she had to pick it up herself. After that, she too stopped asking her neighbors for these sorts of favors. In this regard, she is not alone. I began asking people when they thought this behavior changed, and for many, while they still might have gone to the neighbor 10 years ago, nearly everyone that I asked said they would not have gone to the neighbor 5 years ago. This seems to suggest that in the span of a decade or less, the practice of going to one's neighbors to ask a favor has significantly decreased in prevalence.

Much uniformity existed in people's description of their own behavior in these situations. Similarly, there was a pervasive belief that most other people felt and acted the same way (interviewees noted that their neighbors did not come to them anymore either to borrow these small items). And while there was also a relatively uniform belief that the underlying cause of this change is a sense of pride or shame, the possible explanations for why this change has manifested varied more widely. What follows is a brief description and commentary on some of the possible causes of this phenomenon as identified by Rota residents.

Economic Shifts
Several people believed that, in some way, economic factors contributed to the development. I found it remarkable that during several interviews, when respondents considered why people stopped asking favors of their neighbors or why there might be a sense of pride or shame in doing so, a fear of being viewed as unable to provide for themselves was articulated. In the words of one interviewee, "You have a job with a high salary and you need to ask me for salt?" Another said the neighbors would think, "She just got paid yesterday. She can't even buy ketchup?" This feeling seems to suggest that as more people acquire gainful and reasonably well-compensated employment, they should be able to afford these necessities. That people might not have these necessities would thereby imply they were somehow irresponsible with their finances, rather than a simple coincidence that one unexpectedly ran out of a basic item. Economic data from the CNMI might provide additional evidence suggesting this phenomenon took root around a decade ago and has since strengthened. The first decade of the 21st century in the CNMI was a period of growth, followed by a rapid downturn in the economy that reached a nadir in the aftermath of the global housing market collapse. Since that time, the local economy—in Rota and the wider CNMI—has steadily grown. Between 2005 and 2016, Rota saw an overall increase in employment of more than 10%, according to the 2016 HIES report, while the CNMI, as a whole, saw a similar decrease (though this decrease is largely due to the closing of the garment industry). A higher percentage of workers in Rota are employed by the government than in the other islands, though this percentage decreased over that same period. The data are somewhat mixed in that it seems more people are employed today than they were a decade ago, but the median and mean incomes for Rota have decreased significantly over that same period, much more significantly than for the CNMI as a whole (CNMI Department of Commerce/Central Statistics

Division, 2017, pp. 24-29). This could suggest that while more people are working, money for households has become more scarce, which might explain why people have such a sense of shame if they need to ask a neighbor for a favor.

Americanization

The rising influence of American values was another oft-cited contributing factor to this phenomenon. As people shared their perspectives, the American values in question seemed to be those of capitalism, individualism, and self-reliance rather than the more traditional communal values of the islands. When I asked Tony why so many people no longer asked their neighbors for favors, she said, "Time[s] change, everything change[d], money talks and bullshit walks." Her sentiment, and use of this quintessential American trope, was echoed by several other people, and she was not the only person to utter, verbatim, this saying. Other people also mentioned that they or their family members had, in the last few decades, spent a significant amount of time in the United States working, studying, or living with relatives, which invariably impacted their worldview and practices. This is increasingly the case for the islands, as more and more Indigenous people move to the mainland for better education and employment opportunities, bringing back with them some of the values acquired during their time away. The degree of cultural decline in the islands may well be seen as proportional to the degree of American influence in those islands. Guam, by most accounts, has undergone the greatest deterioration of Indigenous culture (it has been a US territorial possession for over a century and is home to large US military installations), while Saipan in the CNMI has seen it less so, and Rota the least.

Another way to consider the impact of Americanization (and to a degree the next topic, modernization), is according to age. As I spoke with people about this phenomenon, I noticed a strong correlation between age and intensity—a kind of age gradient. Younger people expressed the most resistance to the idea of asking their neighbors for favors, and thereby tended to exhibit the most shame at the prospect of doing so. Magdelena, the Director of DCCA, had indicated that her son was the reason this matter came to her attention, and her recounting of the experience would indicate that his resistance and shame over asking a neighbor for a favor was intense. So too, for the young man I spoke with in the bird sanctuary. At the other end of the spectrum, manåmko' were more likely to view such behavior as acceptable, while people of middle age tended to present a more mixed set of feelings. It would seem that the more steeped in American and modern ways a person is, the more likely he or she is to find the practice of asking neighbors for favors objectionable.

Modernization

Some impact on this phenomenon also comes from the inevitable effects of modernity, including the technological revolution and globalization. Though more indefinite in its parameters or effects, the role of modernization cannot be understated, in particular the rise of the internet and social media. Several interviewees mentioned, with dismay, the potential criticism or slights on social media they might receive were they to go to their neighbors for a favor. The inevitable gossip that happens in communities, coupled with the wider reach of social media and the increasing prominence of full-time employment in the islands, seems to have made this a potent barrier to earlier modes of neighborly interaction.

Demographic Shifts

The composition of neighborhoods, of whom one might have as neighbors, has also been changing over the past several decades in Rota. Several people mentioned the likely impact of familial dispersion as a cause of this behavior change. As recently as 20 years ago, it was likely that many of one's neighbors were not just family, but close family—parents and offspring, siblings, first cousins. More recently, as people come of age, they often move away from the principal residence to start their own families. This movement, whether to another island or the US mainland, or to another village or part of the village in Rota, means that more people are living in proximity to people who are not family or close relations. Tony indicated that was very much the case for her family: "In our culture, the Chamorro culture ... the families are really close ... and people surrounding they're just like family, but now: no more." Later, she went on to say, "I live by myself right now. And that's one thing that's hurting me. I'm all by myself, nobody is coming to see me or keep me company. Before, they used to give the mother, the grandmother, to borrow their kids to be with, but now no more."

One factor in this dynamic is the CNMI Village Homesteading Program. The program, a consequence of Public Law No. 1-42 and promulgated in 1979, provides homestead lots to persons of Northern Marianas descent who meet certain criteria. According to the office of the Rota District of the Department of Public Lands (personal communication, February 14, 2018), several villages in Rota are almost exclusively comprised of homestead lots, and over 1,000 homesteads have been allotted to date. These figures, given Rota's population, account for roughly half of all homes. The lots are typically created in undeveloped areas, and are awarded randomly via lotteries, further increasing the chance of someone having neighbors who are not close familial relations. This lack of familiarity—despite knowing one's neighbors and their daily routines, as one person mentioned—could contribute to the sense of pride or shame one might feel in asking for a favor.

We may never know why, ultimately, the practice of asking one's neighbors for a favor—once so common in the small, communal society on Rota—seems to be dying out. While the reasons offered by residents themselves are logical and compelling, the dynamics are complex. There are also some lingering conundrums, such as why the aversion to this practice seems to have so quickly spread, or why this particular practice seems to be so associated with America and American values. With regard to this study, it also suffers from sample size limitations, in particular a lack of socio-economic diversity. Most of the people I interviewed were gainfully employed. Perspectives might differ among the unemployed or underemployed, or in more rural parts of the island, where people are not so directly integrated into the economy and workforce.

Despite this lingering uncertainty, a few truths remain. The first is that this phenomenon seems to have taken hold within a significant portion of the population on Rota, and that this change is a divergence from previous practice. While the degree to which it has taken place may be up for debate, as well as its prevalence among the younger people, one other truth remains and is perhaps even more consistent: sadness. The people of Rota with whom I spoke about this phenomenon were almost universally saddened by it. They felt that they were losing an essential element of their culture. A couple even wondered aloud what it meant or what else they might be losing but are unaware of. As the small prop plane for my thirty-minute flight home taxied down the runway and lifted off, the seats behind me filled mostly with jovial Rota residents making a trip to Saipan for a Christmas work party, I felt a sinking sensation in the pit of my stomach stronger than the mere Newtonian pull of the plane against gravity. It felt like loss. And sadness.

References

CNMI Department of Commerce/Central Statistics Division. (2012, December) *2010 Census demographics profile summary by district.* http://ver1.cnmicommerce.com/wp-content/uploads/2012/12/2010-Census-Demographics-Profile-Summary-by-District.pdf

CNMI Department of Commerce/Central Statistics Division. (2017, April). *2016 Commonwealth of the Northern Mariana Islands household income and expenditures survey (HIES) report.* https://commerce.gov.mp/sites/default/files/2016-hies-final-report.pdf

Farrell, D. A. (2011). *Modern history of the Northern Mariana Islands* (2nd ed.). CNMI Public School System.

Guam State Data Center, Bureau of Statistics and Plans. (2012, December). *2010 Census Guam demographic profile summary file.* http://cnas-re.uog.edu/wp-content/uploads/2015/10/KGI_2010-Guam-Demographic-Profile-Study.pdf

Lévesque, R (Ed.). (1999). *History of Micronesia: A collection of source documents* (Vol. 14). Lévesque Publications.

Madrid, C. (2014). Ritidian and Songsong across the Rota Channel: Historic significance and culture of historic preservation. In M. T. Carson (Ed.), *Guam's hidden gem: Archaeological and historical studies at Ritidian* (pp. 44–52). British Archaeological Reports.

Russell, S. (1994). *Proposed historic periods for the islands of Saipan, Tinian, and Rota* [Unpublished manuscript]. CNMI Division of Historic Preservation.

Russell, S. (1998). *Tiempon, i manmofo'na: Ancient Chamorro culture and history of the Northern Mariana Islands.* CNMI Division of Historic Preservation.

Russell, S. (2002). *The island of Rota: An archaeological and historical overview.* CNMI Division of Historic Preservation.

Spennemann, D. H. R. (2008). *Luta: I tiempon aleman. Rota as seen through German eyes 1899–1914.* Heritage Futures.

Militarism and Sovereignty in the Contemporary Northern Mariana Islands

Theresa "Isa" Arriola

Every few weeks in the CNMI, the US military publishes an inconspicuous notice in the local newspapers that include the dates and times they will be using the northern island of Farallon de Medinilla or FDM (No'os in Chamorro)[46] for target practice. FDM is located approximately 45 nautical miles (80 km) north of Saipan in the Marianas archipelago and has been used as a live and inert range by the Department of Defense since 1971 despite being home to a number of bird species including the endangered Micronesian Megapode (Megapodius laperouse) (Lusk et al., 2000). During the drafting of the CNMI Covenant, FDM was to be used for defense responsibilities and cost the military a total of $20,600.[47] The DOD currently maintains an active lease with the CNMI Government that began in 1983 and has an option to renew for another 50 years (Hofschneider, 2016). Due to the military's testing, fishing vessels, tour operators, and the public are advised not to enter the general location of the maneuvers which includes up to 12 nautical miles around the island. These notices are published fairly often but quickly fade into the background to make way for other more pressing news stories. I draw attention to this particular notice as a way to highlight how militarization promotes a routinization of violence that is easily glossed over as a necessary component of the political agreement between the CNMI and the United States rather than an ongoing and contingent negotiation.

This chapter's main intervention within this line of argument then is to disrupt the common narrative that sovereignty was "given up" for United States citizenship at the time of the CNMI Covenant's creation and that military planning is a "necessary evil"[48] that we bargained for when we signed the 1975 Covenant agreement. Rather than accepting the Covenant as a stranglehold on future discussions of our political status and increased militarization, I instead call the concept of sovereignty into question beginning at the time of the creation of the Covenant agreement[49] in an attempt to reconceptualize the sociopolitical potential of sovereignty for our people. In doing so, I advocate for indigenizing sovereignty (Nadasdy, 2017)—a perspective that is grounded in an Indigenous epistemology of land, and I argue that processes of decolonization must examine the role of militarism in shaping the trajectory of Indigenous sovereignties throughout the entire Marianas. This is a vision of sovereignty as dynamic and emergent: sovereignty measured by how well Indigenous peoples in the Marianas are empowered to maintain ownership and control over their lands, rather than sovereignty defined by political status. I draw on historical documentation regarding the CNMI Covenant throughout the CNMI community, contemporary discussions regarding political status in news media, informal interviews, and participant observation in Saipan from 2016 to 2020. I draw heavily from theories of sovereignty within Indigenous and Native Studies to critique the conventional understanding of Euro-American sovereignty and explore its possibilities for our political presents and futures in the Northern Mariana Islands.

Indigenous Sovereignty

Sovereignty is a fraught topic that is both political and personal, particularly as it pertains to Indigenous peoples who continue to negotiate its meaning within the context of settler societies where juridical notions of sovereignty often contradict notions of Native sovereignty. In order to work through this contradiction, Teves et al. (2015) ask "Is Native sovereignty the same sovereignty articulated within Western political discourse?" and "If not, can Native peoples rearticulate sovereignty given its ideological baggage?" (pg. 3). These questions raise important insights into the meaning of sovereignty within the context of Indigenous political systems nested within United States political frameworks (A. Simpson, 2014). In these contexts, Euro-American conceptions of sovereignty continue to dominate the sociopolitical narratives while simultaneously undercutting Indigenous political systems that do not fit neatly within the bounds of its definition (Deloria, 1979).

In its most conventional and popularized form, sovereignty is defined primarily as "Supremacy or pre-eminence in respect of excellence or efficacy"; a second definition is, "Supremacy in respect of power, domination, or rank; supreme dominion, authority, or rule" (Oxford, n.d.). By definition the state is characterized as having enough power to exist independently and "regulate one's own internal functions in the field of domestic relations" (Deloria, 1979, p. 22). The state is presumed to be the apex of power and even "the precondition for politics" itself (Nadasdy, 2017, p. 3). Sovereignty then as a concept is inseparably enmeshed with the production of the "modern" nation state, in which the nation is viewed as a supreme authority that rules over an easily demarcated or bounded territory. The roots of this concept can be traced back to the Enlightenment and the Age of Discovery, and is "directly tied to the need to codify and regulate the practices of conquest and the settlement of lands with peoples deemed uncivilized—and hence unsovereign" (Bonilla, 2017, p. 332).

The history of colonization within Indigenous communities flips the definition of sovereignty on its head by highlighting how the term is both historically contingent and dynamic where Indigenous expressions of sovereignty are often in direct confrontation with the state and even precede European conceptions (Nadasdy, 2017). As Kanaka Maoli (Native Hawaiian) scholar J. Ke'haulani Kauanui (2017) has pointed out, "Any discussion of sovereignty is sure to entail competing epistemological frames, and thus different ontological orientations and diverse political forms in theorizing our political present" (p. 326). Sovereignty is therefore negotiable, fluid and ever-changing, yet deeply meaningful and real. At any particular moment in history, the term means different things to different peoples, but has tremendous capacity to inform Indigenous political life and futurity through its possibilities. Defining sovereignty is therefore an exercise in power itself and is a form of negotiation rooted in one's experience within a changing society and especially in the context of decolonization. Indigenous perspectives have much to offer to the concept of sovereignty because of the ways that they both transform and challenge traditional statist ideologies that envision statehood as a political end goal.

Sovereign Limits

Indigenous theorists have long recognized the inherent limits of employing European concepts of sovereignty to understand the politics of Indigenous nations, territories, and commonwealths where sovereignties are deeply interdependent (Cattelino, 2008), emergent (Uperesa & Garriga-López, 2017), nested (A. Simpson, 2014), entangled (Nadasdy, 2017), paradoxical (Kauanui, 2018), and interact with statist ideologies in complex ways. Many of these political arrangements exist outside the normative notions of a sovereign nation-state and defy the "universal norm" of sovereignty (Bonilla, 2013). This is because for many Indigenous peoples, sovereignty is not simply a political concept but "is at its core about relationships—relationships with each other and with plant and animal nations, with our lands and waters and with the spiritual" (L. Simpson, 2015, as cited in Hiller & Carlson, 2018, p. 49). Such perspectives reveal the political possibilities and limitations of sovereignty and have been a critical component of theorizing Indigenous political resurgence, resistance, and negotiation against colonial concepts of sovereignty that seek to codify Indigenous political systems and forms of governance (Trask, 1999).

Because of these historical complexities and competing epistemological positions, I do not attempt to *define* sovereignty within Chamorro and Refaluwasch communities, but to examine the stakes of contemporary renderings of sovereignty in the Northern Mariana Islands, particularly amidst ongoing militarization—a process that is often in direct conflict with movements towards the protection of Indigenous land. This examination requires an unsettling of current assumptions that undergird definitions of sovereignty and decolonization in the context of the CNMI Covenant, as well as in the context of Indigenous theory-making more broadly. For the territories and commonwealths that are popularly characterized as living *under* United States sovereignty, such as Guam and the CNMI, these realities are often complicated by the fact that the United States does not view itself as an empire and "is often presented as an exception to the colonial model of state power" (Uperesa & Garriga-López, 2017, p. 39). The mere existence of places like Guam and the CNMI in the political imaginary as we know them today, like other "discontiguous States of America" (Lai, 2011), do much to trouble this perception of exceptionalism and debunk this myth about American history (Kiste, 1993, p. 66).

On February 15, 1975, when the CNMI Covenant was signed, a headline in the *New York Times* read, "The United States signed a covenant today that will eventually make the Northern Marianas [sic] Islands in the Pacific a commonwealth, under American sovereignty, much like Puerto Rico" ("Pact", 1975). As an unincorporated territory, *under* American sovereignty, these designations secured a political distancing between the CNMI and the United States that continues to characterize our contemporary social and political relationship. Sovereignty in the CNMI is therefore complicated by the fact that federal legislation can supersede local self-governance, despite the fact that self-governance implies a level of political autonomy (at least in theory) to the people of the Northern Marianas. This legal paradox has led to much debate within United States legal circles, leading one legal analyst to question, "... in the event of an irreconcilable conflict arising between the Northern Marianas people and the United States government regarding an internal matter of the CNMI, who must prevail?" (Horey, 2003, p. 182). In reference to this ambiguity within the CNMI Covenant, Horey (2003) writes that there was no "suggestion or agreement as to precisely how, as a practical matter, local self-government *would* be secured from federal interference. The only agreement was that, somehow, it would" (p. 241). This legal quandary is relevant to the contemporary context of troop "repositioning" in the Pacific as part of the ongoing military build-up as the superseding of federal legislation over local laws has historically occurred because of increased militarization in the name of national defense. This quandary also calls into question the very notion of ownership over marine resources, submerged lands, and other "federalized" spaces such as marine monuments within the United States Insular Areas in the context of militarization. As Bonilla (2017) explains, to define the boundaries of its territory, nation-states rely on certain "territorializing assumptions" and "constitutive exclusions" that define who can and cannot become part of the nation.

(Un)incorporated into the Nation

The United States designation of islands as *insular territories* to be administered by the War Department's Bureau of Insular Affairs in the late 19th and early 20th centuries is one such form of demarcation. By including the category of *unincorporated territory* into the political vocabulary, territories remained in spaces of "liminality" and "deferral" (Goldstein, 2014, p. 15). This has manifested in what Fallon (1991) argues is an "ambivalent, if not antagonistic, attitude toward granting independence to these territories" (p. 31).[50] Such designations, which produced a sense of being half in and half out of political decision-making, is evident in the juridical recognition of territories as "foreign ... in a domestic sense" when discussions surrounding the much-debated Insular Cases were under way (Burnett & Marshall, 2001; Kaplan, 2005) In reference to Puerto Ricans, Amy Kaplan (2005) describes this legal paradox as a "limbo in space and time" that allows the United States to interpret the political futures of the territories and commonwealths in ways that both deny them the ability to become a state but also the ability to become an autonomous nation (p. 3). Kaplan's (2005) analysis in *The Anarchy of Empire in the Making of US Culture* highlights how such paradoxes are not anomalies at all, but rather part and parcel of United States' empire building and that far from being contradictory, the foreign and the domestic are co-constitutive (p. 4). By touching on the Insular Cases in this discussion, my point is not simply to re-hash the imperial and racist roots from which these legal opinions and juridical categories have sprung. Instead, I wish to highlight how these discourses pervade current discussions of self-determination among the Chamorro and Refaluwasch people in the CNMI by framing sovereignty as subsumed by and through United States political frameworks.[51] The legacy of the Insular Cases continues to provide the foundation for the flourishing of other imperial formations (Stoler et al., 2007) that do not easily fit within the context of colonialism as it is typically imagined. One such manifestation in our contemporary world is the assimilationist discourse of inclusivity into an "American political family." Such discourses have long been detrimental to Native peoples whose struggles are framed within the context of exclusion/inclusion into the broader nation state (Byrd, 2011, p. xxv) and work to foreclose Indigenous political imaginaries.

Assimilation into a broader American political family was an influential narrative employed in early Covenant negotiations between the United States and the CNMI in the early 1970s. The Marianas Political Status Commission of 1974 described this commonwealth union as "the name given to a self-governing political entity which is closely attached to another, larger political unit such as a nation." Between 1972–1974, there were five rounds of CNMI Covenant negotiations before the Commonwealth Bill was signed into law (US Public Law 94-241) by US President Gerald Ford on March 24, 1976 (McPhetres, 1997, as cited in Babauta & Babauta, 2008, p. 5). During this time, assimilationist discourses that aimed to incorporate the CNMI into a United States political structure provided powerful narratives that influenced Covenant negotiators in Saipan, which was considered the capitol island of Micronesia at the time. For example, the Honorable Edward De Leon Guerrero Pangelinan, Chairman of the Marianas Political Status Commission (MPSC) at the time, understood Indigenous relations with the United States as something that both expanded economic opportunities and provided a sense of incorporation into a broader American social, political, and economic family. He explained,

> As citizens, we enjoy the benefits of being part of the richest and strongest nation in the world. The geographic boundary of the CNMI is no longer limited to the boundaries of the island's lagoon, it extends from the CNMI to American Samoa to Hawaii, the continental United States and to the American Caribbean of Puerto Rico and the US Virgin Islands. Our lands are the most beautiful and scenic spots on this planet. And what about the communities we have built—our cities, towns, counties, villages and the length and breadth of our country. And finally, the diversity of our people, the Indigenous Chamorro/Carolinians, all are now members of a much larger community of over 300 million Americans. We all benefit from the various cultural and ethnic diversity of our American population. (Babauta & Babauta, 2008, pg. 5)

Mr. Pangelinan's statement links a diverse array of other United States territorial "possessions" with the continental United States through their incorporation into an American political system that he frames as "ours." In the CNMI, where Chamorros and Refaluwasch are often simultaneously understood and self-identify as both Indigenous *and* American, assimilationist discourses are often recapitulated through civil rights frameworks transplanted from the United States of America that effectively erase indigeneity through the racialization of Chamorro/Refaluwasch people as an ethnic group within America. Such discourses continue to be produced through the expansion of federal policies via militarization today and have profound consequences on contemporary Indigenous politics where the power to retain control over Indigenous lands as the ancestral people of the Northern Marianas is complicated by the legal designation as American citizen.

Linking Sovereignty to Decolonization

Sovereignty is fundamentally linked to decolonization since it involves a critical re-thinking of how we envision who we are as a people and how we envision the future of our political systems, particularly in relation to the broader American nation. It entails an unsettling (Bonilla, 2017) of who we are as Indigenous peoples in today's world where decolonization is commonly associated with state-sanctioned processes that often link political independence with a complete disconnection from larger nation states. Sovereignty is thus linked to our relative political agency or ability to continue to negotiate our political futures, much like our community did in the early days of the Covenant negotiations when questions surrounding the exercise of our political power were surfacing. Yarimar Bonilla's (2017) preference for the term unsettling as opposed to decolonizing is instructive here since it "avoids the telos of decolonization. What is unsettled is not necessarily removed, toppled or returned to a previous order but is fundamentally brought into question" (p. 335). The term "unsettling" is a useful analytic to employ in the Pacific where many islands remain technically de-colonized, but remain under US hegemony (Pöllath, 2018) and where some—such as Guam—remain on the United Nations list of Non-Self-Governing Territories (NSGT). In this light, it is helpful to understand decolonization less as a linear political process with a defined end goal than it is to view it as a dynamic and transformative process situated at the complex intersection of sociopolitical and historical circumstances.

In the context of United States-CNMI relations, sovereignty remains an inroad for exploring contemporary changing social dynamics in the Marianas and to unpack the ways that United States sovereign power is asserted over local political decision-making via the powerful sociopolitical influence of militarization. An adequate examination of our political futures must engage with the influential power of militarization on our islands, where United States hegemony manifests itself in ways that are not always so obviously tied to traditional concepts of colonialism. As Na'puti (2013) points out,

> Today colonial control and imperial rule no longer manifest in overt and hostile taking of land as was common in the era of European colonialism. Instead, colonialism operates in more covert ways, through the control of labor markets and neoliberal reforms and by exerting military and political pressures throughout the globe. (p. 56)

Amidst increasing militarization, processes of decolonization can be understood less as *breaks* from the trajectory of larger nation state building, and more a site of political contestation and ongoing negotiation with the United States. Yet the prospects of re-negotiating the CNMI's political status with the United States often led people in Saipan to ask me, "if not the United States military, then who?" In other words, how could we possibly survive, "who would we even be, without the United States?"

This phrase was usually followed up by an assertion that if it were not for the United States presence here on our islands, we would be overtaken or threatened by another nation like China or North Korea—a narrative largely promulgated by the conversations surrounding the United States' Pacific Pivot that capitalizes on the threats posed to the Marianas from the Asian continent. While I do not seek to downplay the real dangers that have been asserted against the islands by countries such as China and North Korea, I do want to contextualize our islands' involvement in the broader geopolitical and military strategy between nation states whose priorities center around the promotion of defense goals rather than Indigenous sovereignty.

Creating a (Trust) Territory, Defining the Common(wealth)

What does decolonization mean when Indigenous homelands have been reconfigured as American territory and where decolonization is foreclosed by commonwealth status? Furthermore, how do we define "the commons" in a territorial possession? In his essay entitled "Against death maps of Empire: Contesting colonial borders through Indigenous sovereignty," Eric Ritskes (2015), writing about Jodi Byrd's concept of the *commons*, asserts,

> Byrd (2011) recognizes indigeneity as a necessary obstacle to 'the commons' as a means of decolonization because the commons is conceptualized on and through lands stolen from Indigenous peoples; the idea of the commons was not only always exclusionary, as Kim Christen (2012) argues, but always already embedded in colonial dispossession.

In the case of the CNMI, Indigenous experiences living in an unincorporated territory push the limits of the terms like "decolonization" in productive ways by challenging what it means to be part of a broader commons defined by a larger nation state. What decolonization actually means in a United States territory[52]— where the full spectrum of constitutional rights is not present—has long been up for debate. Fallon (1991) expands on the paradoxical nature of this political agreement when he writes,

> The necessary basis of equality is missing because the islands do not have equal representation in the US Congress, the inhabitants of the Northern Marianas cannot vote for president, the islands may be subject to federal laws not applicable to the states, and the legislature of the "Commonwealth of the Northern Marianas" does not conform in its structure and nature to the state legislatures. (p. 29)

The various United States territorial statuses of the islands that comprise the Pacific therefore exist within a "murky" political zone "lying between formal statehood and official independence" (Fallon, 1991, p. 23). As a commonwealth—a term which in itself is rather nebulous[53] —the people of the CNMI opted for a closer political union with the United States that recognized local self-government, but in many ways privileged United States citizenship.

Discussions surrounding decolonization in the Marianas are complicated by the meaning of colonization itself, especially in the CNMI, where United States political hegemony is often framed as a necessary component of securitization in the region rather than a form of occupation. Banivanua-Mar (2016) argues that this perspective was exemplified by the US Secretary of War Henry L. Stimson's characterization of the Pacific Islands as critical defense "outposts" to detract from the problematic use of the label "colonies." (p. 117) Thus, Northern Marianas history is conventionally understood as moving in teleological fashion from conquest to colonization to self-government. Importantly, colonization in the case of the Northern Marianas usually refers to Spanish, German and Japanese occupation, rather than the United States, which is commonly viewed as a nation state that negotiated with the CNMI rather than as a colonizer. It has been argued, for example, that the Northern Mariana Islands were "no longer true colonies" (Horey, 2003, p. 21) under the jurisdiction of the League of Nations, since the Indigenous peoples were seen as desiring to integrate "American ideals of democracy, equality and popular sovereignty ... and that there be a break from the colonial past, not a continuation of it under another name" (Horey, 2003, p. 242). From this perspective, the creation of the Covenant symbolized for many in the Northern Marianas a move towards incorporation into a broader nation that signified the end of colonization, rather than another beginning.

Having been framed in the language of self-determination, the ideological and political transformation of the Mariana Islands, from its status within the Trust Territory of the Pacific Islands (TTPI) to a United States commonwealth, also symbolized for many an exercise in sovereign power that had not been afforded under any other previous colonial regime. As Chamorro legal scholar Nicole Torres (2012) points out, "the CNMI acted as a sovereign in negotiating the Covenant with the United States, which specifically acknowledges the CNMI's inherent sovereignty." (p. 173) This process is viewed as a distinguishing political feature between the CNMI and the largest and southernmost island of Guam, which is undergoing a political status education campaign regarding a formal path to decolonization through the United Nations due to its non-self-governing territorial status.[54] While the 1950 Organic Act granted US citizenship to those living in Guam, it allowed for only a limited form of "self-government" and one non-voting delegate in Congress. Thus, the CNMI's political status can be viewed as "temporalized in a moment" (A. Simpson, 2010) and the Covenant codified sovereignty by framing it as something that was given up in favor of citizenship.

The Sovereignty/Citizenship Trade-off and the Dependency Dilemma

In an attempt to learn more about the perception of sovereignty as something that was traded for citizenship during Covenant negotiations, I conducted an interview with Chamorro lawyer and sovereignty scholar Mr. Robert Torres from Saipan. I began by asking Mr. Torres about his views regarding the history of sovereignty and its implications for contemporary society in the CNMI. He responded,

> you ask yourself ... when has a people ever had an opportunity for true independence and forsake independence and bargain away their own sovereignty in favor of a favorable political relationship with its former trustee ... never ... this commonwealth was a kind of anomaly in this history, and so Guam never had an opportunity to negotiate for this.

In his explanation, Mr. Torres frames this unique history as one in which we entered into a bargaining relationship with the United States as a former trustee by *giving up* our sovereignty. CNMI historian Samuel McPhetres (1997) also notes this agreement in his popularly referenced history book entitled *Self-Government and Citizenship in the Commonwealth of the Northern Mariana Islands*. He explains that this decision

> was an act of self-determination by a sovereign Indigenous population who voluntarily opted for union with the United States knowing that they had independence as an alternative. It was the first time that this had ever happened in the history of the United States.

Despite the fact that the Marianas was not considered self-governing at the time, the decision to enter into a political union with the United States was viewed as an act of "inherent sovereignty" (McPhetres, 1997, p. 48). Guam on the other hand was viewed as never having had the opportunity to participate in such a historical moment. Given this fact, I continued to inquire as to why independence was such a controversial idea at the time.

T.A.: It's interesting that independence was immediately associated with having no connection with the United States, like you are turning your back on the country. I'm curious as to why independence was so controversial.

R.T.: The majority of people did not see independence as the path of opportunity, progress or development ... The fact of the matter is, when we bargained for the Covenant, we signed onto a deal that wholesale adopted the American system of governance, laws and jurisprudence and economic benefits and everything. We did. And now it can't be terminated unless there is a mutual consent provision which it's obviously not going to happen that the United States would have a mutual agreement to terminate the Covenant ... so we have to now work within a system of laws and rules and finances that is affected by US policies, on immigration, on labor, on an environment, and as the ebb and flow goes in the United States so too goes the CNMI ... So we bargained for this, and we signed on for it and that's the deal we made.

In his discussion, Mr. Torres highlights the deep legal entanglements that have emerged from the Covenant negotiations. While the mutual consent provision offers us a level of protection against unlawful Congressional power, Indigenous political lives are now so inextricably linked to United States political systems that the implementation of the provision is now often viewed as an impossibility. Covenant expert and co-author of *An Honorable Accord: The Covenant Between the Northern Mariana Islands and the United States*, Howard P. Willens (2003) explains that the CNMI's political arrangement is both "constitutional and successful" and that the mutual consent provision "protects the Northern Marianas people from having the fundamental terms of their relationship with the United States being unilaterally altered by the US Congress—as Congress is presently free to do with respect to Guam and the other US territories" (p. 376). I highlight Willens' analysis here to point out that while contemporary debates surrounding the CNMI's political status center around issues of US constitutionality, this analysis misses out on the broader issue of dependency that militarism produces. Put another way, legal provisions—even the ones meant to protect the CNMI—cannot be divorced from the broader history of imperialism throughout the Marianas, where US military goals remain preeminent. Without contextualizing the history of the Covenant in this way, arguments over whether or not the CNMI's status remains constitutional will do little to expand the horizons of decolonization in the Pacific. Chamorro scholar Michael Bevacqua (2017) has characterized the similar situation in Guam as a "decolonial deadlock," which people liken to suicide, and can be described as "a discursive formation that circles around the idea that the best possible political and social configuration in Guam has already been reached through its colonial relationship to the United States and that hence, nothing more need be done" (p. 107). In the CNMI, discussions surrounding the Covenant often foreclose possibilities for future dialogue about Indigenous futures by placing a stranglehold on discussions of decolonization. The formation of commonwealth in the CNMI and territorial status in Guam are viewed as meaningful political arrangements that make it difficult to speak about our contemporary relations with the United States as imperial in nature. This stifling of the political imagination also frames decolonization as a simplified "choice between national independence in isolation and emancipation in association or integration with the colonizing power" (Heim, 2017, p. 915). In the CNMI, our militarized legal entanglements with the United States remind us that decolonization has never been a simple question of what is legal or not.

The Limits of a Commonwealth Status

In 2008, the US Congress federalized the CNMI immigration system despite the CNMI government's popular disapproval of this legislation. One year earlier, at a hearing before the Committee on Energy and Natural Resources, David B. Cohen (Deputy Assistant Secretary for Insular Affairs) testified that while the CNMI had made improvements to working conditions since the 1990s, serious concerns over homeland security, human trafficking and mistreatment of refugees throughout the islands still remained. For these reasons, Cohen concluded that with the help of the US Congress, the CNMI's immigration system must be federalized as soon as possible through the passing of bill S.1634, the Northern Mariana Islands Covenant Implementation Act. This was an important moment for the people of the CNMI, who lacked representation in Congress yet were being subjected to federal oversight over immigration policies that were seen as failing. While Cohen was clear about the need to federalize, his statement also highlighted the inequitable political relationship between the US and CNMI. He explained,

> we're concerned about the message that would be sent if Congress were to pass this legislation while the CNMI remains the only US territory or commonwealth without a delegate in Congress. At a time when young men and women from the CNMI are sacrificing their lives in Iraq in proportions that

far exceed the national average, we hope that Congress will consider granting them a seat at the table at which their fate will be decided. (United States/CNMI Political Union, 2007)

At the conclusion of the federalization process, CNMI residents remained uneasy about what this controversial change meant in terms of federal encroachment over local laws even amidst the criticism of the local government's failings.

In a *Marianas Variety* article entitled "CNMI Lawmaker Advises Review of US Ties," CNMI Representative Stanley T. Torres framed the issue in terms of an unequal relationship between the US and the CNMI. He crafted House Bill 17-7, calling for the creation of a Second Marianas Political Status Commission that would re-evaluate this political relationship. In a telling interview, Torres stated,

> [the] timing is very right to bring this proposal up because it appears that the federal government has been screwing us for a long time ... The feds give us money but instead of letting us make the best use of it ourselves, they put a lot of restrictions. (Erediano, 2011)

Torres' comments reflect the CNMI's inability to adequately exercise the right to self-government, and similar sentiments continued to remain a theme into the mid-2000s as US military planning burgeoned alongside these concerns. In 2015, House Bill 19-2 was submitted[55] to the Nineteenth Northern Mariana Commonwealth Legislature. In short, the bill was titled the Second Marianas Political Status Commission Act of 2015[56], whose purpose was to reinvigorate the call to create a Second Marianas Political Status Commission

> that the people desire to reexamine whether continuing, in a "Political Union with the United States of America" under the Covenant is in their best interest, or whether some other political status will better enable them to fulfill their hope and aspirations in attaining full and meaningful self-government, as stated by the late US Senator Jacob Javits of the State of New York in the deliberations of the Covenant and as amended.

Recognizing that the current political time in which we find ourselves no longer accommodates the CNMI's desires for self-determination, the goal of the Second Marianas Political Status Commission was to meaningfully engage in discussions regarding contemporary political relations with the United States. Authored by Rep. Felicidad Ogumoro (R-Saipan), the CNMI Senate passed the House bill by a vote of 6-1 on December 19, 2014. The Commission consists of nine voting members and two non-voting ex-officio members, including two persons from Rota, two from Tinian, and five from Saipan. The bill came on the heels of a number of important changes in the CNMI, among which "Submerged land control, rampant militarization, and the federal immigration takeover" ranked as the most pressing (Chan, 2016).[57] Arguably, while all three political concerns are presented as separate issues, they can be viewed as falling under the same umbrella of militarism.[58] In an interview about her experiences regarding the authoring of House Bill 19-2, Rep. Ogumoro (personal communication, July 6, 2020) explained,

> The US continues to make policies without proper consultation and if there is consultation and we say no, just like in the case of the military ... when we are trying to make a point ... they keep going, as if we are talking to the birds.

Having personally heard her express similar concerns about the Covenant in past gatherings, I inquired about her experience with the Covenant negotiations as well. According to Rep. Ogumoro (personal communication, July 6, 2020), she explained,

> look back into the reports even in our books, it only took ... oh my gosh ... less than a year ... such a short time for public education for the people to understand what the Covenant really means. You see what is happening now for the other [Pacific] entities such as the Republic of the Marshall Islands, Palau and the Federated States of Micronesia ... they are on equal footing with US ... with us, the US is speaking on our behalf and that is so obvious when we go to the United Nations ... we sit *behind* the US and they speak on our behalf.

Rep. Ogumoro's sentiments echo the much longer resistance that existed in Saipan to accepting commonwealth status as the best option for the people of the CNMI. In particular, it has been noted that the Saipan Women's Association (SWA) and the United Carolinian Association (UCA) were vocal opponents of the Covenant while major support came from the Marianas Political Status Commission (McPhetres, 1997, p. 54). This history is helpful for understanding how resistance to political negotiations with the US has historically manifested itself among different groups in ways that do not always fit neatly into a pro-US narrative.

In a *Saipan Tribune* article entitled "Meaning of Covenant Questioned," John Tagabuel, executive director of the Carolinian Affairs Office, stated that the "US is treating us like a US territory" (Chan, 2016) like Guam or Samoa, which are non-governing entities. In comparing our status to Guam, Mr. Tagabuel's comments reveal a number of complex social and political realities that continue to shape discussions of Indigenous self-governance in the Marianas. First, as previously mentioned, as a commonwealth, the CNMI is viewed as having more political autonomy than the neighboring island of Guam, which remains on the UN list of Non-Self-Governing Territories (NSGT). Similarly, Tagabuel's comments reveal the relative political disadvantage that American Samoans, as American nationals (as opposed to US citizens), have in comparison to those living in the Northern Marianas. This perspective has also frequently been brought up by Saipan residents in personal conversations when referring to Guam's political status by stating, "At *least* we are a commonwealth." In fact, when applied to the CNMI, the label of territory is considered offensive to some since it elides important differences between the CNMI and Guam regarding self-governance. At a public presentation about the legal status of the US territories in which I was in attendance on Saipan in 2018,[59] John Gonzales (president of the Northern Marianas Descent Corporation) stated that to call the CNMI a "territory is an insult ... who went through a process unlike any other" islands in the region. In this regard, commonwealth status is often a mark of distinction that is upheld as a source of pride for the people of the CNMI.

In legal terms, the designation of commonwealth status along with the creation of the CNMI Covenant, the Constitution, and the ensuing political union with the United States bestow upon the CNMI a level of political autonomy that simply is not present in many other "territories." In fact, in a 1975 plebiscite vote to become a US commonwealth, the Indigenous populations of the Northern Mariana Islands were understood as the only people ever known to have "voluntarily opted for union with the United States knowing that they had independence as an alternative" (McPhetres, 1997, p. 57). This autonomous decision was understood as an "act of self-determination by a sovereign Indigenous population" (McPhetres, 1997, p. 57) and is tied to the fact that the political union between the CNMI and the United States could not be altered unless by agreement on behalf of both parties. This was defined as a mutual consent agreement (or mutual consent clause) written into the Covenant as a way to thwart an abuse of power should it ever arise. As a result, Guam is sometimes upheld as an exemplar of what the CNMI does not want in regard to self-determination, as its official status remains an unincorporated, organized territory in which the Organic Act of 1950 was imposed upon the island. As Mr. Rudy Sablan in the *Saipan Tribune*, explained,

> There exists a misconception about our CNMI. Many people believe that because we are a commonwealth, we belong to the United States, as if we are property or territory of the US Wrong. We don't belong to the USA. Neither the US Congress, nor the US President, has yet to agree that we are a US-owned territory. The CNMI is not just US soil. (Chan, 2016)

Legal scholar Horey (2003) has argued that politically this has been an outcome of the "overall federal tendency ... to ignore the unique circumstances of the CNMI, and lump it together with the traditional US territories" (p. 182). Both Mr. Tagabuel and Mr. Sablan point out the inherent contradiction between the CNMI's self-government and US sovereign power over the CNMI's political system, a paradox that continues to frame contemporary discussions of sovereignty in the CNMI, with one prevailing view being that US citizenship as a worthy trade for sovereignty. This political history is important to re-examine in light of contemporary discussions of self-determination amidst the steady growth of military planning in the region, wherein Indigenous self-governance is couched within the framework of US sovereignty.

The Politics of Indigeneity

Contemporary media coverage of the Mariana Islands tends to center around a few salient themes: US political controversies[60]; the lack of democracy being extended to the United States' territorial possessions; and more recently, the devastating effects of unprecedented typhoons hitting "US soil."[61] Although seemingly disparate, these themes overlap in complex ways and point to the inextricable links between America's imperial reach and its ensuing militarization of the environment. This coverage seeks to portray a more inclusive and historically accurate representation of United States imperial history in US territories where most inhabitants are Indigenous peoples who do not possess the same constitutional rights as American citizens in the continental United States. It also highlights the general unfamiliarity that most Americans have in regard to United States territories, which engenders a sense of disbelief that such political arrangements continue to exist in today's world where overt forms of colonialism are no longer acceptable.

On the March 8, 2015 airing of HBO's "Last Week Tonight," John Oliver picked up on this discrepancy and noted that, while

> more than four million people live in the US territories, more than 98% of them are racial or ethnic minorities, and the more you look into the history of why

their voting rights are restricted, the harder it is to justify, 'cause it goes all the way back to when America first acquired them. (Last Week Tonight, 2015)

By framing Indigenous people in the territories as racial or ethnic minorities that live in places that were "acquired" by the United States, Oliver's comments reflect a common practice of racializing Indigenous peoples (Moreton-Robinson, 2015) in an attempt to underscore the unequal application of democratic rights to *all* Americans. While his sketch was informative of America's imperial reach outside the continental United States, it continues to highlight the complex political realities that Indigenous people in territories and commonwealths must negotiate under American political hegemony that cannot be solved by voting rights.

Such perspectives portray a lack of political representation—specifically inequitable voting rights[62]—in an American system of governance as *the* root of the islands' many social and economic issues. Increasingly, democratization and a growing American consciousness are understood as the panacea to the many social and political problems facing the people of the Marianas. I argue that while the critique of unequal political representation is well founded, it highlights state-centered approaches to decolonization that define political and social equality through the granting of US citizenship and incorporation—a move in which democracy is viewed "as the ever-heralded justification and decisive promise of inclusion in settler states more broadly" (Goldstein, 2014, p. 20). From this perspective, statehood is upheld as the apex of assimilation into a seemingly homogenous American political system—a prospect that presents itself as a legal paradox in overseas insular territories[63] (which include the CNMI, Guam, the US Virgin Islands, American Samoa and Puerto Rico) in which "the promise of statehood" (Goldstein, 2014, p. 16) existed but never manifested through their designation as *unincorporated*.[64] As Stayman (2009, as cited in Pöllath, 2018) points out, "The status of 'unincorporated territory' meant that fundamental individual rights were protected by the Constitution, but Congress need not extend citizenship nor extend a promise of eventual statehood" (p. 237).

Thus, militarism overlaps with the politics of indigeneity in the CNMI in a number of important ways. First, processes of self-determination complicate the politics of indigeneity across the archipelago, where decolonization for Chamorros in Guam, and for Chamorros and Refaluwasch in the CNMI both overlap and diverge due to our different colonial and political histories. Secondly, Chamorros and Refaluwasch peoples must contend with authenticating and differentiating their indigeneity against the background of Americanization. Indigeneity overlaps with racial politics and highlights the influence that settler legacies of racial purity and blood quantum have over the authentication of Indigenous peoples. Lastly, militarism forces both groups to reckon with the sometimes tenuous and paradoxical nature of having two groups fall within the same category of Northern Mariana Descent (NMD)—a category that often becomes conflated with indigeneity in the CNMI.

One of the most important consequences of the differential military and political histories of the Northern Marianas and Guam in terms of Indigenous self-determination has been the formal recognition of two groups of people into the category of Northern Marianas Descent: the Chamorro and Refaluwasch peoples. The emergence of an "Indigenous" label surfaced among Chamorros in the 1980s in Guam as a response to issues of self-determination (Tolentino, n.d.). In the CNMI, however, indigeneity is often conflated with the legal categorization of "Northern Marianas Descent" which designates those individuals who meet the requirements of Article XII in the Northern Mariana Islands Constitution. Article XII is entitled "Restrictions on Alienation of Land" and is comprised of six main sections. In Section 4, a person of Northern Marianas Descent is defined as,

> a citizen or national of the United States and who is of at least one-quarter Northern Marianas Chamorro or Northern Marianas Carolinian blood or a combination thereof or an adopted child of a person of Northern Marianas descent if adopted while under the age of eighteen years.
>
> For purposes of defining Northern Marianas descent, a person shall be considered a full-blooded Northern Marianas Chamorro or Northern Marianas Carolinian if that person was born or domiciled in the Northern Mariana Islands by 1950 and was a citizen of the Trust Territory of the Pacific Islands before the termination of the Trusteeship with respect to the Commonwealth (Commonwealth Law Revision Commission, n.d.).

The definition of NMD, taken directly from the experience of the drafting of the CNMI Constitution during the Trust Territory of the Pacific Islands (TTPI) period, used a combination of time, location, and political status as guidelines for identification of Indigenous peoples in the CNMI. This designation was important for the way that it linked the deeply meaningful and ancestral ties to the land with

Indigenous people. Given the long historical use of blood quantum as a tool for discrimination against Indigenous peoples globally, the use of blood quantum to define NMDs might appear somewhat contradictory. However, a closer examination reveals that the use of blood quantum to define indigeneity need not be discriminatory and, in fact, can work to promote Indigenous self-determination (Villazor, 2010, p. 476). This is an important distinction to make in the context of US political hegemony in the Pacific where Indigenous rights create counter-claims against US constitutional rights such as "equal protection and individual rights" (Villazor, 2018, p. 128).[65] In the CNMI, the definition of NMDs highlights the complexity of both indigeneity as a political and social category that intersects with a broader American national identity and citizenship.

Given this history, the perspectives of Chamorros from Guam often do not address the perspectives of Refaluwasch people who re-located to the Northern Mariana Islands in the early 19th century after a massive typhoon hit their home islands (Alkire, 1984, p. 272). Despite evidence of pre-contact relationships between Carolinians and Chamorros from Guam (Goetzfridt, n.d.), this contemporary Refaluwasch "blind spot" is often unintentionally promulgated by scholarship about Chamorros, particularly in Guam, where the same history between Refaluwasch is not shared. Camacho (2011) touches on this issue when he notes that

> Guam, in their view, persists as the center of Indigenous injury, thereby foreclosing discussion of other "grievable" subjects in the Mariana Islands. The Guam-centrism is widespread. That is, the majority of the Catholic debates, Indigenous literatures, oral traditions, political issues, popular cultures, and women's organizations representing Chamorro society almost exclusively focus on Guam, if not portray Chamorros as Indigenous only to this island. (p. 704)

Teasing out the socio-political differences between Guam and the Northern Mariana Islands has the potential to shed new light on longstanding inequities that continue to shape our relationship with one another both politically and economically, as well as our differential relationships with the United States. Rather than an obstacle, these differences can be a key to shaping self-determination as we negotiate various legal avenues for demilitarization and decolonization. Although outside the scope of this discussion, the differences and similarities between Chamorro and Refaluwasch cultures and political histories have much potential for unpacking how colonization has influenced our understandings of indigeneity in today's world.

As Kanaka Maoli scholar Haunani-Kay Trask (1999) points out, "Because of colonization, the question of *who* defines *what* is Native, has been taken away from Native peoples by Western-trained scholars, government officials and other technicians" (p. 43). In the CNMI, the shared history between Chamorros and Refaluwasch (or mixed "Chamolinians") remain a site of productive tension in which we can expand our visions of Indigenous sovereignty outside the bounds of political recognition.

Conclusion

How would it be possible to exercise self-determination amidst militarization, if only Guam—or if only the CNMI—could technically achieve this goal? What do two different political statuses within the same archipelago mean for decolonization? In the Marianas, reconfiguring the possibilities of sovereignty are critical to confronting United States hegemony. Critiquing the hypermilitarization of the region is key to this confrontation because "militarism and militarization both establish the conditions of the nation-state and claim justification for their further imperial expansion as the defense and redeployment of those conditions and calculated disposal of national sacrifice zones" (Goldstein, 2014, p. 9). Militarism works to construct the discursive formation of such sacrifice zones, military borders, and strategic outposts as necessary to national security through the construction of insular environments ripe for testing and training. The undoing of this particular colonial framing of sovereignty within the Northern Marianas remains critical amidst ongoing militarization, a process which continues to uncritically invoke the islands' political status, size, and geographic location as justification for increased militarization by presenting them as national defense necessities. This perspective also allows us to abandon the settler logic of political incorporation and navigate us away from the notion that *more* political representation in Congress necessarily equates to increased self-determination. It does so by highlighting the primacy of Indigenous relationships through and within our "common wealth"—that is, to recognize that our political power lies in the relative ability to care for our ancestral lands, seas and skies that make possible our connections to this place, rather than a vision of militaristic consumption of island environments based on a loosely defined and problematic ideal of a national commons. To recognize the land as an Indigenous "common wealth" rather than a US commonwealth means to literally break apart the term, wrest back its meanings from its imperial roots, and understand the environment and our surroundings as a communal space that we take responsibility for protecting rather than exploiting or extracting.

Since the first plans regarding the military build-up in the Marianas were made public in 2005, community members throughout the Marianas expressed concerns about militarism as an impediment to decolonization, particularly in Guam. In a statement before the UN Special Committee on Decolonization in 2006, Guam Senator Hope Cristobal noted the absurd situation that surrounds ideals of self-determination on an island as militarized as Guam. Cristobal (2006) explained,

> The sheer number of eligible voters connected to the military, their dependents and contractors is of great concern when implementing the exercise of our inalienable right to self-determination in ... Guam ... Even more disturbing is the military's attitude that they, too, can vote to decolonize a non-self-governing territory! To be sure, the military can surely determinate a US favorable outcome of any election.

Sen. Cristobal's concerns echo the deeply problematic way that self-determination is framed in the context of settler colonialism, whereby the distinctiveness of Indigenous claims are ignored in favor of a seemingly homogenous American citizenship. Furthermore, increasing militarization continues to reveal discrepancies in the way that the CNMI and Guam can engage with processes of self-determination in their distinct political relationships and negotiations with the United States. The collapsing of socio-political differences between the CNMI and Guam risks oversimplifying the struggle for decolonization as one that can be framed only within and through the confines of US legal frameworks. The argument that the CNMI was *never* colonized because we were able to "choose" our political status and that we were not a spoil of war as was Guam is testament to this oversimplification. It restricts how we might imagine self-determination by linking decolonization to political status and depoliticizes the influence of US political power in the archipelago. A myopic focus on political status therefore constrains possibilities for demilitarized futures. By incorporating the land and environment into discussions of self-determination, our viewpoints shift towards a more expansive politics of sovereignty and decolonization that is not shackled to military whims throughout Oceania.

References

Aguon, J. (2009). The power of a dual rights legal strategy for the Chamoru people of Guam. *University of Hawai'i Law Review, 31*(1), 113–154. https://heinonline.org/HOL/Page?collection=journals&handle =hein.journals/uhawlr31&id=114&men_tab=srchresults

Alkire, W. H. (1984). The Carolinians of Saipan and the Commonwealth of the Northern Mariana Islands. *Pacific Affairs, 57*(2), 270. https://doi.org/10.2307/2759128 Article XII, Northern Mariana Islands Constitution. (n.d.). Ballotpedia. https://ballotpedia.org/Article_XII,_Northern_Mariana_Islands _Constitution

Babauta, J. N., & Babauta, C. T. (2008). Edward DLG. Pangelinan shares his thoughts and vision of the NMI under Commonwealth status and the opportunities it presents. *Homeland, 2*(6), 1–11.

Banivanua-Mar, T. (2016). Decolonisation and the Pacific: Indigenous globalisation and the ends of empire (Critical perspectives on empire). Cambridge University Press. https://doi.org/10.1017/ CBO9781139794688

Bevacqua, M. L., (2017). The decolonial deadlock in Guam. In F. Negrón-Muntaner (Ed.), *Sovereign acts: Contesting colonialism across Indigenous Nations and Latinx America* (3rd ed., pp. 107–124). University of Arizona Press.

Bonilla, Y. (2013). Ordinary sovereignty. *Small Axe: A Caribbean Journal of Criticism, 17*(3), 152–165. https://doi.org/10.1215/07990537-2378973

Bonilla, Y. (2017). Unsettling sovereignty. *Cultural Anthropology, 32*(3), 330–339. https://doi.org/10.14506/ca32.3.02

Burnett, C. D., & Marshall, B. (2001). *Foreign in a domestic sense: Puerto Rico, American expansion, and the constitution (American encounters/global interactions)*. Duke University Press Books.

Byrd, J. A. (2011). *The transit of empire: Indigenous critiques of colonialism (First Peoples: New directions Indigenous)*. University of Minnesota Press.

Camacho, K. L. (2011). *Cultures of commemoration: The politics of war, memory, and history in the Mariana Islands (Pacific Islands monograph series)*. University of Hawaii Press.

Cattelino, J. (2018). From Locke to Slots: Money and politics of indigeneity. *Comparative Studies in Society and History, 60*(20), 274-307. https://doi.org/10.1017/S0010417518000051

Chan, D. B. (2016, February 25). Meaning of Covenant questioned. *Saipan Tribune*. https://www.saipantribune. com/index.php/meaning-of-covenant-questioned/

CNMI Covenant. (n.d.). Commonwealth Law Revision Commission. https://cnmilaw.org/cov.php#gsc.tab=0

Commonwealth Economic Development Strategic Planning Commission. (2009, November). *Comprehensive economic development strategic plan 2009-2014 for the US Commonwealth of the Northern Mariana Islands*. US Department of Commerce Economic Development Administration. https://opd.gov.mp/ wp-content/uploads/opd/CNMI-StrategicPlan2009-2014.pdf

Commonwealth Law Revision Commission. (n.d.). *Article XII, Northern Mariana Islands Constitution*. https:// cnmilaw.org/cons.php#gsc.tab=0

Cristobal, H. A. (2006, November 28). *CHamoru self-determination pa'go* [Paper Presentation]. Statement Before the United Nations Special Committee on Decolonization (C-24) 2006 Pacific Regional Seminar, Yanuca, Fiji. http://www.guampedia.com/wp-content/uploads/2017/07/2006-HOPE-CRISTOB- AL-Edit.pdf

Deloria, Jr., V. (1979). Self-Determination and the concept of sovereignty. In R. Dunbar-Ortiz (Ed.), *Economic development in American Indian reservations* (pp. 22–28). University of New Mexico.

Erediano, E. (2011, March 22). Northern Marianas should reassess commonwealth political status, says N. Marianas lawmaker. *Marianas Variety*. http://www.pireport.org/articles/2011/03/15/ cnmi-lawmaker-advises-review-us-ties

Fallon, J. E. (1991). Federal policy and US territories: The political restructuring of the United States of America. *Pacific Affairs, 64*(1), 23. https://doi.org/10.2307/2760361

Goetzfridt, N. J. (n.d.) Carolinians on Guam. In *Guampedia*. https://www.guampedia.com/carolinians-on-guam/

Goldstein, A. (2014). *Formations of United States colonialism*. Duke University Press Books.

Heim, O. (2017). Island logic and the decolonization of the Pacific. *Interventions, 19*(7), 914–929. https://doi.org/10. 1080/1369801X.2017.1401945

Hiller, C., & Carlson, E. (2018). These are Indigenous lands. *Canadian Social Work Review, 35*(1), 45–70. https://doi.

org/10.7202/1051102ar

Hofschneider, A. (2016, December 13). FDM: This island has been military target practice for decades. *Honolulu Civil Beat*. https://www.civilbeat.org/2016/12/fdm-this-island-has-been-military-target-practice-for-decades/

Horey, J. E. (2003). The right of self-government in the Northern Mariana Islands. *Asian-Pacific Law & Policy Journal, 4*(2), 181–245. http://blog.hawaii.edu/aplpj/files/2011/11/APLPJ_04.2_horey.pdf

Kaplan, A. (2005). *The anarchy of empire in the making of US culture (Convergences: Inventories of the present)*. Harvard University Press.

Kauanui, J. K. (2017). Sovereignty: An introduction. *Cultural Anthropology, 32*(3), 323–329. https://doi.org/10.14506/ca32.3.01

Kauanui, J. K. (2018). *Paradoxes of Hawaiian sovereignty: Land, sex, and the colonial politics of state nationalism*. Duke University Press Books.

Kiste, R. C. (1993). New political statuses in American Micronesia. In V. C. Lockwood, T. G. Harding, & B. J. Wallace (Eds.), *Contemporary Pacific societies studies in development and change* (pp. 67–79). Prentice Hall.

Lai, P. (2011). Discontiguous states of America: The paradox of unincorporation in Craig Santos Perez's poetics of Chamorro Guam. *Journal of Transnational American Studies, 3*(2), 1–28. https://escholarship.org/uc/item/02f4v8m3

Last Week Tonight. (2015, March 8). *U.S. territories: Last Week Tonight with John Oliver* [Video]. YouTube. https://www.youtube.com/watch?v=CesHr99ezWE

Lusk, M., Bruner, P., & Kessler, C. (2000, December). The avifauna of Farallon de Medinilla, Mariana Islands. *Journal of Field Ornithology, 71*(1), 22–33. https://doi.org/:10.1648./0273-8570-71.1.22

McPhetres, S. (1997). *Self-government and citizenship in the Commonwealth of the Northern Mariana Islands, USA*. CNMI Public School System.

Moreton-Robinson, A. (2015). *The white possessive: Property, power, and Indigenous sovereignty (Indigenous Americas)*. University of Minnesota Press.

Na'puti, T. R. (2013). *Charting contemporary Chamoru activism: Anti-militarization & social movements in Guåhan*. [Doctoral dissertation, University of Texas at Austin]. Texas Scholar Works. https://repositories.lib.utexas.edu/bitstream/handle/2152/25955/NAPUTI-DISSERTATION-2013.pdf?sequence=1

Nadasdy, P. (2017). *Sovereignty's entailments: First Nation state formation in the Yukon*. University of Toronto Press, Scholarly Publishing Division.

Oxford (n.d.). Sovereignty. In *Oxford English Dictionary*. Retrieved 2020, from https://www.oed.com/view/Entry/185343?redirectedFrom=sovereignty&

Pact is signed to make North Marianas a U. S. Area. (1975, February 16). *The New York Times*. https://www.nytimes.com/1975/02/16/archives/pact-is-signed-to-make-north-marianas-a-us-area.html

Pöllath, M. (2018). Revisiting island decolonization: The pursuit of self-government in Pacific island polities under US hegemony. *Island Studies Journal, 13*(1), 235–250. https://doi.org/10.24043/isj.46

Ritskes, E. (2015). Against the death maps of Empire: Contesting colonial borders through Indigenous sovereignty. *Decolonization*, 1–5. https://decolonization.wordpress.com/2015/10/14/against-the-death-maps-of-empire-contesting-colonial-borders-through-Indigenous-sovereignty/

Second Marianas Political Status Commission Act of 2015, CNMI §11100 (2015). https://cnmilaw.org/pdf/cmc_section/t1/11100.pdf

Simpson, A. (2010). Review: Under the sign of sovereignty: Certainty, ambivalence, and law in Native North America and Indigenous Australia. *Wicazo Sa Review, 25*(2), 107–124. https://www.jstor.org/stable/40891325

Simpson, A. (2014). *Mohawk interruptus*. Duke University Press Books.

Smith, G. (1991). *Micronesia: Decolonisation and US military; Interests in the Trust Territory of the Pacific Islands*. Peace Research Centre, Research School of Pacific Studies, Australian National University.

Stoler, A. L., McGranahan, C., & Perdue, P. C. (2007). *Imperial formations (School for advanced research advanced seminar series)*. School for Advanced Research Press.

Teves, S. N., Smith, A., & Raheja, M. (2015). Introduction. In S. Nohelani Teves, A. Smith, & M. H. Raheja (Eds.), *Native studies keywords (Critical issues in Indigenous studies)* (1st ed., pp. 3–17). University of Arizona Press.

To Approve "The Covenant to Establish a Commonwealth of the Northern Mariana Islands," and for Other Purposes: Hearing Before the Subcommittee on Territorial and Insular Affairs of the Committee on Interior and Insular Affairs, House of Representatives, 94th Cong. 1 (1975)

Tolentino, D. (n.d.). CHamoru quest for self-determination. In Guampedia. https://www.guampedia.com/politics_and_government/chamorro-quest-for-self-determination/

Torres, N. M. (2012). Self-determination challenges to voter classifications in the Marianas after Rice v. Cayetano: A call for a congressional declaration of territorial principles. *Asian-Pacific Law & Policy Journal, 14*(1), 152–202. http://blog.hawaii.edu/aplpj/files/2013/01/APLPJ_14.1_Torres_vFINAL2.pdf

Trask, H. (1999). *From a native daughter: Colonialism and sovereignty in Hawaii (Revised Edition)* (2nd ed.). Latitude 20 Books.

Tuck, E., & Yang, K.W. (2012). Decolonization is not a metaphor. *Decolonization: Indigeneity, Education & Society 1*(1), 1-40.

United States/CNMI Political Union: Hearing Before the Committee on Energy and Natural Resources, United States Senate, 110th Congress, 1 (2007) (Testimony of David B. Cohen).

Uperesa, F. L., & Garriga-López, A. M. (2017). Contested sovereignties: Puerto Rico and American Samoa. In F. Negron-Muntaner (Ed.), *Sovereign acts* (pp. 39–81). University of Arizona Press.

Villazor, R. C. (2010). Reading between the (blood) lines. *Southern California Law Review, 83*, 473–494. https://ssrn.com/abstract=1622009

Villazor, R. C. (2018). Problematizing the protection of culture and the insular cases. *Harvard Law Review Forum, 131*(6), 127–152. https://harvardlawreview.org/2018/04/problematizing-the-protection-of-culture-and-the-insular-cases/

Willens, H. P. (2003). The commonwealth of the Northern Mariana Islands is both constitutional and successful. *The Journal of Pacific History, 38*(3), 375–377. https://doi.org/10.1080/0022334032000154119

Wong, A., & Cruz, L. (2018, November 15). The media barely covered one of the worst storms to hit US soil. *The Atlantic.* https://www.theatlantic.com/science/archive/2018/11/super-typhoon-yutu-mainstream-media-missed-northern-mariana-islands/575692

The Evolution of Respeto (Respect) as Viewed through Three Generations of Refaluwasch (Carolinian) Families

Cinta Matagolai Kaipat

Respeto

Respeto (respect) is one of the cornerstones of Refaluwasch (Carolinian) culture. It dictates what is considered a culturally appropriate or inappropriate manner of interacting with every single being we encounter. For us Refaluwasch, respeto is crucial to our very survival. Based on my own personal observations, I find that there has been a diminished sense of respeto in Refaluwasch culture with each succeeding generation. I fear that the continuation of this trend will lead to the rapid extinction of this important hallmark of Refaluwasch culture. Why is this important? This is important because our culture is what makes us unique; it is what sets us apart from other peoples of the world. Moreover, respeto helps restore peace and harmony, both within and outside of our own Refaluwasch society. Of parallel importance is that it promotes tipiyew—that Refaluwasch "spirit of unity"—of one heart, one mind, and one love for all. To lose appreciation for this important Refaluwasch value threatens the very survival of our culture and unique way of life.

My Parents' Generation

My parents were born in the 1930s during the Japanese occupation of our Mariana Islands. I am certain that what my parents learned about respeto growing up in their respective households was shaped by their cultural environment, as well as later-life influences they experienced as they matured into adulthood.

My Father

My father was born to a Refaluwasch father and a Chamorro mother on the island of Agrigan (also called Agrihan), one of our remote islands north of Saipan in the Northern Islands of our Marianas archipelago. Agrigan was populated almost exclusively by Refaluwasch at the time my father and his family lived there. That is where my paternal grandparents chose to live and raise a family. My father was the second to the youngest child in a family of six boys and one girl.

He was a schoolteacher, a song composer, a farmer, a medic, a traditional local healer, a public official, and a congressman. In his younger years, he worked as a cook on a ship. My father had the privilege of traveling abroad to pursue his education in places such as Chuuk in Micronesia, Fiji, Hawai'i, and Japan. I am certain this experience further shaped his worldview and helped him become a better community leader in service to our people upon his return home from studying abroad. His exposure to the outside world honed his skills as a diplomat, enabling him to navigate skillfully between the more modern world he ventured into and the more traditional world he had been raised in.

My father was also a visionary who was ahead of his time. He believed in developing our islands' natural resources and held strongly to the belief that the peoples' skills had to be developed as well as this was a key element in the communities' achieving self-sufficiency and economic prosperity. My father returned to Saipan in the early 1960s after completing his studies at the University of Hawai'i where he majored in agriculture. He was subsequently hired to help run the Agriculture Program in the Marianas during the Trust Territory era which began after WWII. It was then that he moved our family from Agrigan to Saipan. I was the youngest of five children born at that time. In Saipan, we lived in isolation in Chacha, as Kagman Village was still an undeveloped farm area back then. My father held this position until he was persuaded to run for political office to represent our people of the Northern Islands.

He won a seat in the Legislature and moved our family back to the Northern Islands and resettled us in Pagan (pronounced "Puhgan") in the latter part of July 1968. By this time, our family had expanded to seven children.

Although my father was one of the most highly educated men of his time—especially for a Refaluwasch or a Refaluwasch-Chamorro—he did not limit himself to playing the traditional male role common in Refaluwasch society. On the contrary, upon returning from one of his trips to Saipan to attend a Congressional session, or when he would return home after an off-island trip to Japan or Hawai'i to engage his contemporaries on agricultural matters, he was often seen carrying one of my younger siblings on one hip while stirring a pot on the stove. He even improvised a wood-burning oven so that he could bake bread!

I was 10 years old when we tragically lost my father. He was murdered in April 1972, while protecting a constituent who sought refuge at our house one night following a domestic dispute. I mention my father's death because I include in this writing what I learned from him about respeto as I was growing up, although most of the discussions on this subject will be lessons passed on by my beloved mother, who lived to the age of 75, just 2 months shy of her 76th birthday, before we lost her, too, in April 2010.

My Mother

My mother was born in Saipan to Refaluwasch parents. She was raised by a single mother. She was an only child before a half-sister came along a few years later. It would be a few more years later before her mother would marry and give birth to her youngest half-sister and half-brother. Mom began her formal education during the Japanese administration. She got as far as second grade under the Japanese education system. Like a typical Refaluwasch family, my mother grew up in a humble home where money was hard to come by. Her mother was a tall curly-haired stern woman. Much of her beliefs and teachings were passed on to her by my maternal grandmother and other relatives.

My mother's family lived in Chalan Kanoa in Saipan prior to moving to Agrigan after the end of WWII. As the eldest, she helped take care of her younger siblings. Mom worked hard to take care of her family. She continued this "life work" after she and my father were married and started a family. She was pregnant with her tenth child when my father was killed. While she never took a job outside the house, the "life work" my mother assumed raising all 10 children on her own after my father's death was nothing short of remarkable. She was the glue that held us together when our world was suddenly shattered after my father's death. We owe my mother a debt of gratitude that can never ever be repaid. She was an incredibly strong role model who believed in and lived by the Golden Rule. There is no doubt that she left the biggest influence in shaping our lives.

My Generation

My siblings were born in the 1950s, 1960s, and 1970s. I was born in 1961. I am fond of sharing this piece of trivia with new friends. I tell them that the number 5 plays a significant role in my life. For starters, my parents had five boys and five girls. After having five of us, they waited five years before they had five more children. I am the fifth child of the 10 children born to my parents. Five of us were delivered at home on Agrigan by our Chamorro grandmother and, finally, I was the fifth child that she delivered.

Speaking of my grandparents, unfortunately, all had passed away by the time I was old enough to know and appreciate them. I am sure I would have learned a lot from them. Also, as I mentioned earlier, my father's tragic death when I was 10 years old not only deprived me of a father, but also robbed me of the opportunity to learn so much from him. Hence, most of what I learned about Refaluwasch culture and respeto came from my mother as well as other relatives. I thank God for my mother and all the relatives who took the time to instill Refaluwasch values and lessons, such as respeto, in me and my siblings.

The Next Generation

Members of the next generation include my numerous nieces and nephews in my immediate family, as well as other relatives who were born in the 1970s, 1980s, 1990s, and 2000s.

I. Ttong (Kissing of the Hand)

One of the first things children are taught to do in order to show respeto is to kiss the right hand of a parent or older relatives. When meeting relatives who are a generation or more above you (either while visiting or after church), the first act in paying respeto is to walk up to that individual, gently take and raise his or her right hand towards your nose as you bend down and kiss the hand and say "Ñora" if the person to whom you are according respeto is a female or "Ñot" if the person is a male. These are Spanish-origin Chamorro words. I am sure that this practice was something picked up from our Spanish colonizers who conquered and subjugated my Chamorro ancestors in the 1600s. That my Refaluwasch ancestors share this customary act of showing respeto means that they, too, did not escape Spanish subjugation even though they did not settle in the Marianas permanently until the 1800s.

Refalowasch call this act of according respeto by kissing the hand "ttong." This act is also very important in paying respeto to one's godparents. Being blessed after kissing the hand—with the person bestowing the blessing touching the head and replying "Liyoos faiyéégh" (God bless you)—is culturally important. It is an important symbolic gesture of an ongoing relationship based on respeto. In fact, one of the baptismal godparents will also be the godparent at the godchild's wedding. If the godchild is a female, then the godmother will be involved in the wedding ceremony, and vice versa if the godchild is a male.

There are certain situations when a "proxy godparent" may be called upon to fill in for the actual godparent. For instance, when one of my father's godsons was about to get married, he came to our house and asked if my eldest brother could stand in as a proxy for my father as he knew that my father had long since passed away. Another situation where the "proxy godparent" may be called in is if the actual godparent is either off-island or too ill to attend the wedding ceremony.

My Parents' Generation
While I did not see my father engage in this customary respectful act of ttong while I was growing up in the Northern Islands, I am certain that he performed this act whenever he met up with his aunts and uncles living in Saipan. As to my mother, I did have many chances to observe her engage in this practice when we moved to Saipan permanently in 1972 right after my father was killed.

My Generation
One of the earliest teachings instilled in us by my parents to accord respeto was to

"åmen" or "ttong" whenever we met a relative who was my parents' contemporary or older. Failure to accord respeto was not tolerated. This was all well and good if one knew who amongst the relatives were due to be accorded this act of respeto. However, it gets complicated when you find yourself in a crowd of people feeling bashful because you do not really know to whom to accord this respectful act.

I recall my personal experience with this very dilemma. I was 16 when I left home for Chicago to pursue my education. I finally moved back home after attending school and living and working in the States for almost 20 years. Unfortunately, my long absence from home made attempts to re-assimilate back into my community challenging. I often found myself in awkward and embarrassing situations wherein I did not know most of the people surrounding me at social gatherings or at other public functions, including members of my Refaluwasch community. To play it safe and avoid offending anyone, I mistakenly decided to "åmen" or "ttong" the folks who had gray hair. I assumed they had to be a generation older than me and, therefore, worthy of the respectful gesture. However, that was not a fail-proof method. Much to my chagrin, I ended up having gray-haired folks yank their hands away from me in exasperation. However, some did laugh at me, but, thankfully, they also took the opportunity to educate me and point out that we were contemporaries and so it was, therefore, inappropriate for me to engage in the respectful practice of "ttong" with them. Nevertheless, some others believe that receiving a blessing—albeit from a contemporary—is still a good thing.

The Next Generation

No doubt that unless the practice of ttong is taught and reinforced as the children are growing up, this would not be something that the next generation would automatically value and appreciate and, therefore, feel compelled to perform as appropriate. This generation either ignores this significant cultural component of showing respeto to one's elders or their godparents. Of those who do observe this practice, I would say that, with few exceptions, a vast majority of them complete the act of ttong in a perfunctory manner. For example, my generation would approach the relative or godparent, reach for and raise the right hand while bending down to kiss it and say "Ñiot" or "Ñiora" and then wait for the relative or godparent to put his or her hand on our heads and bless us. Disappointingly, I have observed a number of members of the next generation opt to ttong from a distance, if at all. They simply approach and bend over from a few feet away and say "Ñiora" without walking up to hold the hand and kiss it and wait for the blessing.

Another dramatic departure from the traditional hand kissing in ttong that I have observed in this generation is the quick peck on the cheek while saying "Ñiora." We know that this is a customary greeting in many other countries, including the United States. But, while there is nothing wrong with this manner of greeting friends and loved ones, the symbolic act of kissing the hand in ttong is done for a completely different purpose—to accord respeto and to receive a blessing in return. Today, this important cultural act of according respeto and receiving a blessing in return has somehow morphed into a mere greeting with a peck on the cheek. Again, I emphasize that the two are not interchangeable. They are mutually exclusive—each done for a completely different purpose.

For obvious reasons, I am not a fan of this trend, as it takes away from the significance of what is supposed to be a meaningful mutual exchange of paying respect and receiving a blessing in return. A peck on the cheek is simply that—a greeting—which is different from and does not equate to ttong, which is the giving of respect and then receiving a blessing in return. Thinking about this issue opened my eyes to how my mother must have felt whenever my siblings and I failed to live up to her expectations of how we ought to practice and observe respeto in all its various forms and nuances.

II. Rankings by Gender and Birth Order

Refaluwasch society is a matrilineal society wherein the eldest woman within each clan is entrusted with the powerful position of being the "trustee of the family land." Despite this, the plain fact is that men still outrank women in Refaluwasch society. This is just the way it is and has been this way for many, many generations. The man is the head of the household. Male children outrank female children. Sisters are taught to respect their brothers and to act in a respectful manner toward them, such as using respectful language when speaking to them or about them and monitoring their behavior to remain respectful at all times. Conversely, the men are expected to be mindful of their language and behavior around their sisters to ensure that respeto is also observed at all times.

But this is not the only ranking system that must be followed. Another ranking system also exists within each gender. If there are five brothers, for example, the eldest brother would outrank the younger brothers and so forth on down the pecking order. This is the same with sisters. In theory, this is the way things are supposed to work. However, within my parents' generation, younger male siblings still accord their older female siblings respeto in the same manner that they would accord respeto to older male siblings. This, too, is proper and acceptable. While this may seem like a contradiction, I say it is more of an exception rather than a contradiction.

These rankings apply to other relatives as well. If one were to look at a family tree, the children of the eldest male relative would outrank the children born to younger siblings and the rankings would extend down the family tree to the very last branch. The next in line in terms of this ranking system would be the children of the second eldest male and so forth. Finally, after the children of the youngest male would come the children of the oldest female. The rankings continue with the children of the second oldest female, then down to the children of the youngest female being last.

These ranking systems can get complicated, and some might even say it is a convoluted system that is impossible to truly grasp. However, serious attempts at learning and understanding these systems are important, as one must do everything possible to avoid offending anyone and shaming the family. For example, it would be highly improper for the children of any younger sibling to ask the children of the older male siblings to perform any chores for them. Yet, it is perfectly appropriate for the children of the older siblings to ask the children of the younger siblings to perform chores for them. This applies to the rest of the families on down the line. Hence, knowing such rankings is crucial in "saving face," as to act improperly or disrespectfully would bring shame and dishonor to the family. Obviously, this is to be avoided at all costs.

My Parents' Generation

I recall that my father always remained respectful of his siblings, including his only sister who was older than him. Again, this was the exception I mentioned earlier about brothers according respeto to their sisters as well, which is perfectly acceptable. This same deference also extended to my father's relatives. Also, as I mentioned above, my mother was the oldest child in her family, so I saw her younger siblings, including my uncle who was the youngest child in my mother's family, accord my mother a lot of deference. My mother practiced the Refaluwasch customs of awóówó (respectful language) and appwóro (respectful behavior) where my uncle was concerned, and so both accorded respeto toward one another. My mother also accorded respeto to her other male relatives.

My Generation
In my family, the ranking system was also observed in terms of recognizing that our eldest brother commanded the highest respeto of all. All of us accorded him the respeto that he was entitled to by virtue of his birth order, as well as the fact that he was also a male. But while our mother and other relatives attempted to teach us women to practice the custom of appwóro to accord respeto to all our brothers, with few exceptions, my generation was less rigid in applying this practice, if at all. For instance, in my immediate family, none of my brothers was ever required to stand up in order for us to pass by. However, my brothers would definitely stand up for our female cousins who were practicing appwóro. Nevertheless, my sisters and I also understood that we should not and would not walk past our brothers or other male relatives if they were sitting on the floor without first politely asking them to get up off the floor and at least sit in a chair while we walk past them. My other male siblings who are younger than our eldest male sibling are also expected to observe the same practice when it comes to our eldest brother and so forth down the line.

The Next Generation
In our family, we were met with mediocre results when trying to teach the ranking system to our children. The next generation lives in a far different world than my generation or my parents' generation lived in.

III. Kkapasal Faluwasch
In Refaluwasch culture, there is an everyday language that everyone uses. We call this language "kappasal falwasch" (language of our island). While kappasal faluwasch may be used among peers and in communications between older and younger generations, depending on the family's respeto practices that rank family members, there may be limitations or variations in how widely this everyday language is used.

For example, some Refaluwasch families are more traditional than others; therefore, they may adhere to a more rigid custom of speaking kappasal faluwasch when addressing certain individuals to avoid being disrespectful in their manner of communication. For instance, kappasal faluwasch may be peppered with the respectful language of awóówó where appropriate to accord respeto to whomever the intended audience is. Some may also use kappasal faluwasch when they are in the exclusive presence of their respective gender's company, where the rigidity and importance of choosing one's words carefully is far more relaxed. Yet, another situation in which kappasal faluwasch is spoken without peppering it with awóówó is communication between spouses.

My Parents' Generation

Regarding my parents, I know that they communicated with each other in kappasal faluwasch. There was no requirement for either of them to speak the language of awóówó when communicating with each other.

My Generation

My generation's first spoken language is also kappasal faluwasch. Both parents spoke to us in kappasal faluwasch and we also spoke it amongst each other, as well as with friends and relatives.

The Next Generation

Cultural advocates and preservationists say, "You lose your language, you lose your culture." I believe this is true. Perhaps in our zeal to push our children to excel in school, where English is the only language taught and spoken in virtually all subjects, we began speaking English to our children at home almost to the exclusion of our own Refaluwasch language. This was and IS a big mistake. I believe this has shortchanged our children's opportunity to learn their first language at home while simultaneously learning English in school. The addition of the television in our homes also contributed to the replacement of our Refaluwasch language with English. While it is good that our toddlers learn to speak English while watching children's shows on televisions, iPads and cell phones, imagine how much better it would have been if our children also watched similar programs in our own Native languages.

Additionally, almost all the books the kids read in school are written in English. Consequently, it became more and more of a struggle and almost a losing battle to attempt to teach the Refaluwasch language to the next generation, who seemed to have less and less interest in learning the language. When you speak in kappasal faluwasch to members of the next generation, you are more likely to be met with blank stares or question marks written on their faces as they are often virtually clueless as to what you are saying to them. If you speak to them in kappasal faluwasch, some will respond in English with, "I don't understand what you're saying." When this became apparent in our own family decades ago, one of my brothers, who opened my eyes as well as the eyes of some of our other siblings, decided that it was time to take drastic measures to stem and reverse the tide.

To do this, we decided that whenever our nieces or nephews would call the house, we would say "Refaluwasch" once they began speaking in English. This startled them at first. In fact, we endured weeks of their stammering on the phone, followed by silence that culminated in the kids hanging up on us in frustration. However, a line had been drawn, and, for everyone's sake, especially our children's, it was important to stand our ground. My brother even required some of the younger kids in our family to begin writing daily journals in Refaluwasch about what happened in school. This made for some hilarious reading, but the kids got the point.

Of course, it did not happen overnight, but eventually, it began to pay off. Today, these once-young members of the next generation are fluent in kappasal faluwasch and those who have become parents are now able to pass on kappasal faluwasch to their own children.

Although we averted the total loss of kappasal faluwasch in the next generation in our immediate family (and perhaps other families might have also met with similar success), unfortunately, there are still some gaps. Ongoing efforts to teach our children kappasal faluwasch must continue. We know that some parents of my generation still speak English exclusively or almost exclusively to their children who were born in the next generation. My hope is that we make every effort to collectively encourage and remind such parents that their assistance and cooperation in this regard are crucial. I am mindful, however, that this effort to preserve our indigenous language will succeed only if the parents believe it is something valuable and worth preserving.

With optimism, I can say that not all is lost. I cannot emphasize this enough—we MUST bring back our bilingual classes to our schools. At one time, our Public School System offered bilingual classes which, in my opinion, proved to be invaluable in providing many young children with some kappasal faluwasch lessons that they were not exposed to at home. It was far better than nothing. Ideally, kappasal faluwasch lessons ought to begin at home and should be reinforced or augmented in school, as well as through other community programs that could be offered or sponsored by the Carolinian Affairs Office, the Indigenous Office, the Language Policy Commission, or some other programs funded both locally and federally. I also understand that there were some schools in our Public School System that offered language immersion classes as part of their bilingual classes. I applaud this move and believe should be revived with the return of our bilingual programs to our schools.

IV. Awóówó

There is a respectful language in Refaluwasch culture called "awóówó." This honorific language must be used to accord respeto when interacting with certain family members, as well as members of the general public. This language is also essential in communicating with male relatives, including older relatives who must be accorded respeto. The same applies to communicating with children. However, it is not appropriate to apply the honorific language of awóówó to oneself. For example, in the everyday language of kappasal faluwasch, a person may say "Ibwe mwongo" (I'm going to eat), but one may not apply the awóówó language when referring to oneself by saying "Ibwe ilitiyáy."

Moreover, when inviting someone to eat, one might say in kappasal faluwasch "Itto mwongo" (Come eat), depending on whom the person is addressing. For instance, an older sister may say this to her younger sister or perhaps an older brother may say this to a younger brother. However, a Refaluwasch woman may never use such language to invite her brother, parents, older relatives, a child, or members of the public to eat, as that would be very impolite. So, instead, she must use the respectful language of awóówó and say "Itto ilitúgh" (Come eat) if she were addressing a single person. If she were inviting individuals from any of the aforementioned categories of persons, however, she would say "Aw itto ilitúghámi" (Come eat, everyone). When addressing a child, she would say "Itto mamma" (Come eat), and if she were addressing more than one child, she would say "Aw itto mamma" (Come eat, everyone).

My Parents' Generation

Generally speaking, whenever my parents communicated with others, they would speak in kappasal faluwasch, although awóówó was also spoken whenever the situation dictated such. And, while I did not observe my father speak the awóówó language, I certainly observed my mother utilizing this language in her everyday communications with family members. As explained above, rankings do play an important role in how awóówó is used. So, while my mother was required to use the language of awóówó at all times in communicating with her brothers, elders, relatives, and members of the public, she was not required to use awóówó when communicating with her younger sisters because, as the eldest female in her family, my mother outranked her two younger sisters. However, my mother's younger sisters were required to address her in the language of awóówó.

My Generation

My generation speaks the everyday kappasal faluwasch with some words of awóówó when called for. However, I know that the awóówó language is spoken less and less frequently. Despite my mother's best efforts to teach us awóówó, it is my firm belief that unless the language is spoken regularly in the house, it is easy to lose it—assuming one acquired it to begin with. This is why I see fewer and fewer people speaking awóówó today. In other words, there needs to be a constant teaching and reinforcement of this awóówó language for it to remain relevant and to prevent it from fading into obscurity. If we do not use it, we lose it. It is as simple as that.

I know that there is great admiration for those who still speak awóówó today. This is especially true of children. Children who speak awóówó today garner high praise and much respect and admiration for themselves as well as their families. There is this belief that a child who speaks awóówó is a child who has been brought up right. Though admirable for the respeto values it promotes, one of the reasons awóówó is losing its popularity with each generation is that it is a difficult language to understand and master. English has become a necessary language of education and modern-day survival. It is the world's common language used to connect peoples of all walks of life from practically every nation on Earth. Thus, unlike my parents' generation and previous generations, there is more emphasis on teaching and learning English as opposed to teaching and learning awóówó.

The Next Generation

For those members of the next generation who are proficient in awóówó, I commend them and their parents or relatives who imparted such knowledge to them. They are rare gems. This shows that there are some members of the next generation who value our culture enough to invest in learning about our culture and languages. They made sure they spent quality time with their elders who effectively imparted such knowledge to them. They are the stewards who keep the cultural links connected. This is a very worthwhile endeavor.

One such steward I have met and interviewed is an impressive young man in his mid-20s who is able to write and speak eloquently in both Chamorro and Refaluwasch. He epitomizes the bright hope for the future and is a credit to the next generation. After I spoke with him, this young gentleman revealed to me that his desire to preserve his Refaluwasch and Chamorro heritage was inspired by *Lieweila: A Micronesian Story*, the historical cultural documentary film that I co-produced and released in 1998 with Dr. Beret E. Strong, her husband John Tweedy, Esq., and my brother, Gus. The film traces the emigration of my Refaluwasch ancestors from the central Carolines to the Marianas in the 1800s. Led by Chief Aghurubw and two other chiefs, the Marianas is where they resettled after they were forced to escape from earthquakes, floods and devastating typhoons. The film also traces my Refaluwasch ancestors' shared history with my Chamorro ancestors under various colonial regimes that ruled the Marianas, starting with the Spanish, followed by the Germans, the Japanese and then the Americans.

This particular young man had an impressive appreciation and knowledge of both his Chamorro and Refaluwasch cultures and languages. He speaks and writes in both languages fluently, which has garnered even more respect and admiration from me. I conducted my interview with him via social media and immediately regretted not having met him in person before he returned to the States to care for his elderly grandparents. I would say that this young man represented the exception rather than the rule. He especially impressed me with his command and use of awóówó as we conversed, as well as his understanding of respeto and the importance of using appropriate language in public debates, such as on social media.

The young man caught my attention when I first read his comments on social media reminding another individual of the importance of minding our language in public debates. He spoke of how disappointed our elders would have been had they heard the coarse language being used in public debates today. When I asked him about this, he lamented that someone told him a long time ago that if he truly wanted to learn about his culture, then he would have to go and live with the elders who could teach him what he needed to learn. And that is exactly what he did. That he was able to confidently use his knowledge and maturity to remind or teach others how to communicate properly in public is a testament to the fine job that his elders had done in imparting valuable life lessons to him. This is truly commendable on the part of the student and his teachers.

Within my own family, the members of the next generation are communicating in kappasal faluwasch mixed with some English, though we continue to encourage them to use kappasal falwasch as the main language at home. Unfortunately, their knowledge and use of awóówó is still somewhat limited, but some are making some progress.

V. Off-color Jokes and Cuss Words
In Refaluwasch culture, there is a divide between proper male and female behaviors that dictates what each gender ought to say and how each should behave. This is done to accord mutual respeto to one another and to avoid committing cultural taboos. For example, men and women must never tell off-color jokes in mixed company. Men and women may use provocative language to tell jokes, but such language must be restricted to the privacy of same-gender gatherings. To do otherwise is taboo. The rationale behind this is that violating this taboo will erode respeto. For brothers and sisters, maintaining respeto is especially important and something that must be safeguarded at all times.

Refaluwasch people also believe that respeto demands that one never use cuss words with one's parents, brothers, elder sisters, or young children. Of course, it is considered in poor taste and taboo to cuss in public. Not only would cussing be a breach of respeto, but it is also believed that sisters should never cuss out their brothers as this could result in dire consequences for the brothers. Why? This is because Refaluwasch people believe that a woman's words are very strong and powerful and, therefore, directing cuss words at one's brother could potentially bring some illness upon him. It is tantamount to casting a curse upon one's brother. In some instances, it is believed that this may even lead to sickness and death.

Additionally, such risqué language and jokes must also be avoided in the presence of elders and children. There is a reason that gender segregation exists in Refaluwasch society when people are socializing. This is done to avoid the risk of offending anyone with "loose" language in a more relaxed atmosphere, especially in situations where alcohol is involved and there is typically a lot of teasing and joking around, sometimes using cuss words and delving into subject matters that are best not discussed in mixed company. Hence, both genders accept that there are certain cultural practices both genders must observe in order to preserve respeto. Thus, gender segregation is one way of upholding and ensuring respeto.

Moreover, Refaluwasch people believe that there is a strong correlation between what one might say and how one might act. Thus, if the genders communicate in a respectful language to each other, then a corresponding respectful behavior towards one another follows. Conversely, if the males or females do not accord each other proper respectful language, then the erosion or lack of respeto amongst the two may inevitably lead to risqué behavior, which is forbidden in Refaluwasch society. This is a fine line that must never ever be crossed. To do so brings with it "loss of face" and shame to the families on both sides.

My Parents' Generation

For obvious reasons, my parents would not or did not engage in any of these types of joking and teasing, much less cussing. Otherwise, such behaviors would have registered in my or my siblings' conscious memories. The fact that my memory is devoid of any personal anecdotes where one or both of my parents either engaged in hurling cuss words at each other or at others or telling risqué jokes in mixed company or in public arenas assures me that they both acted properly and responsibly. This says a lot given that both of my parents were known for their great sense of humor and quick wit. My father was also quite a prankster, though all in good, clean fun. My mother was also quick with a smile. She liked to laugh, tease and joke as well. But as I said, throughout the years, I never saw either parent act inappropriately.

My Generation

My generation is also expected to operate within the same cultural constraints that prohibit the telling of off-color jokes or using cuss words in much the same way as my parents' generation or previous generations. However, there were some instances I was privy to where I would say that there were lapses in good judgment. For example, I once observed a fellow Refaluwasch woman going along with and engaging in sharing off-color jokes with our male Chamorro colleagues at a social gathering in order to fit in. This made me uncomfortable as a Refaluwasch woman, but it was not my place to say anything to her. In this regard, my Refaluwasch culture clashed with my Chamorro culture in a major way.

In my Chamorro culture, sharing off-color jokes in mixed company is perfectly fine. In fact, the more you engage in it, the more you are accepted into the circle. However, this is the antithesis of how to fit in in my Refaluwasch culture. It is one of the big taboos that my Refaluwasch culture preaches directly against. I have also personally experienced this culture clash.

Several years ago, while briefly working for the same employer as one of my brothers, we ended up finding ourselves in the most awkward and embarrassing situations whenever our Chamorro co-workers would tell off-color jokes with the two of us present in the same room. Obviously, we could not stop our Chamorro colleagues from telling such jokes, which they considered to be harmless and all in good fun. But, in order to minimize such awkward situations and adhere to our own Refaluwasch cultural values, my brother and I made a point of taking turns leaving the room periodically whenever we were in social gatherings. This way, our colleagues continued to enjoy themselves without my brother and me being embarrassed. Perhaps this solution may seem drastic, but to us, it was a necessary compromise that worked for us.

On another matter, I have also come across a number of folks in my generation who sometimes post on social media to blast an anonymous person they were angry at using strong cuss words that were disturbing and embarrassing. Not only is this in poor taste, but it often reflected poorly on the very person or persons launching the attacks. Social media platforms, such as Facebook, have shrunk the world by connecting everyone from near and far in this virtual world. However, when used improperly, social media can give some a false sense of courage. It emboldens some to spew hate and disrespectful language online, which the individuals might think twice about doing in person. When used properly, social media can be a great tool for the education of others and staying connected with friends and loved ones. However, when used carelessly, it can become a formidable weapon of cultural destruction. It goes without saying that the key here is to use social media responsibly.

The Next Generation
As much as we do our best to teach our children about awóówó and other respectful manners, unfortunately, like adults, they also sometimes exhibit lapses in good judgement and engage in inappropriate joking. For example, I believe that the popularity of explicit or vulgar rap music has had a negative impact on younger generations. Music is one way in which children acquire language and without the expletives in popular music, our children would probably not have this type of language or speech in their daily vocabularies. Western comedians are also partly to blame. Comedy using foul language attracts younger generations who get caught up in the humor of the jokes, regardless of the way they may run counter to the values within their own culture.

Again, I reiterate that social media plays a role in the erosion of respeto by providing an easy and convenient vehicle with a built-in audience in which one can log-in and spew hatred and foul language in the relative comfort of one's home with almost total impunity. This not something that the impressionable next generation ought to emulate.

VI. Addressing Elders and Children
In our Refaluwasch culture, elders and children are to be addressed using respectful language at all times. However, there is a slight variation in the respectful language that is used to communicate with elders versus that which is used to communicate with children. For example, the word "mamma" (eat) is often used when communicating with children. As stated earlier, to invite an adult to eat, one ought to use the polite word "ilitúgh" (eat) or "yááyá" (partake). However, over time, the same

word used to invite children to eat—"mamma"—has gained acceptance while communicating with elders or visitors in general. Again, generally speaking, the use of the word "mwongo" (eat) when addressing everyone else but oneself is considered very impolite.

My Parents' Generation

While I did not observe my father use the language of awóówó while I was growing up, my mother certainly utilized the awóówó language extensively whenever she communicated with elders or children.

My Generation

My generation still uses awóówó to communicate with elders and children, so the practice continues. However, there may be some irregularities depending on the household one is brought up in. In other words, if the parents or a parent teaches awóówó to their children as they are growing up, then they would most likely use this tool. Otherwise, if the children were never exposed to awóówó, then they would not use it. With regard to my own immediate family, my mother did her part to instill awóówó lessons in us with varying degrees of success. I can state unequivocally that I know a lot more and also a lot less about speaking awóówó than some of my siblings.

The Next Generation

With some exceptions, the next generation is generally lacking in the knowledge of awóówó, which leads me to my earlier point expressing that many parents do not teach this respectful language in the home as often as previous generations have. However, teaching awóówó to the next generation is not as simple as one might think given that English has become the preferred language within many of Refaluwasch homes today. I attribute this to the home environment having changed drastically in numerous ways for many members of the next generation.

For one thing, having both parents working to earn a living outside the house meant that the next generation is being raised by foreign houseworkers who speak English, not Refaluwasch, to the children. Another reason is that, in our zeal to propel ourselves forward in keeping pace with modern society, we have imported beliefs from other cultures without considering what consequences this might have on our respective cultures in our communities. For instance, we thought it was a good idea to build a Manåmku' (Senior Citizens) Center to provide a place where our elders could gather socially. However, the unintended disadvantage was that this took the elders out of their family homes and resulted in lost opportunities for them to interact with younger generations on a daily basis. Thus, a number of children were deprived of prime opportunities to learn awóówó and other valuable lessons of our Refaluwasch culture from their elders.

Another challenge is that there are more mixed marriages between Refaluwasch and persons from other countries, including the United States. Obviously, English is the primary language used to communicate in our diverse society, and, unless efforts are made by either parent to teach the children their respective languages, English will be the only language spoken by the children. In such situations, even the most fluent speaker of awóówó would be hard-pressed to force awóówó lessons on the English-speaking children who may not have the slightest inclination to learn the language. As the popular saying goes, "You can lead a horse to water, but you can't make it drink."

VII. "Bostus" or "Tarapaas" Language or Behavior

In situations where someone callously spews disrespectful language or acts in an indecent manner without regard to audience or venue, this behavior is often met with heavy criticism and scorn as this definitely goes against everything that one is taught about practicing respeto. I have heard this manner of speaking being referred to as "bostus" (rough) or "tarapaas" (scattered). For example, in a public setting, if one were to invite everyone to eat, one should never use the everyday language of kappasal falwasch and say "Aw itto mwongo" (Come eat, everyone) for that would be frowned upon and the speaker would be denounced as being very disrespectful for using bostus or tarapaas language. Whether in gatherings at home or in a public arena, but most especially when in a public setting, the speaker must always accord respeto by addressing the people using the respectful language of awóówó. The host or hostess may say something like "Sa yááya milikka pattiisch" (Let's all partake in our feast).

My Parents' Generation

In all my years with my parents, not once did I ever see them act in this bostus or tarapaas manner that would have brought shame to the family. As a matter of fact, this is precisely the type of unacceptable behavior that my mother would have been horrified to see any family member engage in.

My Generation

My parents endeavored to teach and mold us into model citizens and to behave in a manner that would not dishonor our family. Family pride was very important to them and they instilled this value in all of us. Therefore, they would be aghast if we were to engage in speech or behavior that would be considered bostus or tarapaas.

However, like other generations, my generation is also vulnerable to the influences of alcohol. We know that alcohol can have negative influences on people's behaviors regardless if they are at home or out in public. Therefore, some people—male or female—under the influence of alcohol may be susceptible to engaging in such bostus or tarapaas speech or behavior that they normally would not engage in when sober. It goes without saying that we must be mindful at all times that we must all endeavor to use alcohol responsibly, whether in social settings or while driving on our highways.

The Next Generation

I believe that one's family and upbringing play a major role in how one is expected to behave in public or in family social gatherings. The next generation must be guided and encouraged to walk the straight and narrow path. Not surprisingly, the absence of proper guidance or positive role models in a child's life may manifest itself in socially unacceptable language and behavior that are labeled bostus or tarapaas.

Unfortunately, alcohol is not the only threat to the success of the next generation. While teenage drinking is something that is common amongst the members of the next generation, another threat that preys on such young lives is drugs. Peer pressure is the devil in disguise. As a former prosecutor, I was privy to sad situations in which I saw members of the next generation throw their lives and future away by getting involved in alcohol, drugs and petty crime because they lacked a stable home environment and a family support system to nurture and guide them. Unfortunately, unless these basic needs are met, such troubled members of the next generation will be prone to engage in tarapaas behaviors and bostus speech.

VIII. Appwóro (To Respectfully Bow Down)

Just as there is a respectful language called awóówó, another way to accord respeto is in how both genders conform their behaviors toward one another. Refaluwasch call this "appwóro" (to respectfully bow down). For example, it is a cultural taboo for a sister to walk upright and past her brother upon entering a room while he is sitting down. For the sister to properly and respectfully proceed, she would first humbly ask her brother to stand up before she enters the room. Of course, if her brother were alert and saw his sister approaching, he would have taken his cue to stand up before she arrived to accord his sister proper respeto in return. Standing to accord a lady respeto upon her entering a room is analogous to the chivalrous act of a Western gentleman who stands up when a woman enters a room. We see this depicted in Western movies or television shows often. With that said, the same appwóro requirements do not apply to the sister's children with regard to their uncle (the mother's brother).

Under certain circumstances, when it is impossible for a brother stand up, such as when a brother in bed due to an illness, his sister is expected to approach him or go past him on her knees or, in some instances, crawl past him on all fours until she is some distance away before resuming her upright standing position. In other cases, however, the sister would refrain altogether from entering the room upon seeing her brother lying on the floor. Moreover, consideration is also accorded to persons with disabilities who need to be accommodated with chairs or a raised seat. Again, a person who adheres to the proper requirements of appwóro not only garners immediate respeto for himself or herself, but also extend respeto to the person's family.

Appwóro is also practiced in public settings. For example, during wakes, family members (such as elder women and children) usually gather on mats on the floor and sit around the coffin. It is customary that a woman, whether young or old, who enters a room must never simply enter assuming a regular upright posture, but must show respeto by bowing upon entering the room, by walking on her knees, or by crawling to join family members sitting around the coffin. Failure to accord respeto this way should be avoided, since such behavior is frowned upon. I cannot emphasize this point enough—behaving in a disrespectful manner not only casts aspersions on the character of the "offender," but also reflects poorly on the offender's family. This is because people will assume that the family was negligent in teaching proper manners of respeto to the "offender." Otherwise, the "offender" would have known better.

My Parents' Generation

Perhaps it is because I lost my father when I was only 10 years old and was, therefore, deprived of the joy of a life lived with him that I have no specific knowledge or recollection of him ever practicing appwóro. My mother, on the other hand, most definitely practiced appwóro throughout her life. She not only practiced appwóro with her youngest brother, but also with the male and female relatives who were her contemporaries.

My Generation

As stated earlier, appwóro was something taught and encouraged by my mother as we grew up. However, my generation's version of appwóro is not as strict or rigid as the version practiced by my mother and women of her generation. The reason for this is that many women of my generation have not found the more rigid and traditional form of appwóro practical for our lives today.

When I asked one of my relatives whether she practiced appwóro, she responded immediately with a hearty chuckle. After regaining her composure, she told me that, on the contrary, she would deliberately go out of her way to avoid practicing appwóro because she would not conform to behaviors of bending, kneeling and crawling just to get past her brothers or other males who were entitled to be accorded such acts of respeto. In fact, she said she specifically avoided practicing appwóro by steering clear of the vicinities where she knew the men gathered.

In today's modern world, many Refaluwasch women have entered the workforce in greater numbers than before. The reason for this is not just a matter of choice. It is a matter of necessity in most cases, as many families find it virtually impossible to survive on a single income. Also, some women now hold key leadership positions in government, as well as in the private sector. Speaking from personal experience, I know that I, and others like me, found that practicing appwóro in its rigid form is impractical in today's diverse heterogeneous society.

For example, when I worked as an Assistant Attorney General in the Criminal Division of the Office of the Attorney General in the CNMI, my job as a prosecutor necessitated that I stand up in the courtroom while addressing the jurors or the court. A number of my male relatives work in law enforcement. Therefore, it was not unusual for me to interact with male relatives while working on a particular case. Some male relatives who are not in law enforcement have also appeared in court when summoned for jury duty. Had I been practicing appwóro, I would have had to ask all male relatives present in the courtroom who are my contemporaries to stand and remain standing before I could stand to perform my job in the courtroom. Culturally speaking, they would not have been allowed to sit down until I sat down. Obviously, that would have been impractical, not to mention awkward.

This would have been true in other public settings as well. For instance, there were numerous occasions when I was called upon to stand and speak publicly as a member of the Legislature or during political events. I did not find it practical to stand on a stage or at the podium and assume the appwóro posture, even if my brothers were in the audience. Yet, according them and the members of the public, respeto in the way that I addressed them through language was always expected.

Nevertheless, I acknowledge that other Refaluwasch women may choose a different path. The Refaluwasch woman has the ultimate choice—regardless of where she is doing her public speaking—to choose to either stand on stage like I did or stand offstage at the same level as the audience if that is her preference. This is also acceptable and keeps with Refaluwasch values of humility and never putting oneself above others.

The Next Generation

I am certain that some parents do teach members of the next generation in their families some important socially polite behaviors, but from my observations, the strict mandates of appwóro are mostly ignored. Again, this is something that our Refaluwasch society must examine and determine whether these rules are worth preserving, and, if the answer is "yes," then meaningful steps should be taken to bring about the desired results. Otherwise, not teaching it is analogous to discarding it.

IX. Sharing Cups, Dishes and Utensils

Traditional Refaluwasch culture also has strict etiquette governing the sharing of cups, dishes and utensils between brothers and sisters. It is considered a cultural taboo for sisters to share cups, dishes, or utensils with their brothers. If a brother visits a sister's house, he is prohibited from using any cup except for the cup that has been specifically designated as "his." The brother is also restricted from using any silverware or plate aside from those designated as "his." If he uses a cup, dish or utensil that is not specifically designated as "his," his sister is forbidden from using that same cup, dish or utensil. Regardless of whether it was an unintentional use by the brother, the sister would still not be allowed to use the item(s) for a few days before such item(s) is/are considered "cleansed." Only then may his sister use the item(s) again.

My Parents' Generation

My father did not observe this cultural practice. However, my mother most certainly observed this cultural practice as applied to her brother, as well as her contemporary male relatives. Such restrictions only governed the relationship between the sister and her brother. No such restrictions applied to the children.

My Generation

With some exceptions, I would say that my generation made a complete departure from our parents' generation when it came to sharing utensils, cups and dishes. This was a cultural practice that my siblings and I never followed. All of us drank from the same cups, ate from the same dishes, and used the same utensils. For some reason, my mother decided not to enforce this practice that she and women of her generation practiced. Besides, disposable cups, dishes and flatware made this a non-issue for most of us.

The Next Generation

As happened in my generation, the cultural restrictions prohibiting the sharing of cups, dishes and utensils among male and female siblings also disappeared among the next generation.

X. Using the Outhouse or Bathroom

In traditional Refaluwasch culture, sisters must navigate their way to the outhouse without their brothers knowing or seeing them. Imagine the difficulty of pulling this off successfully every time her brother happens to be near the outhouse. In such cases, the sister must be resourceful in enlisting the help of others to distract her brother and lure him away from the vicinity of the outhouse in order for her dash toward it. However, no such restrictions apply to the men.

My Parents' Generation
To my knowledge, my father never engaged in this practice. Of course, my mother, the more traditional of the two, complied with such cultural practices as she was raised to understand observing these customs is important. I do recall some instances when she was forced to enlist the help of other family members to redirect our uncle away from the outhouse in order for her to use it without his knowledge. This later ceased being an issue after we moved to a house with an indoor bathroom and my uncle moved in with his other sister and her family.

My Generation
This is another area of my generation's marked departure from the rigid cultural mandates practiced by my mother and members of her generation. While we do not go out of our way to advertise when Mother Nature calls, we certainly are not required to hide it anymore or to enlist the help of others to distract our brothers as we scurry off to "powder our noses" (to use a Western euphemism). Nevertheless, common decency and respeto demand that discretion be exercised.

Perhaps the main reason for this departure from tradition is the current prevalence of indoor toilets instead of outhouses. With few exceptions, most contemporary Refaluwasch households have one or two indoor bathrooms. Therefore, everyone takes turns using the bathroom. In large families, one never knows who is going to answer when someone knocks on the bathroom door. Had my sisters and I practiced the outhouse etiquette of my mother's generation, this would have presented quite a dilemma, perhaps forcing me or one of my sisters to disguise our voices while in the bathroom to avoid giving ourselves away if a male sibling came knocking on the bathroom door. Once again, I believe that practicality won out over cultural restrictions.

The Next Generation
As with my generation, the taboos that existed in my parents' generation with

regard to the use of the outhouse or bathroom facilities have disappeared in the next generation.

XI. Socializing

In traditional Refaluwasch culture, women and men never intermingle when they socialize. Men often gather in a group or groups outside the house and away from where the women typically gather, which is usually inside the house. This is done for the purpose of ensuring that respeto is always maintained during such social gatherings. Hence, loose language, dirty jokes, etc. may be shared in a relaxed manner without fear of offending the opposite sex or eroding respeto.

My Parents' Generation

In my early years, growing up on the island of Pagan in the Northern Islands, I observed that my father socialized both in an all-male setting as well as in a mixed-gender setting. At that time, my father was the elected Congressman representing the people of the Northern Islands and was also the District Administrator's Representative (DistAd Rep). His position called for him to socialize within a wide circle of people from the Northern Marianas, Guam, other islands of Micronesia, Hawai'i, and other US states, as well as other foreign countries, such as Japan and Australia. My mother, on the other hand, was more comfortable socializing in an environment segregated by gender. Nevertheless, she had to adjust her comfort level and adapt to the wider social settings when called upon to host gatherings required of my father's position as a public official.

My Generation

Today, my family socializes in both gender-segregated and mixed-gender gatherings. If there was a gathering that included other relatives, the men would segregate themselves from the women as they typically do. As my youngest sister recalled, one teaching from my mother regarding respeto while socializing in segregated gatherings is that it would be inappropriate for my sister to join the men, even if her husband were part of the group. In gatherings of immediate family members, however, my family usually socializes in a mixed-gender setting. Our family loves to gather and sing, so all of my siblings frequently sit together to socialize and sing with our nieces and nephews. No matter what, we must always be mindful of treating each other with dignity and respect, in manner as well as in speech. This is absolutely non-negotiable.

The Next Generation
I would say that, depending on the situation and the setting, the intermixing or segregation of the two genders of the next generation is similar to that of my generation.

XII. Entering the Brother's or Sister's Bedroom
In traditional Refaluwasch culture, it is generally taboo for a sister to enter her brother's bedroom, especially if he is married. However, some exceptions apply. For example, the sister may enter the single brother's bedroom if she were to retrieve his dirty laundry or clean his room. Otherwise, the sister is expected to stay out of the bedroom. Moreover, the sister is prohibited from sitting on or lying down on her brother's bed. Doing so would be disrespectful to her brother. In cases where the brother is married, it would be his wife's responsibility to retrieve something from the bedroom instead of his sister's. This would include the dirty laundry, as the wife takes over the laundry duties for herself and her spouse.

Conversely, the brother is also culturally prohibited from entering his sister's bedroom. This is strictly taboo, although this taboo might be relaxed in certain emergency situations, such as in the event of a fire or a medical emergency. Other than according respeto, there is also the expectation that barring the brother's entrance into the sister's bedroom acts as a preventive measure against the possibility of inappropriate incestuous behaviors. Hence, one must be vigilant against this at all times. Generally speaking, this taboo also includes other male relatives.

My Parents' Generation
This was less of an issue for my parents as we lived apart from their siblings. However, much later, when we moved to Saipan after my father's death, there came a time when my uncle (my mother's brother) came to live with us, but he lived in his own small shack that was detached from our house. Hence, there was no need for him to enter the main house unless he was invited in, much less enter my mother's bedroom. My mother certainly had no intentions of entering his little shack.

My Generation

In my immediate family, certain reasons provide the "justification" for entering a brother's bedroom, such as, if the only phone in the house is located in one brother's bedroom. Entering the bedroom to answer the phone is a must. Another "justifiable" reason is entering the bedroom to use the desktop computer or printer. Another reason would be to retrieve something. Beyond these reasons, the brother's room is still considered off-limits out of respect for him and as a preventive measure against any inappropriate and unwanted incestuous incidents.

The Next Generation

With the next generation members in my immediate family, respeto is observed in that siblings—males and females—are taught to respect the bedrooms of married siblings. They are taught that they should not enter such domains unless consent is expressly given. For instance, the bedroom occupied by one of my nephews and his spouse is also shared with other family members who often stay over on the weekends. Hence, the rules are more relaxed. Otherwise, on any normal weeknight, respeto must be accorded to give the couple their privacy. Another exception where entering the married couple's bedroom is acceptable is when the parents of an infant are both away at work while their baby is still asleep in the bedroom. In this scenario, it is perfectly fine to enter the bedroom to care for the baby.

XIII. Attire

In traditional Refaluwasch culture, men wear a red loin cloth called a "ttughumagh." Typically, no shirts are worn with the ttughumagh. The traditional women's outfit consists of a red wrap-around skirt with hem lines that extend either down to the calves or the ankles. The skirt is called an "apelipel." The women, especially older women, also are topless. The skirt alone is considered an entire outfit.

Subsequent generations later ditched the ttughumaghs and the apelipels as everyday wear. This is especially true for Refaluwasch who have moved to Saipan from the Northern Islands and find themselves living with other diverse cultures and populations who primarily wear modern Western-style clothes. Obviously, dressing in traditional clothing while everyone else is dressed in Western-style clothing makes one stand out and would not facilitate successful assimilation into the community.

It would be awkward for both the Refaluwasch woman or man to appear at work topless in their traditional ttughumagh or an apelipel.

My Parents' Generation

As a young child growing up in Agrigan, I recall seeing the elder men of my parents' generation (and even older) wearing the ttughumagh as they went about their daily lives. They were often topless. I also recall seeing the women on Agrigan, especially the elder women, wearing the apelipel on a daily basis. They, too, went topless.

However, I never saw my father wearing a ttughumagh until decades later, when I visited the American Memorial Park Museum in Saipan one day and came across a series of black and white photographs taken on Agrigan immediately after WWII. Two of the photographs that are included in the series show one of my aunts (my mother's first cousin, who was married to one of my father's elder brothers) holding a radio as she stood next to an American GI. In two of the photographs, there were two teenage boys kneeling in front while looking back at my aunt and the GI. My father was one of the boys in the photographs. He was 14 years old when the photographs were taken. Incidentally, one of the photographs taken that day with just my aunt and the GI became part of the photo exhibits that hung on the wall for a time at the American Memorial Park's WWII Museum. I have never once seen my father wearing a ttughumagh in person.

On the other hand, I did see my mother wearing the apelipel in Agrigan. I even recall her telling us a story about when she wore an apelipel to church with one of her cousins when they were teenagers. However, she only dressed in contemporary Western dresses when we lived in Pagan and Saipan.

My Generation

One of the major differences in the manner of dressing between my parents' generation and my generation is that the males no longer wear the ttughumagh and women no longer wear the apelipel on a daily basis. The only time that these traditional outfits are worn is when either gender is part of a traditional dance group that performs to entertain tourists or at some other special cultural events. Other occasions calling for the wearing of the ttughumagh or apelipel would be during performances at our yearly Cultural Heritage Month celebrations or as part of the entertainment at annual events, such as the Flame Tree Arts Festival or Taste of the Marianas.

Other changes include some folks wearing the ttughumagh as if it were a wrap-around skirt instead of as a loincloth style that exposes the buttocks. The women still wear the traditional apelipel, although instead of the wrap-around style, some find it more practical to have a seamstress sew the apelipel so that it is more fitted, and any risk of it coming loose and falling off the hips is eliminated. Otherwise, the horizontal-striped wrap-around apelipel also worn by previous generations even older than my parents' generation is the other preferred style also used today. Another marked change is that the female dancers of today never go topless.

My eldest sister recalled the story of how my father had to convince my mother to allow my sister to wear pants (As I write this, I marvel at how far we have truly come). When my eldest sister was in high school in the early 1970s, my father had to explain to my mother that my sister needed to climb some stairs to get to her classes on the second floor of Marianas High School. Therefore, it was necessary for her to wear pants to preserve her modesty and dignity.

As the second oldest of five girls, I consider myself fortunate that I did not have to fight that battle, as my mother had been won over on the practicality of wearing pants. However, she remained stubborn about hemlines. While she accepted the traditional mandates on where appropriate hemlines should be as she was growing up, this was a topic that she was adamant about. She made sure that all of her daughters knew her opinion on the matter. Her rule was that the hemline had to be below the knee and shorts were off-limits, unless the pant legs were also cut below the knee.

My eldest sister bore the brunt of our mother's rigid teachings on the subject of hemlines. As my sister explained, it was the belief that any outfit worn with the hemline above the knee invited unwanted temptation from the opposite sex. Therefore, due care must be taken to avoid putting oneself in such a vulnerable situation. The main goal is to avoid putting the idea into the minds of those who may be tempted to engage in inappropriate behaviors. As the saying goes—"Better to be safe than sorry."

When my eldest sister asked for an explanation of the rationale behind this custom of keeping hemlines below the knees, my mother's reply was that this was strictly necessary as a "deterrent"—a "preventive measure"—aimed at discouraging the male eye from seeing the woman's exposed knees and being tempted to engage in lewd thoughts that might then lead to an unwanted sexual attack. However, given that Refaluwasch women of my mother's generation and previous generations often exposed their breasts fully as they went about their daily chores without any fear of triggering inappropriate sexual temptations, it strikes me as an odd contradiction that a woman's exposed knees would be considered more provocative than her exposed breasts.

Today, I would say that the generational conflict about where the proper hemline ought to be has diminished with the popularity of wearing long pants or long Western-style skirts. However, the conflict continues regarding wearing "hot pants" or "short-shorts." This is still frowned upon within our immediate family, as well as within Refaluwasch society as a whole.

The Next Generation

I have noticed that the rules have relaxed quite a bit with regard to how the next generation dresses today. While dressing provocatively is still frowned upon, members of the next generation have been able to get away with far more and treated with way more leniency than previous generations, including my own. The hemlines are shorter now, resting above the knee and half-way up the thigh in some instances. So, too, have the hemlines for short pants, which have become shorter as well. There is even the sharing of clothing, such as t-shirts or socks, amongst the two genders that appears to have gained casual acceptance. Broadly speaking, the Refaluwasch community has become more tolerant and less traditional, mirroring today's more tolerant society.

One of the signs of the changing times in which we and the next generation now live is the acceptance of transgender dress that would have raised eyebrows not long ago. Today, some Refaluwasch boys now pierce one or both of their ears, pluck their eyebrows, wear make-up, and paint their nails without raising concern. But, to cultural purists or traditionalists, this behavior clashes with traditional

Refaluwasch culture wherein clothes are meant to conform closely to each respective gender's masculine or feminine identity without any blurring of lines.

XIV. Body Parts

Traditional Refaluwasch culture teaches women that sisters accord their brothers respeto by not touching anywhere on their brothers' body from their upper torso up to their hair. Unless a brother is sick and in need of being nursed back to health, touching the brother's upper torso, face or head is taboo. Another exception to this taboo is when the brother is a young child in need of care, such as being bathed or being nursed back to health.

One of the most important things for others to be aware of about Refaluwasch culture is that the face is very sacred to the Refaluwasch people. One must never touch another person's face—adults or children—and, if one must do so, then one must preface such action by saying "Tirow." While most people typically hear the word "Tirow" used as a greeting (Hello), used in this context, however, the word means "Excuse me" or "Pardon me."

This Refaluwasch cultural belief that the face must never be touched clashes with other cultures that believe it is perfectly okay to pinch a baby's cheeks to convey one's affection or opinion of the baby's cuteness, or even those who pinch an adult's cheeks in a playful manner. What one culture may deem to be an appropriate act to convey affection is something that Refaluwasch people regard as rude. This is especially true in cases where the pinches result in the baby's screaming in pain.

My Parents' Generation

In both his medical profession and role as a local healer, my father was accorded the privilege of touching the face and other body parts in order to treat his patients. For instance, I saw my father touch a patient's face as he pulled an abscessed tooth. I was also at the house when he delivered one of my sisters at our home in Pagan.

My mother's only brother was the youngest child in her family. She helped to raise and take care of him, but as he got older and could groom himself, my mother's help became unnecessary. I have no doubt that my mother would have initiated the switch at the appropriate time to conform to the appropriate cultural etiquette of respeto concerning touching the face and other body parts.

My Generation
Respecting our brothers' faces and not touching their upper torso up to their hair were things that my mother emphasized as we were growing up. This is a practice that we still maintain today, although with a lot less rigidity, as we live in a society where we (brothers and sisters, nieces and nephews, etc.) hug and kiss each other on the cheek. So, obviously, we do not subscribe to the rigid "no upper-body contact" of our parents' generation.

The Next Generation
While according respeto by not touching another person's face is still encouraged amongst the next generation, there is less emphasis on the rest of the restrictions that had been observed in previous generations, including my own.

XV. Visiting Other People's Homes
When visiting other people's homes, regardless of whether it is a visit to a relative's house or not, Refaluwasch culture forbids entering the house without waiting to be invited in first. Moreover, the visitor is also forbidden from going beyond a certain point in the house. The visitor should accord proper respeto by remaining near the entrance or, if the kitchen were right near the entrance, then refraining from wandering beyond the kitchen area.

Another important cultural mandate is that visitors are absolutely forbidden from entering the bedroom, which is considered the most private and intimate part of the house. Additionally, another respeto etiquette that is part of Refaluwasch culture is that visitors are expected to behave respectfully at all times and refrain from being nosy.

My Parents' Generation
My observation of how my parents behaved while visiting other people's homes is wholly consistent with the cultural mandates expected of good and polite house guests.

My Generation

One of my relatives who was raised by his paternal grandmother recounted that whenever he and his grandmother arrived at someone's home, he would knock on the door politely and they would wait to be invited into the house. He said that upon entering, the first thing that his grandmother would do was glance surreptitiously around the top four corners of the room near the ceiling to quickly and discreetly scan the room for any protective local medicines that might be harmful to her or him. A discovery of medicines—with potentially harmful spirits there to protect only the members of that particular household—often resulted in a quick termination of the visit.

Upon visiting other people's homes, my mother repeatedly expressed that we were to remain either near the entrance or in the kitchen for the entire duration of the visit. We were also taught that we should be polite and not go to people's homes on an empty stomach or to be greedy if food was offered. Another thing my mother was adamant about was that under no circumstances were we to ever take anything that did not belong to us or to think about coveting anything that did not belong to us. Such transgressions would have been met with either a severe verbal tongue lashing or, in some instances, a "good" spanking. One must never shame the family.

The Next Generation

We, too, have taught and continue to encourage the next generation of our immediate family to observe respeto behaviors when visiting other people's homes. We often remind them to stay within the established boundaries. Obviously, it is our wish and desire that our children remember the lessons even when we are not with them as they visit other people's homes.

XVI. Visitors to Our Home

Visitors to a Refaluwasch home can expect to be welcomed hospitably. It is customary to offer food and beverages to visitors.

My Parents' Generation

Growing up in Kagman, Saipan in the mid-1960s, I recall that our isolation from the rest of the population was periodically broken when we had visitors on weekends. Few people owned cars at the time and the travel distance encouraged relatives to stay the weekend when they visited. My parents were gracious hosts who ensured that our guests had a pleasant stay with us.

When we moved to Pagan after my father's election to Congress and his appointment as the District Administrator's Representative for the Northern Islands, I observed the way my parents went out of their way to be gracious hosts to our visitors. Days before the off-island visitors would arrive, my father would go hunting with my relatives for coconut crabs and other delicacies, which my mother would cook up and serve our guests. My father would also go fishing with relatives so that our visitors could also eat fish. Because we had a farm, visitors never left without a cargo of watermelons, mangoes and oranges, as well as coconut crabs, fish and other delicacies that were harvested from our island and waters. As to our local on-island visitors, they, too, were often welcomed to the house with coffee, other beverages and food.

My Generation

When I was growing up, my mother kept us on a very short leash. This was especially true after we moved to Saipan following my father's death. We were restricted from going to the neighbors' houses to play. Our yard was the extent of our boundary. Hence, we hosted childhood friends at our home rather than us visiting them at their homes. Whenever childhood friends came over to our house to play, my mother would insist that we offer them food and beverages the minute they appeared at our house. To my mother's way of thinking, offering our visitors food and drinks is a good host's first obligation in keeping with respeto practices. However, inviting our friends beyond the confines of the kitchen or main common areas was still taboo. Under no circumstances were we to ever invite our friends into the bedroom area, and this is another practice that we maintain to this day.

The Next Generation

Despite our teachings, I cannot say that the members of the next generation in our family have always adhered to our cultural teachings in this area. Sometimes, they invited their friends beyond the points where visitors are normally allowed access. It is only a problem when we learn about this breach after the fact. Some members of the next generation choose to ignore this mandate or are completely oblivious to the teachings that my mother was very strict about.

XVII. Conclusion

The 2010 Census, which includes the census figures for the Commonwealth of the Northern Mariana Islands, reported that the total population of Refaluwasch (Carolinians) was 2,461, as compared to the total population of 12,902 Chamorros. Historically, the Refaluwasch population has always been small, and it has remained this way today. Given that we have been in the Marianas since the 1800s, the very small size of our Refaluwasch population is an enigma. I maintain that there continues to be a threat that we will either perish as a people if our population dwindles every generation, or that we perish because we have allowed our unique cultural identities to die out. So, what can we do about this?

I maintain that culture is not static; it is organic—a "living thing"—that evolves constantly and is shaped by societal and environmental influences of the time. Therefore, it is our responsibility to identify those important core values of our Refaluwasch culture worth preserving and take decisive actions to teach and perpetuate them while allowing our culture to evolve with the times. In other words, we must adapt in order to survive.

I asked members of the next generation to share what lessons of respeto they had learned from their parents and relatives, and I received the following answers:

- Behaving respectfully when visiting other people's homes;
- Listening and not talking back to their parents;
- Doing their chores in a timely manner when asked;
- Behaving in school;
- Staying off drugs and alcohol;
- Staying out of gangs;
- Choosing the right friends; and
- Attending church on a regular basis.

This is highly encouraging. What this tells me is that some parents are doing a fine job of communicating with their children and imparting important cultural values to them. And the good thing about this is that it shows the children are listening.

Though no child is expected to absorb all of the teachings imparted to them, I nevertheless commend parents who take the time to actively engage their children in lessons on our Refaluwasch cultural beliefs and teachings. And while this is all good and positive, we must also remind ourselves that we should not rest on our laurels, but remain vigilant in teaching and passing on important core cultural values. It is imperative that we continue to reinforce our cultural beliefs and traditions to the next generations.

I attribute some of the next generation's lack of full compliance with our cultural teachings to the fact that they are still young and still in training. Despite this understanding, it is quite difficult to assuage feelings of apprehension when a member of the next generation in our family commits a cultural faux pas that reflects poorly on the family. An example of this would be sitting down to eat in front of visitors without inviting them to share the meal. In the absence of a polite invitation to partake in the meal, the young "offender" ought to have just waited to eat after the visitors had left. This is an example of such cringeworthy moments. However, such awkward instances also provide us with opportune moments to reinforce the lessons of respeto with renewed vigor. Like one of the perennial favorite mottos often quoted in high school student yearbooks says, "If at first you don't succeed, try and try again."

Respeto is critical in preserving the way that family members are supposed to interact with one another. Applied outside of the family, it helps maintain harmonious relationships within our own society, as well as during our interactions with other societies. It is easier to teach and pass on what we still have than it is to reinvent what we have lost. We ought to choose the path of least resistance. Like our language, teaching respeto must begin at home. This is where it must start. Then, it ought to be reinforced by our schools, churches and the community at large. Our government must also be actively involved in this objective. All Refaluwasch have a stake in this; everyone must get involved. We can do this together. As another popular saying goes, "It takes a village to raise a child."

Our history teaches us that we are survivors. We are alive today because our Refaluwasch ancestors boldly set sail across open ocean in search of a new, safer home here in the Marianas. If we can survive devastating earthquakes, floods and typhoons, we can surely survive modernity, too! Let us continue to navigate through life's modernity without losing the Refaluwasch identity.

Lastly, allow me to take this moment to acknowledge and thank the following people who made my contribution to this book possible. First, a huge danke and olomwaay to NMC's Ajani S. Burrell for his guidance, support and sheer persistence in recruiting me to participate in this book project, thereby ensuring that a Refaluwasch (Carolinian) voice is also heard; to Dr. Kimberly Bunts-Anderson, also of NMC, for her helpful edits and guidance; to Dr. Don Rubinstein at the University of Guam for his immensely helpful edits; to the CNMI Humanities Council for making these types of valuable community projects possible; to my anonymous Refaluwasch interviewees and consultants whose invaluable time, input and substantive reviews made me strive even harder to produce a more inclusive and accurate contribution to this book project; to Representative Sheila J. Babauta for her invaluable support; and, last, but not least, I extend a huge olomwaay to Mrs. Margarita Olopai-Taitano, my Refaluwasch Editor, not only for her substantive reviews and invaluable input, but also for patiently and painstakingly correcting most of my horrible Refaluwasch spellings. You all have my immense humble gratitude and respeto.

Misan Ánimasan Ásuli: field notes and conversations from the Talakhaya Watershed, Luta

Malcolm Johnson

Topographic map of Talakhaya, missing streams and stories, produced by the United States Geological Survey, 1983

*"The same stream of life that runs through my veins night and day
runs through the world and dances in rhythmic measures.
It is the same life that shoots in joy through the dust of the earth in numberless blades of grass and breaks into tumultuous waves of leaves and flowers.
It is the same life that is rocked in the ocean-cradle of birth and of death, in ebb and in flow.
I feel my limbs are made glorious by the touch of this world of life.
And my pride is from the life-throb of ages dancing in my blood this moment."*

— Rabindranath Tagore, *Gitanjali: Song Offerings*

The åsuli (freshwater eels) live here, it is their home. Does my presence frighten them? Do they know I am just passing through, scribbling notes of their existence in the margins of a tattered map? Where will they go if the streams stop flowing year-round and access between the ridges and sea vanishes? They have a long journey ahead of them—we all do.

Sitting carefully on the jagged karst every week for the last few years has turned the uncomfortable familiar, the karst and my discomfort worn smooth by our time together. In the freshwater pool, a ripple disrupts the fogged mirror-like water. Drops trickling against polished stone echo among the surrounding cliffs, disrupted only by the occasional call of one small silk-feathered såli, a native bird in Luta (Rota). I sink the metal-encased end of a multiparameter water quality meter into the water. Delicately calibrated to calculate aquatic chemistry, the instrument garners curiosity from the uhang (shrimp) with their little claws and delicate pereiopods. They climb and crawl on the instrument without fear. Can they remember it from the week before? Sinking to the muddy bottom, the machine works a neoteric kind of wizardry to offer me information whose meaning remains confined to spreadsheets or my limited baseline knowledge.

When I first arrived in Rota a few years back, I regularly ventured out of the office to conduct fieldwork necessary for building both intimacy and awareness of the Talakhaya coastalscape, the place where land, sea, and the more-than-human assemblage meet. Although researchers have been here for decades, there remains a sense of mystery emanating from the limestone forests, as though no accumulation of knowledge could ever quite encapsulate the spirit of the island. Unlike many of my colleagues here, who are dedicated to the monitoring and recovery of the endangered åga (Marianas crow) or fanihi (Marianas fruit bat), my commitments revolve around the priority watershed on the south side of the island. Fires, clear-cutting, sugar cane, more fires, erosion, another fire, and the seemingly endless pursuit to stabilize the soils with non-native grasses and nursery-grown native tree species have left the watershed in a perpetual state of recovery. These pursuits are not mine alone, the burden of growth and loss shared across generations and between islands.

"Everything is part of a watershed." This innocuous statement is radical in nature, particularly given the fact that many of us know very little about the watershed we inhabit, let alone watersheds in general. Watershed is loosely defined as the "line separating waters flowing into different rivers," where a *shed* represents the "ridge of high ground between two valleys or lower ground, a divide" (Soanes & Stevenson, 2004, p. 1632). A quick search of catchment area maps or drainage divides or water basins, which are watersheds of a different name, will produce images such as Figure 1 of countries and communities redrawn with colorful, chaotic shapes that rarely share similarities with the borders of states or countries that we are familiar with. Hydro-cartographies could not care less about politics and nationalism.

Figure 1

Major Water Basins of the World

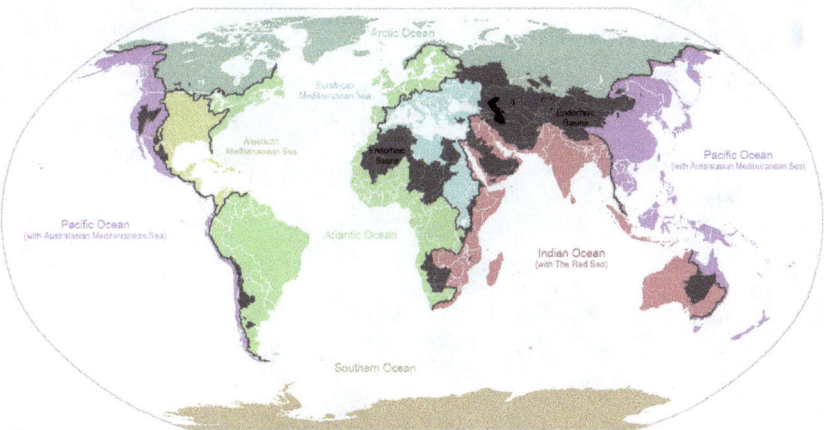

Note. Major continental divides, showing drainage into the major oceans and seas of the world. Grey areas are endorheic basins that do not drain to the ocean. From *Ocean drainage* [Image], by Citynoise, 2007, Wikimedia Commons. https://commons.wikimedia.org/wiki/File:Ocean_drainage.png . Public Domain.

The Talakhaya Watershed is one of five watersheds on Rota (Figure 2) and is located in the south of the island, where there are no paved roads and few permanent structures. Turning the corner at Poña Point, you can look up at the steep slopes that define the watershed, deep green in the wet season and an eerie brown in the midst of the dry season. A decade ago, the community came together with support from government agencies to establish Talakhaya as a "priority watershed," a term related to NOAA's Coral Reef Initiative, which allowed for a steady stream of funding to recover and revegetate the exposed soils of the watershed in the hopes of reducing erosion and conserving the adjacent coral reefs. The process led to the Conservation Area designation, the publication of the Conservation Action Plan, and implementation of the annual revegetation project. However, success for the project, for a return to the pristine limestone forests that once graced the southern coast, is dependent on the commitments of community members to care for the slopes as they would their own homes.

Figure 2

The Five Drainage Divides or Catchment Areas of Luta

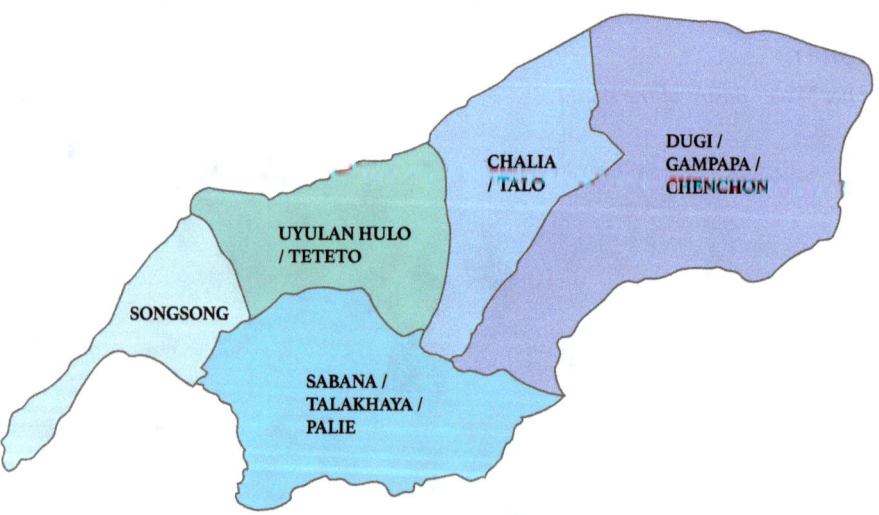

Note. Each area is defined by a combination of geological, topological, and fluvial aspects. The Talakhaya watershed is of particular interest because it is the only place on the island where the water flows on the surface. From *The watersheds of Rota* [Image], by CNMI Bureau of Environmental and Costal Quality (BECQ) – Division of Coastal Resources Management (DCRM), 2020, https://opd.gov.mp/wp-content/uploads/opd/Talakhaya-2020-WMP_final-internal-draft.pdf . Public Domain.

To know a watershed, from a data-driven natural-science perspective, demands familiarity with a wide range of disciplines: geology to understand the way stones and aquifers alter the hyporheic flows where the water moves beneath the surface; hydrology to grasp the influence of sediments and nutrients on the quality of flowing water and the resulting change in its chemistry; biology to sense the way fish and shrimp and trees and birds all depend on the ecosystem that encompasses them.; ecology to comprehend the depth of interconnectedness; and sociology to discern the human bond with the coastalscape. Soil composition, historical land-use changes, impacts on coral reefs, and the infrastructure that allows us to pass through, study, grow, and depend on the watershed also have dedicated life-long pursuits of knowledge.

The Talakhaya Watershed is overflowing with these knowledges, much of it hidden, but enough sensually accessible for me as a researcher. Squatting on the edge of the freshwater pool, I am struck by how much I do not know. What species of fish is that? Why is the water suddenly so turbid? Has this shoreline erosion increased since the first people wandered these same veins? Notebook in one hand, camera attached to my backpack, dirt under my fingernails. There are divides everywhere, each stream its own watershed. Stories are woven into the roots holding streambanks in place. Watersheds turn into subwatersheds that turn into subsubwatersheds that turn into innocuous pools of water that vanish when it is either too hot or too wet to sustain their borders.

Leaning over the muddled waters with a small plastic bag to gather water samples, I freeze as something flashes out of sight beneath the sunken leaves and stones. Was that just an apparition, a trick caused by shifting light and waterlogged branches? No, this anguillid has been carefully documented in my notes, defying its nocturnal habits to make its presence known to the visitor that returns once again. Åsuli, more commonly known as giant mottled eels or *Anguilla marmorata*, spend the majority of their lives hidden in the muddy depths of freshwater pools, where they can sustain themselves on a steady supply of uhang and avoid the impacts of oppressive dry seasons. While it is often hard to discern the age of an åsuli just by looking at them, they can live for decades in the slopes and streams of Talakhaya.

During my first trek into the jungle accompanied by a young taotao tåno' (Indigenous person, literally "people of the land") trained to understand the equipment and scientific procedures, I asked questions like "how many waterfalls are there?" or "what unique species call these streams home?" He offered relatively few answers while acknowledging a lack of expertise in such things, which he attributed to his age and education. "Faisen i mañaina, ask the elders," he advised. I soon came to learn that the knowledge of this ecosystem had been lost over time, from the Spanish colonization to the American standardized testing system. Only in the last decade has local ecological knowledge been incorporated into the school curriculum, with only a few species and habitats getting recognized. In many cases, it comes down to the passion of an individual teacher to make sure åsuli or fanihi or åga are even mentioned in the classroom.

While my work partner stood on the streambank and I knelt in the stream with my hands clasped around the multiparameter instrument, he shared his story about getting to know the watershed more in the last year than he had in his whole life. His position was bound to Talakhaya and the revegetation project, supported by the local environmental agencies. Trained to raise plants in the nursery, collect stream water samples, and monitor the revegetation efforts, he acknowledged how little his friends knew about the way the streams change and shift throughout the year. There are few, if any, lesson plans dedicated to the streams of Luta and even fewer opportunities for students to travel the relatively short distance to the southern side of the island to gain familiarity with Talakhaya. And with climatic changes on the horizon, there are some lessons that will only make their way into history books.

The dry season is in full swing as I trek along the stream towards higher ground. During the months when the rains are sporadic and the soils are vulnerable, majestic falls become mud pits tainted with the scent of rotting fish and occupied by ravenous hilitai, the mangrove monitor lizards, with their sharp claws and jagged teeth. Babbling streams turn speechless, streambanks collapse under their own weight, the scientific instruments (Figure 3) used to measure water quality lose their telos. While the more serious impacts of climate change are still on the horizon, others have already made themselves known. Even during my geologically fleeting presence in the watershed the last few years, change arrived drastically compared to the historical records describing the ecosystem. One landowner, whose surname is synonymous with one of the island's villages, called the changes unprecedented in the many decades he had been there. Watching the rheic, the aboveground flow, creep meter by meter further inland every week, I would leave the jungle full of sadness and confusion, uncertain that my efforts to craft a management plan to protect this place for future generations would matter. How will the åsuli find their way without flowing water, I wondered. What will sustain the residents of Rota if the waters run dry?

Figure 3

Equipment Used to Measure Water Quality

Note. From Malcolm Johnson, 2017

During a stakeholder planning workshop held in the mayor's office, the participants grapple with similar questions. Standing around a plastic table draped in a printed map of the entire conservation area of Talakhaya, including symbols for streams, properties, and critical habitats for a few of the endangered and endemic species of Talakhaya, debate ensues over the biggest threats to watershed health: invasive ungulates, intentionally set fires, erosion of the badlands, climate change, politics. Sticky notes scribbled with these very words are placed in their rightful locations and concern mounts as the map vanishes beneath the yellow and pink pieces of paper. In a room full of community members who have the greatest familiarity with the watershed, we all feel humbled by the sheer challenge of managing the coastalscape, particularly given the diminishing resources available. Just like the streams drying up, so too are our chances to reverse course and establish a resilient future for the watershed and its human and non-human inhabitants.

In my attempt to more accurately map the freshwater veins of the watershed, upon whose source every human resident of the island depends, I stick as close to the stream edge as I can. While it is fairly common knowledge that 90% of the island's drinking water comes from Talakhaya, it became abundantly clear at the stakeholder workshops that accurate and micro-level maps of the various features of the watershed are non-existent and are needed. From missing streams to vague allusions to the locations of invasive species, our current maps are not sufficient for the goals. The streams are dangerously inaccessible to most people, the biologists and the deer hunters notwithstanding. Eventually, the dense foliage completely thwarts my progress, forcing me to fumble forward on my hands and knees until the tropical limestone forest gives way to colossal grasses and treacherous ridgelines. The familiar warmth and brilliance of the sun disorient me after hours protected beneath the canopy.

Pulling my tired legs up the steep incline, I approach a cluster of stones situated higher than the jungle below. Sitting down and looking out across the rolling hills with scattered emerald patches left intact after decades of habitat destruction, I wonder what this land looked like before all the clear-cutting. Massive scrapes of exposed rock remain where the depleted topsoil has vanished, leaving behind barren uninhabitable earth, glaring scars when seen from above. From my pocket, I unfold a map and begin to trace my finger along the dark green veins, canopied sanctuaries for freshwater pumping fertility into the region, and the barren patches of brown denoting the dried-out savannah.

The neighboring ridges obscure the decades of monumental effort taken to secure the exposed soils and eventually return the landscape to limestone forest. Hundreds of thousands of non-native grasses specifically chosen for their ability to hold soils and prevent erosion have been transplanted from nurseries on the other side of the island. A group of nursery assistants are hired every year to propagate the seeds of Bahiagrass and Vetiver in addition to as many endemic trees as the germination of seeds can provide. A few months later, a dozen volunteers drive up the treacherous trails and carry the seedlings over ridges and through valleys to reach the next area requiring revegetation. Their hands are saving the watershed, their efforts are giving the åsuli and all the native species a fighting chance in the face of climate change.

The revegetation efforts are situated on ground once ravished by human invaders, occupiers of these islands, who clear-cut large swaths of the native jungle that once existed on the ridges between each valley. It is hard to say when the landscape level changes really started, but the small monuments demarcating the existence of an old Japanese sugarcane company may signal the last major alteration. The revegetation project is transitioning towards planting more trees next year, with the stated goal of returning the area to its past existence, a lush forest that may only ever exist in stories. We debate feasibility and fundability and capability in a small office, while the whole future of the watershed is clouded in uncertainty. Our efforts sometimes feel like an Anguillidian ouroboros, an eel eating its own tail.

Most years, they are able to bring a group of students up to the area to assist in the project. Under the glare of the sun, without any nearby canopy, the young volunteers get dirt under their nails as they place the grasses into divots dug out by an experienced Luta Livelihoods volunteer. After only a few hours, they are exhausted, sweat falling from their arms and chins. One young woman sitting nearby taking a needed break mentions to me how she had no idea people were planting trees in Talakhaya to prevent erosion from destroying the adjacent reefs. "Is this all that we can do?" she questions. The following day, the same students gather on a beach to don snorkels and explore one of the nearby reefs, after a brief lecture about what we as individuals can do to help protect corals. Maybe there is still hope.

On my last workday in Rota, I sat on exposed karst stones with James Manglona, Rota's Forester for CNMI Forestry (Figure 4). The sun was irradiating us, grass whispered with the occasional breeze, volunteers chatted while they worked nearby. The sweat puddled on our brows, and I expressed concern that I had accomplished so little, that what I had learned over the last few years painted a grim scene for the Talakhaya watershed. James, the coastalscape's greatest champion, reassured me that every person who has dedicated time to protecting the watershed matters, particularly when change is already present. Without him, there would be no restoration, no soil-securing grasses, no hope for the myriad of non-humans that grace the lands and seas around us. "Will you come back?" It sounded more like an invitation than a question. We both recognize the persistent difficulty of conservation when capacity continues to recede like streams in the dry season. With his support and the commitments of the stakeholders, a plan is in place that should ensure funds for the foreseeable future. The silence between us faded as we got back to the work at hand, continuing along the perimeter of the annual revegetation project to more accurately map that year's success.

Figure 4

James Manglona Amongst a Revegetated Hillside

Note. From Malcolm Johnson, 2019

The sound of approaching rainfall forces me from my perch on the exposed stones as I quickly tuck away the map. The rain carries both life and destruction for this collection of Strahler-numbered watersheds (the Strahler-number is a mathematical approach to identify and label the branching network of tributaries within streams, rivers, or watersheds). As the droplets seep into the arid soils, the flora exalts for sustenance in the midst of the dry season. At the same time, along the edges of the delicately carved streams, the weight of the moisture begins to rip trees and shrubs and stones from their once-stable banks. As the rainwater rushes down from the mountain it fills with sediment, altering the mapped streamlines and eventually suffocating the increasingly vulnerable corals that seem worlds away. Lasting for only a brief moment, the clouds disappear over a few ridges in the distance, leaving behind the comforting scent of petrichor and a drenched desire to reverse course, head back down into the veins below, and return to the parked truck.

Carefully navigating downstream, the scent of moss and decomposing leaves and water teeming with a microbial universe refreshes and soothes me. Suddenly, I glimpse the marbled form of an åsuli caught in a pool no larger than itself, cut off from the flowing waters that just rushed through this sheltered valley. Crouching down no more than an arm's length away, I cause the anguillid to recoil in its limited space, trapped and separated. A familiar predicament for this isolated scientist. Eating freshwater eels was historically undertaken by the lower mañåchang caste of the archipelago, allowed only if caught by hand since they were forbidden from using fishing tools and spears (Cunningham, 1992). Stories told by the inhabitants of another island lament the harvesting of the reclusive creatures, sold to markets in distant places that had already exhausted their local eel populations (Pacific Worlds, n.d.). Some believe that the *Anguilla marmorata* (Figure 5) dig deep holes to open up the underground artesian wells, leukocytes ensuring the caves continue to supply blood to this ecosystem.

Figure 5
Juvenile Åsuli Found in One of Talakhaya's Streams

Note. From Malcolm Johnson, 2018.

The small black eyes meet my own and stillness overtakes us both. I wonder if it would be best to continue onward, taking a wide arc away from the confused giant mottled eel and allowing fate to take its course. Fleetingly, I contemplate reaching in and grasping my companion, if I could be so bold to find solidarity with such a magnificent being, in order to assist in relocation to a more abundant body of freshwater. Or would my attempt just result in distress for the åsuli and the stream, which have found a delicate balance without my intrusion? Just when I have decided on how to respond, a flicker of brown and yellow dances between my legs, shimmies across polished stones, and vanishes over a ledge in the distance that conceals a shallow pool inhabited by uhang. The dry season will come to an end soon and access to food and the sea will be in reach.

Continuing towards the forest's exit, the murmur of the stream fades and all that is left is the scraping of stones beneath my boots and the occasional joyful cry from the fluttering såli (starling) that seems to have followed me throughout the day's journey. Signs of the hyporheic zone—the spongy sub-streambed— manifest in the sinking of footprints into the muddy streambed and the stoic cane toads wallowing in moistened crevices, a species native to the Americas, introduced to this liminal space in order to control pernicious beetles from decimating the fields of sugar cane. Hitchhiking across oceans with their human counterparts, the highly toxic toads have colonized islands all over the world, outcompeting the indigenous amphibians, filling puddles with countless eggs, consuming anything that will fit in their massive mouths, including the juvenile åsuli. There is no plan to curb their population here, just to accept their existence and pray that they do not cause any more ecological damage.

Managing, protecting, and conserving watersheds is a monumental task. It can take dozens of people, multiple meetings, and hundreds of hours researching, writing, and monitoring just to reach some kind of consensus on what needs to be done to ensure resilience for a single species, let alone an entire coastalscape. Yet the interconnectedness of all the flora, fauna, waters, soils, infrastructure, histories, and humans that move in and out of the basin makes every response to the identified threats subject to conflict and uncertainty. We need to repair the road to reach the water cave, but what about the endangered damselfly? No hunting is allowed in the conservation area, yet the deer keep eating all the endemic trees that are out-planted. In passing, someone mentions climate change at a stakeholder meeting, and everyone shifts uneasily in their seats. The streams ran dry again this year and the corpses of åsuli were found in one of the deepest dried-out pools.

Competing cultures reign supreme in stakeholder meetings in Rota, with one constituency arguing for the need to protect wildlife so that it can be harvested as the ancestors had done, while another sees the "undeveloped" areas of Talakhaya as an opportunity for a new hotel, without mentioning the two abandoned hotels passed on the way to the meeting. Someone in the room will distrust the government for letting the habitat destruction continue in one area or for neglecting to repair a road in desperate need of stabilization. Another person sits silently and only leans in to remind everyone of the importance of a particular cultural site or an endemic species habitat. There are arguments over the use of pesticides, debates over who is the responsible entity, and disagreements over the lack of enforcement. Even the most knowledgeable residents struggle to agree on what is best for everyone and everything in Talakhaya.

As I duck beneath the cement footbridge, the rolling sound of waves in the distance begins to echo through the depths of the dynamic world hidden beneath the dark green veins of the map. Hearing the latching of a car door, I peak over the rocky bank and decide to climb out and introduce myself to the couple loading bunches of bananas and pugua (betelnut) into the back of their corroded pickup truck. They tell me about harvesting dozens of different species, catching freshwater prawns, and utilizing the land for decades based on knowledge passed down from their parents. I tell them about my research on the streams, and the goal of establishing a management plan for the watershed. The man reminisces: "When I was younger, I counted all the waterfalls for a class project with the help of my father." He had forgotten the exact number by now, guessing, "Fifty maybe?" This was one of the recurring questions I asked friends and colleagues and community members: "How many waterfalls do you think Rota has?"

Sitting in one of the restaurants in town on Sunday mornings early in my stay, I would introduce myself to fellow diners and talk about my hopes for my next 3 years in Rota. I would always inquire about their local knowledge of the watershed, usually starting with that simple waterfall question. I asked the same question to kids in all the schools. The answer was always "one," or maybe "five" if they assumed each major stream had one. In the second year, I conducted a survey about the watershed and the environmental resources of Rota in general. Still the same answers on the number of waterfalls, which made sense given that the most frequent responses for "time spent in the watershed" were "never" or "once a year." If you define waterfalls by a height taller than your average male, there are close to 70—some taller than 20 meters—and nearly all traversed by åsuli.

The couple and I speak about changes in the climate they have experienced in their lifetime, like the once perennial streams now dry more days of the year than flowing, and our fears for future climatic disturbances inevitably submerging the island's village beneath the tides. She asks me about the water cave, the source of the wetlands, which secures the precious waters for human usage. "What impacts are our actions having on the streams?" she asks. Offering only predictions and hypotheses, I encourage them to participate in the next stakeholder meeting to share their thoughts with the rest of the community. Before continuing my descent, I question them about their familiarity with the åsuli inhabiting the waters. He recalls how his family would ensnare only the largest, taking no more than once per year from the same green vein, yet they have become so rare he can no longer recall the last time one was caught.

Conversations like this were rare when venturing out into the watershed, a place on the island where I would most easily achieve solitude. On one occasion, I stumbled upon two older gentlemen wearing wetsuits torn to shreds, floating in water only a few feet deep and filling woven baskets with uhang. I asked them how often they collect the freshwater prawns. "A few times a year, although it is much easier when the streams run partially dry" was the response. On another occasion, I surprised a couple newly arrived on the island eating their lunch next to the most popular waterfall on the island. After reminding them to not leave behind trash, I asked how often they came out here. "This is our first time," they told me. I wondered if it would be their only time. I questioned others I encountered. A non-local guide taking a group of tourists wearing zoris and carrying umbrellas up the main trail. A Public Works employee on his way to clear foliage hanging over the dirt road. My questions always have the same intention, attempts at piecing together the story of the watershed through their stories and their relationships with Talakhaya.

When I am not wandering around the watershed, my questions seem to garner a similar sentiment, whether I am sitting in one of the restaurants or waiting at the post office or presenting at the school or conducting surveys. The watershed and the revegetation project are held in high esteem by the people of Rota, regardless of familiarity. After 10 years of volunteers spending their summers planting grasses and trees in the badlands, most of the community is aware of the project and the value of the watershed. However, only a select few have a comprehensive understanding of what was, is, and can be. While I am sitting alone for breakfast on a Sunday morning, a manåmko' (an elder) waves me over and asks me how the revegetation is going. He used to work for CNMI Forestry and was impressed with how much the landscape has changed since the inception of the project. "What comes next for Talakhaya?" he wondered. A transition to planting only native trees, renovations to the roads in order to reduce sedimentation, or nothing much at all. The future is still very uncertain. Who will champion the watershed's future? Who can?

Passing a few more cane toads, who frantically hop whichever direction they are facing, a large shadow swoops across my path. I catch a glimpse of the blackened wingspan of the endemic åga who laughs and teases me from the sparse canopy while I stumble through the jungle. Recording the location in a small waterproof notebook, to be passed on later to the endangered crow researchers also dedicated to the maps and blemishes of this island, I step out into the looming sunlight once again. Trust from the community does not come easy for scientists from the mainland—trust eroded by fights over land and over the protection of endangered species. Sometimes seen as another symptom of the federal government's possession of the islands, we must be careful not to take ownership over our findings—information does not exist in isolation.

As I try to piece together the history of the watershed, it became increasingly evident that the knowledge of the landscape existed in the silos of academia, was forgotten over time, or never even reached the community. Scouring dusty documents written in the late 1980s, I would find information that no one on the island seemed to remember, maybe because it was never shared beyond the academic publication. The biologists did not connect with the sociologists who neglected the geologists who could not care less about the farmers tilling their land. As the management plan came together, we tried to weave a tapestry out of peer-reviewed papers, the conversations with residents, and åkgak (pandanus leaves). Even if a plan cannot provide lasting protection for an ecosystem, it can serve as a repository for all the stories, facts, figures, maps, and hopes for Talakhaya. Maybe in a few years, drawn by the tides, someone will pick up the plan and feel inspired to let the streams flow through their veins, to find joy in the non-native grasses, and to dance for the health of the watershed.

With the sea breeze pushing against me and the limestone forest to my back, I scan the exposed coral reefs being hammered by waves. How do the fragile åsuli navigate these tumultuous waters? Hatching from eggs in an unknown location in the middle of the ocean west of the archipelago, the larval *leptocephali* drift with the currents until they reach islands throughout the Pacific Ocean. Through some kind of magic, they discover this small watershed in the vastness, morph into elvers so they can swim up one of the five streams and their towering waterfalls, and live demersally for two to four decades in freshwater pools as yellow eels. Eventually, their mucus-covered bodies undergo one last metamorphosis that signals their need to swim out to sea. Transforming into silver eels, they return to the same bearings in the middle of the sea to spawn and perish, their corpses serving as nutrients for their offspring, an ocean cradle of birth and of death (Schofield & Fuller, 2021).

Returning to my beat-up red truck that survived an onslaught of falling breadfruit from the neighboring tree, I think about the familiar journey of the åsuli. We both found this island by chance, becoming our home the moment we felt the freshwater flowing upon our faces, both destined one day to leave towards the sea. My muddied fingers trace the dark greens of the map once more, remembering each tempestuous encounter solely by touch. What if the åsuli cannot reach the ocean due to the changing climate? When the elders sink to the bottom of the pools and are consumed by microbial decomposers, who will feel the impacts of the last scaled spirit vanishing from the ecosystem? When all that remains of the anguillidae are points scribbled on maps and stories shared in classrooms full of distracted children, how will my intrusion on the banks and cliffs be measured? I am just another impact of the Anthropocene, one more visitor carving lines and points out of the living landscape. Watershed management plans cannot restore the connection between humans and the giant mottled eel, severed with each successive ruinous colonization, be it human or non-native species.

Managing a watershed or an ecosystem or even a single species seems near impossible from this vantage point. Charting stakeholder relationships generates a complex web of interconnected yet competing interests not unlike the multifaceted food webs gracing science textbooks. Strategic actions can only answer questions that we know, yet the complex coastalscape demands more. Like the åsuli, with their lives spread across massive spatiotemporal scales, management plans must grasp at the extant knowledge, informed by the past, with eyes towards the future. Climate change expectations, casino projects covered in gold leaf, the collapse of fisheries, clashes over freshwater resources. The stories from Talakhaya have changed every decade and will continue to transform. A 10-year-old stands before Okgok Falls for the first time, smiling as her elementary school teacher excitedly snaps pictures of Gua'a, the largest waterfall on the island. A lifelong landowner sits attentively during a workshop about funding for watershed-friendly land use changes. A local biologist presents her findings in the mayor's office to a small group of interested community members. Thousands of human lives, to say nothing of untold other species, all connected to the watershed and its uncertain future.

The truck and I bounce along the pothole-ravaged road constructed from the crushed remains of deceased coral colonies. Approaching the aircon-chilled office sheltering all the daily threnody for the åsuli, sights of the horizon prompts thoughts of future watershed acquaintances. On some islands the eels are invasive, on others they are endangered. What would I whisper in those vascular jungles to ask for permission and forgiveness for my incursions? These streams are the veins that flow through my hands, finding comfort in the well-known axilla of this limestone temple. The patterns are versant, the flow prosaic. Yet the attempts to gather knowledge mar the landscape, another outsider bearing the gift of colonization in the guise of conservation, arriving and leaving like many of the other researchers who temporarily call this place home. It only takes a few months for the eels to float to their freshwater sanctuary, satisfied to remain until their final gambol beyond the lagoon.

References

Citynoise. (2007). *Ocean drainage* [Image]. Wikimedia Commons. https://commons.wikimedia.org/wiki/File:Ocean_drainage.png .

CNMI Bureau of Environmental and Costal Quality (BECQ) – Division of Coastal Resources Management (DCRM). (2020). "The five watersheds of Rota" [Image]. *Talakhaya integrated watershed management plan (TWMP)*, p. 21. https://opd.gov.mp/wp-content/uploads/opd/Talakhaya-2020-WMP_final-internal-draft.pdf

Cunningham, L. J. (1992). *Ancient Chamorro society*. Bess Press.

Pacific Worlds. (n.d.). *CNMI: Tanapag — The land: Water*. Retrieved April 29, 2018, from http://www.pacificworlds.com/cnmi/land/water.cfm

Schofield, P.J., & Fuller, P. (2021). *Anguilla marmorata (Quoy and Gaimard, 1824)*. US Geological Survey, Nonindigenous Aquatic Species Database. https://nas.er.usgs.gov/queries/factsheet.aspx?SpeciesID=2291

Soanes, C., & Stevenson, A. (Eds.). (2004). Watershed. In *Concise Oxford English dictionary* (11th ed., p. 1632). Oxford University Press.

Hågu, Guåhu, yan Hita (You, Me, and We): What Does it Mean to be Part of Guåhan's (Guam's) Multi-faceted Community?

Kelly G. Marsh-Taitano

I Tinituhon (In the Beginning): Homelands
Some 3,500 or more years ago, i Manaotaomo'na (the People of Before; Chamorro or CHamoru ancestors) voyaged to and made their home in what we today call the Mariana Islands (Historic Resources Division, 2006, p. 7). I Manaotaomo'na had their own way of referring to their home islands—Låguas for the southern islands or perhaps the entire archipelago (meaning long and slender), and Gåni for the group of islands north of Sa'ipan (Chamisso, 1817, as cited in Barratt, 1984, p. 28; L. Cunningham, personal communication, March 14, 2017; Russell, 1998). Following Indigenous protocols, i Manaotaomo'na fished and voyaged throughout the 550-mile length of the archipelago, from the northernmost island of Uråkas to the southernmost, Guåhan, or Guam (Figure 1) (Coomans, 1997; Furey, 2006, p. 44; Russell, 1998). They gathered and cultivated åmot (traditional medicines) and foods like dokdok (native seeded breadfruit), lemmai (seedless breadfruit), and suni (taro) in coastal plains and interior portions of the islands. They also hunted various paluma siha (birds) and other delicacies such as fanihi (fruit bat) and harvested other valued

resources like åkgak (pandanus) for weaving, fotfot siha (trees) to carve into canoes, and ålutong (volcanic rock) to utilize as stone tools.

Figure 1

The Sakman (Chamorro Ocean-going Canoe) SAINA

Note. The SAINA, seen sailing here between Guåhan and Luta (Rota), was the first sakman crafted in Låguas yan Gåni in over 250 years owing to the intensive missionization and colonization of CHamorus (Chamorros; the Chamorro people) from 1698 on. Those foreign impositions greatly transformed aspects of traditional culture and at times, specifically banned oceangoing voyaging (Cepeda et al., n.d.; Cunningham, personal communication, March 14, 2017). From Ron Castro, personal communication, March 14, 2017. Copyright 2017 by Ron Castro and TÅSI (Traditions About Seafaring Islands).

Låguas yan Gåni are where i Manaotaomo'na became uniquely Taotao Tåno' (People of the Land), or CHamoru (Chamorros; the Chamorro people) as is described in the traditional oral narrative Fo'na and Pontan (B. Cruz, personal communication, 2016; Hattori, 2021; G. E. Taitano, n.d.b). Låguas yan Gåni are thus a homeland for i Manaotaomo'na and their descendants. Former Governor of Guåhan Ricardo J. Bordallo expressed the depth of the CHamoru sentiment for their homeland, which can be applied to Låguas and Gåni more broadly, when he said,

> Guam is not just a piece of real estate to be exploited for its money-making potential. Above all else, Guam is the homeland of the Chamorro people. That is a fundamental, undeniable truth. We are profoundly "taotao [tåno']"—people of the land. This land ... belongs to us just as surely, just as inseparably, as we belong to it. No tragedy of history or declaration of conquest, no legalistic double-talk can change that fact. (Phillips, n.d.)

At some point in those ancestral times, i Manaotaomo'na developed trading relationships with others in the region including neighboring Refaluwasch (Carolinian Islanders) who voyaged to Låguas yan Gåni seeking i Manaotaomo'na pottery, medicine, and more. After centuries of this relationship, in the early 1800s, Refaluwásch voyaged to settle the islands to the north of Guåhan and are also thus formally recognized as Indigenous to those islands (Figure 2) (Farrell, 2011, pp. 192–201).

Figure 2
CHamoru, Refaluwasch, and Other Festival of Pacific Arts 2016 Delegates on Guåhan

Note. Delegates were welcoming traditional canoes as they entered the Hagåtña marina during part of the Festival's opening ceremonies. The Festival provided an opportunity for Guåhan's wider community to understand themselves as being part of a Pacific Island community and to encounter Pacific Islanders from other parts of Oceania. Photo from Kelly G. Marsh-Taitano.

I Matulalaikan i Måtan Guåhan (The Changing Face of Guåhan)

I Manaotaomo'na thrived in their homelands, over time settling islands throughout the archipelago as attested by the latte (stone foundational supports for structures), lusong (stone mortars), stone paved areas, åcho' atupat (slingstones), haguet (fishhooks), and other heritage items that exist there still. Their sphere of contact with others further expanded in 1521, when i Manaotaomo'na discovered a Spanish exploratory expedition in their waters. This encounter initiated semi-regular trade with the Spanish, which then eventually led to missionization and colonization of Låguas yan Gåni (1695-1899), despite nearly three decades of resistance by sizeable numbers of i Manaotaomo'na (Atienza, 2013; García, 2004). Although significant features of CHamoru culture, like ocean voyaging and traditional dance, were lost or otherwise challenged and transformed in this and later colonial administrations, i Manaotaomo'na and their descendants have consistently maintained key aspects of their culture and customs, such as retaining the centrality of family in their lives (Souder, 1992; Underwood, n.d.). Further, many of the impositions or desired outside cultural features were CHamorucized to suit CHamoru sensibilities and preferences rather than adopted wholesale (see, for example, Figure 3).

Figure 3

Preparing the CHamorucized Version of Tortillas (Titiyas)

Note. Preparation took place at the 9th Annual Gupot Fanha'aniyan Pulan Chamorro (Chamorro Lunar Calendar Festival) held January 2017. Tortillas were introduced to the Mariana Islands during the Spanish colonial administration from "New Spain" (Mexico). The Spanish at the time also had colonies in parts of the Americas, including what is now referred to as Mexico. From Edward B. San Nicolas, personal communication, 2017, February 17. Copyright 2017 by Edward B. San Nicolas.

The lengthy Spanish administration of i Taotao Guåhan (Chamorros of Guam) ended abruptly with the Spanish-American War of 1898. The United States seized Guåhan while the northern islands were sold to Germany shortly thereafter (and then subsequently taken over by Japan in World War I, and administered by the United States following WWII. Over time, these two divisions of Låguas yan Gåni developed into the US unincorporated Territory of Guam and the US Commonwealth of the Northern Mariana Islands (CNMI or NMI), as they are known today (Farrell, 2011; Hattori, 2006). This political divvying up of a homeland and the peoples upon it tore apart a society and the families within it, without the involvement of the very CHamorus, Refaluwasch, and others present who were directly affected. At times, these borders imposed by outside forces have been closed by administering powers, thereby slowing or stopping completely the traditional flow and reciprocation among families. Such circumstances have produced some distinctions over time between the i Taotao Guåhan and those of the northern islands.

Perhaps indicative of pre-colonial population patterns and later colonial reinforcement, Guåhan is the most heavily populated island within Låguas yan Gåni. The 2020 Census of Guam tallied 153,836 CHamorus, Refaluwásch, other Micronesians and Pacific Islanders, and peoples from islands and continents near and far who call Guåhan home (US Census Bureau, 2021). However, similar to other Pacific Islanders, a majority of CHamorus (from both Guåhan and NMI) now reside outside their homeland islands, with at least 63% living in the United States, a trend that appears to be on the rise (Figures 4 & 5). CHamorus live in every state in the United States, from California and Washington to Texas, New York, and Florida, with an unknown number living within other US territories such as Puerto Rico and American Samoa (Hixson et al., 2012). If it were possible to count the thousands of other CHamorus living abroad outside the United States, the percentages would shift even further, maybe markedly so. Many find this trend of Indigenous depopulation of their homeland for both for Guåhan and NMI disturbing (F. Untalan, personal communication, March 17, 2017). Conversely, there are some CHamorus from the States or elsewhere who intentionally return home to connect with the land, know their families, and learn the culture as it is practiced in the islands.

Figure 4

CHamoru Distribution in the United States (2000)

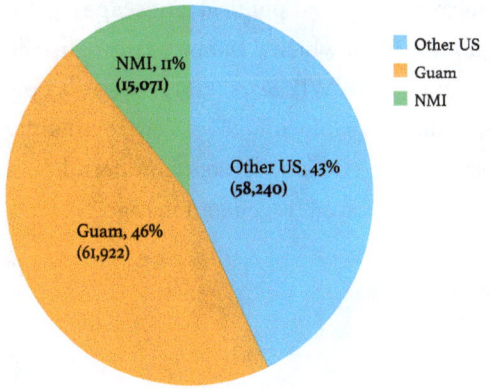

Note. In 2000, the majority of those who self-identified as CHamoru for the US Census were still living in their home islands. Some of these figures may be misleading, however, owing to factors related to lack of self-identification or inadequacy in census race/ethnicity categories. "Other US" does not include the territories of Puerto Rico, US Virgin Islands, or American Samoa as US Census agents were not able to verify whether any CHamoru resided in those areas. Percentages may not add up to 100% due to rounding off of figures. Adapted from *Chamorro Migration to the US*, by F. Untalan, n.d. (http://guampedia.com/chamorro-migration-to-the-u-s/). Copyright 2009–2019 by Guampedia.

Figure 5

CHamoru Distribution in the United States (2010)

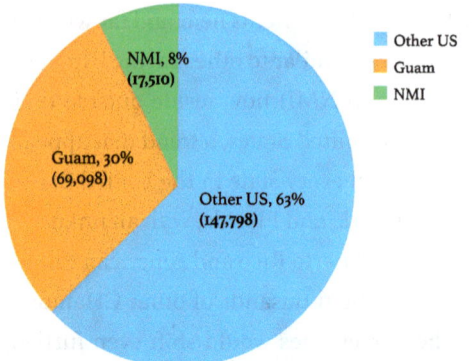

Note. Some of the rise in numbers of those who identify as CHamoru in US areas other than Guåhan and NMI might be due to improved census race/ethnicity categories and increased self-identification as CHamoru since 2000. "Other US" does not include the territories of Puerto Rico, US Virgin Islands, or American Samoa as contacted US Census agents were not able to verify whether any CHamoru resided in those areas. Percentages may not add up to 100% due to rounding off of figures. Adapted from *The Native Hawaiian and Other Pacific Islander Population: 2010*, by L. Hixson et al., 2012, 2010 Census Briefs (https://www.census.gov/prod/cen2010/briefs/c2010br-12.pdf).

While there have long been fluctuations in Guåhan's population, major shifts have taken place within the lifetimes of our elders that have radically reshaped and restructured many aspects of Guåhan's socio-cultural and political landscape (Bettis, 1996, p. 112; Untalan, n.d.). Guåhan, a homeland in which CHamorus made up the vast majority of the island's population up to pre-WWII years (91% in 1940), is now one where CHamorus are outnumbered due to sizeable influxes of new community members, including those from the NMI (Table 1). Many facets of modern life in Guåhan would be unrecognizable to those alive just a few generations ago.

Table 1

CHamoru Population in Guåhan Since 1920 According to US Census

Year	Total Population of Guåhan	CHamoru
1920	13,275	92%
1930	18,509	89%
1940	22,290	91%
1950	59,498	45%
1960	34,762	52%
1980	105.979	45%
1990	133,152	43%
2000	154,805	42%
2010	159,358	42%
2020	153,836	Pending US Census data

Note. Percentages are rounded off. Different censuses may use varying standards and methodology. The 1970 Census was omitted as it only identified the population as "native" or "foreign born," which did not allow for an accurate counting of CHamorus versus other ethnic populations on island. Adapted from *The Native Hawaiian and Other Pacific Islander Population: 2010*, by L. Hixson et al., 2012, 2010 Census Briefs (https://www.census.gov/prod/cen2010/briefs/c2010br-12.pdf), *Chamorro Migration to the US*, by F.F. Untalan, n.d., Guampedia (https://www.guampedia.com/chamorro-migration-to-the-u-s/). Copyright 2009-2019 by Guampedia, and Census of Guam, 2020.

During our great-grandparents' time, very few in the community did not identify as CHamoru—speaking the language fluently as their first language, practicing the CHamoru culture, and living a CHamoru pre-WWII lifestyle. However, early influxes caused the status of the CHamoru population to plummet to that of being a plurality by 1950, just a few years after WWII, a status that has remained true up to 2010 (Figure 6 & Table 1) (Bettis, 1996, pp. 106-107). Many are waiting to see if the 2020 census tabulations will challenge this long-standing status. It has now long been the combined non-CHamoru peoples that make up the majority of the island's population. Currently, the second largest group on island (26%) are those who have emigrated from the Philippine Islands, mainly in the decades following WWII, a marked change from comprising just 2.6% of Guahån's 1940 population (Quan, n.d.).

Figure 6
Guåhan's Festival of Pacific Arts 2016 Delegation

Note. The delegation was about 500 people strong. Recognizing the island's history of colonialism, immigration, and emigration, Guåhan decided that, in addition to Indigenous Pacific Islander CHamoru delegates, other community members who practiced or performed CHamoru arts and culture would also qualify to serve as delegates, regardless of their ethnicity or whether they resided off-island or not. From Monica Okada Guzman, personal communication, 2017, February 22. Copyright 2016 12th Festival of Pacific Arts Guam 2016.

Some scholars, such as the Honorable (former Congressman) Dr. Robert A. Underwood (1997) have stated that such trends of dramatic population growth and change may not bode well for the survival of the CHamoru people. He further said, "It may simply not be healthy for a society to change with such rapidity regardless of the characteristics of the incoming migrants or the ostensible economic benefits they bring" (p. 131).

Hågu, Guåhu yan Hita (You, Me, and We): Social and Cultural Impacts
CHamorus as a people are often described by others as "welcoming" and "hospitable" toward newcomers and visitors (DCA, 2003, p. 63). And while we can point to many ways in which other peoples and their cultural ways have added to the variety of life and experiences in Guåhan over the centuries, and continue to contribute to the island society and economy, we must also remember that non-CHamorus create other types of impacts as well. Adding to the challenges of globalization, modernization, and other forces, the rapid influx of others is straining Guåhan's natural and governmental resources as well as, to some degree, repressing the practice and maintenance of i kostumbren CHamoru (the Chamorro culture) (Underwood, 1997, p. 131).

Inagofli'e': CHamoru Caring for Each Other

Much in keeping with Pacific Island cultural ways, CHamorus will often open their houses, arms, and families in looking after new community members and visitors. This is often referred to as being "hospitable" or "generous," but it really is so much more than that. One will typically not be thirsty or go hungry if there is a CHamoru nearby with drink or food in hand. At an event, a CHamoru host and their relatives will periodically check in on guests, hand out more refreshments, offer to dispose of guests' used plates, and offer food to take home (Mendiola, n.d.a). The goal is for the guest to be "comfortable and wanting for nothing" (DCA, 2003, p. 63). Not often discussed, however, is that the rules of host-guest etiquette extend in both directions and involve a custom of reciprocity, a key CHamoru cultural value alongside interdependence, and a sense of obligation (Souder, 1994, p. 194). Those brought up within similar cultures know these rules inherently. Many others have learned these unwritten rules along the way or are continuing to learn.

However, there are a growing number of community members coming from other US areas and other countries who do not know about certain customs prevalent in i kustombren CHamoru, including rules about not being able to easily say "no" in Island cultures so one has to develop a sense of not asking for more than is appropriate to receive; rules about deferring the first and second offers of a gift or offer of food, as a means of gauging whether accepting that which is being offered would unnecessarily burden the host; rules that relationships are, at their best, reciprocal and generational; and other such Islander codes of conduct (Hezel, 2001; Hezel, 2013; Mendiola, n.d.a). While CHamoru younger generations continue such protocols to a degree, at least some of the CHamoru manåmko' (elders) and others express the view that they see some of the finer details or intentions of customary protocol as they knew it to be eroding, such as when it is proper to balutan (term informally used to describe packing up food to carry out after an event) and who should be prioritized in benefiting from balutan (e.g., Paulino et al., 2010). Mindful of this, cultural leaders are working to ensure transmission of these finer elements.

CHamoru Culture and Our Multi-Faceted Island Community

A variety of cultural features from elsewhere have been, in whole or in part, woven into the tapestry of island life, many of which have been CHamorucized. For instance, a look at our island fiesta tables shows a sampling of the many peoples and cultures that have come to the island (see Figure 3) (Mendiola, n.d.b). Added to traditional CHamoru fare like fish, taro, breadfruit, and katupat (rice cooked in a small basket of woven coconut leaves), have been CHamorucized dishes like titiyas, tamåles, and red rice, as well as the introduction of pancit, lumpia, Kentucky Fried Chicken, sushi, kimchi, and much more.

New names and new family members have made their way into CHamoru clans (Forbes, n.d.). The CHamoru language has, as living languages do, adopted and adapted from other languages that were imposed or otherwise introduced (Underwood, n.d., p. 10). Holidays from elsewhere have replaced or been added to traditional ones that are still celebrated or are in the process of being reinstituted (such as ancestral processions of commemoration). And a broad range of new events and activities have been added to the continuation of core values, such as respecting elders, and the maintenance, perpetuation, or revitalization of traditional practices and lifeways (Figure 7) (Souder, 1992; Underwood, n.d.).

Figure 7

Guma' Fuetsan I Acho' Latte, Tulu Na Nåpu

Note. Guma' Fuetsan I Acho' Latte, Tulu Na Nåpu (House of the Strength from within in the Latte Stone, the Third Generation) under the direction of Ma'gas Group Leader Patrick "Somnak" Camacho. It is one of the many dance groups that now exist in Guåhan. They showcase the success of the last several decades of effort that revitalized CHamoru dance, chant, and other traditions after centuries of suppression of aspects of CHamoru culture by colonial and other agents. The multi-storied hotels and developed residential neighborhoods in the background convey the continuation of the CHamoru people and lifeways in modern times. From Edward B. San Nicolas, personal communication, 2017, February 17. Copyright 2017 by Edward B. San Nicolas.

These cultural exchanges go both ways. For newcomers and visitors, it may be their first chance to try local and localized foods such as kelaguen månnok (chicken mixed with lemon, onion, and pepper); fina'denne' (local hot sauce); empanadas; and pickled papaya, daigo (radish), mangoes, eggs, and even pickles (Figure 8). Living in Guåhan may be their first foray out of the US mainland or their first venture from another country or a neighboring island to become, essentially, immigrants or settlers to an Indigenous homeland, (e.g., Bettis, 1996; Underwood, 1997).

Figure 8
Locally Grown Produce and Jars of Pickled Papaya and Mango

Note. The fresh and pickled produce at the 9th Annual Gupot Fanha'aniyan Pulan Chamorro (Chamorro Lunar Calendar Festival) held January 2017 are local favorites and a fun experience for others to try as well. From Edward B. San Nicolas, personal communication, 2017, February 17. Copyright 2017 by Edward B. San Nicolas.

For some, island life evokes a slower-paced style of living in comparison to the city they left behind, while for others, Guåhan is the big city compared to the smaller island or other community they moved from. What has become Guåhan's multi-ethnic, multi-cultural community may be familiar to some newcomers in its being a very cosmopolitan mix of people, while for others it may be a new experience in diversity and their first time to live as part of a minority, which may take some getting used to.

On the other hand, numerous non-CHamoru members of Guåhan's community have called the island their home for decades. Quite a few have raised children in Guåhan and perhaps even have grandchildren or great-grandchildren here, or, having been born in Guåhan or having arrived as a child, know no other "home." Some of these long-time community members now refer to themselves as Guamanian (a term with a complex history, as for decades, i Taotao Guåhan were referred to as such), or are at times referred to as Che'lu (sibling), Chamaoli (Chamorro + haoli, an adopted Hawaiian term for outsider, or foreigner), or other such terms meant to show their long-term connection with the community (G.E. Taitano, n.d.a; Borja, 2017).

Long-term residents, though perhaps identifying as an American, Australian, Filipino, Japanese, Thai, Pohnpeian, German, or another ethnicity on the one hand, may also identify, on the other hand, as someone who grew up in a Pacific Island community, or in Guåhan specifically, thus perhaps considering themselves a bit different than their fellow ethnic or national "kin." Many long-time community members marry into the CHamoru culture or marry another long-term resident, at times creating identifiable groups within the larger community. Though our community handles all these changes—and new levels of diversity that have happened rapidly—relatively well, there are tensions and serious issues such as a certain amount of division based on ethnic lines as well as various challenges to the Indigenous CHamoru culture and to Guåhan's quest for decolonization (Bettis, 1996, p. 111).

Socio-cultural and Political Impacts

CHamorus, both in the Marianas and abroad, as any other people, have a wide range of ways of looking at issues such as Guåhan's social, cultural and political conditions—each of which is a complex mix of inside and outside forces at work. Some of the overarching concerns held by portions of the community over the years are related to issues of dilution, domination, and diversion, each of which are discussed briefly below (Table 2).

Table 2

Concerns Held by Some Regarding Socio-cultural and Political Impacts of Rapid Demographic Changes to Guåhan as a Homeland

Type of Impact	Issue
Dilution	Worry of loss of CHamoru political control
	Treated as a minority in their own homeland

Type of Impact	Issue
Domination	People with non-CHamoru cultural views of CHamoru/Indigenous/Island culture & ways
	People with their own priorities & views of proper socio-political and cultural order
Diversion	People with their own social & cultural interests
	People with political diversions—affiliations, beliefs, & interests

Note. Adapted from "The Guam Dilemma: The Need for a Pacific Island Education Perspective," by K.B. Aguon, 1993, Hale'-ta, Hinasso': Tinige' Put Chamorro, Insights: The Chamorro Identity, pp. 89–101; "Colonial Immigration in Guam," by L. Bettis, 1996, Hale'-ta: Kinalamten Pulitikåt: Siñenten Chamorro, Issues in Guam's Political Development: The Chamorro Perspective, 1st ed., pp. 102–124; "Pacific Identities, Beyond US Racial Formations: The Case of Chamorro Ambivalence and Flux," by M. P. Perez, 2002, Social Identities, 8(3), pp. 457–479; "Chamorro Ambivalence and Diaspora: Beyond US Racial Formations," by M. P. Perez, 2003, In L.-H. N. Chiang, J. Lidstone, & R. A. Stephenson (Eds.), Global Processes, Local Impacts: The Effects of Globalization in the Pacific-Asia Region, pp. 31–44; "Psyche Under Siege: Uncle Sam, Look What You've Done to Us," by L. M. T. Souder, 1994, Sustainable Development or Malignant Growth?, pp. 193–195; and "Immigration and Guam's Future," by R. A. Underwood, 1997, In Political Status Education Coordinating Commission (Ed.), Hale'-ta, Hinasso': Tinigei Put Chamorro, Insights: The Chamorro Identity, pp. 131–136.

Dilution

There are several ways in which the concept of dilution impacts i Taotao Guåhan both locally and within the nation. Impacts caused by those who have migrated to the island since 1898 and 1940 are why the United Nations adopted particular resolutions and plans of action for non-self-governing areas, such as "instructing member states to prevent migration to colonial territories" precisely because it is understood that their presence is in general "disruptive" and can be a "major obstacle" when it comes to exercising the right to self-determination in a genuine way for the peoples of that area to whom the right of self-determination belongs (J. Aguon, 2012; Bettis, 1996, p. 112).

However, the United States has allowed migration to its territories to be largely unregulated (outside of national immigration laws and regulations) and the large influx of non-CHamorus who have become the majority of Guåhan's community have indeed muddied the understanding of many socio-cultural and political issues. Guam's history illustrates how "colonial powers have often used immigration to distract, confuse, and subvert the issues of decolonization, especially when they wish to remain in control of the territory" with immigrants as "part of the colonizing process" (Bettis, 1996, p. 111). Many i Taotao Guåhan have worried over the decades about the dilution of their political control over their homeland, control that was hard fought for and has only briefly been regained (1950-present) in a limited fashion after over 300 years of colonial rule (Bettis, 1996, p. 111).

At the national level, the peoples of Guåhan are only allowed a diluted form of participation in Congress (with a nonvoting delegate to the House of Representatives and no presence in the Senate) and are not allowed to participate in the vote for president. Instead, Congress has plenary (absolute) authority over US territories like Guåhan, and has thus far provided only a limited set of rights and privileges to their residents (Bevacqua, n.d.; C.P. Taitano, 1996).

CHamoru standing within the United States is further diluted as in many ways they are treated as a minority, not only abroad, but in their own homeland. This is largely due to the way that the US federal government and prevailing ideology frame race, indigeneity, recognition of Indigenous lands, and notions of equality (e.g., K.B. Aguon, 1993; Perez, 2002; Perez, 2003). Despite decades of local efforts to have a real voice within a US government proclaimed to be based on the democratic principles of equality and representation, CHamorus, among other Indigenous Peoples in the United States, have been provided little consideration and recognition (Waldman, 1985).

CHamorus, along with other Pacific Islanders, have been and continue to be, in some ways, considered "non-White" in the United States. Parents, grandparents, and great-grandparents within many CHamoru families served in the US military in "Colored" troops, or were relegated to the same or similar limitations as "Coloreds" by being able to serve only as mess attendants or personal aides to officers; were denied service at establishments that did not serve "Coloreds" during the Jim Crow years in the continental United States; and, at home in Guåhan, have had to contend with, during much of the island's history under the United States, segregated spaces and facilities that have been, at their core, separate and unequal (e.g., Quitugua, 1991, pp. 75–76; Sanchez, 1989, p. 145; Vance & Manning, 2015, p. 135).

Domination

Furthermore, the large influx of non-CHamorus who have arrived in the last 70 or so years, came with or developed their own views about what is or what should be CHamoru, Indigenous, or Islander ways, which may run alongside, dominate, or overlap with the range of CHamoru views about these same issues. Some of these newcomers are supportive of the maintenance of the CHamoru culture , while others may still be trying to figure out what constitutes island life and I kustombren i Taotao Guåhan (the culture of the CHamorus of Guam). Still others may have their own notions of what being productive should look like (e.g., whether Islanders use their time "productively" or not); which cultural "measuring stick" should be used in assessing i Taotao Guåhan and their culture and language (e.g., whether they are truly CHamoru and to what degree); or what aspects of life should be prioritized and when (e.g., the time and place for family and familial obligations which are primary considerations in i kostumbren CHamoru), and so forth (Aguon, 1993). Added to the presence of these notions is that some of the island's community members may be quite vocal about their precepts and dominate the community conversation about where their notions should figure into the consideration of local matters (Bettis, 1996, p. 106).

A lot of energy can thus be spent sorting through island issues to make sense of them, or negating the disruption these competing notions cause. Some of this energy is spent reminding the community at large and each other, that the CHamorus as a people have the right to, and that there is value in, recognizing and maintaining their own Indigenous set of core values, philosophies, and lifeways (Aguon, 1993; Bevacqua, n.d.; Borja, 2017; Underwood, 1991, Underwood, n.d.).

An example of muddied issues and competing notions is the political issue of determining who will partake in Guåhan's act of self-determination. The United States placed the island on the UN list of non-self-governing territories in 1946 just after WWII, thereby creating international recognition that the people of the island have the right to decolonize (see Benavente, n.d.; The Organic Act of Guam, n.d.; The Treaty of Paris of 1898, Article IX; United Nations, n.d.). The Government of Guåhan's position has long been that the "Native Inhabitants" of the island, a category of people referred to and defined by the United States in pertinent legal documents, are those who will vote in a decolonization plebiscite (Native Inhabitants are defined as those that were present during germane historical events of 1950 or 1898, and their descendants) (V.-L. Leon Guerero, 2014). Others have stated that the right belongs to the CHamoru people, while still others feel that every US citizen who is a resident should participate in the vote. For many, the latter position is extremely controversial given the rapid demographic changes since 1940 which have created the potential for non-Native Inhabitants and non-CHamorus to drown out Native Inhabitant and CHamoru political will regarding the future status of a CHamoru homeland.

In 2011, a non-Native Inhabitant, non-CHamoru resident filed a suit in court to defend his claimed right to vote in the people of Guåhan's decolonization process. Although self-determination is an international right, the ruling of the case was decided following US domestic law with the 9th Circuit Court of Appeals ruling against the Government of Guåhan, striking down the island's decolonization law as unconstitutional. The case came to a close when, in 2020, the Supreme Court denied to review the case. This meant that the 9th Circuit 2019 ruling currently stands. For many, the issues are still far from settled.

Diversion
While recognizing that CHamorus, like all groups of people, embrace a wide range of traditional values and practices, it is also true that, to varying degrees and in varying ways, customary CHamoru values, philosophies, and lifeways are impacted by the presence of the large number of non-CHamorus in Guåhan (and by having large numbers of CHamorus living outside the Marianas archipelago). These short- and long-term community members from other cultures, or even from neighboring Mariana Islands to the north, arrive in Guåhan with their own cultural, personal, or other sets of social, political, and cultural interests that may or may not align with those who are i Taotao Guåhan.

Within this matrix of CHamorus and diverse community members, are a wide variety of positions depending on a host of factors like cultural identity, family or political party affiliation, level or type of education, and personal convictions, among others, as they weigh in on issues like what types of directions the island economy should go in, what decolonized political status is the best option for us, and more. The end result, thus, is often a mixture of Indigenous and non-Indigenous community members alongside each other in a diversity of social, political, and economic positions.

Part of what has become perhaps more evident in recent years is the dilemma that, even if long-time residents and newcomers respect the local culture and issues of Guåhan, they may feel like they do not have a real stake in, or want to interfere in, particular issues such as militarization, especially regarding Indigenous i Taotao Guåhan claims to land. These dilemmas can have real consequences in and of themselves.

Take, for example, the public review and comment periods that are a part of the environmental impact statements prepared for militarization processes that have been ongoing for the last decade. If community members do not participate or comment because they do not feel they have a right to weigh in on i Taotao Guåhan issues or issues they may not be present for in the future, their non-involvement may be read as consent for the proposed actions. Or, conversely, if they do weigh in, such thoughts may impact the outcome based on their different non-Indigenous connections to and ways of conceiving of the land, which can be distinct from that of the CHamoru worldview, which holds that, "Land is the soul of Chamorro culture. It, together with the sea, gives life to the Chamorro." (For further detail regarding these CHamoru concepts see, Cabrera, et al., 2015; Phillips, n.d.)

Examples of Socio-Cultural and Political Impacts on Daily Life

Many facets of life in Guåhan have been impacted by the history and circumstances of colonial systems, modernization, and island demographics, each deserving to be examined in detail to provide nuanced understandings. Here, however, I will briefly introduce just a few important issues that are part of our daily lives, those revolving around where we live and around work life and school life, which perhaps feel so familiar and basic to modern-day living that we may not typically view them as impacting the CHamoru culture and family structure.

Where We Live

In the big picture, it is readily apparent that the core CHamoru value of the primacy of family still has a strong presence, though it has changed in certain ways (Iyechad, 2001; Marsh, 2019; Souder, 1992, p. 144; Underwood, n.d., p. 14). For example, owing to the influence of the concept of an American nuclear family and other influences, "extended" families are less likely to live in family compounds nowadays. It is now more common for family members to live not only farther apart but in different villages, islands, states, or even countries (Souder, 1992, p. 144). These more recent residential patterns are impacting to some degree the time, energy, and types of resources contributed toward fulfilling family obligations that bond and reinforce the CHamoru family. Advances in technology along with the growth of social media, and their increased use in response to the COVID-19 pandemic, are adding their own dynamics to these issues allowing for more types of connectivity between family and friends on-island and off-island.

Work Life

For centuries, a good number of CHamorus resisted fully participating in the cash economy in many ways during the Spanish and early US colonial administrations, though there had been a number of extremely successful CHamoru families during both administrations (A. Leon Guerero, n.d.; Sanchez, 1989, pp. 272–281). The cash economy gained a stronger foothold during the US administration after WWII when the CHamoru people and other locals dealt with issues such as bombed and burned-out lands, dislocation owing to a high number of US military land takings (including whole villages), and relocation within the island (A. Leon Guerero, n.d.; Sanchez, 1989, pp. 277–281).

While numerous i Taotao Guåhan have succeeded and earned recognition for excelling in the workplace (such as within the US military), modern work life has impacted traditional timelines and motivations for and methods of conducting "work" in particular ways. For instance, familial and other celebrations nowadays may have to consider whether they will occur during times outside of working hours or whether it is now perhaps more convenient or otherwise beneficial to meet family obligations by contributing cash rather than labor or something personally fished or hunted, gathered, or harvested (Iyechad, 2001, pp. 172-174).

School Life

While perhaps no one in Guåhan challenges the value of formal education per se, modern schools operate as cultural entities unto themselves, complete with their own rules of conduct, processes, and standards (Aguon, 1993). Over the centuries, i Taotao Guåhan have seen education shift from traditional informal practices of mentoring and guiding family youth to formal systems instructing youth in which teachers may spend more time with children than the children's family.

Island students today receive lessons in classrooms from a mixture of i Taotao Guåhan, Taotao Sa'ipan, or other CHamorus; long-term residents; newcomers; or transient instructors who utilize textbooks written, more often than not, for a continental US setting that does not always translate well to local conditions (though there are ongoing efforts to more actively develop local curricula). For example, students may never learn about CHamoru authors such as Peter Onedera, despite Señot Onedera being formally recognized as Sainan Minenhalom Sinangan Ginen i Hila' (Master Storyteller), but the students will perhaps instead be taught about Shakespeare. They will be taught about "spring," "summer," "fall," and "winter" rather than fañomnåkan and fanuchånan (the "sunny" and "rainy" seasons of the Mariana Islands). Foreign socio-political and cultural ways of thinking can be embedded in such situations and can challenge Pacific Island cultures and settings if we do not all work to recognize and mitigate them (Aguon, 1993).

Sa Håfa? What Does It All Mean?
There are many ways we could explore these issues further. Each of the facets of life discussed above have certain costs and benefits: salaries provide the ability to support families and fulfill familial obligations, perhaps even in an enhanced fashion; work provides services and goods to Guåhan's community members; education and training programs open doors to jobs and careers that are personally satisfying, benefit the community, and provide salaries that, as noted above, allow us to fulfill familial obligations; and so on. While no one is necessarily calling for the end to new residents arriving on Guåhan's shores, to formal education, or for the end of a cash economy in Guåhan, it is important to be conscious of the ways that these forces and the diversity of our community impact cultural philosophies, traditions and lifeways that are foundational to i Taotao Guåhan culture and the island way of life. Further, it is important to be aware that the historical circumstances, colonization, and rapid shifts in demographics have had even wider impacts than those discussed here.

It is no coincidence that communities that suffer historical trauma, rapid changes, and other events as happened in Låguas yan Gåni end up with wounds and scars that take concerted effort to address and heal. The story is all too common among Indigenous communities, wherein a toll is exacted upon the physical and mental health of Indigenous Peoples as individuals, as families, and as communities. I Taotao Guåhan and other CHamorus now suffer the highest rates of diabetes, obesity, hypertension, and cancer, in addition to the highest rates of adult and juvenile crime within Guåhan's diverse ethnic communities (Rapadas et al., 2005). As i Taotao Guåhan work to heal and move forward, many express an appreciation of those who recognize the validity of their culture that deserves to be assessed according to its own "measuring stick," and of those who do not treat their culture as a failed attempt according to someone else's standards (Figure 9).

Figure 9
CHamoru Dance House Group from Japan

Note. Revitalization of CHamoru dance has been so successful that guma' (houses) are now being established outside of the Mariana Islands—in other US areas like California and Washington, but also in other countries like Japan. Above are members of the Japan-based Guma' Famagu'on Tåno' Yan I Tasi (House of the Children of the Land and the Sea) who performed at Gef Pago February 2017. Also present are a few CHamoru and other Guåhan community members. From Edward B. San Nicolas, personal communication, 2017, February 17. Copyright 2017 by Edward B. San Nicolas.

Un Dångkolo' Na Si Yu'os Ma'åse' to: Drs. Michael Clement, Jr., Elizabeth 'Isa' Bowman, and David Atienza and PhD Candidate Becka Garrison for their time and expertise in reviewing an earlier version of this essay; Dr. Faye Flores Untalan for allowing me to use data from her demographic tables and for generously setting aside time to share perspectives about CHamorus abroad and demographic changes in the Mariana Islands; Kumision i Fino' CHamoru (Chamorro Language Commission [of Guåhan]) members Rosa Palomo and Teresita Flores, as well as Flo Mesa and Ignacio R. Camacho for guiding me in the CHamoru language; photographers Edward B. San Nicolas and Ron Castro, along with TÅSI, for graciously sharing their photos; Ma'gas Group Leader Patrick "Somnak"

Camacho for his support of the use of a photo of Guma' Fuetsan I Acho' Latte, Tulu Na Nåpu; Nieves Materne for authorizing usage of a photo with her; Ignacio R. Camacho and Cheryl and Dr. Lawrence J. Cunningham, for searching through their photo collections; Sam Ilesugam for guidance regarding the Central Carolines; and Linda Taitano Reyes, Zina Ruiz, and Elyssa J. Santos for connecting me to Dr. Untalan and Ma'gas Group Leader Patrick "Somnak" Camacho.

References

Aguon, J. (2012). *The commerce of recognition (buy one ethos, get one free): Toward curing the harm of the United States' international wrongful acts in the Hawaiian Islands.* 'Ohia. Ka Huli Ao Center or Excellence in Native Hawaiian Law. https://www.law.hawaii.edu/sites/www.law.hawaii.edu/files/content/Programs%2CClinics%2CInstitutes/108622%20L1%20Aguon%20r5.pdf

Aguon, K. B. (1993). The Guam dilemma: The need for a Pacific Island education perspective. In Political Status Education Coordinating Commission (Ed.), *Hale'-ta, hinasso': Tinige' put Chamorro, Insights: The Chamorro identity* (pp. 89-101). Political Status Education Coordinating Commission.

Atienza, D. (2013, August). *The Mariana Islands militia and the establishment of the 'Pueblos de Indios': Indigenous agency in Guam from 1668 to 1758* [Conference paper presentation]. 2nd Marianas History Conference: One Archipelago, Many Stories, Integrating Our Narratives, University of Guam, Mangilao, Guam. www.uog.edu/sites/default/files/pai5-atienza-priests-mayors-indigenous.pdf

Barratt, G. (Trans. & Ed.) (1984). *Russian exploration in the Mariana Islands, 1817-1828.* CNMI Division of Historic Preservation.

Benavente, E. L. G. (n.d.) Interpretive essay: Chamoru self-determination. In *Guampedia.* http://www.guampedia.com/interpretive-essay-commission-on-self-determination-2/

Bettis, L. (1996). Colonial immigration in Guam. In Political Status Education Coordinating Commission (Ed.), *Kinalamten pulitikåt: Siñenten i Chamorro* (pp. 102-124). Guam Political Status Education Coordinating Commission.

Bevacqua, M. L. (n.d.). American-style colonialism. In *Guampedia.* http://guampedia.com/american-style-colonialism/

Borja, J. (2017, March 21). *TheJohnnyBubble On: Guam's future political status.* Odyssey. https://www.theodysseyonline.com/thejonnybubble-guams-future-political-status.

Cabrera, G. S., Kaipat, C. M., Marsh-Taitano, K. G., & Perez, R. (2015, June 16). Facts you need to know about gathering community input. *Saipan Tribune.* http://www.saipantribune.com/index.php/facts-you-need-to-know-about-gathering-community-input/

Cepeda, J., Iriarte, L. Z., & Cunningham, L. J. (n.d.). Chamorro sidereal direction terminology. In *Guampedia.* http://www.guampedia.com/chamorro-sidereal-direction-terminology/

Coomans, P. (1997). *History of the mission in the Mariana Islands: 1667-1673* (R. Lévesque, Trans.). CNMI Division of Historic Preservation.

DCA, The Department of Chamorro Affairs, Research, Publication, and Training Division. (2003). Culture & hospitality. In *Chamorro heritage, a sense of place: Guidelines, procedures and recommendations for authenticating Chamorro heritage* (pp. 61-66). Department of Chamorro Affairs, Research, Publication, and Training Division.

Farrell, D. A. (2011). *History of the Mariana Islands to partition.* CNMI Public School System.

Forbes, E. (n.d.). *The origin, meaning, and history of Chamorro names* [Lecture Series Presentation]. MARC Research Library Video Collection.

Furey, J. (2006). *Island ecology & resource management.* Northern Marianas College Press.

García, F. (2004). *The life and martyrdom of the Venerable Father Diego Luis de San Vitores of the Society of Jesus, First Apostle of the Mariana Islands and events of these islands from the year sixteen hundred and sixty-eight through the year sixteen hundred and eighty-one* (M. M. Higgins, F. Plaza, & J. Ledesma, Trans.). University of Guam Richard Flores Taitano Micronesian Area Research Center.

Hattori, A. P. (2006). The politics of preservation: Historical memory and division in the Mariana Islands. *Micronesian Journal of the Humanities and Social Sciences, 5*(1/2), 1-4.

Hattori, A. P. (2021, September 13). Folktale: Puntan and Fu'una: Gods of creation. In *Guampedia.* https://www.guampedia.com/puntan-and-fuuna-gods-of-creation/

Hezel, F. X. (2001). *The new shape of old island cultures: A half century of social change in Micronesia.* University of Hawai'i Press.

Hezel, F. X. (2013). *Making sense of Micronesia: The logic of Pacific Island culture.* University of Hawai'i Press.

Historic Resources Division (2006). *Historic preservation review.* Guam Historic Resources Division.

Hixson, L., Hepler, B. B., & Kim, M. O. (2012). *The Native Hawaiian and Other Pacific Islander Population: 2010* (Report No. C2010BR-12). US Census Bureau.

Iyechad, L. P. (2001). *An historical perspective of helping practices associated with birth, marriage and death among Chamorros in Guam* (Vol. 27). The Edwin Mellen Press.

Leon Guerrero, A. (n.d.). Early American economic history. In *Guampedia*. http://www.guampedia.com/early-american-economic-history/

Leon Guerrero, V.-L. (2014). CHamoru registry and the decolonization registry. In *Guampedia*. https://www.guampedia.com/chamorro-registry-and-the-decolonization-registry/

Marsh, K. G. (2009, November 18). Familia. In *Guampedia*. http://guampedia.com/familia/

Mendiola, T. M. C. (n.d.a). Geftao: Unselfishness. In *Guampedia*. http://guampedia.com/geftao-unselfishness/

Mendiola, T. M. C. (n.d.b). Guam's fiesta table. In *Guampedia*. http://www.guampedia.com/chamorro-food/fiesta-table-overview/

The Organic Act of Guam and related federal laws affecting the governmental structure of Guam, Current through USP.L. 108-378. (n.d.). Judiciary of Guam. http://www.guamcourts.org/CompilerofLaws/GCA/OrganicAct/Organic%20Act.PDF

Paulino, L., Ecle, G., Cepeda, J., Perez, K., Pangelinan, J., Gogue J., Borja J., & Santos V. (2010, 3 July). Please don't abuse balutan generosity. *Pacific Daily News*. http://archive.guampdn.com/article/20100703/OPINION02/7030319/Please-don-t-abuse-balutan-generosity

Perez, M. P. (2002). Pacific identities, beyond US racial formations: The case of Chamorro ambivalence and flux. *Social Identities, 8*(3), 457-479.

Perez, M. P. (2003). Chamorro ambivalence and diaspora: Beyond US racial formations. In L.-H. N. Chiang, J. Lidstone, & R. A. Stephenson (Eds.), *Global processes, local impacts: The effects of globalization in the Pacific-Asia region* (pp. 31-44). Graduate School and Research, Richard Flores Taitano Micronesian Area Research Center, University of Guam.

Phillips, M. (n.d.) Land ownership on Guam. In *Guampedia*. http://www.guampedia.com/land-ownership-on-guam/

Quan, C. G. (n.d.) Filipinos of Guam. In *Guampedia*. https://www.guampedia.com/filipinos-on-guam/

Quitugua, F. J. A. (1991). History of American education on Guam, the impact of military presence and its level of financial support, and the effort we are exerting to improve education on Guam. In D. H. Rubinstein, & V. L. Dames (Eds.), *Uncle Sam in Micronesia: Social benefits, social costs* (pp. 74-80). University of Guam Micronesian Area Research Center.

Rapadas, J., Balajadia, M., & Rubinstein, D. (2005). Guam: Caught amidst change and transition. In A. J. Marsella, A. A. Austin, & B. Grant (Eds.), *Social change and psychosocial adaptation in the Pacific Islands cultures in transition* (pp. 145-170). Springer.

Russell, S. (1998). Gani revisited: A historical overview of the Mariana archipelago's northern islands. *Pacific Studies, 21*(4), 83-105.

Sanchez, P. C. (1989). *Guahan, Guam: The history of our island*. HM Capital Printers, Ltd.

Souder, L. M. T. (1992). Unveiling herstory: Chamorro women in historical perspective. In D. H. Rubinstein (Ed.), *Pacific History: Papers from the 8th Pacific History Association Conference* (pp. 143-161). University of Guam Press and Micronesian Area Research Center.

Souder, L. M. T. (1994). Psyche under siege: Uncle Sam, look what you've done to us. In A. Emberson-Bain (Ed.), *Sustainable development or malignant growth? : Perspectives of Pacific Island women* (pp. 193-195). Marama Publications.

Taitano, C. P. (1996). Political development. In Guam Political Status Education Coordinating Commission (Ed.), *Kinalamten pulitikåt: Siñenten i Chamorro, (Issues in Guam's political development: The Chamorro perspective)* (pp. 45-56). PSECC.

Taitano, G. E. (n.d.a) Adoption of "Guamanian." In *Guampedia*. http://www.guampedia.com/adoption-of-guamanian/

Taitano, G. E. (n.d.b) Origin of Chamorro as an ethnic identifier. In *Guampedia*. http://guampedia.com/origin-of-chamorro-as-an-ethnic-identifier/

The Treaty of Paris of 1898, United States-Spain, December 10, 1898. http://www.msc.edu.ph/centennial/treaty1898.html

Underwood, R. A. (1991). Entroduksion. In M. Crisostomo (Ed.), *Legacy of Guam, i kustumbren Chamoru* (pp. 14-15). Legacy Publications.

Underwood, R. A. (n.d.). *Hispanicization as a socio-historical process on Guam*. [Unpublished manuscript].
Underwood, R. A. (1997). Immigration and Guam's future. In Political Status Education Coordinating Commission (Ed.), *Hale'-ta, Hinasso': Tinige' put Chamorro, Insights: The Chamorro identity* (2nd ed., pp. 131-136). Guam Political Status Education Coordinating Commission.
United Nations. (n.d.). *The United Nations and decolonization: Non-self-governing territories*. Retrieved March 29, 2017, from http://www.un.org/en/decolonization/nonselfgovterritories.shtml
Untalan, F. F. (n.d.). Chamorro migration to the US. In *Guampedia*. http://guampedia.com/chamorro-migration-to-the-u-s/
US Census Bureau. (2021). *Guam's 2020 housing unit and population counts*. Census of Guam. https://bsp.guam.gov/census-of-guam/
Vance, J., & Manning, A. (2015). Pacific Islanders and the Civil War. In Official National Park Service Handbook (Ed.), *Asians and Pacific Islanders and the Civil War* (pp. 130–135). The National Park Service.
Waldman, C. (1985). *Atlas of the North American Indian*. Facts on File, Inc.

Notes

¹Micronesian poets, on the other hand, have made significant contributions to Pacific literature, led by writers such as Craig Santos Perez and Cecilia Taitano Perez of Guam, Kathy Jetnil-Kijiner of the Marshall Islands, and Emelihter Kihleng of Pohnpei.

²See, for example, http://www.hawaii.edu/cpis/psi/, a site sponsored by the Pacific Studies Initiative, a joint project of the University of Hawai'i Center for Pacific Islands Studies and the East-West Center Pacific Islands Development Program (PIDP) that provides online instructional support, including sample syllabi, for Pacific-related courses.

³The 11 novels were read as e-books on a Kindle reader, thus the references included in this paper all refer to the "location number" of the text, rather than the page number.

⁴For elaboration on *duendes,* see "I Duendes" by Pale Eric Forbes. <http:paleric.blogspot.com/2011/10/i-dendes.html>.

⁵See, for example, the writings of Michael Lujan Bevacqua.

⁶Craig Santos Perez's works are especially noteworthy. See, in particular, his three collections of poetry: 1) *from unincorporated territory [hacha]* (2008), 2) *from unincorporated territory [saina]* (2010), and 3) *from unincorporated territory [guma']* (2014)–for which he was honored with the prestigious American Book Award in 2015. He was also recognized with the 2011 PEN Center USA Literary Award for Poetry and, most recently, the 2016 Lannen Literary Fellowship.

⁷Tabios (2000) creates a poem by collaging phrases from the authors represented in *Babaylan: An Anthology of Filipina and Filipina American Writers.*

⁸My reference to ube as symbolic of Filipino cultural "roots" is because ube is made from the root of the purple yam. This metaphor is in accordance with my

article, "The *Ube* ("Roots") Generation," published in the December 2016 volume of *Humanities Diliman*.

[9] In *Identity Formation, Agency, and Culture: A Social Psychological Synthesis*, James E. Côté and Charles G. Levine (2002) describe the numerous difficulties faced by the descendants of immigrants.

[10] The songs in my album were written by my mother, Alpha Espina. Helen Chaco provided the CHamoru translation in the lyrics.

[11] The use of personal experience as an introspective, self-reflexive process is not uncommon in research involving identity and its negotiation, particularly within diasporic communities. See Nadal (2010), David (2013), Rath (2000), Hall (1989), and Skinner (2009).

[12] Portes and Rumbaut (2001) found that a thoroughly acculturated third generation lacks the drive and social resources of their immigrant ancestors, and thus their perspectives on American imperialism are largely conditioned by what happened to their parents and grandparents.

[13] See Constantino (1970).

[14] I composed the lyrics, while my mother composed the music.

[15] Capitalization is reproduced exactly as it appears in the original.

[16] Internalized oppression is defined by David (2013) as a condition in which an oppressed individual or group come to believe that they are inferior to those of the dominant group; it is possibly the most insidious consequence of oppression.

[17] According to David (2013), colonial mentality can be perpetuated though the generations, and these attitudes become more pronounced and exacerbated through the generations.

[18] Through personal census conducted by Mr. Rian Charoenkhai, a local volunteer for the Royal Thai Consulate General (Labor Section) in Hong Kong, who oversees the census for the Consulate.

[19] "The CW-1 nonimmigrant visa program permits employers who meet program requirements to hire nonimmigrant workers temporarily in the Commonwealth of the Northern Mariana Island (CNMI or 'Commonwealth') to perform services or labor based on the employer's need. Job opportunities for the CW-1 program can have validity periods of up to one year and may be renewed for two additional periods of up to one year, with the exception of statutorily defined 'long-term workers' who may receive a certification with a validity period of up to three years, which may be renewed for additional periods of up to three years" (United States Department of Labor, n.d.).

[20] In modern orthography in Guam, the spelling would be "Tåno' i CHamoru."

[21] There is a significant amount of detail to this case that this brief description does not provide.

[22] Empty Land.

[23] In seeing how these arguments can work in the CHamoru case, it is important to note the differences between CHamorus and "domestic dependent nations."

[24] The Project "English in paradise?: Emergent varieties in Micronesia," for which the data was compiled, is funded by the Swiss National Science Foundation (SNSF).

[25] Speaker code: *Island* (here: Sa = Saipan), *Speaker number, Sex, Age*

[26] The most frequent languages spoken in Saipan at home (population 5 years and over: 43,871 = 100%) are the Philippine languages with 33%, Chamorro with 22% and English only with 17% (CNMI Department of Commerce 2010, p. 181; p. 186). The rest of the languages are spoken less frequently than 10% and are not listed here.

[27] English as a lingua franca is described as "a 'contact language' between persons who share neither a common Native tongue nor a common (national) culture, and for whom English is the chosen *foreign* language of communication" (Firth, 1996, p. 240).

[28] Speakers adjust their accent or other aspects of language production according to listener's speaker style or a desired variety.

[29] The Peace Corps, however, also were the people who brought about a change in language attitude towards the Indigenous languages: The value of the local languages was re-discovered and appreciated (Topping, 1985, p. 119).

[30] For further information about the history of the Saipan Carolinian language and its possible vanishing, see (Ellis, 2016).

[31] The Carolinians in Saipan call themselves Refaluwasch, the "people of our land," which refers to Saipan (cf. Kuehling, 2012, p. 57).

[32] This chapter specifically focuses on women and women-led organized resistance to militarization. I do not include statements or documentation from the US Department of Defense. The official documentation and justification for the build-up is available online at http://www.cnmijointmilitarytrainingeis.com.

[33] In March 2015, a federal court ruled that these sonar exercises and underwater detonations in the waters surrounding Hawai'i and off the coast of California violate the Marine Mammal Protection Act and the Endangered Species Act (Martinez, 2015). However, the Navy continues to use the same methods within the Mariana Islands Training and Testing (MITT) program. See: https://www.nrdc.org/media/2015/150331-0. Also see Chapter 1 of the Special Report, Pacific Outpost in the *Civil Beat* by Anita Hofschneider, 12 December 2016. (Hofschneider, 2016a). For an explanation of MITT: http://islandbreath.blogspot.co.nz/2013/11/help-save-mariana-islands.html (Paik, 2014).

[34] In addition, the US military must follow Section 106 of the National Historic Preservation Act, a separate consultation process to determine the "potential effects of the proposed action on historic properties." Available at http://

www.cnmijointmilitarytrainingeis.com/get-involved (US Marine Corps Forces Pacific, 2015).

[35] In April 2017, the DOD scheduled additional meetings before the revision EIS has been released. In addition, they were scheduled with very short notice and took place from 2–4 pm during the workday (Villahermosa, 2017). For more, see Rep. Demapan's concerns: http://www.mvariety.com/cnmi/cnmi-news/local/94776-rep-angel-demapan-questions-cjmt-meetings.

[36] Adams also says that the CNMI is "one of the poorest, most isolated and least well-represented entities in the US." Brian Turner, an attorney at the National Trust for Historic Preservation, says the EIS proposal demonstrates "environmental injustice" and "if this sort of thing were proposed in North Carolina [the continental United States], it just would never happen" (Hofschneider, 2016a).

[37] In addition to the LFTRC on Tinian, another example of the US Military environmental contamination legacy are the 42 leaking oil fuel tanks abandoned by the US Navy in the 1960s in Saipan, known as the "Tanapag Fuel Farm." This is in addition to the millions of pounds of Unexploded Ordnance (UXOs) (Hofschneider, 2016a).

[38] It would also (ironically) destroy the first peace monument built by US Navy Seabees in 1945 in Tinian after the Japanese Imperial Forces surrendered. In addition, the training would potentially destroy 200 sites that are eligible for the National Register for Historic Places (Hofschneider, 2016c).

[39] See the short video with residents from Tinian, accessible online: http://www.aljazeera.com/blogs/asia/2016/08/voices-northern-mariana-islands-160831152622901.html (Ortigas, 2016).

[40] Mayor Aldan suffered a fatal heart attack on February 20, 2017 at 46 years old. The community was in shock, and the future of the Pågan homestead program is uncertain (Pagarao, 2017).

[41] View the online petition at https://www.change.org/p/united-states-department-

of-defense-do-not-use-the-inhabited-us-islands-of-tinian-pagan-as-a-high-impact-bombing-range.

[42] According to the 2015 *Mariana Islands Training and Testing* (MITT) proposal every island in the archipelago is categorized as a "potential location" for a Live Fire Training Range Complex (LFTRC).

[43] I believe online petitions do serve a purpose, since this petition was a post I shared on the *Oceania Resistance* Facebook page and reached hundreds of people beyond the archipelago.

[44] This is highlighted in the article, "Resisting Political Colonization and American Militarization in the Marianas Archipelago," I created for *AlterNative: International Journal of Indigenous Studies* (Frain, 2016).

[45] On December 5, 2016, the US Department of the Navy filed a motion to dismiss the lawsuit of four environmental groups for lack of jurisdiction (Manabat, 2016). However, the groups maintain their right to sue (Torre, 2017).

[46] Farallon de Medenilla, or FDM as it is commonly referenced, was a name given to the island under Spanish colonial rule, but the Indigenous Chamorro name for the island is No'os (personal communication with historian Genevieve S. Cabrera).

[47] Specifically, Section 802 of the CNMI Covenant reads: "(a) The following property will be made available to the Government of the United States by lease to enable it to carry out its defense responsibilities: (1) on Tinian Island, approximately 17,799 acres (7,203 hectares) and the waters immediately adjacent thereto; (2) on Saipan Island, approximately 177 acres (72 hectares) at Tanapag Harbor; and (3) on Farallon de Medinilla Island, approximately 206 acres (83 hectares) encompassing the entire island, and the waters immediately adjacent thereto (b) The United States affirms that it has no present need for or present intention to acquire any greater interest in property listed above than that which is granted to it under Subsection 803(a), or to acquire any property in addition to that listed in Subsection (a), above, in order to carry out its defense responsibilities" (CNMI Covenant, n.d.).

⁴⁸This terminology was employed in a number of personal communications on Saipan during conversations that took place beginning in 2006 onward when community members were describing the military's presence in the Marianas after WWII.

⁴⁹The Marianas Political Status Commission in 1975, defined the "Covenant" as a "binding agreement like a contract or compact and the title used for this agreement is not intended to have independent legal significance. This title seems appropriate because the relationship between the United States and the Northern Marianas will be a permanent one, which in its fundamental respects will not be able to be changed by one party without the consent of the other" (*To Approve*, 1975).

⁵⁰It should be noted that, according to Smith (1991), "The Marianas plebiscite on future status held in 1975, notwithstanding the size of the vote for a Commonwealth (78.8% with a turnout of over 90%) failed to include independence or free association options. The options required by UN decolonization principles were not offered and the status of this act of 'self-determination' was criticized by a number of legal scholars. The failure to present other options reflects an agreement by both the United States and political leaders in the Northern Marianas to push the matter through as quickly as possible, and implied some lack of confidence in the islander's support for Commonwealth status" (p. 36). Historically, it is understood that the members of the Congress of Micronesia (a bicameral legislature created in 1965 during the TTPI) were not in agreement with the members of the Marianas delegation in the 1960's about the Northern Marianas desiring a closer political union with the United States. (McPhetres, 1997).

⁵¹The importance of the Insular Cases also highlights the court's reliance on *Rice vs. Cayetano* as a tool for understanding indigeneity in the Marianas. While the formation of a Northern Marianas Descent identity was not intended to map onto race, it has sometimes been conflated with race and is viewed as a direct violation of the U.S. fourteenth and fifteenth amendments. However, the use of *Rice vs. Cayetano* to understand race relations in the CNMI is problematic and has been problematized by a number of legal scholars (Aguon, 2009; Torres, 2012; Villazor, 2018).

⁵²While I am not suggesting that the CNMI is legally defined as a territory, it has often been presented as undistinguishable from other territories in terms of federal

policies. Horey (2003) has argued that politically, this has been an outcome of the "overall federal tendency ... to ignore the unique circumstances of the CNMI, and lump it together with the traditional U.S. territories." (p. 182) In theory, this distinction is important, since commonwealth status affords the Northern Mariana Islands with a level of autonomy that other territories do not have, such as the right to self-government and the creation of the CNMI Covenant and Constitution.

[53] Fallon (1991) argues that the term "'commonwealth' has no precise definition for the U.S. Government" (p. 26) and points to the historically arbitrary use of the term by other U.S. states such as Kentucky, Maryland, Massachusetts, Pennsylvania, and Virginia; as well as the Philippines' short-term use of the term between 1935–1946. For further discussion of the "graded, political limbo" that "the federal government has consigned" to it's eight insular territories, including American Samoa, the Federated States of Micronesia, Guam, the Marshall Islands, the Northern Marianas, Palau, Puerto Rico, and the U.S. Virgin Islands, see Joseph E. Fallon's (1991) "Federal Policy and U.S. Territories: The Political Restructuring of the United States of America." A similar assessment of national belonging is addressed by Barreto and Lazaro who write that there are "varying degrees of national belonging."

[54] At the time of this writing, Guam was listed under Chapter XI of the Charter of the United Nation's list of Non-Self-Governing Territories (NSGT) which are defined by the United Nations as "territories whose people have not yet attained a full measure of self-government."

[55] This bill was submitted around the same time that major increases in military planning were being discussed. For example, it was submitted shortly before the Final Record of Decision (ROD) for the Marine Relocation and the Final Environmental Impact Statement (EIS) for the Mariana Islands Training and Testing (MITT) was released.

[56] The first political status commission refers to the original Covenant agreement made in 1975 between the CNMI and the United States of America.

[57] The three issues being referred to are: 1) The CNMI's legal struggle to retain control over the submerged lands surrounding the Marianas 2) the increasing

militarization of the islands and surrounding sea and airspace, and 3) the U.S.'s decision to federalize the CNMI immigration system which up until 2008, had been run by the CNMI Government.

[58] Chamorro scholar Keith Camacho (2011) conducted an analysis of Chamorro and Filipino social movements in the Marianas and argues that the ensuing federalization of the CNMI immigration system due to labor violations can be understood as a move to further militarize the region through the logic of border policing. This argument is instructive of the way in which all three issues fall under the umbrella of militarism. It is also worthwhile to note that the precarious economic situation in the CNMI that was left in the wake of federal immigration, has produced a further reliance on militarization as a means for economic revenue. For example, in the CNMI's Comprehensive Economic Development Plan 2009–2014, the document notes that, "Although faced with many economic challenges the Commonwealth looks to an opportunity which is already bringing in new investment to the region. The planned military buildup, which is the planned move of Marines from Okinawa to Guam, will undoubtedly bring both positive and negative challenges" (Commonwealth Economic Development Strategic Planning Commission, 2009).

[59] This public presentation was entitled "U.S. Constitutional Rights in the Territories and the CNMI," and was held at American Memorial Park on July 8, 2018. It was hosted by the Honorable Gustavo A. Gelpi from Puerto Rico and the Honorable Jose S. Dela Cruz from Saipan (CNMI).

[60] The largest of these incidents is now described as the "Jack Abramoff CNMI scandal," which involved U.S. lobbyists and other government officials swaying Congressional actions in the CNMI.

[61] See Alia Wong and Lenika Cruz's (2018) critique of mainland America's scant coverage of Typhoon Yutu in their article entitled "The Media Barely Covered One of the Worst Storms to Hit U.S. Soil" published in *The Atlantic*: https://www.theatlantic.com/science/archive/2018/11/super-typhoon-yutu-mainstream-media-missed-northern-mariana-islands/575692/

[62] To be clear, I am not arguing that voting rights are not important, but instead that fighting for equality based on an assimilationist discourse propounded by United States policies does not go "far enough" in alleviating the deeply asymmetrical socio-political and economic structural relations that characterize the US-CNMI relationship. This argument aligns itself with Indigenous scholarship in North America that recognizes both the possibilities and limitations of describing Indigenous struggles within the framework of "human and civil rights based social justice projects" (Tuck & Yang, 2012, p. 1).

[63] The eight insular territories include American Samoa, the Federated States of Micronesia (FSM), Guam, the Marshall Islands, the Northern Marianas, Palau, Puerto Rico, and the U.S. Virgin Islands. The political status of the islands are as follows: FSM (Free Association), Marshall Islands (Free Association), Palau (Free Association), Northern Marianas (Commonwealth, unincorporated), Puerto Rico (Commonwealth, unincorporated), Guam (unincorporated), U.S. Virgin Islands (unincorporated), American Samoa (unincorporated).

[64] Both the CNMI and Guam are considered "organized and unincorporated" (Fallon, 1991, p. 25) despite their different political statuses.

[65] For an in-depth discussion of Article XII and its usage in the local court system in the CNMI and Guam, see "Problematizing the Protection of Culture and the *Insular Cases*" by Rose Cuison Villazor (2018) and "Reading Between the (Blood) Lines" by Rose Cuison Villazor (2010). While the legal ramifications of these tensions have continued to play out at the time of this writing, the question of whether US laws can accommodate for Indigenous rights in the CNMI is outside the scope of this writing. However, I draw attention to Article XII to highlight the longer and more enduring role of US political power and its ability to transform the politics of indigeneity in the CNMI.

Contributors

Poonsri Algaier has lived in Saipan since 1994. She is a graduate of Chulalongkorn University in Thailand and Ohio University in Athens, Ohio. Poonsri has worked in the Languages and Humanities Department of the Northern Marianas College an ESL teacher, and is a founding member of Thai Community, Inc., a benevolent organization created by the Thai community in Saipan.

Theresa "Isa" Arriola, Ph.D. was born and raised on the island of Saipan in the Northern Mariana Islands. She earned her doctorate from the University of California at Los Angeles in sociocultural anthropology. Her research focuses on the socio-political implications of contemporary militarization on Indigenous sovereignty throughout the Marianas archipelago and Oceania more broadly. She is currently an assistant professor in the Sociology and Anthropology Department at Concordia University, where she teaches about militarism, Indigeneity and Oceania.

Kimberly Bunts-Anderson, Ph.D. is an Associate Professor in the Social Sciences and Fine Arts (SSFA) department at Northern Marianas College, Saipan where she has worked as a full-time faculty instructor for over a decade. She holds a Ph.D. in Linguistics and Psychology from Macquarie University, an M.Ed. in TESOL/TEFOL from the University of Sydney, and a B.A. in Mass Communications and Journalism from New Mexico State University. Her research interests include sociolinguistics, language cognition, and investigating how technology integration impacts higher education learning and teaching. Kimberly has published in several international academic journals and monographs. She served as co-editor for this collection. Kimberly first traveled to the Marianas in 1994 and fell in love with the islands and people. She returned with her family in 2006.

Ajani Burrell is an assistant professor at the Northern Marianas College (NMC). He currently chairs the Languages and Humanities department and the Academic Council at NMC. He also served as the lead editor for this collection. He has published prose in several literary magazines and journals. When not working or writing, he enjoys traveling, spending time with his family, and all manner of outdoor activities.

Royce Camacho is a Chamoru scholar and instructor of composition and research writing at the University of Guam. In the classroom, he aims to teach students about indigenous rights and research produced in Micronesia. His work outside the classroom involves community-based stewardship of natural resources and culturally significant sites in the Marianas. He is the grandson of Rosario "Laling" Camacho on his father's side and Profita "Fita" Roberto on his mother's side.

Tabitha Caser Espina, Ph.D. is a Postdoctoral Teaching Associate in the English Department and Affiliate Faculty in the Asian Studies Program at Northeastern University. She previously taught as an instructor at Guam Community College, University of Guam, and Washington State University, and as an assistant professor of Rhetoric and Composition at Eastern Oregon University. She has published in *College English*, *Race and Pedagogy Journal*, *Asian Studies*, *Humanities Diliman*, *Pacific Asia Inquiry*, and *Micronesian Educator*. She has also worked with Humanities Washington, Oregon Humanities, Humanities Guåhan, and the Humanities Center at Wesleyan University and has presented her work throughout the US and in 11 countries.

Sylvia C. Frain, Ph.D. earned her doctorate with the National Centre for Peace and Conflict Studies from the University of Otago in Aotearoa, New Zealand. She published her doctoral thesis on women's resistance to United States militarization as a free e-book on the website *Guampedia*. In 2021, she received the CNMI Governor's Humanities Award for Research and Publication in the Humanities. Currently, she is a New Zealand Science Whitinga Fellow in the School of Art + Design at Auckland University of Technology and is a producer for the documentary film, *Tip of the Spear*. She also curates the research-oriented Facebook page, Oceania Resistance.

Anne Perez Hattori, Ph.D., familian Titang, is a professor at the University of Guam who teaches in the History program as well as the CHamoru Studies and Micronesian Studies programs. Her research interests surround US colonialism in Guam in the early 20th century, particularly its impact on health and culture. She authored *Colonial Dis-Ease: US Navy Health Policies and the Chamorros of Guam, 1898-1941*, published in the Pacific Islands Monograph Series, University of Hawaii Press. Dr. Hattori is also co-editor of the forthcoming *The Cambridge History of the Pacific Ocean*. This 2-volume, 64-chapter publication will be unveiled by Cambridge University Press in November 2022.

Mary Therese Perez Hattori, Ph.D. is Interim Director of the Pacific Islands Development Program in the East-West Center in Honolulu. She is a native CHamoru of Guåhan, of Familian Titang, born to Paul Mitsuo Hattori and Fermina Leon Guerrero Perez Hattori. She is an advocate for Pacific islanders in Hawai'i, co-organizer of cultural events, such as the annual Cultural Animation Film Festival, the annual Celebrate Micronesia Festival, Micronesian Women's Summit, and Oceania on the Reel, and Affiliate Graduate Faculty of the University of Hawai'i at Mānoa and the USC Rossier School of Education. Dr. Hattori is also an author, poet, mentor, public speaker, and philanthropist.

Dominique B. Hess is a research associate at the Center for the Study of Language and Society (CSLS) at the University of Bern, Switzerland. Her research interests include sociolinguistics, (grammatical) language variation and change, varieties of English, studies of contact language, youth language as well as language planning and policy. She currently works as a research associate and lecturer at the University of Teacher Education in Bern.

Malcolm Johnson is an interdisciplinary human and physical geographer with publications in academic journals, books, humanities magazines, websites, technical reports, and management plans. He is currently affiliated with the University of Tasmania and the Centre for Marine Socioecology, where his research focuses on perceptions of climate change, landscape value discourses, and coastalscape planning. Malcolm first encountered the Åsuli while serving for three years as the National Coral Reef Management Fellow in Rota. His time there has significantly inspired the trajectory of his life, offering a better understanding of place, self, and the complex challenges we are all facing

Cinta Matagolai Kaipat is a Refaluwasch-Chamorro artist, fashion designer, music composer, filmmaker, and community advocate. She is a former labor hearing officer, congresswoman, and prosecutor. Cinta was born on Agrigan in the Northern Islands and spent a number of her childhood years on Pågan. She moved with her family to Saipan in 1972 after her father's death. She moved to Chicago the summer of 1978 and earned her high school diploma from Evanston Township High School in 1979, her B.A. from DePaul University in Chicago in 1993, and a J.D. from the University of Minnesota Law School in 1997. Cinta returned to Saipan where she has lived since 1999 and sings with her family as a founding member of the renowned Olomwaay Family Choir.

Kenneth Gofigan Kuper, Ph.D. is an Assistant Professor of Political Science (specializing in International Relations), CHamoru Studies, and Micronesian Studies at the University of Guam. He holds a Ph.D. in Political Science and an M.A. in Pacific Islands Studies from the University of Hawai'i at Mānoa. His dissertation focused on the complexities of military presence and security in Guam through the concept of "sustainable insecurity." His research interests include the role of islands in global politics, Indo-Pacific geopolitics, militarization of the Pacific Islands, decolonization, and the reconceptualization of security. He was born, raised, and lives in Guam, where he proudly speaks Fino' CHamoru to his two children.

Angelyn Labadan is a Tokyo based multidisciplinary artist who works across illustration, design, writing and publishing. She graduated from Temple University Japan Campus with a Bachelor of Fine Arts and Communications Media. Angelyn has worked on a variety of projects for Temple University Japan Campus, Uprizine, and TokyoDex. She has also written for media such as *The Japan Times*, *Metropolis Japan*, and *Tokyo Weekender*. In her free time, she enjoys drawing, watching dramas, writing, and reading tarot cards.

Victoria-Lola M. Leon Guerrero is the director of publishing at the University of Guam Press. She has been a published writer, professional editor, educator, and community organizer for more than 20 years, and is currently the co-chairperson for the Independence for Guam Task Force and the Educational Development and Research Committee co-chairperson for the larger organization, Independent Guåhan. When she isn't working, writing, or visiting her mom in To'to, Victoria-Lola loves laying on a guåfak beneath the fragrant canopy of her ylang-ylang tree with her three sons, husband, and a good book.

Tricia Lizama, Ph.D. is an associate professor of Social Work at the University of Guam (UOG). She earned her doctorate in Human Services from Capella University, her Master's in Social Work from the University of Hawai'i at Mānoa, and her bachelor's degree with a double major in Social Work and Psychology from UOG. Prior to her work at UOG, Dr. Lizama was a team leader/social worker for the

Department of Veterans Affairs. She also served as a psychiatric social worker for the Department of Education, Division of Special Education, Program for Students with Emotional Disabilities. Dr. Lizama currently provides behavioral health services on a part-time basis. She is a Licensed Professional Counselor (LPC) and a Licensed Clinical Social Worker (LCSW). Dr. Lizama is married to Troy Lizama and they have six beautiful children.

Kelly G. Marsh-Taitano, Ph.D. is a Research Associate of the Micronesian Area Research Center, Unibetsidåt Guåhån (UOG) where, for numerous years as an Adjunct Professor, she has taught courses such as the History of Guam, Introduction to Anthropology, and a course she developed on recapturing the carving of latte. Her PhD in Cultural Heritage Studies from Charles Sturt University, Australia builds on her MA in Micronesian Studies and BAs in History and Anthropology from UOG. She advocates safeguarding and promoting that which is special in our region, served as a senator for the 35th Guam Legislature, was co-Chair of the History Subcommittee of the 12th Festival of Pacific Arts which Guåhån hosted, and conducts cultural and historical community outreach.

Lisa Linda S. Natividad, Ph.D. is a Professor of Social Work and CHamoru Studies at the University of Guam. She has taught a course in Family Violence for over a decade. She is a licensed clinical social worker, mental health counselor, professional counselor, and marriage and family therapist. She is a founding member and past President of the National Association of Social Workers, Guam chapter. She is a consultant to the Department of Youth Services in the CNMI, providing assessment, counseling, and staff training. Her research interests include cultural competency, decolonization, demilitarization, and creating peace in families and communities.

Craig Santos Perez, Ph.D., familian Gollo, is a Chamoru writer and scholar from Mongmong, Guam. He is the co-editor of six anthologies, and the author of five books of poetry and the monograph *Navigating Chamoru Poetry: Indigeneity, Aesthetics, and Decolonization* (University of Arizona Press, 2022). He has received the American Book Award, the PEN Center USA literary Prize, and the Nautilus Book Award. He is a professor in the English department and affiliate faculty with the Center for Pacific Islands Studies and the Indigenous Politics program at the University of Hawai'i at Mānoa.

Sharleen Santos-Bamba, Ph.D. is the Interim Vice Provost for Academic Excellence, Graduate Studies, and Online Learning at the University of Guam, and an Associate Professor of English, CHamoru Studies, and Micronesian Studies. Sharleen has publications that have contributed to discourse on language and literacy, roles of women, and culture. As an educational consultant, she has been contracted to provide training in literacy, assessment, and culturally sustainable education for the Guam Department of Education, the FSM school system, and ETS. She is an advocate of the production of indigenous literature and art and engages in initiatives that promote language, literacy, and indigenous ways of knowing. She is married to Vincent Bamba, and they reside in Pago Bay.

Gerard van Gils is a former teacher at Kagman High School and is the 2017 State Teacher of the Year - Northern Mariana Islands. While working as a teacher, he collaborated with his peers to found the Million Dollar Scholars and Mentor for a Meal programs. He is an avid chainsaw enthusiast and loves the islands of the Northern Marianas.

www.ingramcontent.com/pod-product-compliance
Lightning Source LLC
Chambersburg PA
CBHW051523020426
42333CB00016B/1748